LAST TRAIN OVER

LAST TRAIN
OVER ROSTOV BRIDGE

by

Captain Marion Aten, DFC
and Arthur Orrmont

Thin Red Line Books
London

To
Air Vice Marshal Raymond Collishaw,
CB, DSO, OBE, DSC, DFC, RAF,
and the late Captain S M Kinkead,
DSO, DSC, DFC, RAF.

Contents

*

The Camels would go in first, bombing and strafing the enemy, and Ulayai would then follow up with a wild cavalry charge, sabres flashing as the White horsemen descended on the by-now disorganized Reds. … Watching one of these cavalry charges from the cockpit of a Camel was an exhilerating but odd sensation, almost as if one had suddenly turned the controls of some Wellsian time machine and was watching a battle that had taken place a hundred years or more before.

Raymond Collishaw, from his autobiography,
Air Command: A Fighter Pilot's Story

Publisher's Note

*

Since the first US & UK editions of *Last Train Over Rostov Bridge*, a wealth of new material has become available including much of the original research as well as critical reactions and further eyewitness' accounts which appeared in response to the book's publication.

This new edition of the book has evolved into much more than a revised version of the original work due to the collegiate effort of the following contributors (listed below alphabetically):

Michael Aten, an aerospace engineer and distant relative of Marion Aten, through research into Marion's life, technical knowledge and study of the Russian Civil War, has provided the new Introduction, Appendices I & III, as well as editing the Notes to the Text.

Dr Julian Lewis MP , in the midst of a very busy schedule, always found time to help with numerous queries about B Flight and its personnel from information gathered through painstaking research for his biography of B Flight's commander, *Racing Ace: The Fights and Flights of 'Kink' Kinkead DSO DSC★ DFC★*.

Gary Boyce Radder, Marion Aten's nephew and closest living relative, enthusiastically opened the family archives to share new material, including letters and photographs, as well as offering his reminiscences of Marion's later years.

Dr Léonie Rosenstiel, Arthur Orrmont's widow, brought enormous energy and a highly trained eye to all aspects of the project as well as unearthing (and transcribing) a mountain of material pertaining to the original edition including the correspondence and taped interviews between Marion and Arthur.

Professor David Treloar graciously provided full access to the notes his father, Colonel George Treloar DSO MC, made on the original edition of *Last Train Over Rostov Bridge*, as well as supplying photographs taken by his father during the course of the campaign in South Russia.

The publisher would like to thank these contributors for making this greatly expanded edition possible.

A Note on Russian Placenames

*

Batum (in Georgia) is now known as Batumi.

Brest-Litovsk (in Belarus) is now Brest.

Constantinople is modern-day Istanbul.

Debaltsevo now is more commonly called by
its Ukranian name, Debaltseve.

Ekaterinodar is now Krasnodar

Orel is more commonly known as Oryol today.

Petrograd was St Petersburg during Tsarist times, was called
Petrograd (1914-24), then Leningrad (1924-91), and since
then has reverted to St. Petersburg.

Sebastopol today is more commonly known as Sevastopol.

Tiflis is now Tblisi.

Tsaritsyn was renamed Stalingrad in 1925,
and has been called Volgograd since 1961.

Introduction to the New Edition

*

The Russian Civil War of 1918-1921 brought forth a bitter harvest of destruction, disease, famine, death, and profound social upheaval. The human cost during this short period of conflict, with large rival armies fighting across the vast Russian Empire, was in excess of 5 million deaths and may have been far higher. By 1922, there were an estimated seven million 'streetchildren' in Russia as a result of the Civil War and the famines that followed. Yet today, neither the events nor the significance of this brutal clash of military forces and political ideologies is well known to the general public. It has been fifty years since the writing of *Last Train Over Rostov Bridge*, and we can now see even more clearly how the outcome of this Civil War became a turning point of the 20th century, profoundly influencing its future political course.

The Civil War was born out of the collapse of the 600-year-old Tsarist regime and the subsequent revolution that brought Vladimir Lenin and his Marxist-based Bolshevik communist government to tenuous power in 1917. Various disenfranchised and disillusioned political groups, among them democrats, liberals, and Tsarist sup-porting monarchists, as well as many officers of the Tsar's former Russian Imperial Army and ethnic minorities such as the Cossacks, resisted the communist revolution and formed their own loosely allied combat forces. These forces were led primarily by former Im-perial Army and Navy officers, most notably, General Yudenich, Admiral Kolchak and General Denikin. Collectively, these groups were known as the 'Whites', a name derived from a derisive Bol-shevik term that referred to the colour standard adopted by the monarchist-supporting upper class in France during the late 1800s. The Bolsheviks coined the term in order to create the (false) im-pression that all Whites supported the re-establishment of the Tsarist monarchy.

The Whites controlled large areas of Russia throughout much of the Civil War period. With the Bolsheviks only in firm control of Petrograd (St Petersburg) and Moscow, and the area of land between these cities, the conflict was fought primarily on three fronts: in the north, around St Petersburg, with White forces led by General Yudenich; in the east, in Siberia, where forces were led by Admiral Kolchak; and on the southern front, south of Moscow, where a loose confederation of Cossack and White Armies was led by General Anton Denikin. The southern Russian and Volga River countryside where Denikin's forces operated is the crucible for the events in this book.

Lenin's young government knew that it would struggle to consolidate power in Russia but did not anticipate the extent to which foreign governments would attempt to intervene in this internal conflict. The United States, France, Great Britain and even Japan, sent a variety of military aid to the disparate White Russian forces. Great Britain sent money, arms, military advisors, troops and equipment, and to southern Russia they sent several aircraft units that were loosely part of a training mission to support the efforts of General Anton Denikin's White 'Volunteer' Army, which had been recently operating with some success against the Bolsheviks in that region.

One of the units that the British committed to the conflict was 47 Squadron, a Royal Air Force unit that had been formed during WWI and had previously operated in Greece. While in Russia, this unit flew mostly De-Havilland DH-9s and DH-9As, both used as two-seat observation and bombing aircraft, with one flight in the unit operating the infamously touchy – yet supremely manoeuvreable – Sopwith Camel fighter plane. Marion Hughes Aten, a young California rancher who had enlisted in the RAF (then known as the Royal Flying Corp, or RFC) in 1917, was assigned as a Sopwith Camel pilot and instructor when he accepted a personal invitation to join the unit from WWI ace and 47 Squadron Commander, Raymond Collishaw.

What spurred this young Californian to seek adventure in the British Royal Air Force?

Perhaps Marion's wanderlust was a natural outgrowth of his early family life. He was the eldest son of a famous Texas Ranger, Ira Aten, who, while serving as an officer in the Rangers, had pioneered parts of west Texas in the 1880s. It was in Ira's and his wife Imogen's modest Texas sod dugout that Marion was born in 1892. He would grow up witnessing his father riding after the bad guys – rustlers, thieves, fence cutters, and even murderers – and bringing them in for justice. Here, in the still untamed west, Marion's sense of adventure, his self-confidence and his bravery grew.

Ira, Imogen and family pulled up stakes in 1904 and relocated to the then-remote Imperial Valley, in the desert back-country of San Diego, California. There the Atens pioneered all over again, establishing the prosperous 8N Bar Ranch. Ira became actively involved in the growing farm community and participated in the local water board (a major political force in any desert area), eventually becoming its director.

Amongst Marion's suggestions to Arthur Orrmont for the blurb on the book, he wrote of himself: 'When he was riding the western range, before the age of ten, he longed to see more of a world than one tenanted by cattle and buffalo grass.' Marion also recalled that he, 'Always wanted to fly! I wanted to get close enough to an airplane to touch it. Just to put my hand on it!'

A few years later he attempted to enlist in the US Army Signal Corps as a trainee pilot but was unsuccessful as they were, by and large, accepting only trained pilots. Undeterred, in 1917 he travelled to Canada with a group of friends and while there joined the Royal Flying Corps with an eye to being part of the fight in the Great War.

Having completed his training late in the war, Marion received his full pilot's-license one day after the Armistice, too late to prove his flying skills in the skies over France and Belgium. Consequently, he was eager to accept the offer to join 47 Squadron in its support of the disorganized and beleaguered White forces of southern Russia.

The months that young Aten would spend in Russia would test his bravery as he and his comrades were thrust into a situation of profound chaos – where for a time anarchy, violence, pestilence and atrocity engulfed civilians and the military alike. Under the most challenging of circumstances – and certainly beyond anything in his previous experience – Marion Aten would prove himself in a strange land by performing heroic service that would be recognized by both the British and White Russian high commands.

When his service in Russia was at an end, Aten again accepted an assignment that promised danger and adventure, only this time in the unmapped deserts of the Middle East, where he became part of the British force that was being deployed to put down a growing Arab and Kurdish uprising in the area of modern-day Iraq. He retired from active duty with the RAF in 1927 and returned to help his father at the 8N Bar Ranch.

Aten reflected on his experiences in Russia in a 1935 five-part serialization in *Liberty* magazine. As he was not a professional writer, these are as-told-to pieces, written by H. Bedford-Jones in the florid purple-prose style that was so popular at that time. He later went on to write a short story based on his experiences of flying in 1920's Iraq which appeared in *Short Stories* magazine in 1938. Expanding his writing horizons, Marion also penned an epic poem based on the same subject that was published in book form in 1949.

But late in his life he returned once again to the events of southern Russia in 1919–1920. Under circumstances that are still not known, he had created an outline for a book based on his Russian experiences, along with descriptions of some of the events. Although this work was utilised during the writing of *LTORB*, all copies of this manuscript of more than 200 pages now seem to be lost.

Encouraged and aided by non-fiction writer, editor, novelist and author's agent, Arthur Orrmont, the pair fashioned, through conversation and voluminous correspondence, this narrative memoir in the best tradition of the genre. In *Last Train Over Rostov Bridge,* some liberties with historical accuracy were taken to give us a dramatic and exciting story. The characters are real (though names, dates and places were often changed to spare the living) as are the setting and most of the events. This is a rousing yarn of adventure for the sake of adventure, of companionship and bravery, and ultimately of heartbreak and death. It tells us of a time when the world was perceived to be a much larger place.

As Arthur Orrmont wrote after Marion's death in May, 1961: 'He was a deliberate man, a fearless man and an infinitely gracious one; a man of warmth and humour. He was perhaps the last of the pre-Freudian adventurers, a man who sought experience – of men, of war, of distant places – for itself and not for any complicated reason of the psyche.'

Last Train Over Rostov Bridge brilliantly captures the character of Captain Marion Aten, his comrades-in-arms and the terrible and momentous events of the Russian Civil War.

Michael Aten,
San Diego, California, June, 2011

Foreword to the Original Edition

✳

The great Russian Civil War (1918–1921) was probably the worst reported conflict of modern times. Few correspondents were with either the Bolshevik forces (later the name was changed to Communist) or with the White Russian Army, and those who were with the troops were plagued by lack of communications and with strict censorship. Later a few generals of both sides did write memoirs of those dreadful days; they were not only hopelessly biased, but for the most part emphasized the complex political ramifications of the struggle.

At long last a book has been written that humanizes that war; that tells of it in terms of air and ground battles, in terms of the gallantry, the cowardice and the suffering of the millions of Russians who found themselves caught up in a flow of tragic events over which they had no control. Strangely enough, an American, Captain Marion Aten, who flew for the RAF, was a witness to these events. His story has been skillfully shepherded through the typewriter by professional writer Arthur Orrmont. You can read *Last Train Over Rostov Bridge* as merely an exciting personal narrative of a young adventurous pilot who not only became dedicated to the cause of the White Army forces but who found time to fall in love with an attractive Russian nurse. You can also read it as a perceptive footnote to history, for Marion Aten, even then, had an inquiring mind which forced him to the conclusion that a Russian Bolshevik state could only be a menace to the eventual peace of the world.

A few words about Marion Aten. His father was a famous Texas Ranger, Captain Ira Aten, who eventually retired from the service and bought and developed the successful 8 N Bar Ranch in El Centro, California. Shortly after World I broke out young Aten, by then equally at home on a horse or in the cockpit of a plane, went to Toronto to enlist in the Royal Flying Corps. When he arrived in France he was lucky enough to be assigned to Squadron 203 led by Canadian Raymond Collishaw, the No. 3 Allied fighter ace of World War I. Collishaw wound up with a record of sixty-eight downed

German aircraft even though he only had one eye (the medical examiners never knew this until after the war was over).★ His second-in-command was Sam Kinkead who had accounted for thirty-nine enemy planes. These two and the young pilot from California became a convivial trio, always ready for a fight or a frolic.

Marion Aten's war came to an embarrassing end when a flying accident, having nothing to do with combat, resulted in his left arm being broken in four places. When Armistice Day came Aten was in the Eastchurch Hospital outside of London, but he knew that his old squadron mates would be celebrating the end of hostilities at the Royal Automobile Club Bar. With his arm in a sling he joined them, and after a few drinks Collishaw broached the subject of flying against the Bolsheviks. He, Kinkead and several of the squadron had already faced the bleak prospect of peace and had joined the fighting forces of the White Russian Air Force who were fighting the Bolsheviks with the unofficial blessing of England (which was sending supplies to the enemies of Bolshevism).

The boy from California didn't know a damn thing about Russia except that the Tsar had abdicated and was now dead. He knew that there had been a confusing revolution and that a man named Lenin had signed a separate peace treaty with the Germans at Brest-Litovsk. Collishaw, whom Aten idolized, explained the difference between the 'good guys' and the 'bad guys'. The Bolsheviks or the Reds as they were even called then were the 'bad guys' and the Whites were the 'good guys'. When Collishaw told Aten that he would be commanding officer of 47 Squadron,★★ three flights with a total of 300 men (including pilots, ground crew and maintenance personnel) and suggested that he go along, the young American ordered another drink and said, 'Why not'. A few months later Aten went to South Russia to join Lieutenant-Colonel Raymond Collishaw and his fighter pilots who were flying the British Camels, fractious planes that only responded properly to the hands of skilled pilots. For some time this was a gay and dashing war, with Collishaw's group completely dominating the air protecting the ground troops of General Peter Nicholaivich Wrangel's Cossacks.

★   Collishaw has been variously credited with 60 through to 68 downed planes.

★★ It was Collishaw who commanded 47 Squadron and Captain Samuel Kinkead was in the officer in charge of B Flight to which Marion Aten was posted.

There were caviar and vodka and acquiescent and lovely Russian girls. General Anton Ivanovich Denikin commanded the White Army. His No. 2 man was Baron Wrangel, a brilliant officer with an illustrious World War I record.

At first the White Army gained a succession of quick victories, but then General Simeon Mikhailevich Budenny, head of the Red Army under Leon Trotsky (Commissar of War), conscripted thousands and thousands of workers, to whom the Bolsheviks had promised paradise, and put guns in their hands. Suddenly Aten and the other RAF pilots grew up and began to realize this wasn't fun and games. He flew every day but at night came to know officers of the White Army (including General Wrangel) and in this book he tells us a story of lost opportunities that might well have changed the course of the Russian Civil War. Had these opportunities been seized, the Bolsheviks might conceivably have been defeated, thereby completely exterminating the threat of what we know as Communism.

This part of the story I have never heard before. General Denikin had exhilarated his troops with the slogan, 'We will be in Moscow by Christmas', as Napoleon had once said. He determined to push full steam ahead for Moscow, but decided to divide his troops into three forces along the way. In vain Wrangel objected that such a course was suicide. He was a professional military man who realized that when a sharp thrust was made at an enemy position the thrust must be single, not divided. Denikin accused him of wanting to capture Moscow by himself. Wrangel shrugged his shoulders and obeyed orders.

Wrangel, according to the authors, was a truly great general, but he couldn't cope with General Budenny and his rapidly increasing forces. Wrangel asked his headquarters for new orders countermanding those which insisted that he advance on Moscow. He felt he might accomplish the mission with Denikin's reserve troops, but the Commander-in-Chief was adamant and insisted that Wrangel aim for what had now become the capital of the Bolshevik government with the troops that he had.

The authors bring up an interesting question. Had Denikin thrown all of his troops behind Wrangel this brilliant general might have taken Moscow and what we know today as Communism might never have existed. This is pure conjecture, but the authors make out a good case for it. Had Wrangel won, the whole course of history might have been changed. Or had the Allies who were giving token assistance to the White Army really put their whole strength behind the fight, Russia today well might be a relatively democratic state.

The writers of this book, in the midst of their exciting narrative, raise these provocative points. They are worth considering.

Quentin Reynolds
[1961]

BOOK ONE

*

Journey to Russia

At the Quai d'Orsay Clemenceau coughed into his yellow hand and returned his eyes to the official dispatches. At 1600 Pennsylvania Avenue Wilson drew a shawl around his bowed shoulders and reached for his pen. At 10 Downing Street Lloyd George impatiently pressed the buzzer that summoned his first and second secretaries. Force without stint or limit, force to the utmost had won the war, along with Almighty God, Right, Truth, Justice, Freedom, the Self-Determination of Nations, no Indemnities or Annexations. Now it was time for work in the new world eleven million dead had made safe for democracy.

Chapter One

*

In London on November 11, 1918, as in Paris, in Rome and in New York, there was celebration. At eleven o'clock that morning, blazoned by the Fleet Street extras, the news had come, and at eleven that night the church bells were still ringing, the boat whistles still blowing, the pubs still roaring, and people still danced in the streets. They had poppies in their buttonholes and in their hats, and London was a sea of poppies from Bayswater Road through Oxford Street, across the Haymarket and through Trafalgar Square into Whitehall. Grocers stood by while small boys stole oranges. Tram conductors refused to take fares. Bowler-hatted clerks pressed flasks upon strangers, and the women kisses and sometimes more than kisses, if the strangers were young and wore khaki and had eyes haunted by Belleau Wood or Vimy Ridge or Chateau-Thierry.

If you were that stranger it was good to be alive and young and whole; a survivor. Oh, it was true enough the world was a poorer place to live in: so the thinkers had said. The youth were betrayed and the dream of human perfectibility forever shattered, and optimism – except in the empty words of the proclamations – dead. From now on it would be fashionable to believe in nothing. But one could believe in nothing and still have a rattling good time, and that, for a disillusioned optimist, was the important thing to remember. For the young back from the war there was youth to spend, youth so far unsquandered like the combat pay in your pocket, and if money was exhaustible, youth was not, now that the trenches were empty and the air above them still, and now that it was time again for old men to do the dying as the old men should.

At Pall Mall I got out of the cab that had stopped for my slinged arm outside of Victoria Station. As I paid my fare the cabby repeated his friendly warning: 'Now you be sure and stay away from Piccadilly tonight, Lieutenant. The crowd'll bust yer other arm.' I thanked him and turned down Pall Mall. I had no intention of going to Piccadilly Circus, certain this evening to be the most crowded place in London, and in triumphant Christendom, to boot. I planned merely to have a few drinks with the squadron mates I expected to find at the Royal Automobile Club bar, and then turn in fairly early at a nearby hotel.[1] My arm, broken in four places in a flying accident, was still far from mended. It would be some time before I could hope to be discharged from the RAF hospital at Eastchurch,[2] which had given me a forty-eight-hour pass to go into London and celebrate the defeat of the Hun.

Pall Mall looked like the set for a naughty revue. Overhead hung a big yellow Schubert moon: by the light of such the Zeppelins had lately bombed the city. Down the street, each against a tin-hatted street light, leaned ardent couples. They embraced, and parted only to drink from flask or bottle. As I passed one street light, a young lady in floppy hat and suit skirt tight at the ankles dropped a pint bottle at my feet. It smashed, splashing Scotch against my boots. I smiled in encouragement and passed on.

'Harry, just because you won the bloomin' war don't give you any right to paw so,' the girl protested.

At the next lamppost a stunning brunette with a Modigliani neck snaked her arm in mine and held me there, captive. I looked down into smoky eyes like smoky eyes that had made me foolish one Imperial Valley spring and the memory of which had driven me away to join the circus. There was a wise man who said that young boys must join circuses, and he said it right.[3]

'Darling blueboy,' the Modigliani said, 'were you very badly wounded?'[4] She was very drunk, but lovely.

'Come now, Claris, the Lieutenant's busy,' said her colonel, a white-moustached War Office type much too old for Claris. He distinctly emphasized the 'Lieutenant'.

'Blueboy,' Claris asked, ignoring him, 'was it a Hun bullet from one of those horrid black machines with the crosses on them? Were you very *badly* hurt?'

'"My body only,"' I quoted gallantly from Rupert Brooke, '"but your eyes do wound my soul."' With a contemptuous salute to the colonel, I retrieved my good arm and continued on, edging past a group of fellow-countrymen in khaki bawling out 'Mademoiselle from Armentières'.

The uniformed carriage attendant was shooing a couple of leather-capped roisterers away from the Automobile Club's marble steps. 'I don't care if it's bloody Armageddon,' he was saying firmly, 'this here's a gentleman's club, and we don't tolerate no disturbances.' He prodded one of the roisterers with a disdainful toe.

'Good evening, Eastman,' I said, answering his greeting, and passed through the monogrammed door he held open for me into the tiled entrance hall.

It was like coming out of the storm into the calm of an aquarium, and the decorous silence hit me like a blow. Off to the right, in the reading room, superannuated baronets with brandies at their elbows sat absorbed in the evening papers, deaf to the sound of revelry and debauch that filtered in through the French windows. One was reading a bound edition of Surtees from the library shelves which offered nothing more recent than Meredith and Gissing. Beyond, in the billiard room, baldheaded gentlemen prodded coloured balls with sticks of wood, while stiff-backed waiters stood patiently by with refreshments.

At the back of the entrance hall two young sapper officers sat ensconced in telephone booths, arguing young ladies into doing the town. One wiped a forehead that had most likely been dry at Ypres.

In the bar, where I had known they would be, sat Colly, Kink, Bill Daly and Tommy Burns Thomson.[5] The bar was a small one and had room for only five; they had saved a seat for me. 203 Squadron looked after its own.

Kink, the witty one, was first to see me come into the room. 'It's Bunny's ghost! I knew they'd send him West at Eastchurch.'

'Bunny, you bastard, come have a drink,' said Collishaw, the hero and the handsome one.

'Strewth, two drinks for Lieutenant Aten,' said Daly, the rounder, and pounded the bar.

Burns Thomson, the baby, sat with a grin that managed to be both wide and sickly. He had just lost ten quid, having bet me that I would celebrate Armistice at Eastchurch with a copy of *La Vie Parisienne*. I was a 'poor mender', he said.

George, the bartender, set before me a single Scotch and soda, silently reminding Bill Daly that at the Royal Automobile only one drink was served at a time.

Kink shook his head in disbelief. 'The Flying Cowboy made it to London by Armistice. The man who thought he could fly into a Bessonneau and out the other side.'

He was referring to my accident. At Eastchurch field, trying to avoid a landing plane, I had tried to fly through a canvas hangar, a trick only Colly, and perhaps Kink, could have attempted with any prospect of success.[6]

'Where's Bunny's ten quid?' Kink inquired of Tommy blandly.

Tommy groaned, and reaching for his billfold, counted out fresh white notes on the bar. He was an Edinburgh Scotsman, and though as reckless with a bet as an aeroplane, it pained him to lose money.

I ordered another round. And another. We drank to the Armistice, and to the end of the war. To the downfall of the Hun. To peace, and to the Allied victory. We drank to the demoiselles of Paris and to the girls of Mayfair. We drank to practically everything but home, and I was beginning to wonder why when Colly began to ask me some strange questions.

'Bunny, do you really plan to go back to that ranch in California?'

'It looks that way, Colly. *La guerre a fini.*' Outside someone smashed a street lamp, and it sounded so much like the pop of a Very pistol that we all grinned.

Colly frowned. 'You didn't see much action, did you, on the Western Front? A month's combat, a couple of Hun bullets in your tail. Nothing spectacular, I mean. No kills in the air.'[7]

'You know that, Colly,' I said. The conversation depressed me. Raymond Collishaw was the third leading Allied ace of the war. Though sightless in one eye – a fact the Medical Board had failed to discover – he had shot down sixty-eight German aircraft. And the man who sat beside him, Sam Kinkead, had scored thirty-nine victories in Turkey and on the Western Front. Even Bill Daly had two Hun planes to his credit, and Tommy, one. 203 Squadron was one of the best known fighter squadrons at the front, and had ended the war with the second highest bag of enemy machines. The other boys had fought well for the King; I had only cost him money.

Colly sniffed. 'Ranches sound like a deadly bore. Five to one you'll get sick of all those cattle and want to join up again.' Kink, who had been raised on a South African farm, objected. 'Hold on now, Colly, ranching's not as bad as all that.'

Colly turned to face him, raised an eyebrow, and then returned his attention to me.

'Bunny, you like flying, don't you?'

'Love it,' I told him truthfully. I had never been the same since that day in 1911 when, a boy of sixteen, I had seen and touched my first machine: Bob Fowler's Wright Model B biplane that had landed in Pasadena on the first cross-country flight in the United States. When war had broken out I had left El Centro for Toronto to enlist in the RFC, and though my father had put the train fare in my pocket, had it been necessary I would have made it to Camp Mohawk on foot.[8] Caring as much as I did for flying a plane, it was going to be difficult to give it up for ranching.

'Got a girl back home?' Colly asked me after a pause.

I shook my head, wondering what he was up to. Colly knew that romantically I was as free as a tailwind.

'I understand,' Colly went on, 'that your father was a Texas Ranger.'

'Dad pioneered Texas after the Civil War,' I said. 'He was one of the best cattlemen in the West.'

Colly rubbed his chin reflectively. 'Must have been a pretty independent fellow. Strong individualist, and all that. Didn't stick close to home and hearth. Went adventuring, you might say, into the wilderness.'

'You might say that. Colly, what in hell are you getting at? Out with it.'

Tommy sniggered, and Colly quelled him with a look.

'Suppose another war came along?' Colly said, his grey, long-lashed eyes narrowing. 'You wouldn't exactly mind flying in it, would you?'

'Good Lord,' I said. 'Have the Serbs or Montenegrins broken loose again?'

'You haven't answered my question.'

'Give me another war and I'll tear up my demob papers tomorrow.'

'Good,' Colly said. 'Then how would you like to fly against the Bolshies?'[9]

'The Bolshies?' I repeated stupidly.

'With the Whites against the Reds, Bunny,'' Kink explained.

I had no interest in politics and knew next to nothing about Russia and its current internal affairs. The Tsar, I knew, had abdicated, and now was dead; there had been a confusing revolution; a sinister man named Lenin had passed through Germany in a sealed railway car and signed a separate peace with the Germans at Brest-Litovsk; a rather unsporting gesture. I didn't know how to spell Brest-Litovsk, which had a faintly indecent ring. I knew the Russian winters were cold, and the people, bundled up in bear rugs, went about in sleighs. Much vodka was consumed, both in Moscow and in the provinces.

'I didn't know,' I said, 'that we were at war with the Reds.'

'We're not,' Colly said patiently, 'and it's not likely we will be. With our help the Whites can do the job. This summer Allied intervention and support got seriously under way. Allied troops landed at Murmansk and Archangel, where they've overthrown the local soviet and set up a provisional government of the north. We've got Allied forces in Vladivostok, and the Japanese are holding strategic points in eastern Siberia. American troops are guarding the railroads out there, and there are several thousand British supporting and instructing Admiral Kolchak – the White muckamuck of the north.'

'Colly,' I said, 'how the devil would you fly in all that snow?'

'We're not going to Siberia,' Kink said. 'We're going to the south, the Cossack country. We'll be supporting the counter-revolution that's started up there under General Denikin.'

Taking his time about it, Colly lit a Gold Flake, 'I'll be commanding officer of three flights with a total of about three hundred men. That includes officers, ground crew, and maintenance personnel. You'd be flying Camels under Kink in B Flight with Bill, Tommy, and a chap named Eddie Fulford,10 who'll be joining us later on. The other boys of A and C Flights will be flying DH-9 and DH-9A bombers. It should be a damn good show and we shouldn't have too much trouble getting the mess over with around this time next year. Want to come? What do you say we fox 'em?'

Did I want to come? Colly's invitation was an honour; I knew that only the best pilots of 203 Squadron were being asked to make the trip. But I temporized, not wanting to show how eager I actually was.

'A year, you say. I promised the folks I'd get back home as soon as the fighting was over.'

'A year if that,' Colly said. 'The Whites have all the military brains and mountains of Allied munitions and equipment. We could be in Moscow by next Christmas.'

'Think of all the Russian women, Bunny,' Bill Daly said. 'Throwing themselves at their brave foreign defenders, begging for a kiss. Countesses, baronesses by the dozen. Might even bag yourself a princess.'

'Combat pay too,' Tommy said. 'A quid extra a day.'

'Temporary rank of Captain,' Bill put in.

'New Camels?' I asked Colly.

'Not quite,' he told me. 'Our ships have seen a lot of action in Salonika during the war. They're a little bashed. But to service them we'll have the best damn crews in the RAF'

'All right, count me in,' I said. Pandemonium. Kink threw his arms around me and Bill pounded my back so hard I fell off the stool. Tommy, helping me to get up, slipped himself, and we rolled over the blue carpet. Colly managed to spill half his Scotch and soda on my head.

'Gentlemen! Gentlemen!' George pleaded. 'Rules of the club! Rules of the club!'

In the doorway stood two of the old walruses from the reading room, staring at us in shock and amazement. The Times in their liver-spotted hands were like huge warrants for our arrest. One never shouted in the Royal Automobile, not even on Armistice night. It was a rule of the club.

Colly raised his glass to the walruses and invited them to have a drink. Slowly, in concert, shaking their heads and flanks, the walruses waddled away.

We drank to the walruses. And to Mother Russia, and to the Tsar and the Tsarina, dead though they might be. We drank to the princesses, the duchesses, the countesses, the baronesses. And even to the Bolshies.

Turning unsteadily to the bartender, Colly asked for a bar chit and a pencil. He scrawled something on the back of the chit, and handed it to me. The message read:

> *Kindly provide Lt. Aten in Dover with transportation to Boulogne.*
> *His eventual destination is South Russia.*
> Raymond Collishaw, Lt.-Col., RAF

Colly put his hand on my shoulder. 'Sorry you can't leave with us, Bunny; we're taking off in a couple of weeks, and I doubt if you'll be discharged by then from Eastchurch.[11] But I'll leave instructions along the route, and you can just hop along after us.'

I looked at the chit doubtfully. 'The handwriting's rather drunken, and it doesn't look very official. Can I really get to Russia on a bar chit?'

'Colly's got direct orders from the Air Ministry,' Kink said. 'Don't worry about a thing.'

Colly put down his glass and straightened his tie. 'I am late,' he said, 'for a pressing appointment with a marchioness. Will you warriors excuse me?'

In respectful silence we watched him leave the room.

'There goes a great man,' Kink said. 'A man of unconquerable spirit and incredible powers of recovery. He'll be sober when he pays off the cabby at Berkeley Square.'

'Shall we drink to the marchioness?' asked Bill Daly.

So we drank to that lady, and to her honourable sister, too. Then, showering George with pound notes, we left the bar, bound for whatever adventure the night, still young, might bring.

In the lobby one of the two pleading sappers was still on the telephone. Tommy suddenly sat down in an armchair and turned green, and we hurried him into the washroom, where he threw up in a healthy manner. Outside the club, we found a taxi at the curb.

'Well, boys,' Kink said, 'is it on to Piccadilly, to bow to the whores and pinch the ladies?'

'On to Piccadilly!' we shouted, and piled in.

It wasn't easy to get into Piccadilly. The place was mobbed. Khaki pushed serge and serge jostled khaki, and chenille and jersey pushed and jostled both, all shouting, sweating, and exalted. There were French sailors in red pompons and French officers in braided képis and Polish legionnaires, doughboys, Canucks, Anzacs, and Red Cross officers with a shine on their Sam Browne belts and leather puttees that hurt the eyes. For the first time in years the signs were lit, and Schweppes, Oxo and Bovril bathed the crowd in a bright yellow glow. We pressed forward, impelled by the same atavistic compulsion as our neighbors, toward the Fountain of Eros in the centre of the Square; it seemed as though all London meant to renew itself at the springs of the God of Love.

Around us voices swelled in incessant song. Tommies sang 'It's A Long Way To Tipperary', Frenchmen chorused 'La Marseillaise' and 'Madelon', American doughboys bellowed:

> *Ho! for the coonyac, ho! for the wine.*
> *Ho! for the Mam'selles*
> *Every one is fine.*
> *Ho! for the hardtack, bully beef and beans.*
> *To hell with the Kaiser and the goddamn Marines!*

And into the stupendous uproar we four shouted the old RAF battle song of the Western Front, 'It's The Only, Only Way':

It's the only, only way,
It's the only trick to play;
He's the only Hun, you're the only Pup
And he's only getting the wind right up:
So go on and do not stop
Till his tail's damn near your prop.
If he only crashes this side in flames,
Well, you'll only know they'll believe your planes –
So keep him right
In the Aldis sight,
It's the oh, oh, only way!

The crowd was no respecter of RAF blue. I got an elbow in my ribs that knocked the wind out, and Kink was stabbed in the ear by an umbrella. Bill Daly got kneed in the groin and Tommy was knocked off his feet. We reformed our line and continued forward towards the fountain, Kink holding a slightly bloodied handkerchief to the side of his head.

A drunken Canuck corporal had climbed the fountain to the figure of Eros at the top, and was vainly trying to tug the god from his pedestal. Thoroughly soaked from the jet of water that came from Eros' mouth, the corporal was finding his perch a slippery one, and as we and thousands watched, his foot slipped and he barely caught himself from falling into the basin below. Again he grappled with Eros, tugging with inebriate persistence, while the crowd shouted encouragement and advice:

'He'll come off you do 'im easy.'

'A Canuck couldn't do it, but an Englishman could!'

'Let a man up there to do a man's job – a bloody sailor!'

Around us bets were being made on how long it would be before the Canuck slipped and fell. An infantryman of the Fourth King's counted seconds on his watch, and an engineer wearing the shoulder patch of the Thirteenth Royal Fusiliers checked him for honesty. The Canuck, waterlogged and disconsolate, was losing his grip again when the firemen arrived, carrying ladders.

Three firemen in slickers and hip boots climbed into the base of the fountain and set up the ladder against the lip of the next basin. One of them mounted the ladder and started up, and the crowd, anxious to see, pressed forward.

There was no help for it; we were too close to the fountain, and the mass of onlookers pushed us over the edge of the bottom basin, together with a civil servant carrying a rolled umbrella and a young lady of fashion separated from her escort. Her shrieks were worthier of a more desperate situation. But all of us got soaked up to our knees in the foot-deep basin, except for Tommy, who lost his balance and sprawled full-length. With the help of the firemen we clambered out, dripping.

The firemen, decent chaps, provided escort through the laughing crowd, and one of them hailed a taxi. We headed up Shaftesbury Avenue, bound for Soho.

'What time is it?' Kink asked, wringing water from his whipcord breeks.

I looked at my watch, but the fountain escapade had put it out of commission.

'Can't be later than one-ish,' said Bill Daly. Taking out his roll of soggy pound notes, he examined them ruefully.

Tommy sneezed. 'Hell of an early hour to be turning in,' he grumbled. 'We should have brought a change of uniform from the base.'

'Say,' Bill said, 'did anybody see what happened to the corporal?'

None of us had, and we all felt somewhat cheated. An atmosphere of damp sobriety had settled over us when the cab pulled up at the hotel.

The receptionist's eyes were cool as we approached the desk, leaving a trail of wet footprints over the carpet. Tommy had begun to sneeze violently.

'We'd like four single rooms,' Kink told the receptionist. 'If you don't have them, we'll take a couple of doubles.'

'Sorry, Sir,' the receptionist said, 'all filled up. Thousands of men in the city.'

I had thought the place looked too damn respectable for the likes of four dripping flying officers. I said to Kink, 'Come on, we'll try the Devonshire.'

'The Devonshire's too far away, and Tommy's got a weakness for pneumonia.' He turned back to the desk clerk. 'Tell the manager I'd like to see him.'

'The receptionist hesitated, and Kink said, in his tone of command which shattered ordinary mortals, 'The manager, man, are you deaf?'

The receptionist left the desk and returned with a middle-aged man with cheerful eyes. Without a word he swung the register toward us. 'Catching a cold, eh?' he said to Tommy. 'Better get you into bed.' After we had signed, he waved away the bellboy and took us up in the elevator to our first floor rooms.

I had noticed that he walked with a limp. When he opened the door of my room and switched on the light, he tapped his leg significantly. It gave off a hollow sound.

'Grateful to you RAF chaps,' he said. 'Ruddy Fokker strafed our trench one day, got me in the leg, and turned to come in a second time. I was lying there helpless. If one of your boys hadn't come from out of the blue and pounced him, I might not be here today. Sleep well, Lieutenant. Enjoy the peace.'

I had sat down on the bed and taken off my jacket before it occurred to me that the war was over, but not for Marion Hughes Aten. I was going half way round the world to fight in another.

For a moment – but only a moment – it seemed like a silly idea.

Tomorrow, as soon as I got back to Eastchurch hospital, I would write a letter home. Father would understand, but not mother. For more than one reason I wished my brother Boyce hadn't died of a machine-gun bullet near Apromont in the Argonne Forest the previous September.[12]

Chapter Two

＊

Colly's promised telegram arrived two and a half weeks later. It read:

HUNGOVER BUT DETERMINED, LEFT DOVER TODAY FOR BOULOGNE. SUGGEST YOU DEPART EASTCHURCH SOON AS POSSIBLE FOR DOVER WHERE MARINE LANDING OFFICER WILL ISSUE TICKET FOR BOULOGNE. FURTHER INSTRUCTIONS AWAIT YOU THERE.
NICHOLAS II.

The wire was delivered to me the day I was discharged from the hospital and an hour before I was put under arrest and confined to the base for 'an indefinite period at the commanding officer's discretion'. My offense had been to disobey the regulation that forbade 'social conversation and intercourse with the auxiliary female force in uniform', namely the WRAFs who cooked and served our meals, did our laundry, signed out our library books, typed our records, and filed our papers.

That evening a barracks' mate and I were talking desultorily with a WRAF who enjoyed local fame and popularity for having spat most often into the soup of Colonel Dudgeon, the most detested officer on the Isle of Sheppey. I was just about to excuse myself when Colonel Dudgeon happened by, swinging his swagger stick and humming 'Auprès de ma blonde'. My companion bolted cravenly into the darkness, but I stayed on to face the colonel's wrath. As it turned out I should have bolted too, but it is a constitutional inability of mine to show so intimate a portion of my anatomy as my backside to anyone whom I despise.

'Lieutenant,' said the colonel, after dismissing the WRAF, 'are you cognizant of regulations regarding this offense?'

'Yes, Sir. I am put under open arrest and ordered to report to the adjutant every twenty-four hours. I am confined to Eastchurch until further notice, but I may, meanwhile, request a court martial.'

The colonel tapped his stick against his boot. 'That is correct. Your knowledge of regulations is commendable. Your obedience to them is not.'

'Am I dismissed, Sir?'

'Presently, Lieutenant. What's this I hear about your going to Russia?'

'It's true, Sir. But I'm surprised. I didn't know personal messages were opened at headquarters.'

Dudgeon reddened. 'Are you accusing me of reading your mail?'

'No, Sir. Just my telegrams.'

'Aten,' the colonel said softly, with menace, 'don't count on leaving for Russia for a while. Quite a while. It distresses me to say this, but by the time you get there the war might well be over. Open arrest has been known to last for months at Eastchurch, and the court martial section, should you ask for a trial, is badly jammed up. Struthers, the chap who talked to the librarian, waited a jolly long time for his. Dismissed, Lieutenant. Carry on.'

The next morning I asked for a court martial, but the schedule, as the colonel had said, was crowded. The soonest date the adjutant could give me was in March. I wrote to Colly, care of the Marine Landing Officer in Boulogne, but the weeks passed and there was no reply, and I had no idea of B Flight's itinerary thereafter. I pulled a string in Whitehall, but it proved a loose one, and Dudgeon had the satisfaction of telling me that the Air Vice-Marshal believed that discipline in the RAF was of paramount importance. I seethed and I moped and I contemplated murder, and spent a miserable Christmas and New Year's Eve in quarters reading a bad translation of a Turgenev novel.

I don't know when it occurred to me that I could simply walk out of Eastchurch by the back door, but one night in late January I did just that;[1] I picked up the kit my friend had checked with the station master, and caught the train with seconds to spare. As it rattled over the drawbridge that separated the Isle of Sheppey from the mainland I began to relax but checked myself; I was hardly safe till I left Sittingbourne Junction behind me, and Sittingbourne was two hours away. Dudgeon might have discovered my escape and called ahead to the Junction Military Police.

At Sittingbourne the line branched one way to Dover, the other to London. On the platform an MP officer approached me as I was lugging my kit to the waiting room; and my heart beat madly for a moment and then seemed to stop. But the alarm was a false one: he had a brother at Eastchurch and wondered if I knew him and how Edgar was getting along.

There was only a short wait for the Dover train. I shared a compartment with an old lady from London who was going to visit her married daughter in the Cinque Ports town.

'Are you goin' home?' she asked me pleasantly.

'No, well yes, as a matter of fact, I am.'

'Must be good to be goin' home after this horrible war. Henry, that's my boy, he just about got away with a whole skin, fighting for that butcher Haig.' She brightened. 'Think how fine it'll be to see your mum and dad.'

'Yes, it will be.'

'They'll be thrilled to see their soldier lad,' she said, and went on to tell me how glad Henry had been to see his mum, dad being dead these six years last Christmas. It was conversation I found less than cheering, remembering mother's plea in her last letter that I change my mind about freebooting to a war that was no concern of mine, and excusing myself to the old lady, I went into the dining car for a glass of ale and a smoke.

I sat there for the entire trip. The train passed over the Dour and came into the town, and I saw the white cliffs of Dover that fringe the coast on either hand, and on the eastern height the Castle with its Roman *pharos* which had once signaled ships at sea. In the failing light the remains of the Saxon fort and Norman keep were still visible.

It came to me that Roman and British and Saxon and Norman had conquered here in turn only to be forgotten. If that was so, in a hundred years what heart would beat faster at the reliquaries of the Great War that had just ended? History moved too fast, and time corrupted it; in another hundred years how many greater wars would have been fought and unremembered? I had no talent for prevision, and yet I saw before me now the plane I flew and loved, the Sopwith Camel, reposing antediluvian as a dinosaur in the darkest hall of some museum, and children, back from a weekend on the moon, come to laugh at it, doubting that such a fragile patchwork of canvas, wood and baling wire could rise, much less fight, in the air. Why, you could poke your finger through the wing! Look, Daddy, at that old-fashioned propeller!

From Dover station I took a taxi to the Marine Landing office on Admiralty Pier. The assistant was on duty. He knew of no message from Lt.-Col. Collishaw, but perhaps the senior officer, due to return shortly, did.

'You don't plan on getting across to Boulogne tonight, I hope?' the assistant said. 'Last steamer left ten minutes ago, packed to the gunnels with demobs bound for the fleshpots of Paris.'

'Then I'll have to wait till morning.'

'You been demobbed?'

'No, I'm signing on for another year or so of bully beef and hard-tack.'

He looked at me as if I were slightly mad. 'A pity,' he said, and shuffled some papers.

I asked him for the name of the best hotel in town.

'The King's Arms. You'd best call for a reservation, Lieutenant. The town's hopping with demobs.'

As I put down the telephone the MLO came in. He remembered a message from Colly, but had mislaid it. After a long search he found it in the bottom drawer of the files, under a dirty teacup and a canister of sugar.

It was written on the back of a Gold Flake's packet. 'Proceed to Boulogne,' it read.

> *Avoid there a coquette in red named Mignonette. Tommy unfortunately did not. Further instructions M.L.O. Boulogne.*
> Boris Godunov.

'High-spirited fellow, that Collishaw,' the MLO said. 'Entertained us royally. We were sorry to see him go. From all the ribbons on his chest he must have seen a fair bit of action. What was the white one for?'

'Stefansson's Arctic Expedition,' I said shortly.

He hadn't heard of Colly, and it annoyed me. The panjandrums of propaganda had made Billy Bishop and William Barker the official Canadian heroes of the air, but for some unfathomable reason crossed Colly off their list. In day-in-day-out fighting, Colly's record stood first among British airmen. And yet his name was unfamiliar to the British army in France, and almost completely unknown to the British and Canadian public.

'Yes,' I said, 'He saw a fair bit of action,' and swinging up my kit, left the pier office.

At the King's Arms the desk clerk gave me the last bed in the house, a camp-bed set up in the laundry room. I had dinner, and then went into the oak-panelled bar.

It was packed and very lively. There was no room at the bar itself, and a girl seated with a couple of British naval officers asked me to join their party.

I thanked her and sat down. One of the officers, who was fairly drunk, squinted belligerently at my RAF insignia.

'Flyer, eh? Well, we're Dover Patrol.' He said it as if I owed him not only respect but money.

When I nodded pleasantly, his lip curled. 'You mean to say you've never heard of the Dover Patrol?'

'Can't say I have.'

'Well, we fed London during the war, damn it.'

The other officer winked at me. 'That's enough, Rowland. He probably saved London. Shot down all those Zeps and Gothas.'

'He sounds like an American,' the other said accusingly. 'And if he's an American, he believes in Prohibition.'

The girl, who had been looking at me intently, spoke for the first time. 'He looks like a rabbit, a handsome rabbit. Do they call you "Bunny", Ducks?'

'As a matter of fact,' I said, 'they do.'

'Flyers mostly rabbits,' the belligerent Dover Patroler said. 'Rabbits of the air. Up there stunting, showing off. Not Dover Patrol. We fed London. Got through nine and a half million mail bags and didn't lose a parcel or a letter. Hunted submarines, damn it. Attacked Zeebrugge. I was on the *Swift* when it sank a Hun destroyer.' He glowered at me. 'Lieutenant Rabbit, you ever sink a Hun destroyer?'

'His name's Lieutenant Bunny,' the girl said, reaching out her hand to cover mine. 'He's a perfectly lovely rabbit who flies in the air. He's going to take me away from these nasty seafaring bores, isn't he, to dance and dance till dawn?'

I got up from the table, grateful that the barmaid hadn't yet brought my drink. 'If you'll excuse me, I've got to turn in early for the steamer to Boulogne.'

'Sorry, old man,' the sober officer said. 'Buy you a drink when the next war comes around.' The girl pouted.

'Flying rabbits almost lost the war, damn it,' the drunken officer said. 'Couldn't stay in the air against Richthofen's circus. Dover patrol won the war, I tell you. Fed London, got through nine and a half million bags of mail…'

His voice faded as I left the bar. I spent an hour or so in a crowded pub down the street, and then turned in early. The steamer left at seven.

It was only an hour's trip across the Channel to Boulogne, but the sea was rough. In the lounge I began to feel queasy, and went out on deck for a little fresh air. Abruptly the steamer wallowed, sank in a deep trough, and rose again, lifting me three feet in the air and knocking my head against an unyielding obstruction. I came to in a forest of tree trunks that turned out to be British and French civilian legs.

'*Pauvre soldat.*'

'Pretty bad blow there.'

'He's coming round now. Give me a hand and we'll carry him inside.'

The accident had raised on the top of my head a bump so large that my garrison cap barely fit over it. For the rest of the trip I sat in the galley drinking tea, rubbing my bump, and feeling sorry for myself. My trip to Russia had started out, I thought, poorly.

At Boulogne the MLO handed me Colly's message. It said:

> *At Hotel Edouard VII, Paris. Instructions there if you happen to miss us. Kinkead warns you not to fall into clutches of the avaricious French. When drunk keep money sewed to inside pocket.* Trotsky.

I asked directions to the railway station, and there handed Colly's chit to an earnest young assistant Railway Transport Officer.

'Lieutenant, this is rather irregular,' he told me. 'I think we'd better wait for the senior officer's approval.'

'But the train to Paris pulls out in five minutes,' I protested.

He was sorry, but there was nothing he could do.

The next train was three hours later, and I had no intention of sticking around Boulogne station while the RTO perhaps got it in his head to check with Eastchurch.

When the train pulled out I was on it, holding my fare ready in my hand.

In Paris, at the Edouard VII, I learned from Colly's message that 47 Squadron had by-passed Paris for Marseilles.

In sheer disgust I decided on a few days rest in the City of Light. Foolishly, I neglected to take Kink's advice about money. Candle-lit dinners at Maxim's and the banks of violins at Tour d'Argent were a delight, and I had every confidence in Mimi till she disappeared with five hundred francs.

Life was '*très dure, mon petit lapin*,' her farewell note reminded me.

'Bunny,' I could hear Kink's lecture, 'you'll never understand women. You weren't born to. You treat a whore like a countess and a countess like a countess. Damn it all, man, at least try!'

In Marseilles I picked up another message from Colly at the RTO's:

> *Kink bets you played the fool in Paris. Burns Thomson bets not. On our way to Taranto, Italy. No idea how long there before embarking for Constantinople.* Peter the Great.

'How soon can I get a train for Taranto, Italy?' I asked the RTO.

He scratched his head. 'Trains are booked solid for the next two weeks. The demobbing, you know. Looks like you're stuck here for a while.'

Making the best of it, I got myself a room at the Splendide and went out to the promenoir at the Apollo. When I got sick of the gold-toothed whores and oysters and *vin de cassis* I started on the sights.

They occupied me only by day, and Marseilles is a tough town by night. One evening I was peacefully drinking a Pernod in a bistro near the harbour when a villainous French stevedore swaggered up to my table, and without a word, spat in my glass.

As Colly would have said, it was 'a bit too much'. Swinging from my boots, I hit the stevedore back into another table; it crashed over, depositing him and his two friends on the floor. They scrambled to their feet and came at me with knives, and I might have been floating in the Golfe du Lion next morning with all my problems solved, had not two *gendarmes* passed by at that moment.

My intended assassins were profusely apologetic when they learned I was not a '*sale Limey*' but an American. The captain of police turned me over to the British, and I was shown into the office of an MP major with brand new pips.

He glanced at Colly's bar chit and I saw the familiar look of doubt come into his eyes.

'You say you're on your way to Russia via Eastchurch?'

'That's right, Sir.'

'These orders don't look terribly official.' He reached for the phone, and put a call through to Eastchurch base.

'My assignment's very hush-hush, Sir,' I said hastily. 'State secret, and all that. If you'd care to, please check with General Comerford at the War Office. He told me I was to refer all inquiries to him.'

He hung up the phone as if it had scalded his fingers. 'Oh, well, in that case, no need to pursue it further. You can go now, Lieutenant, and good luck.'

The Marseilles RTO came through sooner than I had expected, and five days later I was on my way to Taranto. Waiting for me at the MLO's was another message from Colly.

> *Keep a weather eye on dancing girls and Levantines selling diamonds. Take passage immediately for Constantinople. Instructions there MLO.* Ivan the Terrible.

The MLO was doubtful about getting passage for me on the Princess Ina, leaving for Constantinople in three days.[2] But he would try. If he failed, I would be stuck in Taranto, probably for another two weeks.

That night for dinner I had *cozze*, Taranto's celebrated large mussel, and rather too much wine. Later I dropped into the bar of the hotel.

The toothy, moustached British officer sitting beside me borrowed a match and then introduced himself. 'Harcourt-Williams, Royal 72nd,' he said. 'Due to be demobbed?'

I told him I was waiting for a ship to Constantinople.

'Ah, great place for history, Marvelous Byzantine and Roman ruins. But Taranto's got some history, too, you know. Are you keen for history?'

'Every now and then.'

'Don't sell Taranto short. Why in 927 this town was destroyed utterly by the Saracens, and then rebuilt in 967 by Nicephorus Phocas. He built that bridge over the channel, toward the northeast of town, and the aqueduct that passes over it. Fine bit of construction that, I can tell you. Do you know when the town was conquered by Robert Guiscard?'

'Can't say I do,' I said, looking around for rescue.

'Guess,' Harcourt-Williams said smugly, and signaled the bartender for another round.

He looked at me expectantly.

'Around 1000?' I guessed.

Grinning, he slapped me on the shoulder. 'Not far off the mark. It was 1063, actually. Guiscard's son Behemund succeeded in Taranto, and after his death Roger II of Sicily gave the town to his son William the Bad. Then, in 1301 Philip, son of Charles II of Anjou, became Prince of the City. He…'

'All this is very interesting,' I interrupted, 'but could we perhaps skip on over to Russia? I'm on my way there, and I don't know a thing about it.'

'Russia.' Harcourt-Williams looked disappointed.

'I mean,' I said quickly, 'starting with the Revolution.'

'The Revolution.' He frowned into his campari. 'Well, to get up to the Revolution, you'll have to bear with me from the beginning. It's a quirk of mine; otherwise I can't order my dates. Let's see. Russia starts with the Slavs. No definite date there, but the Slavs appeared not on the steppe but in the forest…'

He went on to the Antae, the First Federated people, and from there to the Avars, and the Khazars, too. 'I see,' I interrupted him, 'but can't we move up just a little faster?'

He looked at me bleakly. 'But dear chap, you've got to consider the Yaroslav era. It was damned important around 1000. Svyatopolk the Damned killed his brothers, Boris and Gleb, but Yaroslav, another brother, assassinated *him*. Then there was Izyaslav, died in '73.

I let him go on for a while, then I said, 'I'm getting a bit confused by all these people and dates. Perhaps if we could jump to the Revolution of 1905, or was it 1906?'

'It was 1905. But dear fellow, in all conscience I couldn't possibly do that. Got to cover Ivan the Terrible, Boris Godunov, and Catherine the II, and then there are the Alexanders.'

'Was Catherine the II Catherine the Great?'

'Righto. Died in 1796.'

We went back to Ivan the Terrible. It was some time before we got to Alexander II (died 1881), and along about midnight Harcourt-

Williams launched into a disquisition on the Russo-Turkish wars. He was outlining the provisions of the treaty of San Stefano (1878), when I gave up and asked for the bill.

The Englishman was indignant. 'But my dear fellow, we were just getting to 1905!'

I yawned as I got down from the stool. 'You'll have to forgive me, Captain. I've got to catch a ship. It's the SS *Ennui*, bound for Tedium, and she's carrying a cargo of dates.'

I regretted my harshness to the captain by the time I reached my room. But the days were passing, it was taking ages to get to Russia, and I was beginning to wonder if I was going to get there at all.

For the rest of my time in Taranto I avoided the hotel bar, but on one occasion, passing by, I glanced inside to see Harcourt-Williams deep in historical monologue with a trapped lieutenant of the British fleet. I passed on quickly.

The MLO wrangled passage for me on the earlier sailing of the *Princess Ina*. A week later I was in Constantinople.

Colly had left a message with the MLO:

> *Come on to Novorossiisk, Russia. You are now where Europe and Asia meet, so watch out for foul Asiatic diseases.* Rasputin.

'How soon,' I asked the MLO wearily, 'can I get a ship for Novorossiisk?'

'You can't,' he told me, and my heart dropped to my boots until he explained himself. In a week I could get passage on a mule transport to Batum, on the east coast of the Black Sea, and from there I could probably board a tramp steamer to Novorossiisk. There was no direct route to Novorossiisk itself.

He wouldn't, however, advise that I go to Batum: not only was it a very dirty town but malaria infested. He had known of several people who had gone to Batum and never come back.[3]

I thanked him and went out to hail a taxi to the Hotel Pera Plaza, in the European section of the city.

In the shower the nozzle flew off and cut me in the cheek, and in a bad humour I went down to the bar. There I met a Mr. Poulas, a wealthy Greek businessman of international connections. Mr. Poulas was a short, well-dressed man with heavy eyebrows and unstartled, I might almost say, cynical, eyes. Almost immediately he offered to show me the town, but companionably enough agreed to devote this afternoon at least to pursuits of the less touristic variety. I found him a most pleasant drinking companion, with a capacity far superior to my own.

We had dinner, with which Mr. Poulas ordered the best champagne, and then he told me he had some business to attend to for the evening. He would be glad to put his car at my disposal.

I said I would probably be turning in early, and he nodded in his grave way. 'Early tomorrow we shall begin with the Mosque of Mohammed, and devote the day to various Moslem points of interest, saving the Byzantine and Roman for another time.'

'But Mr. Poulas,' I objected, 'you're here on a business trip.'

He smiled. 'Business and pleasure, they are for me the same. You will learn that, Lieutenant. Goodnight.'

I left the hotel for a stroll around the European quarter, ending up for some drinks at the Jardin Petits-Champs. Then I returned to the hotel, had a brandy, and went to bed.

Next morning I came from the dining room to find a glittering black Rolls parked before the hotel entrance. Mr. Poulas was sitting in the curtained back seat behind a uniformed chauffeur.

'Ah, Lieutenant, you slept well? Were you bothered by the roaches?'

'A little. Especially in the bathroom. I must have killed ten of them.'

He sighed. 'It is criminal for the best hotel in Constantinople to be roach infested. I will send up to your room a paste which you will find most efficient.'

We set off for the Mosque of Mohammed. I found Mr. Poulas to be an excellent guide, and I enjoyed the sights, but in the afternoon, after the Shah Zadek, my feet began to give out from treading miles of mosaic floors, and I begged off for a bath and a nap.

Mr. Poulas returned me to the hotel, where he again invited me to dinner. This time I insisted that he be my guest.

He said nothing that evening of what his real purpose was in entertaining me so royally. But the next evening, after we had covered the Seraglio, St. Sophia and the Hippodrome, he came out with his amazing offer over brandy and cigars.

It was nothing less than that I take over the London office of his shipbuilding business, at a magnificent salary, after, of course, my 'little tour' in Russia was over.

'I can see your main interests do not lie in business,' Mr. Poulas said. 'But you can learn. You are intelligent and adaptable; you are also a gentleman. You have charm. These are qualities that can carry you far in the shipping business, where one must deal with many people.'

I stared at him, taken at a loss. 'But Sir, you can't be serious. I'm hardly the executive type. Nor do I have any feeling for ships. I'm a flier, Mr. Poulas. My medium is the air, and I love it. Not the sea.'

'Flying is too dangerous. It is about time that you gave up the pursuit of danger and settled down. One can settle down very nicely in the shipping business.' He paused. 'I also, I must tell you, have a daughter.'

He brought out her photograph. I doubt if I have ever seen a more amazing family resemblance; Mr. Poulas' daughter, whose name was Athena, looked exactly like her father, even to the eyebrows.

I returned the picture to him, saying, 'She looks like a very nice girl.'

Undiscouraged, he said, 'She is an only child and very wealthy. That is better than "nice". My boy, it does not pay to play the romantic and the world does not turn on dreams. Idealism is dead. We are entering a time in which men will fight to become nothing, in which they will find their comfort in nothingness, their peace. Man is striving to make himself inhuman, and he will succeed. You go to fight that nothingness, that inhumanity, and I applaud your misguided courage. But the battle is lost before it is begun. Return from it, then, to whatever reality stands among the ruins. Serve a master who will continue to survive. My boy, do you understand me?'

He interpreted my silence tolerantly and got to his feet. 'I shall see you then for breakfast, tomorrow. At eight o'clock? We still have much to see.'

I had my answer for him at breakfast, and it in no way affected his hospitality. We saw the Golden Gate, the Pege, the gate of St. Romanus, the tower of Isaac Angelus and the wall of Leo, against which the Fourth Crusade had attacked. At noontime the chauffeur produced a magnificent hamper of wine, cheese and game, and we lunched in the limousine. It was dusk before Mr. Poulas' tour ended, at the ruins of the palace of Hermisdas.

'I will drop you off at the hotel,' he said, 'since I am leaving the city immediately.' At the Plaza he held out his hand.

'Goodbye, Icarus who would fly too close to the sun. We shall see who is the wiser, you, or I, the earthbound.'

I watched the limousine glide away, and went upstairs to pack my kit for my midnight sailing on the *Anglo-Egyptian* to Batum.

After the Pera Palace, roaches and all, the British merchant vessel was a comedown. It was built for mules, not passengers; and myself and the dozen British officers bound for Batum, and from there to the oil fields of Tiflis and Baku, were issued camp-beds for sleeping in the mess. We lifted anchor and headed into seven days of heavy ground swell and driving rain. The only consolation was that there was no necessity to watch out for submarines – only floating mines.

The beds were hard and lumpy, but the smell was worse. The whole ship stank of mules, and we drank mule in our coffee and ate mule with our eggs. Even when we went out on the hurricane deck for a breath of air, we breathed mule.

An officer named Baker, a tense, thin chap in his thirties, found the accommodations and atmosphere particularly offensive. Also, as I discovered by the second day out, he detested Americans.

'It's an insult to the dignity of His Majesty's army,' Baker kept insisting. 'Tell me now, Aten, don't you think so? I mean, I can see you Americans doing something like this, but a mule transport for British officers… its a bit too thick. I even saw a rat this morning.'

Sargent, a fair, mild butterball of a man with an unexpectedly sadistic sense of humour, snorted. 'Think of the Greek muleteers below decks, Baker; they've got it much worse. Why, the rats nibble at their toes for dessert.'

'At least you can't say the rats are American,' I said to Baker. 'They're too lean for that.'

Baker would have replied, except that he spied a rat flitting past the companionway. 'Another rat! A big black one! My God, they're taking over!'

'I understand,' said Sargent, lazily turning over on his side, 'that when you get rats and mules together on an unclean ship the result is often bubonic plague.'

To escape the mess I would often talk with Mattson, the first mate, a slow, stolid briarwood of a man who had some knowledge of Russia. He told me it was a bad place to go.

'It's been hell and it'll be worse before it's over. Former shipmate of mine took a load of them refugees from Novo to Constantinople, and he told me some terrible things. Them Reds has killed and tortured thousands. There isn't hardly a family that hasn't got one in it dead.' He glanced significantly at my uniform. 'Them togs won't keep 'em from roasting you over a slow fire, Lieutenant, unless you've got some poison to take first.'

The mate shrugged when I asked him about rats as disease carriers. He was used to the beasts. 'If you've got a ruddy skin,' he said, 'you don't need to worry yourself about the plague. The impurities flush out nice from a ruddy skin; it's the sallow, dark ones, like Baker, who catch it.'

On the fourth day I saw my fourth rat, and on the fifth, my fifteenth. They had begun to swarm up from the holds, and though Mattson told us that was nothing in particular to worry about, Baker was terrified. He warned us to keep away from him, and after every meal he washed his own dishes and utensils. He smoked Gold Flakes incessantly to keep off 'the germs'.

We would look up to find him studying us intently. 'Sargent,' he would say, 'you're looking greenish.' And to me, 'Don't lie, Aten, you've got cramps. That's the first sign.'

Sargent kicked my foot under the table. 'The mate says three muleteers are dying below. One's green already. Once he gets convulsions he'll kick the bucket in less than an hour.'

Baker swallowed uneasily. 'Do I look green? I feel green.'

Sargent regarded him critically. 'Around the gills, slightly. Yes, I can definitely see a little verdigris there. Don't you think so, Aten?'

'Not so much green as blue, I'd say.'

'Blue's the second and final stage,' Sargent said gravely.

Baker groaned and pillowed his head in his arms. His voice came muffled. 'And no doctor on this disgusting British tub. At least the bloody Americans would have had a bloody butcher of a doctor.'

The next day, three muleteers died in convulsions. At Constanta, Rumania, our first port of call, the authorities took note of our yellow flag and refused us permission to dock for refueling. A gasoline lighter set out from shore with a single man on it, a bandana tied around the lower part of his face. The crew of the Anglo-Egyptian did the job of refueling.

From the deck we looked upon the grimy quays, coal wharfs and warehouses of Constanta. To the eyes of landlubbers confined aboard a ship flying the yellow flag they looked inviting.

Suddenly Baker dashed to the rail and began shouting to the lighter crewman: 'Send a doctor! A doctor! Englishmen are dying!'

The Rumanian looked up at him, puzzled.

'I tell you Englishmen are dying! For God's sake send help!'

When Mattson and a crewmember moved toward him, Baker, making a tremendous effort, tried to hoist himself over the side. The mate grabbed his belt just in time, and took him, sobbing, below to the captain's cabin.

Later Mattson told me that they had managed to calm Baker down with several shots of whisky. The next day Baker came back to the mess, where he lay for hours on his cot, staring up at the ceiling.

In Batum harbour, the first Russian territory we had so far seen, a quarantine launch, flying the Union Jack, pulled up alongside the *Anglo-Egyptian*. The MLO gave us instructions through a megaphone while the cold February rain slanted down.

The entire crew and passengers, the MLO said, were to be held in quarantine camp.

'For how long?' the captain shouted from his bridge.

'A month at least,' the MLO bellowed. 'If you live. There's lots of malaria in this bloody town, if you don't come down with the bubonic.'

'And I thought we'd live happily ever after, after the war was done,' Sargent grumbled.

First to land from the ship were the six dead muleteers, strapped down on stretchers. Though twisted in the final throes of convulsions, with their mouths gaping wide and their eyes staring with horror, each one wore a gayly coloured bandana, neatly tied at the chin. Stinking of mule, their countrymen shoved off in the launch after them, and then we followed.

The stench of waste from the oil refineries made us sneeze and cough as the launch took us into an empty tanker berth; there were no docks at Batum. Baker snarled something unintelligible at me as I tried to help him over the side.

The MLO took a wire to Colly at Novorossiisk giving him my whereabouts, and then we went on by lorry to the camp.

The quarantine camp was a desolate straggle of tents at the foot of a mountain behind the town. Barbed wire and a company of Sikhs kept us prisoner. I was assigned to a tent with Sargent and Baker, and decided to make the best of it.

It took a certain amount of doing. Baker began to be troublesome again, conceiving a violent dislike for the camp doctor, and then there was the rain, which was worse than Baker. Average yearly rainfall on the east coast of the Black Sea is over ninety-three inches, the highest in the Caucasus, and for two weeks the rain never stopped: it poured straight down or was blown by gusts of wind through our tent flap, wetting our clothes, mildewing our boots, and turning our tempers from grey to black. We settled deep into the ruts of melancholy, ignoring one another for hours for Russian newspapers we couldn't read, and snapping out insults when we did deign to talk. The conviction grew upon me that I would still be in Batum when the Bolsheviks surrendered.

One morning there were four inches of water on the dirt floor. Baker got up, calmly sloshed in bare feet to the tent flap, and went outside.

'Baker!' I yelled to him, 'you forgot your boots!'

Sargent leaped up from his cot. 'He's gone balmy again!' Motioning for me to follow, he plunged through the flap.

We weren't a minute too soon. Baker was talking to one of the Sikhs on his post at the end of the tent row. As we approached he grabbed the Sikh's rifle and ran away with it, firing into the air.

'He's trying to kill God for all this rain,' Sargent said hoarsely. 'When God doesn't come falling down he'll start shooting up the camp.'

The rifleless Sikh had already blown his whistle, but the shots were alarm enough. Turbaned guards poured from the headquarters shack, and men poked tousled heads out of tent flaps.

Sargent and I were only a few yards from Baker when he turned the rifle on us. He was perfectly composed; he might have been potting at ducks in a shooting gallery. A bullet tore past my ear, and one slammed into the mud at Sargent's feet.

It stopped Sargent's forward action, but I was going too fast to stop. Baker had pulled the trigger on me a second time when I left my feet in a tackle and brought him down in the mud. His head slammed against a barbed wire fence post and he was suddenly still.

The doctor came hurrying up, squatted down beside Baker, and lifted up one of his eyelids.

'Blotto for a while, but he'll be all right. Bring a stretcher,' he ordered the Sikhs.

They took Baker to the hospital in Batum and from there to the hospital in Tiflis, for an operation on his brain. Our quarantine was over three weeks later, and though Sargent promised to write from Tiflis, I never found out what happened to Baker.

The MLO got me passage on the SS *Konslavtina*, a Black Sea tramp, to Novorossiisk. The *Konslavtina* had come from the Crimea to pick up passengers in Batum, and its decks were packed with refugees returning to the cities recently reconquered by the Whites. I shared a cabin deluxe with seven British officers who, though they were all gentlemen, had left the worst berth for me. The drain pipe from the lavatory of the deck above passed above the head of my berth, and it leaked. I spent the three nights of the trip to Novoroissiisk sitting at the foot of the bed with my back propped up against the wall.

The days were more interesting. I was fascinated by the returning refugees, the first Russians I had seen in a group. It was easy to separate the bourgeois from the aristocrats; the bourgeois families always left a child to watch their belongings while mama or papa went to the lavatory or for a stroll, while the upper classes had a certain contempt for possessions, and made little or no effort to protect them against theft. Once an elegant baron returned to find a young man going through his steamer trunk. Without a word and with no evident anger, he kicked him down the nearest companionway.

One afternoon on the top deck I made the acquaintance of Count Krosilev, a retired Tsarist colonel returning from the Crimea. The count, who spoke English perfectly, was tall, ramrod straight, and wore a monocle with aristocratic dash. At first I disliked him for a rather sublime arrogance, but as we talked I saw that his self-assurance was at least half the product of his class. The pride and sense of honour mixed in with his rigidities were, I thought, Russian virtues that would be valuable in a fight.

He told me the story of the rise of the White Volunteer Army under Kornilov and Alexeyev. It was an epic one. Kornilov, born into a poor Cossack family in Siberia, had made his way by sheer ability to the top rank of the Russian army, distinguishing himself both in the Japanese and the European war. Captured by the Austrians with a remnant of men after saving a whole army from destruction, the general had escaped in the disguise of an Austrian soldier. Immediately after the revolution he had been chosen, as the most popular general in Russia, to command the garrison at Petrograd, but had resigned in disgust and returned to the front. There, as commander in chief of the armies, he had been betrayed into an attempt to force the government to restore discipline in the army and order at home. Imprisoned with his staff at Bykhov, Kornilov had escaped from there on the eve of the Bolshevik triumph, and ridden across country to the Don, joining Alexeyev in an attempt to form an anti-German and anti-Red army of officers and Cossacks. In February, 1918, he had walked out of Rostov at the head of three and a half thousand men, the nucleus of the Volunteer Army, which I was soon to join.

The general's army had marched into the steppe surrounded by a large Red force, far more numerous and better armed and equipped than themselves. Yet Kornilov's leadership had made his men invincible, and despite the huge odds against them 200,000 to 3000 – the Reds broke at their approach. Often a dozen of Kornilov's men would fight, and defeat, many scores of the enemy. After Kornilov had been killed by shell fire outside Ekaterinodar on April 13th of last year, General Anton Denikin had taken over the command of the White armies. By this time the Cossacks of the southern steppes were in revolt against the Reds, and had come to the aid of the Volunteer Army.

About the future Krosilev was supremely confident.

'Now that we have reached the Donets and broken the front at Kharkov, we have the Reds on the run. Yet only a few months ago it seemed as if that devil Lenin's prediction was coming true – the Central Powers and treaty of Brest-Litovsk were crumbling together, and the European revolution was at hand. What Lenin didn't reckon with was substantial help from the Allies.'

The colonel filled me in on the White plan of attack. The Whites hoped to reach Moscow and Petrograd by a military advance simultaneously from the south, east and north-west. In the south Denikin's armies were to advance northwards to the Ukraine, occupied by the Red Army when the Germans had withdrawn last year. The left wing of Denikin's forces was to make for Kiev and Kharkov; the right, under General Wrangel, was to push along the Volga and link up with the armies of General Yudenich, striking down from Estonia. Meanwhile Kolchack, in Siberia, was organizing a mass advance westwards across the Volga, aiming directly at Moscow.

'We shall have taken Moscow,' Krosilev said, 'by next Christmas.'

'What about the Red armies?' I asked. 'Aren't they building up?'

'I hear Trotsky's a very capable soldier, especially for a man who had had no actual military experience. The Red armies will be more dangerous as time goes on, but not dangerous enough.'

I asked Krosilev to tell me what he knew about Denikin. Probably 47 Squadron would be flying under either the commander-in-chief or under the orders of Baron Wrangel.

'A good soldier, a hard worker. A bit too liberal for my tastes; he's said some harsh things about the so-called aristocrats and officers of the guard. But that's because of his bourgeois origins – Denikin is the son of minor officer of the line.'

'And Baron Wrangel?' Somehow Wrangel interested me more.

Krosilev took off his monocle and polished it with a mono-grammed handkerchief. 'A man of iron, and probably the most brilliant officer we have. Wrangel isn't, perhaps, as Russian as most of us; he comes from an international family of German and Scandinavian lines, a family that has produced outstanding statesmen and soldiers for centuries. In the war he was a guardsman, and rose to the command of a brigade. My brother fought under him at Galatz; he never knew a man who more commanded the devotion of his men. I wish he, rather than Denikin, were in supreme command.'[4]

The baron, Krosilev told me, was fortunate to have an extraordinary wife. During the revolution he had been arrested in Yalta and hauled before the people's court. Several other prisoners, including an old Tsarist general and a prince, had been condemned to death by the tribunal. The tribunal chief asked the baroness, who wasn't under arrest, why she was here with her husband, and she had told him she wanted to stay with him until the end. So impressed had the chief been by her devotion that he had released the baron, telling him that he owed his life to his wife.

Like Krosilev, the other refugees aboard ship seemed to take a White victory for granted. There was singing all day long, and at night, the *kazachok* and wild gypsy dances. Under the brittle stars concertinas wailed '*Ochi Chornie*', and lovers slipped into lifeboats while the old people nodded over memories. Taking a turn on deck before going back to my leaky berth, I would see Krosilev standing on the quarter-deck, hands clasped behind his back and shoulders straight, observing the festivities like the lord of the manor at one of his peasant's weddings.

The *Konslavtina* docked at Novorossiisk in early March in bitterly cold weather that pierced my winter greatcoat.[5] To the music of a splendidly uniformed brass band, the refugees trooped down from the gangplank, wiping their eyes. More than one bent down and kissed the ground.

Krosilev pumped my hand and wished me good luck. 'You will love Russia,' he said, 'and Russia will love you. But remember, those who have a love affair with us become a little Russian themselves.'

I laughed. 'Is that a prophecy?'

'It is a warning,' he said, and clicking his heels, saluted and strode away down the pier.

At the MLO's office there was a brief, unhumourous message for me from Colly:

> *Report to British Mission Novorossiisk for further instructions.*
> R. Collishaw, Lt.-Col., RAF

My war had finally begun.

★

I shared a *droshky* to the British Mission with a Russian-speaking English officer. He talked with the driver, a lugubrious fellow with a straggling brown mustache, who told us that conditions under the Whites were the same as they had been under the Reds before the latter left the town, except that the Bolshies had put the grumblers up against the wall and shot them.

'When they arrested me,' the driver said, the officer translating for my benefit, 'I said, "Shoot me if you want, I have a nasty wife and not too much to live for. But think – what good will it do you?" So they let me go.'

The driver said that we should send back the Tsar as the only man capable of keeping order, and when the officer said that the Tsar was dead, he refused to believe him. The Englishman turned to me with an amused shrug. 'Ivan here insists the Tsar's in England, as guest of the King.'

I asked my taxi companion the time, and he grinned in answer. 'Take your pick,' he said. 'We have five "times" in Novorossiisk. One is local, and the second ship. The third's Petrograd time, standard throughout Russia for the railways, and the White army. The fourth's the cement-works' time, announced by the blowing of an hourly whistle, and the fifth, British Mission time, which is unreliable. There's an hour and a half difference between the fastest and the slowest of these various times, so I'd suggest that you merely put your wristwatch in your pocket and wait till we've won the war.'

At the Mission I learned that Colly and the Squadron were at Ekaterinodar, base headquarters of Wrangel's army. My instructions were to join them there.

'You'll have to provide the fare,' I told the Mission staff captain. 'I spent my last brass farthing on taxi fare here.'

I pulled out my pockets to prove it to him. They were completely empty, except for a small grey bug, native to the *Konslavtina*, which crawled trustingly out into my hand.

BOOK TWO

*

The Sky above the Volga

Chapter Three

*

The spurs of the Caucasus abut deeply on the Black Sea. The double-engined train, cutting through the notch that overhung the town, climbed to a considerable altitude in what seemed a matter of minutes. The seaward flanking ranges were only around four thousand feet high, but the main snow-covered ranges were close to twelve thousand.

As a Texas and California boy I had never seen such mountains; the Chocolate Mountains of the Imperial Valley were dwarfed in comparison.[1]

It was still sunset as we came to the main ranges, and I saw, below me, fifty or sixty miles of snowfield changing colour in the dying light. Rocks, cliffs, pinnacles, gleaming fields of snow were rose, then violet, and deep gentian. There were pine forests in a smooth bluish plain, and where it ran white with its rapids, a river. I sat lost in admiration till the light failed and a draft on my shoulder nudged me into putting on my greatcoat.

My ticket was first class but I sat in a third class coach that was dirty, cushionless and cold. The ordinary third-class passengers had worse accommodations. At the station in Novorossiisk they had filed docilely into incredibly filthy cattle cars, with what I assumed was typical Russian resignation, allowing themselves to be packed inside with hardly enough room to turn round. Those unable to get in had struggled for a place on the platform between the coaches, on the buffers, and even on the roofs. I wondered how many of them, should they escape death by freezing, would manage to stay on during the overnight trip to Ekaterinodar.

Down in front, near the lavatory that was out of order, sat a fat man in a luxurious fur coat who every now and then lifted a flask to his lips from which he drank greedily. The conductor had turned away a family of four so that Furcoat could travel in two seats with his luggage heaped around him.

'He – how you call him? – speculator,' said the small, smooth-shaven Russian officer who sat beside me. He shook his head in disgust. 'Is no more aristocrats who have the money, but worse, since the Revolution; is bad man like such.'

I nodded sympathetically, and pulling my greatcoat up around my ears, arranged myself for sleep.

Waking up later with hunger pangs, I shared the chocolate bars in my pocket with the officer. Speculator Furcoat had opened a big straw hamper of table delicacies, and a little girl from the back of the coach came up to stand beside him and salivate wistfully. With a grunt he motioned to her to go away. As she passed by my seat I gave her the last of the chocolate.

'*Spasibo*,' she whispered, and went on back to her seat.

'She meaning "thank you",' said the officer.

From above on the coach roof we heard a scream, and then, more faintly, the thud of a fallen body. The train clacked on, and I got up with the intention of pulling the emergency cord, but the Russian took hold of my sleeve.

'That only *muzhik* who has fallen off.'

Well, aren't they going to stop for him?'

He shook his head. 'Train must keep to schedule. Is regret.'

I sat down again. Is regret, I thought uneasily, and tried to settle back to sleep.

Shots woke me. The train now was running over the flat, level, treeless steppe, lightly dusted with snow, and out the window I saw a group of mounted men riding along with the coaches. Tall and well-built, they wore long grey coats with cartridge belts across their chests, and high karakul hats. Each had pistols at his belt and in one hand flourished a rifle, in the other, a long whip. The whip cracks sounded like pistol shots. And how they rode! Like perfect horse-men in a dream of perfect horsemen riding perfect mounts. Before seeing these men I had thought myself a good horseman.

'*Dobroye utro!*' they shouted at us.

'Kuban Cossacks,' my seatmate said, rubbing his eyes, 'They tell us good morning.'

'Those boys know how to ride.'

'Very good fighters, too. And – how you say?,' – he pantomimed emptying a bottle, 'good men for the drink.'

The Cossacks veered off into the steppe, firing a rifle volley in salute.

In another half hour we crossed the Kuban River, and came into

Ekaterinodar, named for Catherine II, great and lascivious Empress of the Russias. Kink and Bill Daly were waiting for me in a Red Cross van at the station.

Kink returned my burlesque salute somberly. 'I have the honour,' he said, 'to present the respects of Colonel Henry Dudgeon, who requests your presence *instanter* in Eastchurch for court-martial proceedings.'

Bill looked at his watch. 'There's a train back to Novo at seven tonight.'

I turned white. Had I come all this way only to be shipped back under arrest to Eastchurch?

'Kink, Bill,' I pleaded. 'For God's sake say you're not serious.'

As Bill swung my kit into the back of the van Kink said, 'Hop in, Bunny. Dudgeon fumed and spluttered, but Colly got it fixed through General Holman of the British Mission. As a matter of fact, Dudgeon's been shipped off to Rhodesia for misappropriation of funds. You're free to fly and die in Russia.'

I relaxed happily in the back seat as Kink drove through the town to the Chernomorskt Aerodrome on its other side. As we passed through the main square I stopped jabbering long enough to point to a large map before which a considerable crowd had collected. 'What's that?' I asked.

'A military map that shows the White advance,' Bill told me. 'At night it's lit up like a Christmas tree.'

'How are things going for our side?' I asked.

'Damn well,' Kink replied. 'The whole of the Northern Caucasus is in Denikin's pocket, and Wrangel's just liberated the Terek region in a brilliant campaign. Kolchak's on the march toward the Volga. It looks like Christmas in Moscow for sure.'

'Now for some of our questions,' Bill said ominously. 'Did Tommy win that bet that you'd make an ass of yourself in Paris? Did you buy diamonds in Constantinople? How did – '

'Hold on, Daly,' Kink interrupted. 'Let the poor fish tell all of us together at the drome. Otherwise it's a double humiliation.'

In the aerodrome mess Colly was having a second breakfast,[2] and Tommy sat beside him, nursing a cup of coffee. Neither said a word as I came in.

Playing along with the game, I let Kink push me down onto the bench on the other side of the table. Kink and Bill then joined Colly and Tommy on the side opposite, the four of them facing me like a tribunal of judges.

'Thanks for the Dudgeon business, Colly,' I said.

He dismissed it with a wave of his hand. 'First things first. Now, how did you like Mignonette in Boulogne?'

'She was occupied.'

'Did you make a fool of yourself in Paris?' asked Tommy.

'I did.'

'Pay Tommy,' Bill said.

'I can't till I cash a check.'

'Were you victimized by Levantine merchants?'

'Positively not.'

Colly turned to Kink. 'Acting-Major Kinkead, will you fill in Acting-Captain Aten[3] on the five points of our squadron incentive plan?'

'Gladly, Sir.' Kink held out his right hand, palm down, and bent down a finger as he ticked off each individual point. 'One: first of the flight to shoot down a Bolshie plane is entitled to the first princess encountered by B Flight. Two: first medal winner of B Flight is entitled to the first duchess. Three and four: second kills and second winners are entitled to the second princess and second duchess, respectively.'

'What about countesses?' I asked.

'This country's rotten with countesses and a lot of types who call themselves countesses but are not. Therefore countesses don't count.'

'What's the fifth point of this incentive plan?'

'Liquor ration. There is none. We've got enough ale, beer, Scotch, brandy, rye and vodka for a regiment of the Royal Irish.'

'Wonderful,' I said. 'I assume we're having a little celebration this evening?'

Colly shook his head. 'No *prazdniks*, as they call them, for a while, Bunny. B Flight train pulls out today for Beketofka at the Tsaritsyn front, and you boys fly up tomorrow morning.[4] A Flight's already at Beketofka drome, waiting for the snow to melt so we can begin Spring operations. I'll be based here in Ekat, outfitting C Flight for action and generally directing things. Every few weeks or so I'll be up to see you.'

'Will we be travelling on these trains?' I asked.

'Living on them. This is a cavalry war, mostly; we'll be following the Cossacks north toward Moscow, and after the Whites take Tsaritsyn, we'll be too much on the move to afford the luxury of a permanent base. When the planes aren't in the air, they'll be packed up on the moving train, or parked on the steppe – our temporary landing fields – trackside. Are you getting the picture?'

'He looks rather stunned,' Kink said. 'I'd better show him the set-up, and get his kit aboard.'

Kink drove me to the Ekaterinodar yards, where B Flight train stood on a siding. It included, he told me, an engine, and tender, two pullman cars, a lounge-mess car, and twenty-five box freights and flatcars. The Pullmans, the pilots' quarters, were on the continental plan with compartments off a passageway. The dining car was a combined mess, lounge and kitchen. In some of the box cars were quartered the hundred-odd ground crewmen and enlisted Tommies assigned to the Flight; others carried ammunition, bombs, petrol, and provisions. The flatcars were for our planes, now in the hangars at Ekaterinodar drome.[5] There were also a number of freights with the letters POW stencilled on their sides.

'Those are the cars for the *plennys*, the prisoners of war,' Kink explained. 'We picked up a batch of *plennys* here in Ekat as labourers, and a couple of them serve as the officers' batmen. You'll get your pick at Beketofka. The monster you see hurtling towards us now is my batman, Ivan.'

Ivan was a huge bearded fellow, at least six-feet-five, wearing a British private's uniform several sizes too small for him. He skidded to a stop before us, and breathing heavily, bowed from the waist. In his eyes, as he looked at Kink, was a look of great canine devotion.

'*Dobroye utro*, Ivan,' Kink said.

Ivan muttered something unintelligible in a *basso profundo* voice.

'They were going to put Ivan into a work crew when I picked him out of the prisoners' compound,' Kink said, 'but I don't think that's the reason for all this extravagant affection. Ivan has a passion for bully beef, eats four tins of the horrid stuff a day, and without me he wouldn't have known it existed.'

Kink pointed to my kit in the van, and then to the first of the Pullmans. Ivan was lifting the heavy kit as though it were a string bag when a stubby, round-faced sergeant major approached us and saluted. I noticed that he limped.

Kink introduced me. 'Sergeant Major Hoskins, the man who gets things done. Sergeant,' he asked Hoskins, 'is everything ready to go?'

'Ready, Sir,' Hoskins said, 'except for one minor detail. Cowderdrill's got all those samovars he bought piled up on his bunk, and I'm thinking that if General Maund came by for a last-minute inspection, they wouldn't look so very soldierlike.'[6]

Kink groaned. 'You tell Cowderdrill that if he doesn't stop worrying about those samovars being stolen and move them immediately to one of the storecars where they belong, I'll have him drawn and quartered.'

'Can't tell him that, Sir,' Hoskins said with an almost imperceptible wink at me.

'Why not?' Kink demanded.

'Because, Sir, he'd believe me, and have a fit of hysterics.'

'All right, then threaten to turn him over to the Bolshies for torture. And Hoskins, will you find Lieutenant Grigoriev and ask him to see me in compartment 9? Not two hours from now but now.'

Ivan brought my kit into compartment 9, adjoining Kink's, and departed, with another low bow to us both. While we waited for Grigoriev, Kink filled me in on the White Russian liaison officer and interpreter who would be in command of the train on its trip from Ekaterinodar to Beketofka. Grigoriev had flown the eastern front during the war and had twice been decorated with the Cross of St. George, Tsarist Russia's highest military honour. When the revolution began he had escaped across Bulgaria to Salonika, where he had flown briefly with the RAF. From Salonika he had returned to south Russia and joined the Volunteer Army. Wrangel had assigned him to 47 Squadron in Ekat.

'Wonderful chap, Grigoriev,' Kink said. 'The only trouble is that Russky – we call him that – is a terrible pest about flying a Camel. I keep telling him that the Russians flew Nieuports during the war and that they'll never get used to the Camel's right-hand turn.[7] But with Russky it's like talking to the wall.'

'With all respects, you can tell me thus till Kingdom went, and still I will not believe. Before we go to Moscow yet I will the Camel fly.'

I turned to see a tall handsome blond standing in the doorway. Good-nature glowed on his face and I liked him immediately.

'I am pleased you meet,' Russky said with evident pride in his English.

'You'll be seeing a lot of Bunny here,' Kink told him. 'He's the curious type and he'll be calling on you for a lot of interpreting.'

'I am very good that,' Russky said, beaming. 'I will with most pleasure interrupt your questions. Now, if you will excuse, much responsibility.'

'Nice chap,' I said to Kink when Russky had disappeared down the passageway, 'but is he the best you could do as an interpreter?'

Kink shrugged. 'You should have seen the one Colly fired before Russky joined us. At least we can understand Russky. How do you like your portable digs?'

'Luxurious,' I said, looking around at the clean and well-appointed compartment. 'All this plush and brass and a batman too! I feel like they're fattening us up for the slaughter.'

'Speaking of food,' Kink grimaced, 'I'd better introduce you to Cowderdrill, the messman. Make a good impression on him, or there'll be hell to pay in more subtle little ways than you can imagine.'

We went from the Pullman to the lounge and mess car, which adjoined it. The lounge was elegant, with comfortable leather-upholstered *banquettes* facing on three sides a gleaming mahogany table. On the table was an assortment of magazines, including copies of *L'Illustration* and *La Vie Parisienne*. In the middle of the car a partition separated the lounge from the dining area. The several tables that would have been in the conventional European dining car had been removed for a single mess table. Against one wall was a bar. Off to the right were the pantry and kitchen, from which we heard a loud banging of pots and pans.

'Cowderdrill!' Kink called.

'Yes, Sir, trotting along immediately,' came the reply.

I couldn't repress a grin at the extraordinary-looking human being who emerged from the pantry. Utterly lacking in coordination, he didn't walk as much as lurch and stumble, as if controlled by the strings of a drunken puppeteer. His mouth hung adenoidally open to show huge horse teeth. From the top of his rather turnip shaped head carrot-coloured hair grew in every direction. His face was more freckles than skin, and his eyes bulged like a frog's surprised in the act of mating.

He saluted, narrowly missing his right eye. 'Yes, Sir, Captain Kinkead, Sir, did you call?'

'Major, Cowderdrill, Major. Did you get rid of those samovars?'

'Yes, Sir, I did Sir, moved 'em to the bomb car. I would appreciate your putting a lock on there, Sir. Wouldn't want them stolen.'

'Nobody's going to steal your damn samovars, Cowderdrill. Will you get this through your head: *Russia is full of samovars!*'

'Yes, Sir, quite, Sir, but you'll lock the bomb car just the same?'

Kink rolled his eyes ceilingward in despair. 'Yes, Cowderdrill, I will. Is there anything else you insist upon?'

'No Sir, nothing, Sir. I thank you.'

'Now this is Captain Aten, Cowderdrill, my adjutant. He likes his eggs soft-boiled and his meat rare. Can you remember that?'

'Yes, Sir. Meat hardboiled and eggs rare. I mean the other way around. Quite, Sir, I'll remember. Glad you're joining us, Lieutenant Hatton.'

'Let's get out of here,' Kink muttered, 'before I go quite mad.'

★

Shortly after dawn the next morning we took off for the Tsaritsyn front. Kink led the formation; I was last. Coming off the runway my foot jammed in the floorboards, and the Camel swung a full ninety degrees to the left. In itself that wouldn't have been so bad, had it not been for the pile of bombs, glistening with yellow paint, that lay directly in my path three hundred yards away in the corner of the drome. Three hundred yards can be covered quickly in a Camel at half throttle, but I had time to think of my blackest sins and wish there had been more of them.

Clearing the bomb pile by inches, I worked my foot free and turned to the right to rejoin the formation. Kink, who always saw all there was to see both fore and aft, waggled his wings and climbed for altitude. The formation followed him along the railway leading across the steppe.

The steppe was bare and cold, lifeless and depressing. The villages we passed at intervals intensified the monotony of earth meeting sky. The houses were identical: square, thatch-roofed, mud-brown. In every village there were two churches, one Russian Orthodox, the other a Mosque. The Orthodox church was big, with white walls, green roof and gables; the Mosque small, with a red roof and a dome. They never varied in design or colour.

Occasionally the railroad made a detour of as much as three or four miles around a town. This struck me as strange, since the flat country presented no resistance to a straight line. I later learned the reason, which was very Russian: when the tracks were laid, the builders of the railroad had demanded a bribe to run them through a particular town. Failing to receive it, they made a detour.

We had been in the air no more than thirty minutes when Tommy dropped out of formation and went down in a long glide. Engine trouble, I assumed. None of our planes was in very good condition; only a short time ago they had been rushed to Ekaterinodar from what had lately been the Salonika front, and the squadron mechanics hadn't had a chance to overhaul them.

Tommy landed in a strip of cultivated field near the road bed. When we arrived at Beketofka Kink would send out a two-seater DH-9 with a mechanic and new parts to get him under way again.

An hour later Bill Daly wagged his wings and went down with what appeared to be another case of engine trouble. I was congratulating myself on my own good fortune when the gas pressure pump on the centre section strut blew off into the slipstream, missing my head by half a foot.

With no regular gas pump, I was obliged to make use of the emergency gas pump lever on the control panel. The pressure gauge began to drop and I started to work the lever up and down. For some time now the steppe had been bare of villages, and I didn't relish the thought of a forced landing.

I closed in on Kink, who had lost altitude to make the most of his fuel supply. My arm was numb from pumping the gas lever; in a few more minutes I would be forced to land.

Kink's oil pressure pump detached itself from his undercarriage strut and darted past my starboard wing, and suddenly the Volga, slow and enormous, was before us, and then, on its west bank, Beketofka drome.

We taxied in on a strip of pasture to a group of canvas hangars camouflaged in grey, brown and green. Off in a corner sat eight DH-9 bombers, half of them with the red, white and black insignia of the White Air Force, the rest with the red, white and blue emblem of the RAF.[8] On a siding to the right were A and B Flight trains. A Flight bombers were being unloaded from the flat cars.

Russky ran up anxiously. 'I see no Tommy, Bill? Something has delayed?'

'Kaput,' Kink said sadly. 'A perfect demon of a Bolshie fighter caught them with their wings down.'

'They're all right,' I reassured the horrified Russian. 'Engine trouble. They'll be here by and by.'

Russky gave Kink a look of infinite reproach, saluted with excessive precision, and stalked away.

Kink frowned. 'Shouldn't have done that. I keep forgetting that Russky hasn't developed an RAF sense of humour. Now he's got something to hold against me, and one of these days I'll have to let him fly that Camel, and he'll break his damn neck.'

Kink left me to send out the rescue crews, and I went to my compartment in B Flight train.

Passing by the window I noticed through the curtains that the lights were on, and that someone was moving around inside. A thief? A spy? Quickly I ran up the steps and down the passageway and flung open the door.

A small, freckled youth with a shock of sorrel hair stared back at me gravely. He was dressed in the black fatigues of a POW, and he was holding a pair of my flying boots in his hand.

I grabbed them from him. 'What the devil are you doing here?' I demanded, though it was perfectly plain. 'Don't you know it's the firing squad for anyone caught looting or stealing?'

He hung his head.

I closed the door and sat down on the edge of my bunk to think the matter over. There was something appealing about the boy: he had that combination of candour and simplicity I had already noticed about the Russians. I had no desire to send him to his death for a crime so minor as the attempted theft of a pair of boots. At the same time I wanted to discourage him from stealing.

There was a knock at the door.

'Quick!' I whispered to the POW, 'Into the closet!'

He looked at me without comprehension. I got up, and opening the shallow closet next to the washstand, motioned him inside. Without the slightest hesitation he obeyed.

I opened the door. It was Russky.

He glanced inside the compartment. '*Plenny* no came?'

'What's that, Russky?'

'I send *plenny* for you to see he is satisfactory. Anikin, his name.'

'You mean you sent me a POW?'

'Yes, he little Bolshie. Red hair – and how you call it? – frecklings. He should polish boots and straighten down, I tell him. If you like, Feodor Anikin become your batman.'

'Oh,' I said, getting the picture finally. I yelled for Feodor to come out.

The closet door opened and Feodor emerged, blinking. Russky's mouth fell open.

I handed Feodor back my pair of boots. 'Tell Feodor,' I told Russky, 'that I am sorry about my mistake. I'd like him very much to be my batman, and if he does a good job on these boots I'll give him a pack of Gold Flakes.'

As Russky translated, Feodor's face lit up with joy. Nodding rapidly, he bowed himself out of the compartment, closing the door behind him.

I explained my mistake to Russky, and he looked at me brightly. 'Good Bolshie, Feodor,' he said, 'and you will not regret. But one thing I am failing in the understanding. Why,' he pointed to the closet, 'works Feodor in closet with the door closed? Is not much crowded there?'

At dinner that evening Kink told us that Eddie Fulford, the Canadian who was joining B Flight, would be flying up from Ekaterinodar the day after tomorrow.[9]

'Colly says he's a hell of a good pilot,' Kink said, 'but something of a deep thinker. Interested in politics and such. Fulford doesn't have a very high opinion of the Whites, especially the aristocrats.'

'I'm inclined to agree with him,' Tommy said. 'I'd swear this Baron Lebedev of the Russian squadron wears perfume.'

I had been introduced to the fliers of the Russian squadron, who were quartered on the A Flight train. They seemed decent enough fellows, except for Lebedev, who when he walked switched his hips and smelled, as Bill said, of perfume.

'Is Lebedev representative of the Russian upper classes?' I asked nobody in particular.

Russky was quick to answer. 'Not,' he said fiercely. 'Lebedev isolated person. Officer class in general middle-class – how you call it? – of substantial substance. Of course reactionaries in White army, but reactionaries everywhere, no?'

It was a question we weren't prepared to argue, and Kink changed the subject by breaking some bad news he had heard over the wireless on A Flight train that afternoon. The French had been defeated by the Reds near Kherson, and together with some Greek troops, had evacuated the city and sailed for Odessa.

'My God,' said Tommy. 'I didn't know the Greeks were in this too.'[10]

'They won't be in it long,' Kink said, 'nor by the looks of it will the French, either. They're fighting with one hand and trying to unlock the exit door with the other. I wouldn't be a bit surprised if they cleared out of South Russia altogether, and soon.'

'Strewth, Kink,' Bill said, 'we're not so permanent ourselves. You know how badly opinion's divided in England on the intervention issue, both among the people and in the Cabinet. Lloyd George thinks armed intervention on a scale large enough to beat the Bolshies is impossible.[11] He says it would take at least four hundred thousand men, and the Allies aren't willing to throw in a fraction of that number.'

'If Denikin and Kolchak keep winning they won't have to,' Kink said. He drew a map from his pocket, changing the subject. 'Here's our flight route for tomorrow's reconnaissance beyond Tsaritsyn. It looks like the Reds have moved some machines into the area. We may have a fight.'

The patrol took off next morning at eight o'clock, with my Number 27 Camel behind Kink in wing position. Minutes later we were over the barbed wire trenches south of Tsaritsyn and then over the city itself. The Red Archies sent up a heavy curtain of German H.E. that emitted a dense, heavy smoke, but their aim was off and we rode through it easily. Tsaritsyn was badly burned out with its factories in ruins. Off to the right, near the curve of the Volga, I saw the broad trench in which, Kink had told us, lay the bodies of twelve thousand civilians slaughtered by the Reds when they had taken the town.[12]

We were over the Volga beyond Tsaritsyn when my engine conked out. There was only one thing to do: turn back and try to land as close to our lines as possible, hoping meanwhile that the engine started up again. Kink signaled his recognition of my predicament, and the flight flew on.

At thirty-five hundred feet I put the ship into a long glide toward the river and breathed a prayer. At my present rate of speed and angle of descent I would land smack in the Volga unless the engine caught again.

It did, miraculously, at two thousand feet. I turned north to regain the flight, and remembering that Red planes might be in the area, began to climb for altitude.

I didn't start climbing a minute too soon. There was the sudden stutter of twin Spandaus, and then a Nieuport shot past, on its fuselage the red star insignia of the Bolshie air force.

It was stupid flying on Mikhail's part. Overconfident, he had expected to get me with his first burst, and now I was in a perfect position to return the favour. I dove, and firing at fifty yards, closed in. My stream of tracers hit. The Nieuport shuddered, faltered, and fell. It went straight into the river bank, exploding with a terrific crash.[13]

Then I thought to look above me. High off to my right a second Nieuport was disappearing into the clouds.

I met the flight coming back from Tsaritsyn. Kink gave me the thumbs up sign; he had seen the burning Nieup on the ground. At the aerodrome I was accorded the honour of first landing.

I had scored 47 Squadron's first victory, and that night we had a *prazdnik* in the lounge. Colly wired congratulations from Ekat, and Cowderdrill broke out the best sixteen-year-old Scotch.

'To Bunny and the princess,' Kink toasted. 'May she be lovely, wicked and rich.'

'Too much to expect,' Bill objected. 'May she be lovely and wicked.'

'That's still too big an order,' Tommy said. 'May she be rich.'

Cowderdrill came sidling out of the galley while I was getting a drink at the bar. 'Sir, I wanted to inquire, that is, I wanted to determine if your Bolshie had an easy death?'

'Comparatively,' I told him. 'He died either from a bullet or in the crash. No flames, Sergeant.'

He visibly relaxed. 'That's good, Sir. I was concerned.'

I decided to josh him along a little. 'Sergeant, I can't say I approve of your attitude.'

'My attitude, Sir?'

'Yes, Cowderdrill, your attitude. I might even say your patriotism, or rather your lack of it. Here we are locked in mortal combat with a godless enemy, and you dare to stand there and feel sympathy for the bloody Red.'

'Sir, it's this way,' Cowderdrill answered me earnestly. 'I just can't stand the shedding of blood. Why, if it was you instead of the Bolshie had gotten his ticket today I would have felt exactly the same way.'

He slid away into the pantry, leaving me there with a glass in my hand and my mouth wide open.

★

'News,' Kink said as we sat down at the breakfast table. 'It came through last night. The French are pulling out of Russia for good. Yesterday they evacuated Odessa.'

He told us as much as had come over the wires from Colly in Ekat. The French commander at Odessa had received orders for the removal of all French troops from the Black Sea port within three days. Anxious to get out, the Frenchman had moved too hastily, and ordered evacuation within forty-eight hours.

As a result the civilian population, only a small number of which could get passage, had panicked. The evacuation had been a shambles. Many of the thousands lining the docks waiting to board the French cruisers, had killed themselves on the spot.

'This is going to affect White morale badly,' Kink went on. 'Not only have the Whites lost one of their chief allies, but the French evacuation leaves the Crimea with its bottom exposed, since White units stranded in Taurida have their left flank unprotected. And now, of course, it's only a matter of time before the French get out of Sebastopol.'[14]

'If the French have given up on getting back their loans,' Eddie Fulford said, 'that means the situation's really hopeless.'[15]

Kink reached for a hunk of hardtack. 'Colly says Wrangel's still after Denikin to push through to Tsaritsyn, join Kolchak's left flank, and go on to Moscow via the Volga route. But Denikin's turned a deaf ear. His main concern is avoiding a threat of a separation between our troops in the Caucasus and the Donets area.'

'Strewth, enough of this major strategy,' Bill said. 'What's our assignment for this morning?'

A light came into Kink's sharp black eyes. 'Something special. We hear there's a big conference of Red Commissars in Tsaritsyn.'[16] He got up and went to the map of the Tsaritsyn area we had tacked up on the lounge car wall, and put his finger on a large public building in the centre of town. 'Trotsky himself might be there. We'll be escorting A Flight DH-9s carrying one-hundred-twelve-pound bombs. Our job's to protect the bombers, so no individual scraps on this one unless I signal. Everything clear?'

'Who's Trotsky?' asked Tommy.

We laughed.

'Any other questions?' Kink wanted to know.

Russky cleared his throat apologetically. 'Kink, with all respects, I could go this time maybe? Fly Russian Nieuport?'

'Sorry, Russky,' Kink said with a straight face, 'you're too valuable as an interpreter.'

We were back forty minutes later with mission accomplished. The A Flight' bombers had dropped their loads on target and, despite heavy Archie fire, completely demolished the commissars' meeting place. If Trotsky had indeed been there, pounding the table, now he was sharing the heat with the Devil in hell.

A couple of Bolshie fighters had come up against us. They were obvious tyros, and Kink, deeming the bombers safe under the protection of Tommy and myself, had collaborated with Eddie Fulford in downing one of them, a lethargic Spad. Then Eddie had chased a Fokker triplane rather deep into Red territory, till he thought better of it and turned around.[17]

That night we had another *prazdnik* for the victors. Some of the A Flight men and Russian pilots showed up, among them Lebedev, the exquisite baron. I noticed that Fulford avoided shaking Lebedev's hand, and ignored the group of Russian pilots.

I went over and sat down beside him. 'What's the matter?' I said, 'don't you like the Russians?'

He grinned at me slowly, and sucked on his pipe, taking his time with an answer. He was a deliberate man and not to be hurried. That tortoise-like quality you might mistake for slow-wittedness, until you saw the way he handled a plane in the air. Then Fulford was all flash and fire, with the anticipation of a Billy Bishop and the quickness of a Collishaw, and you thanked your stars you weren't paired against him. True, today was the first time I had seen him in action, but talents like Fulford's needed only a five-minute dogfight for demonstration.

'You ask me if I like the Russians?' Eddie said. 'If you mean that bunch of thin-blooded aristocrats' – he indicated the White pilots – 'the answer's an unqualified no. If you mean the Bolshies, the answer's also no. If you're speaking of the middle class, the intelligentsia, the Cossacks, and the peasants, then I'd answer like anybody else: some of them. If that doesn't sound too superior. But I warn you, I'm a liberal. I don't like a privileged nobility, a bureaucracy riddled with graft, a secret police, Siberia, a corrupt church, and the throttling of free thought. Forgive me. I seem to be making a speech.'

'No, go on, Eddie,' I told him. 'I'm interested. There isn't anybody else around here who seems to know what this war is all about.'

'There's one – Parker, in Hoskin's company. I was passing by B company train and I heard someone ask Parker what he was fighting for. He said, "A quid a day."'

'Seriously, Eddie,' I said, 'the White army isn't made up only of the nobility. It's the officer and the professional classes, too.'

Eddie nodded. 'And the church, the landowners and manufacturers, the Cossacks, the Mensheviks, the Constitutional-Democrats, Socialist-Revolutionaries, the centre republicans and the liberals. But face up to it, Bunny. This war is basically between two groups of people, the haves and the have-nots.'[18]

'Who do you think's going to win it?'

He grinned at me. 'I've done enough thinking for one night. The British Military Mission frowns on too much thinking. Anyway, we're here to fight.'

Chewing on that, I walked away. At the bar, getting a fresh drink, I had the uncomfortable feeling that Eddie knew who was going to win the war and that for his own reasons he was damned if he would tell me.

★

'We didn't get Trotsky,' Kink told us at breakfast one morning that week. 'White intelligence has it he was in Moscow when we bombed out the commissars. But now the word is he's on his way to Tsaritsyn, coming down the Volga with a flotilla of gunboats. We'll load up with twenty-pound bombs and take out after it as soon as Bunny finishes his tea.'

We caught the forty boat flotilla ten miles above Tsaritsyn and bombed them at one thousand feet, coming down from five thousand one at a time.[19] The Red curtain of fire was heavy. Kink scored a hit astern on the lead ship but our other bombs missed. We turned around and came back for a second try.

The Red flight of six Spads and Nieuports caught us completely by surprise. One riddled Tommy's tail, and he turned home gimpily for Beketofka as another Nieup came in on him for a final pass. I was in time to head off the Nieup, and then there was suddenly a red star in my sights. He rolled, and I shot at him in short bursts; he rolled again and away, and my rudder locked in a spin. Out of the corner of my eye I could see a stubby-winged Spad slipping down, aflame.

Had my spin been less severe another Nieup would have gotten me; as it was he stitched my wing neatly before Kink stole in to scare him away.

I leveled out over the gunboats at a terrifying two hundred feet. Below, the flotilla gunners, lethal dentists, drilled at me with their .30 calibres. Part of my instrument panel dissolved, and a strut flew free.

Then I was past the gunboats and headed for the drome. Glancing back over my shoulder, I saw another Nieup going down and the rest of the Red Flight fleeing into the clouds. B Flight turned and took position behind me, the mother hen seeing the wounded chick home.

'Cor, Sir,' my mechanic Charley Lamston blinked when I landed, 'chewed you up proper they did.'

'Charley,' I said, 'remind me never to go to another dentist as long as I live.'

The flight's two victories, one scored by Kink and the other by Bill Daly, entitled us to a *prazdnik* that night, though we hadn't done so brilliantly with the flotilla. Trotsky was still alive.

Kink had contrived to invite a few refugee girls to the party. All of them were pretty, and two of them were haughty enough to be princesses. They prompted Eddie to a maxim about the Russian nobility: 'They're all princes and princesses or counts and countesses at least. Just like the leaves of a tree; they're there all right, but nowhere near the trunk.'

Tommy played court to one of the Russian girls, a sullen *blondinka* named Katerina in a striking blue silk dress. Towards the end of the evening he took me aside. 'Let me borrow your compartment, Bunny?' he asked, grinning. 'Mine's a mess.'

I gave him carte blanche, including the use of an illustrated volume of Persian love poetry that Kink had lent me.

A few minutes later Katerina's loud scream cut through the hum of conversation. Cowderdrill, the great oaf, had spilled caviar on her blue silk dress. Caviar stains silk badly, as it does almost everything else, and Tommy's fumbling efforts to wipe it off with his handkerchief, moistened with vodka, were only making things worse. Katerina left us shortly thereafter, no doubt to try her luck with A Flight.

From the pantry we heard muffled groans.

Kink laughed. 'Tommy's making Cowderdrill eat all the caviar he didn't spill. And it doesn't agree with him.'

I had drunk more than I should, and on the matter of caviar I agreed with Cowderdrill. White-faced, I listed to the lavatory. Too late; Eddie was inside, having difficulties of his own. I stumbled outside to the tracks. The air revived me. I stood under the Russian stars for a while, breathing in deeply, a little homesick for Bromo-Seltzer.

★

Toward mid-April we heard that the French had evacuated Sebastopol.[20] Sebastopol was the base of the Russian Black Sea Fleet, and so that the Reds should not profit unduly from the evacuation, the French had scrapped over a score of submarines. Russky and the other White officers walked around with long faces and a pessimism we of B Flight refused to dignify with recognition, knowing that the next White victory would send them, just as unreasonably, sky high.

Look at the situation, they told us dolefully. A Bolshie government had been formed in Bavaria, Bela Kun had taken over Hungary, and it looked as though English troops would be pulling out of Armenia and Georgia, leaving only a handful at Batum. *Na Moskvu*? You didn't dare mention the word.

It was May before the pendulum swung back violently in the opposite direction. On the ninth Wrangel scored a brilliant cavalry victory at Velikoknyazheskoye, and Russky told us, his face shining with joy, that it was certain now that Denikin would launch major operations northwards against Kharkov and Tsaritsyn.

'Christmas in Moscow!' he shouted. 'I will myself show you the Kremlin! We will travel the sleigh on the Tverskaya!'

The battle on the Manytsch front, we learned, had been a bitter one. Twice White calvary under General Chatilov had forded the river, and twice they had been beaten back. In late April, Wrangel, not yet fully recovered from a bout with typhus, had gone to report to Denikin, and had been shocked to hear that despite the fact that the Whites had thirty cavalry regiments at the Manytsch River, there was no unity of command. Denikin hadn't dared to put one general under the orders of another. Romanovsky, Denikin's chief of staff, had persuaded him to give Wrangel the Manytsch command, and Wrangel had left for the front promptly.

The situation was a bad one. Red forces were massed in Velikokyazheskoye village, and in its outskirts, on the northern bank of the river. The Red artillery was too powerful for Wrangel to force a passage, and he turned his attention to the east, where the river was muddy and shallow.

It was essential that he get his artillery across the river, and using the wooden fences of the neighborhood, he improvised a causeway. On the dawn of May 4th he made the crossing. By noon two cavalry corps and the artillery had crossed the river; by nightfall the White advance guard had driven the Reds back toward the west and taken more than fifteen hundred prisoners.

The White attack began at dawn on the 5th. Putting up a furious resistance, the Reds turned Wrangel's right flank. The White general was in a predicament; behind him lay the only way of retreat, the right bank of the river was poorly fortified, and he had no fresh reserves.

He resumed the offensive on the 6th, though for three days his men had had no sleep and their horses were exhausted. The White Cavalry, chiefly composed of Don, Circassian and Astrakhan Cossacks, charged to the sound of bugles into the teeth of a tremendous artillery barrage. When the battle was over they had wiped out the 10th Red Army and taken prisoner fifteen thousand men. Wrangel told the exultant Denikin that his Caucasian Army could be at the gates of Tsaritsyn in three weeks' time.

Colly immediately ordered B Flight to step up its operations and destroy as many Red planes as possible in advance of Wrangel's arrival at Tsaritsyn.[21] We were to be especially alert to Red bombers; it was rumoured that the Bolshies had finally managed to outfit and train pilots and observers for a number of German aircraft captured during the European war. If true, this was for us significant news; the Bolshies could now bomb Beketofka, and our immunity from unexpected attack was over.

In the next few weeks, patrolling from Tsaritsyn to Dubovka, base of the Red gunboat fleet seventy miles beyond it up the Volga, we saw no bombers, but we did run into a good bit of fighter plane opposition. Kink downed three red-starred planes, Eddie Fulford and

I, two, and Bill and Tommy shared in a couple of victories. Colly was kept busy wiring congratulations from Ekat.

My most interesting victory during that time was achieved without the firing of a shot. During a dogfight over Dubovka I spotted a Fokker triplane about a thousand yards north of the battle. The Fokker was taking no part in the scrap and apparently observing. I broke off the long-range sporting event I was having with a cautious Nieup, and went for the snobbish tripe.

At four hundred yards the Bolshie saw me coming, and emptied his guns; I could see the tracers going wide to the left and high. Suddenly he dove, and I went down after him. Not sure how much ammunition I had left after my foolish long-distance duel with the Nieuport, I decided to adopt the tactics Kink would have used in the same situation: holding my fire until I came within a very short range. The Camel's telescopic gunsight was set to bull's-eye on a target at one hundred yards; firing at a longer range than that was merely by guess and God. Kink's practice was to hold his fire until he was twenty-five to thirty-five yards from his target. That meant taking chances; once he had pulled out of his dive on a Bolshie plane so late that his under-carriage had hooked the rudder of his victim, and he had landed with shreds of it still clinging to his under-carriage struts.

Now the Bolshie pilot looked back, saw me overhauling him, and increased his angle of descent. I was, however, still gaining; though the triplane had good manoeuvreability and climb at low ceiling, as a diver it was slow, because of the pressure and wind resistance against its triple wings.

As I approached the tripe to short firing range its starboard wing began to flutter up and down. Suddenly, with a terrific boom, the starboard wing folded back against the fuselage, and a clutch of fabric and broken struts came flying back at my ship. To avoid the debris I had to pull straight out of my dive, and one of the triplane's flying wires wound itself around my undercarriage. The tripe spun swiftly down, to crash on the steppe, a huge cloud of dust rising from the wreckage.

A lone Red survivor was fleeing the dogfight, and I re-joined my squadron mates for the flight back home. When I landed my hands were shaking; I had been more affected by the bullet-less encounter than if the enemy had hemstitched my cockpit with .30 calibre lead.

Our patrol two days later to Urbakb drome, where the Red squadrons of the Tsaritsyn area were based, was more dangerous.

We groaned when Kink announced, 'Objective Urbakb. Combined operations with the "Wanderers".'[22] The 'Wanderers' were the White Russian bomber squadron based with us at Beketofka, and it was an understatement to say that we flew with them reluctantly. They were not merely incompetent, they were feckless, and sometimes they endangered our own skins. Incapable of keeping formation, their planes would wander off in all directions, and we would have to shepherd them in like a flock of stupid sheep. In a fight the guns of their observers were likely to jam, and even if they didn't jam, they missed. Sometimes their planes disappeared altogether, and on several occasions we had landed to find them neatly hangared, with the Russians on their third glass of vodka.

It wasn't a question of cowardice. They were all, including the perfumed Lebedev, brave men. They were merely bored by inconvenience and hard work. Russky explained it a little differently: 'With all respects, they not wanting to get in *anglichanie* way.'

Inevitably there were flights from which Lieutenants Arbiev, Olonsky and Chiterin did not return. This both saddened and angered us. We resented being forced to choose between covering the tail of a 47 Squadron man and that of a Russian. We always covered the Russian's, because if we didn't he was a gone goose, while the odds were good that a 47 Squadron man would get away. But we would have relinquished the responsibility with the greatest of pleasure.

'One final warning,' Kink said, before we left the lounge for the field. 'On our last flight with the Russians Lebedev's observer took me for a Bolshie and put a burst right in front of my nose. Anybody sees him about to repeat it, wave a white handkerchief. I'll be grateful.'

We met the Bolshie circus in a sunwashed sky over Urbakb. The White DH-9s dropped their bombs on the drome, demolishing what appeared to be a cookhouse, a latrine and an orderly room, and then the Red planes came up at us with their grab-bag of captured Allied and German ships – Nieuports, Spads, an Albatros, a Sopwith one-and-a-half strutter. They outnumbered us two to one.

We approached one another head-on and the distance between us closed up with suddenness of a snapped rubber band. We fired point blank. The Red planes slipped to our right, and we did likewise, both of us hoping to gain advantage in the turn.

I had a glance at their goggled faces as we passed. One, with a white streamer flying from his helmet, the squadron leader, flew with style, and I wondered if he was a German flying for pay, a bloodthirsty Turk, or an idealistic Bolshevik who believed that Lenin had been born, like Christ, to save the world, but not for God, for man.

I told myself to stop thinking of these men as men like myself, with hopes and fears and private midnight anguishes. They were the enemy.

Kink signaled the turn with a dip of his wing. As we followed him I saw, a thousand feet above, a lone black Fokker circling like a waiting falcon.

The Fokker was a plane that could beat us all for speed and climb, and the pilot had the advantage of altitude. I never saw the Fokker tail, which looked like an ace of clubs, without hoping I had an ace in my own deck to match it. But now I had more immediate and pressing concerns.

When we straightened from the turn it was every man for himself. We caught the Bolshies as their flight whirled to fight; on the turn the Camel could beat anything against it in the air.

I took a quick burst at a Nieup as he came past my sights, trying for a position astern. It was, I saw, the stylish squadron leader.

The Bolshie and I went round and round, alternately taking shots as chance and skill permitted, like boxers in the ring. Quickly we lost height in the tight spiral; in a matter of seconds we had dropped below the level of the other machines.

I began to sweat. We were following each other's tails nip and tuck, the man behind firing frantic bursts at the man before him. I turned desperately to divert the fire from behind, and found the Nieup dead ahead, centred in my sights. I pressed the triggers till my thumb knuckles cracked against the trips. As the bullets struck home the Bolshie looked back at me, it seemed reproachfully, and then slumped forward in his seat. His streamer fluttering gayly, he went down in aimless circles like a scrap of paper in a whirlwind's cone, and slid into the Volga.[23]

A warning shadow fell across my wings and I looked upward, expecting to see a diving Bolshie.

It was a flaming DH-9, its pilot dead in the cockpit, and it was slipping straight into my path. I pulled the Camel into a vertical turn and swerved as the flaming mass plummeted past. As I watched, the observer jumped, tumbling down to the river like a trapezist who had missed his grab for the bar.

Above the Fokker circled triumphantly.

Dry-mouthed I leveled out of the turn, anxious for a breath of cool, fresh air. A bullet-nosed Spad bore straight at me, the pilot making no attempt to turn. His courage was frightening, but I had gone through too much recent discomfort to make things easy for him, and I held to my course with thumbs on triggers.

The Spad dove first, and then I saw the reason: Eddie had cut into his slipstream, his black-nosed guns spitting orange-red. The Spad lurched, turned belly over, and slipped into the river.

I thanked Eddie Fulford's parents fervently for their mutual lust, and looked around for another antagonist. The surviving White Russian planes were grouped now in closer fighting order, and holding their own. Bill and Tommy, in double contest, were playing ring-a-ring-o'-roses with a Nieup and a Spad. Eddie was climbing back up into the main action, and Kink's Camel was engaged with two red stars, giving them a flying lesson.

On the ground, as flat as a pan's bottom except where a ravine cut through to the Volga, were seven flaming gasoline fires, two of them DH-9s.

As I climbed up toward the Fokker he saw me and dove away toward Kink, in position on the first of his Bolshies. Stalling, the Spad slipped away to one side, emitting a wake of the ghost-white smoke that precedes the flames of a fired plane, and Kink turned to burst his second antagonist. As he made his turn, the Fokker, wing tips pointing to earth and sky, raked the Camel.

Kink went down, straight as a falling bucket in a well, the second Bolshie following him for the finishing shot, the Fokker shearing fast away.

It was ridiculous that the best airman of the Turkish front should die under the guns of a second-rater. But he was going to within the next three or four seconds, unless a miracle happened, and I was too far away to help it along.

Sometimes there is justice done. From nowhere appeared a Camel riding Kink's pursuer's tail, and with sure instinct Kink swerved in his glide at the instant the Bolshie, his prop stopped dead, triggered his burst. He missed. Bill Daly's bullets caught the Bolshie, who went into the ground with full throttle on.

Kink, his engine dead, landed safely on the river bank, and Bill followed him down. I circled over them protectively while Kink struck a match to his Camel, then squeezed himself beneath the small centre section atop Bill's guns.

What Bolshie planes were left in the air had broken away and were winging north, including the arrogant Black Fokker. Bill, with Kink aboard, started home, and we followed after.

At Beketofka we toted up the score. Five Bolshie fighters destroyed and two White bombers. From this flight pilots Konov and Gubichev and observers Stoganov and Rimsky had not returned.

We had liked them all, especially Konov, who had played a fine game of chess and was an authority on church iconography.

That night I dreamed of the Black Fokker, and waking the next morning, I knew we would meet again.

Chapter Four

*

Though it was only mid-May, Kink, who always thought ahead, had an idea about making the lounge car comfortable for the winter.

'We need a fireplace in which to burn a merry fire against the Russian cold, and all that. Anybody know where we can get one?'

'Is mansion down near sawmill by river,' Russky said. 'Sacked by Bolshies and looted much, but some things left, maybe.'

Kink glanced at his watch. 'We've got a four-thirty patrol. That gives us a couple of hours. Tommy, you get the van, and Bunny, would you ask Hoskins for a crowbar and some heavy rope? Eddie, you call Ivan; we'll need his strength.'

'What about bringing Feodor along?' I suggested. 'He was a housewrecker before the Revolution.'

'Strewth,' Bill Daly said. 'If Feodor comes along we'll have to ask my Mikhail. We don't want any jealousy among the batmen.'

Eddie rubbed his cheek. 'If you're ringing in Mikhail, than I'll have to ask my Valentin too.'

'All right, all right,' Kink said, throwing up his hands. 'Forget Ivan and the rest of them. But damn it all, fireplaces are heavy. You're going to regret not keeping these batmen in their places.'

Tommy drove the van through the open iron gates and up the graveled drive of a huge English-style manor house. All of its windows had been broken, and there were hammers and sickles smeared in red paint – or blood – on the door, which hung crazily on one hinge. I closed my eyes and imagined I was back in England, and I could see open limousines parked on the driveway and a liveried footman at the door, and inside elegant women sipping sherry with stiff-backed pillars of the Empire. From the tennis court floated an English voice singing out 'Love-thirty, Colonel. Jolly good shot!' and from the kitchen the titter of a downstairs' maid, pinched by the butler.

My fantasy was rudely shattered when we stepped in the door. Machine-gun bullets had riddled the fine panelling of the hall. In the drawing room the hangings, saber-slashed, hung in shreds, and the rugless floors were fouled with horse manure and human excrement; the furniture, what of it had been left behind by the looters, was hacked to splinters. Red cavalrymen had used the mirrors for pistol practice. The paintings were slashed through; one of them, I recognized, was a Venetian scene by Turner. In one corner the corpse of a pet dog, his breed now indistinguishable, lay faintly stinking.

'Like Winter Palace when mobs come through,' said Russky. 'So much beauty, destroyed by madmen. They smashed Venetian mirrors with rifle butts, destroyed old masters, trampled rare manuscripts and love letters. They made love on Tsar and Tsarina's bed; China vases, they were used like chamber pots. Ugh!' He had stepped in a pile of manure.

Tommy laughed. 'Russky, that'll bring you luck.'

Kink told the boys to look through the upstairs rooms; he and I would investigate the lower floor. We moved into the next room, which proved to be the main parlor. There, piles of rubble pushed up against it, was our fireplace.

It was of magnificent black marble with carved cupids on pedestals, bacchic masks and a gilded mirror frame – the mirror itself was broken. Under a heap of half burned leather-bound books were the andirons and pokers.

'It's a beauty, Kink,' I said, 'but it's too big for the lounge car, and how the devil are we going to get it into the van?'

'Call the boys,' Kink said, undiscouraged.

Russky, who had been wandering out back in the garden, came in shaking his head. He had discovered fourteen bodies buried in a shallow trench near the summer house. 'They have murder everyone in house with a bullet in the neck. You must see and believe.'

'It's too depressing, Russky,' Kink told him. 'Come on, let's get to work.'

It took us two hours, but whiplashed by Kink's curses, we got the fireplace out of the house and into the van, though we had to break one of its wooden side boards to do it.

'Strewth, but Kink's a bastard,' Bill Daly muttered when we were under way. He examined a skinned finger. 'Gets it into his head to do something and he'll see it through all the fires of hell.'

Kink, in the front seat, didn't turn his head. 'I heard that, Daly. The fires of hell are just what you'll be wanting, come a Russian winter.'

'With all respects,' said Russky, 'Kink he right. Russian winters like, like – ' He abandoned his search for a comparison, contenting himself with a shiver, which was all the more eloquent for the sweat still streaming down his face.

The fireplace was too big to get through the vestibule of the lounge car. A Flight men stood about shouting noxious advice and encouragement, but not lifting a finger to help. It was obvious that a section of the roof would have to be taken off and the fireplace lowered through it, and a grinning DH-9 pilot quoted an official-sounding regulation which forbade precisely that. Kink ignored him and shook his fist at the other scoffers. 'When it's twenty below and your manhood's freezing you fellows are staying outside! No invitations! Remember that, Black, Carrington, Finch. You too, Lowrey, with your Welshman's black heart! You'll promise us your sisters to get in out of the cold, and we'll laugh at you! Laugh!'

Kink put Sergeant Major Hoskins and five men to work on the lounge car roof while we went off on patrol. We returned from shooting up a locomotive to find the roof already off and the job half done. Cowderdrill, having complained about the noise of hammering, had retired to his bunk with a headache. Two privates of B Company served our dinner, badly, but we solaced ourselves with the knowledge that it wasn't often, in the air force, that you could dine al fresco under the first of the night's pale stars.

Hoskins did his usual fine job and the fireplace was installed, flued and plastered snugly in place against the lounge car sidewall by late afternoon of the next day.[1] There was only one thing wrong: the cherubs, solidly plastered to their bases, were facing the wrong way, with their dimpled backsides to the beholder.

Kink called in Hoskins, and the Sergeant Major disclaimed responsibility. 'It wasn't me, Sir. When I saw them cherubs last, before we did the plastering, they were facing in the right direction. Ain't that true, Stebbins?' he asked his plasterer. Private Stebbins nodded.

Kink's black eyes frosted with understanding. 'Cowderdrill!' he shouted.

In the pantry a dish fell and smashed on the floor. 'You're calling me, Sir?' Cowderdrill quavered.

'Come out of there,' Kink bellowed.

The messman sidled from his galley, and Kink pointed to the cherubs. 'Cowderdrill, I know you did this. Something tells me.

Now I'm not going to court martial you for it. I just want to know why.'

'Yes, Sir, fine, Sir.' Cowderdrill's Adam's apple agitated violently. 'Well, Major, I thought they was just too immoral from the front, Sir. I mean, no fig leaves. So I just turned 'em about. And they look much better. Don't you think so, Captain Kinkead? Sort of less suggestive, Sir, if you follow what I mean.'

★

In another week Wrangel's Cossacks had taken up positions before the barbed wire and trenches that defended Tsaritsyn. Artillery fire became constant night and day.

A Cossack liaison officer arrived to establish his headquarters at A Flight Train, and through Russky we learned from him the near epic story of the general's march from Velikoknyazheskoye.

For days, with very little food and almost no water, Wrangel's troops had marched over three hundred kilometers of barren steppes, uninhabited except for Red strong points which had to be overwhelmed and taken. The nights were cold and damp, and scores of men caught pneumonia. Despite Wrangel's plea for transport, Denikin was already concentrating on the Kharkov front, and headquarters failed to supply him with needed cars and trucks. Wrangel had made most of the journey on horseback, riding with Chatilov's fourth troop. When the stones of the rough road had cut through the tires of his vehicles, he wound rope around the wheels and continued on.

Kink invited a number of Wrangel's officers to share our mess, among them Moslems from the Caucasus who had declared a holy war against the Reds. The Moslems touched no alcohol, and spoke a Russian dialect that Russky was hard pressed to translate. In return the Moslem officers invited us to mess with them in their encampment outside the city, over which flew their green and yellow-crescented flag.

We heard there would be no attack on Tsaritsyn until the artillery, infantry and matériel promised by Denikin arrived. Wrangel's officers were as restive as the general himself, who kept bombarding Denikin with telegrams asking for his promised help; there was a good deal of resentment building up against the commander-in-chief among all the higher ranks of Wrangel's Caucasian Army.

As the days passed no reinforcements came, and our patrols told

Wrangel that fresh Red troops and artillery were daily entering the city. Toward the end of the month we heard that Wrangel had summoned a council of war and asked his generals' advice as to whether they should risk an attack or wait for reinforcements. He told them that the success of an immediate attack was unlikely, but that on the other hand, with the Reds constantly strengthening their position, the odds were that a later attack would certainly fail. Unanimously the council agreed upon attack.

'They won't make it,' Eddie said. 'The Reds are too strong on artillery.'

Rusky was offended. 'With all respects, such talk is bad,' he said stiffly. 'We must possess the hope.'

'I possess the hope, Russky,' Eddie answered, 'but I'd rather have a hole than hope when those shells start pouring in.'

Events proved Eddie right. We did our part, strafing the trenches and rear areas in advance of the attack, shooting up a couple of field guns, and downing the three Bolshie fighters that objected.[2] But the Reds had too many guns and Wrangel suffered heavy casualties. That night there was no *prazdnik* to celebrate the downed Red planes.

Three days later the Reds attacked, driving Wrangel back to the Tchervlennia River. The word was that he would wait there for reinforcements. We were ordered to be ready to pull out of Beketofka at a moment's notice. It was strange that night to get a wire from Colly in Ekat telling us of the success of the Don and Volunteer armies to the west and saying headquarters was optimistic about being in Moscow by late October. October! We couldn't see it. We had identified ourselves with Wrangel and his fortunes, and at the moment, on the Tsaritsyn front at least, we were falling behind.

But Wrangel got his reinforcements. An infantry division and five batteries arrived before the 15th, and he attacked a day later. 47 Squadron was excused from the operation, but only because we had fought our battle the day before.

★

Colly had come up from Ekat to brief us on the mission.

Budenny, the Red's crack cavalry commander, was coming to the aid of Tsaritsyn. He had two or three brigades and three thousand men. Unless he was stopped, his reinforcements might mean the difference between victory and defeat for Wrangel. And if the general was pushed back from Tsaritsyn further than the Tchervlennia River, the whole front would collapse.

'Budenny should be fifteen miles from the city by dawn tomorrow,' Colly told us. 'It's up to you B Flight boys to strafe him dead; in this kind of operation a bomber's useless. They say his sharpshooters can hit a gnat's eye at a thousand yards, so watch yourself when you're coming in. The Cossack cavalry's waiting for him, and they'll reveal themselves to you by forming an 'X' in a square. From there you can play it by inspiration. Any questions?'

'Who's Budenny?' Tommy asked, but this time we didn't laugh.

Next morning we took off into the sun that climbed the marshes beyond Mother Volga. We flew over Tsaritsyn, veered off to the right toward the silver ribbon of the river, and thence over the sunburned steppe. Beyond the city it was flat no longer, but cut and scarred by huge ravines that might have hidden an army.

Suddenly we saw them; a blurred patch below in the ravines and gullies that rapidly metamorphosed into horsemen.

We could see that there were two opposing forces. One group of horsemen, rather smaller than the other, stood in close order; the other was deploying.

Perhaps fifty horsemen detached themselves from the smaller group and hastily arranged themselves into a hollow square inside of which they formed the prearranged 'X'.

Facing them across the steppe was Budenny, preparing to attack.

The Cossacks knew his intention. What they did not know was that his relatively small attacking force was bait. Behind it, in a deep ravine that curved around the Cossack cavalry like the blade of a hand scythe, poured the bulk of Budenny's men.

Kink dipped his wings in command to form a line. He pointed his nose dawnward, throttle wide, and I swung into line after him, the others falling in behind.

We were diving five thousand feet at a speed of three hundred miles an hour.[3] My dive was too steep; I needed a little less right rudder. Cross a hairline over the vertical and my tricky Camel would flip over on its back. I eased back the stick gently; too sudden a jerk would snap the wings off.

My air speed indicator was graduated in miles per hour up to three hundred. The telltale needle had passed that mark and strained against the stop.

The engine meter marked fourteen hundred revolutions per minute, excessive speed for a rotary engine. The engine had ceased to turn the prop; what revolved it now was the blast of air through which I was plunging.

I took a last glance at the oil pressure gauge and noted the pounds of pressure in my gas tank. If the relief valve stuck the tank would explode.

I reached down the starboard side of the cockpit and gave the gun-gear reservoir firing handle a reassuring tug. Should the firing system lose its pressure the Vickers machine guns, synchronized to fire between the prop blades, would cease to function.

The scream of the tortured flying wires had reached a constant pitch that sounded like the whine of a passing shell. Seconds dragged as the ground rushed up. I held my thumbs tight on the two trigger levers attached to the joy stick.

Ahead of me Kink's guns pocked the ground, sending up little exclamations of dust. His ship swerved up and passed me to the right with the suddenness of a camera shutter's click.

Five hundred feet above the ravine. The crowded masses of cavalry gazed up with white faces. I pressed the trips, easing the joy stick back slowly so that my bullets would sweep the line of men. A horse reared, a man began to fall. The horse was still upright, the man still falling when I shot upward out of the dive and my wing blotted them from view.

I zoomed straight up into the brightening sky. Above me Kink cartwheeled into line behind Eddie's anchor machine as it passed him in its dive.

The banshee wail of my wires subsided as my speed cut down. I could hear the roar of the engine. It was deep and smooth, and I blessed Charley and his mechanic's filthy hands.

Then a cartwheel into line behind Kink again, and another start down the hill.

We formed an endless chain of attack. Dive. Shoot. Zoom. Cartwheel. The Red cavalry was helpless. We came so fast they had no chance to defend themselves.

A few raised rifles from pony backs. Some stampeded both forward and back, but Kink had concentrated the attack at both ends of the column, and the narrow gulley was choked with horses and men at entrance and exit.

On my third trip around I saw an officer whipping his horse up the steep side of the gully toward the steppe. I pushed my left rudder slowly. Dust spurted from the dry, eroded earth; the bullets struck a few feet short. I pulled my stick back a fraction and the dust spurts travelled closer and closer in an ineluctable geometry of line until the horse reared and the man flung his arms upward and fell. I was so close I could see the scar on his cheek, the flash of a ring on his finger.

I felt neither elation nor guilt but only a knifesharp sense of concentration. In the air a man exists in a different element of action and response; he is detached from the earth and what he had learned on it of pity and hate; he is himself, and at the same time he is not quite human.

The Cossacks had now charged the decoys before them. Kink signaled Bill Daly out of line, and the two of them raked the decoy columns as the Cossacks galloped in.

The two ammunition belts of eight hundred rounds each I had started out with were now exhausted. My last two dives had been dry ones; I had held my place and pretended to fire for what effect it might have.

Tommy too was dry, but Eddie was firing single bursts of two shots at a time with a single gun. That was smart; he was saving a couple of rounds in his starboard gun against a surprise attack by Bolshie aircraft on the way home. I should have been as prudent.

Bill, back in the line now, was trying to pick off an unhorsed officer who was potting at us with a light machine gun from halfway up the side of the ravine. He missed, and reaching the bottom of his dive, pulled out to follow me around again. I saw him wiping off his telescopic sight for the next try.

On my next run down, a jagged hole appeared in the middle of my port wing. The machine-gunner was beginning to get our range. Eddie fired a single burst as he followed me down. I could hear it through the roar of my exhaust like the faint tap-tapping of a pencil on a window pane.

On my way up again Kink and Bill dove past me on a last strafe of a handful of cavalry that had managed to get clear of the gully and were escaping across the steppe. This time Eddie didn't follow me in the line; flying clear, like myself, of the machine-gunner, he made a wide circle some four or five hundred feet above, and I knew he was clearing a jam.

Tommy and I joined him, pulling in behind, and then followed him down at either wingtip. He dove straight and steep at his target; we lagged a little in a more diagonal descent.

Tommy turned to the left; I did a vertical turn to the right, my wings perpendicular to the ground. I was sitting on the axis of the horizon, pushed deep into my seat by the centrifugal force of the turn. I looked along the trailing edge of my right wing straight down at the ground.

Eddie's dive was carrying him straight into the path of the machine-gunner's bullets. Remorselessly the pencil tapped on the windowpane, and then Eddie's nose suddenly turned up. The slipstream from his prop set the dust swirling.

As Eddie zoomed skyward the machine-gunner sprang to a half erect position, then staggered and fell, rolling down the gully side into a wounded horse spread-eagled at the bottom. The horse's hoofs struck out frantically and the man lay still.

A red Very light shot from Kink's Camel – the signal to break away and regain formation. As we turned back to Beketofka the Cossacks waved. They surrounded a large group of prisoners; to the south, toward the city, fled the last remnants of Budenny's troops.

We had been in the air for almost two hours, Kink told us when he landed at the drome.[4]

That evening Colonel Momontov of Shkura's Wolves, the dreaded Cossack division, regiments of which had fought with us that afternoon, came to Beketofka to thank us. Shkura's men had a wolf's head as their insignia, and their round Cossack caps were made of the Russian wolf's grey fur instead of the usual curly Astrakhan wool. Wolf hair hung shaggily down around the sides and front, and the Cossacks' eyes glared fiercely through the tangled fringe. Shkura's raids were noted for bloodiness and ruthless pillage, and the sensitive Cowderdrill served them vodka and escaped quickly back to the kitchen.

Shkura's Wolves had counted eight hundred dead in the ravine. Eddie asked if there had been any wounded, and Russky said, 'Colonel say they all dead when Wolves have left.'

Momontov gave each of us a Cossack souvenir. Kink received a gold-inlaid *kinzhal*, the Cossack dagger, and I a solid-silver cigarette case engraved with hammer, sickle and red flags that had been looted from one of Budenny's dead.

Next day the battle for Tsaritsyn began. Wrangel's tanks and ar-moured cars attacked followed by the cavalry. The barbed wire down, the fourth division of Kuban Cossacks charged the trenches. The Reds retreated to their last trench line, and by the evening of the eighth, three days later, the Whites were in the town with the Bolshies fleeing north up the Volga.

It was a major victory, as important as the taking of Kharkov by the Volunteer Army a short time before. Wrangel's spoil was immense: over forty thousand prisoners and a mountain of *matériel*.

Denikin arrived to confer with the general and told him his plan of campaign. Wrangel, we heard, was nothing less than stunned. Completely disregarding the general's advice to consolidate the rear and fatten up the thin White reserves before extending the length of the front, Denikin had decided to push full steam ahead for Moscow, dividing his troops into three forces along the way. Wrangel's army was to take Saratov as soon as possible, and move on to Moscow via Nizhni Novgorod; General Sidorin's Army of the Don was to proceed ahead through Voronezh, and Mai-Maievsky, with the Volunteer Army, was to advance directly on Moscow by way of Kursk, Orel and Tula.

In vain Wrangel had objected that such a course was suicide. Denikin was ignoring strategy, choosing no principal direction, and permitting no concentration of troops. The commander-in-chief had glanced at him slyly and said, 'I see. You want to be the first man to set foot in Moscow!'

'Denikin seems to be taking a hell of a chance,' Eddie said. 'One bad licking and the front crumbles and it's all the way back to the Black Sea.'

'Better Wrangel should command than Denikin,' said Russky.

Kink shook his head. 'No chance of that. And if they have another altercation, Wrangel's proud enough to resign.' He circled his wilt-ing collar with a forefinger. 'Well, at least we've earned a little vaca-tion. Anyone for a swim?'

We took the van for the short trip to the river. Kink picked out a sandbar, and we got out of our clothes and into our olive green issue suits.

The water was delightful. We were lolling between dips when Tommy started singing:

Bonjour, ma chérie
Comment allez-vous?
Bonjour, ma chérie
How do you do?
Avez-vous fiancé? Cela ne fait rien.
Voulez-vous coucher avec moi ce soir?
Oui, oui, combien?

As he finished the party of fishermen a little below us pulled in an empty net. We laughed, not at them but at Tommy, and the fishermen scowled blackly.

'Unfriendly blighters,' Bill said.

'They don't like the Reds and they don't like foreign mercenaries either,' Eddie said. 'Either way, Red or White, they still make their pitiful twenty rubles a day.'

'With all respects,' said Russky in the stiff way he spoke when angry, 'difference it exists. Difference of spirit. Materialists cannot sense spirit but exists. White colour of the spirit, of freedom; red colour of blood.'

'All right, you chaps,' Kink interrupted, 'no political arguments. We're here for recreation.'

Tommy whistled, low. 'Speaking of recreation, look to your right.'

A group of girls from Beketofka village had come down to the river to bathe. To our delighted interest they were undressing on the upper end of the sandbar. They paid absolutely no attention to us, not even to Russky, who in proper Russian bathing style was buck naked.

'Oh my, look at that delicious little brunette,' Bill said admiringly. 'Wouldn't you like to go wandering with that in a hay field? Russky, what's Russian for 'My Beautiful One, shall we go wandering in a hayfield?''

'All respects,' frowned Russky, 'I no understand.'

'You understand all right,' said Tommy aggrievedly, 'but you're too much of a rotter to help a poor fellow out.'

Now the girls, all six of them, stood naked in the sunlight. Three were *blondinkas*. Peasants, they were thick in the withers and ankles, but attractive for all that. In careful unison each began to tie a silk kerchief under her chin.

'To keep the hair dry,' explained Russky.

'Reminds me of a story a Russian captain told me in Batum,' Kink said. 'Seems there was this American consul who didn't approve of all this bathing in the nude. He built a bathing box on the beach and changed in it every day. Then he noticed that the Russians were avoiding him, even in the water. He asked his servant to find out the reason, and he reported back, "Sir, the Russians think you must have a dreadful disease, covering yourself up that way, and they're afraid they'll catch it."'

We were all too busy watching the girls wading into the river to respond to Kink's story with more than a perfunctory laugh. We had gotten up to go in after them when suddenly we heard a tremendous explosion in the direction of the drome.

'Strewth,' Bill cried, 'it's the Bolshie bombers!'

There was another great hollow boom, then three or four in succession. Dust rose slowly into the sky.

'Arses up!' Kink shouted, and grabbing our khakis we ran for the van. Russky struggled into his shorts as we bounced over the rough dirt road toward the drome.

It wasn't the Bolshies, but two poor chaps of A Flight who had broken out of formation with engine trouble and returned to the field. As they came in to land at fifty feet, the observer stood up to look ahead over the pilot's shoulder. The bomb toggle at his seat caught in the pocket of his flying suit and released the bomb pull. The first bomb blew the wings off the DH-9; the wingless fuselage fell straight to the ground; and the rest of the full load of one-hundred-twelve-bombs exploded. It was more than an hour before we could get to the blazing wreck.

That night we could see from the lounge to the A Flight headquarters train, where Major Anderson sat writing[5] home to two Canadian wives whose men had gone 'larking in Russia', in the words of a Toronto journalist who had opposed the interference of the Commonwealth in internal Russian affairs.

★

We went into Tsaritsyn for a look at the town that we had so far only seen from the air.

It turned our stomachs. In every street bodies, animal and human, lay rotting. We could smell the unburied Red victims who lay in the ravines on the outskirts. In every breath we took was the heavy, sweetish odor of decay.

The looted shops were empty, the churches, with the exception of the cathedral, desecrated. In the rubbled streets with their shattered houses our whispers came back to us in hollow echoes. People staggered through doorways into the sun, and sat witlessly picking at their rags of clothes. Starving children looked at us blankly. In such a place it seemed a sacrilege to be alive.

'Stay away from the townspeople,' Kink warned us. 'They're rotten with smallpox and typhus.'

'Let's get out of here,' Eddie said. 'The stink's making me sick.'

We had started back for the van, parked in the main square, when a small pig, remarkably dirty and no bigger than a gin bottle, ran across our path. He stopped in front of Bill, braced himself on all four legs, and squealed weakly. Then he fell over on his snout.

Bill took the pig up in his arms. 'Strewth, we've got our mascot. We'll call him Clarence, after Cowderdrill.' He glared around belligerently. 'Any of you types have objections?'

'If Clarence doesn't work out well we can always eat him for Christmas dinner,' Eddie said, grinning.

'But Daly,' Tommy protested, 'how do you housebreak a pig?'

'You don't,' Bill answered.

That afternoon we were expecting Wrangel and his staff at the drome. When the General was an hour late Kink took us in the van into Beketofka village to wait for him at the station.

We found Wrangel on the platform, pacing up and down. He was a very tall, lean borzoi of a man in Cossack's *papakha*, cavalry man's boots, and long-skirted coat; across his chest, bare of medals, was a bandoleer of cartridges. His staff and bodyguard stood on the steps of the train, talking in subdued voices. A half dozen ragged urchins and two tousled peasants at the end of the platform looked on in gaping wonder.

Russky stepped forward and introduced us nervously.

Wrangel cordially shook each of us by the hand. Surprisingly, he knew our names. He apologized for being late; the stationmaster was absent from duty, and it was necessary for him to attend to the scoundrel first. In wartime, he reminded us, a stationmaster's leaving his station was as serious a crime as a sentry's quitting his post.

He resumed his pacing. Russky told us, in an undertone, that only a few days before the general had hanged a stationmaster and his two assistants for the same offense.

In another five minutes the stationmaster appeared, puffing and blowing, from a vodka bout in the village. When he saw the general his fat face turned purple. He put his hand to his heart and dropped to his knees before the conqueror of Tsaritsyn.

'Get up!' Wrangel ordered contemptuously, and the man's babbled *mea culpa* died in his throat. As Wrangel's tongue tore him to shreds the stationmaster looked to us for intercession. We looked away. He turned his eyes helplessly to the gathering crowd of villagers at the far end of the platform. They spat out their sunflower seeds and looked down at the ground.

Finally Wrangel's icy tirade ended. Drawing his *kinzhal* he pointed to the station door. Turning to touch his cap at every step, the stationmaster hurried off and disappeared within.

Russky explained that the general had spared the stationmaster in our honour, but should he ever again be found derelict in his duty, Wrangel would hang him on the spot.

It was completely credible to me that this steel-hard aristocrat had charged, singlehanded, a German battery and sabered its gunners; had, without penalty, coldly and haughtily lectured his commander-in-chief. Never before had I seen such complete dominance of a situation or so absolute an air of command.

Wrangel rejoined us, and Russky translated his remarks. He thanked us for the part we had played in routing Budenny's cavalry; had the Bolshevik general gotten through, his reinforcements might well have made the city impregnable. He regretted that urgent business made it impossible for him to mess with us at the drome, but invited us to a dinner he was giving for his Cossack officers in Tsaritsyn at the end of the week. General Holman, Commander of the British Military Mission, would be present. Again he shook our hands.

What was most extraordinary about the general, I decided, was his ice-blue eyes, their level directness. You thought: tell this man the truth – if you don't, no matter how good a liar you happen to be, he'll know it.[6]

A moment later his train pulled out of the station.

Bill whistled. 'Now wouldn't I hate to get on that fellow's list!'

'You know,' Eddie said, and he sounded surprised, 'he looks like a winner.'

★

There was no morning patrol scheduled, and I came into the lounge for breakfast wearing slippers. Cowderdrill, fussing at the fireplace, didn't hear me. I waited for a moment, my stomach growling, wondering what the devil he was up to, and then pounded my fist down on the mess table. The sergeant jumped, and what he was holding fell to the floor.

I looked, and gasped. Jewellery, scads of it. Bracelets, bangles, pendants with velvet ribbons, brooches, bandeaux, rings, a Russian tiara; earrings, diamond combs and *fourches*; cuff links, scarf pins, gold studs, bejeweled vanity cases. They sparkled and shone in the sunlight, spilling from the small drawer Cowderdrill had dropped to the carpet.

To the right of one of the boldly buttocked cupids, near the ornate mantel, was an open rectangular space. The drawer, one side of which was marble, fit it. Cowderdrill had found the secret hiding place of a fortune in jewels.

He gulped and shuffled his feet nervously. 'It's not what you think, Sir,' he said. 'Them jewels wasn't in the drawer. I mean the drawer didn't have nothing in it when I found it. Them jewels and things I got at the shops in Ekat and Tsaritsyn.'

I got up and picked over the contents of the drawer. He was telling the truth. At a distance the stuff had looked real enough, but it was actually gimcracks, cheap imitation junk jewellery. Russians were poor businessmen, but Cowderdrill had still managed to be had.

'Captain,' he hastened to assure me, 'all I traded for them jewels was some personal drugs I bought me in Constantinople and some Bovril and a few tins of bully beef. The *paruskies*, they love bully beef; they're all like Ivan. Sir, ain't it true we've got enough bully beef to feed the whole of Russia?'

On the proceeds of his fake jewellery and his collection of samovars Cowderdrill was undoubtedly looking forward to retiring from the air force and leading a gilded life in the casinos of the Riviera with a bogus countess on either arm. I couldn't bear to be the one to disillusion him. But if Kink ever found out he was bartering RAF rations on the outside it would go badly for Sergeant Clarence Cowderdrill. I had to put a stop to his peculations.

'Sergeant,' I said, 'if this war goes against us and we have to retreat you're going to be grateful for that carload of bully beef we're hauling. We won't have a damn thing to eat besides bully and caviar.

Now I'll forget our little conversation if you'll promise to stop this jewellery business immediately. Otherwise I'll have to tell the Major, and it'll be a court martial for you as sure as Trotsky wears whiskers.'

'Yes, Sir, thank you, Sir.' He grinned shyly yet proudly. 'Captain, Sir, what do you think of them? Ain't they loverly things, Sir? Look at that diamond tiara. Worth a fortune alone.'

'Um, very nice, Sergeant. Quite a brilliant collection. Now I'd suggest that you get rid of it before the other officers come in.'

Cowderdrill had just closed his secret drawer when Tommy, in his blue silk robe, came in yawning. '*Billet doux* from the Bolshies,' he said. 'A Nieup dropped a flock of them over Tsaritsyn.' He tossed a sheet of paper on the table. It was stencilled in violet ink, and written in English.

The leaflet said that the Reds were very angry about the British airmen who were aiding the reactionary, Tsarist White forces in their foredoomed efforts to crush the glorious Bolshevik Revolution. Should they capture any of us, our fate would be crucifixion, or worse. I reminded myself I was an American, and wondered if it would help.

'What could be worse than crucifixion?' I said.

'Torture,' Tommy said, sipping his tea. 'The Bolshies are first-rate at it. I saw one of their torture rooms in Ekat. They have a special apparatus for taking the skin off your hands and arms. It comes off like a glove. Then they put a rat in a brass bowl against your stomach, and apply hot coals against the bowl till the rat's driven to eat himself out of his cage. They've also got a machine that relieves you of your manhood in a particularly ghastly way, but I won't go into that right now, since the details are rather revolting. Cowderdrill!' he shouted, 'where's my bloody kidneys?'

'Coming, Sir, directly. Right off the fire.'

Cowderdrill set down before Tommy an underdone set of kidneys as red as a commissar's star.

'Ah!' Tommy said with satisfaction, digging in, 'just the way I like them!' I turned green, and leaving my oatmeal half finished, bolted for the lav.

★

Wrangel's party was being held in a chateau by the river occupied by the staff of the 10th Red Army before its hurried departure from

Tsaritsyn. A Cossack officer met us at the door, and showed us up to a second floor ballroom sparkling with silver and cut glass.

'What a place!' Tommy said admiringly. 'These nobles must have all the money in the world.'

'Had,' Eddie corrected dryly. 'And a good thing, too.'

'With all respects,' Russky said coldly, 'you are once again giving birth to anti-sentiments.'

'Hell, Russky,' Kink joshed him, 'Eddie didn't say anything against the Jews. He's got a Jewish girlfriend back home in Ontario.'

'Then that is only thing we have in common,' Russky said with dignity. 'My finance she Jewish. And she more Jewish, I bet, than *yours*!'

We were a little early, but huge crystal bowls of caviar were already set out on the dazzling white tablecloths that covered the long mahogany tables. Before the bowls stood champagne glasses, from which the caviar was to be eaten with spoons. At every place was a decanter of vodka, with a shot glass beside it.

We had started in on the vodka, and I was deploring the Russian lack of imagination in failing to have developed another national drink, when Kink said, 'Here comes the General.'

We rose as Wrangel and his staff entered the room, followed by what seemed to be an interminable column of Cossacks, with pistols and *kinzhals* at their belts.

'Yosefovich, Chatilov, Borodov,' Russky identified the general's staff officers. 'Pokrovsky, Saveliev. Also General Holman.'

Some of Wrangel's staff officers had been with him when the general came to Beketofka, but it was the first time I had seen our British commander. Holman was a huge bear of a man with the reticent competence and God-given assurance of the British professional soldier engraved deeply on his genial face. He was as tall as Wrangel, and though there were no men in the group less than middle height, the two dwarfed the others.

We resumed our seats after the general and his party had taken theirs. Russky introduced me to the Russian officers who sat on either side of B Flight. To my right was a captain of cavalry named Sobolov who spoke English like an Oxonian. He had, he told me, learned the language from his English governess before learning his mother tongue.

The dinner began. There was *zakuski*, the Russian hors d'oeuvres, a meal in itself, and borscht. There were mutton cutlets baked with cabbage, carrots, and other vegetables, and buckwheat-flour pancakes served with melted butter, sour cream and smoked salmon. There were also pancakes stuffed with chopped beef, combined with kidney fat, chopped onions and a Béchamel sauce. There were open tartlets of puff pastry filled with farmers' cheese. Caucasian wine arrived, and with it three kinds of vodka, flavoured with frost-bitten cherries, buffalo grass and red pepper. There was aspic with tongue, salted sardines, and smelts cooked in chicken stock with chopped shrimps and mushrooms. There was sliced cooked salmon and bream baked with *kasha*. There was also a shrimp and fish pie, made with peas, sour cream, lemon and baked between layers of puff pastry. There was a boiled suckling pig, served with a sauce of sour cream, horseradish, salt and pepper. Caviar was served with every course. For dessert there was a pie made with almonds, cherry jam, sour cream, egg yolks and cinnamon; small cheese cakes; a cake made of cream cheese, chopped almonds, candied peels and other ingredients; a cream pudding, and French pastry.

I found I could get through it all by putting one thing on my plate at a time, taking a bite and waiting for the waiter to whisk my plate away and give me a clean one. Then I would repeat the process. Kink caught on to my system, and signaled the rest of B Flight to do the same.

I got talking to Sobolov, and asked him his opinion of Denikin's campaign for the taking of Moscow.

He shook his head grimly. 'I consider it a serious mistake. There's no doubt that for the time being we should entrench ourselves on the Tsaritsyn-Ekaterinoslav front, so that the Volga and Dnieper would be covering our flanks. We could then detach whatever troops were needed for operations toward the southeast, and at the same time maintain a strong garrison at Kharkov. Otherwise we have no organized rear and no bases. And with a disorganized rear there's no way to stop the violence, marauding and other abuses going on behind the lines. The people are bound to hold this lawlessness against us.'

I told Sobolov we had heard that relations between Denikin and Wrangel were pretty badly strained. He grimaced. 'Yes, and it hasn't helped for Denikin to renege on his promise to give us a rest after the taking of Tsaritsyn. We were to have fifteen days and Denikin changed his mind and gave us only two. The 1st Kuban Cossacks are on their way to Saratov now. They don't have a chance to take it; the Reds are pouring troops into the city. Well!' Sobolov lifted his vodka glass. 'Live for the day!'

At the next table a Cossack with a fierce mustache got up on a chair and launched into a ringing speech in Russian.

'Not worth translate,' Russky said. 'Only ordinary sentiments.'

The Cossack tossed off his vodka in a single gulp and shook his head to clear it. Then he smashed his glass to the floor. Other Cossacks rose to make brief speeches and smash their glasses and then silence fell over the room as Wrangel got to his feet. He held up his glass in our direction, and a smile of extraordinary charm lit his severe face with its high cheekbones and ice-blue eyes. 'To my new Cossacks,' he said in English learned for the occasion. 'To my conquerors of Budenny, to my Cossacks of the air!'

The place became a madhouse. The Cossacks jumped from chairs to tables, sending the platters and other dishware flying. The bowls of caviar oozed their black treasure to the tablecloth. On the dais, next to Wrangel, General Holman good-humouredly wiped a blob of caviar from his eye.

'*Za vashe zdorovye! Za vashe zdorovye!*' the long-coated men shouted, and began another series of toasts, all of them talking at the same time with a great deal of grandiloquence and glass-smashing. Several glasses came sailing over our heads, to shatter against the wall beyond. Those cavalrymen who were glassless were drinking vodka straight from the decanters – all three kinds.

'You must excuse them,' Sobolov said. 'We Russians keep sane by periodically becoming insanely loud or sentimental.'

The toast ended, waiters came out to clean the glass from the square of polished floor bounded by the tables.

'Now Cossack dancing,' Russky said. 'The *kazachok*.'

'Watch out for their *kinzhals*,' Sobolov said.

A battery of artillery boomed in the distance as two dancers took the floor. The *kazachok* they danced to an orchestra of accordion, violin and balalaika was a wild, free and explosive thing. The dancers leaped high on their toes, whirled, then squatted on their heels, kicking straight out in front of them first with one foot and then the other. The flashing of boots was so rapid I could hardly follow it.

'Where are the *kinzhals*?' I asked Sobolov.

'Wait,' he told me, 'for the finale.'

Two more dancers had joined those on the floor. The music stepped up in tempo. In their teeth now all four men held the points of three *kinzhals*. Two more Cossack daggers were tucked behind each ear, while each hand, up-raised, grasped another.

The Cossacks beat time, clapping their hands as the dancers did a mad *kazachok*, ending with a flying leap in the air. At the height of their leap the dancers shook themselves like dogs coming out of the water, and the *kinzhals* rained down, sticking their sharp points into the floor. One quivered a bare inch from my foot.

'*Na Moskvu! Na Moskvu!*' cried the dancers, and as the audience took up the cry it became a chant exciting, compelling, irresistible. Even Eddie was on his feet, shouting and waving his glass. Sobolov, his eyes bright, was yelling with the rest of us.

When the shouting died down the orchestra began to play a haunting, plaintive melody, the kind you think you've heard before but haven't. The sudden hush was broken as the Cossacks, bass and baritone, burst into song.

'The song of Stenka Razin,' Sobolov told me. 'He was a Don Cossack, the great Robin Hood of the Volga. Stenka led the Cossack Revolt of 1671. For years he swept the river above and below Tsaritsyn with his flotilla of river craft; when he took a town or a city he redistributed its wealth among the poor and went his way again. When the Volga got too small for him he cruised into the Caspian Sea to plunder the Persians. A Persian princess was one of his prizes, and her fate is the theme of the song.'

As the Cossacks sang, Sobolov recited:

Behind them rose a whisper:
He has left his sword to woo –
One short night and Stenka Razin
Has become a woman too.

What cares he for war or glory,
For spoil or for pelf,
For his princess of the Persians
Is to him all worldly wealth.

Stenka hears the jeering
Of his discontented band,

And the lovely Persian princess
He has circled with his hand.

His black brows have come together
As the waves of anger rise,
And the blood has mounted swiftly
To his piercing, jet black eyes.

'I will give you all you wanted,
Life and heart, and head and hand,'
In echo rolls the pealing thunder
Of his voice across the land.

'Volga, Volga, mother Volga
Deep and wide beneath the sun,
You have never seen a gift given
By the Cossacks of the Don.

And that peace might rule as always,
All my free-born men and brave,
Volga, Volga, mother Volga,
Make my love a grave.

With a sudden, mighty movement
Stenka lifts the beauty high,
And casts her where the waters
Of the Volga sigh.

Dance, you fools, and men, make merry,
What shadow darks your eyes?
Let us thunder out a shanty
Of a place where beauty lies.'

The song was over, dying in a melancholy whisper, and as befits a somber moment, there was no applause.

I saw Tommy wipe a bit of moisture from his eye. 'That's a good story,' he said to Sobolov. 'Is it true?'

The Russian nodded. 'It's also true that when Stenka came out of his solitude weeks later he was a changed man, more violent and bloodthirsty than ever before. He was finally caught and brought to Moscow for trial by torture. The night before they quartered him alive he composed his epitaph. It went, "He who rests here, Stenka Razin Timofief, was an adventurer and an outlaw, but withal a good fellow. And he loved."'

Sobolov sighed. 'But let us not be sad. Have you any English songs to sing?'

Bill let out his belt for the second time. 'There's one I can think of might interest the Cossacks if they could understand it. It describes the duping and betrayal of a nameless cockney maiden, at length and quite intimately.'

'Good, Let's hear it.'

'Won't the General mind?' Kink asked Sobolov.

'Not a bit. Stenka put something of a damper on the party.'

To the tune of 'Stenka Razin' Bill began, falteringly, to sing:

> She was poor but she was honest,
> Victim of a rich man's whim.
> He loved her and he left her,
> And she had a ch-i-ld by him.

We joined in, and so did the orchestra and the Cossacks, the latter humming the tune in their great, booming voices, not understanding a word we said but certain it was no church hymn we were singing. Twenty-five verses after they pounded on the table, demanding more.

The party broke up at two. We assured Sobolov maudlinly that should he ever get fed up with the cavalry, there was plenty of room for him aboard B Flight train. Kink, who had stayed relatively sober, swung the van down the drive, but mistook a ditch for the gate, and five sweating Cossacks helped us out of it.

Leaving the chateau, we roared out 'It's the Only, Only Way.' The night was very black and still. The artillery fire lighting in flashes on the horizon was like the sleepy growling of an immense watchdog we had inconsiderately disturbed.

Chapter Five

＊

Sobolov was right; the 1st Kuban Cossacks failed to take Saratov and were, in fact, thrown back at Kamyshin. Wrangel reinforced his exhausted troops, and after three days of vicious fighting, the Cossack cavalry captured Kamyshin and took thirteen thousand prisoners. B Flight did its part, strafing and harassing the Red railway supply lines and rear areas. A Red machine-gunner creased my helmet and chewed up Bill's instrument panel, but otherwise none of us was touched.

Over his sharp objections Wrangel was ordered to continue the advance on Saratov. 'Telegrams, they keep going forth and back,' Russky told us. 'Wrangel say he have too few men and the Bolshies in Saratov have thousands. He begs for fresh troops.'

In late July the Bolshies counterattacked in the Kamyshin area. The White cavalry beat them back, and the outnumbered Pekrovsky defeated Budenny in three days of bloody battle. But Wrangel was not elated. He reported to Denikin that a few more such apparent successes would force him to fall back on the defensive for lack of men.

The Reds attacked all along the line at dawn of August 1st, and the Baron fell back slowly toward Tsaritsyn. B Flight was in the air for most of the day,[1] coming back to Beketofka to refuel and then taking off again for the front to attack the troop trains bringing up Red reinforcements. Few of the Red machine-gunners were accurate, and we would come in lower and lower on the trains with increasing effect.

During the retreat to Tsaritsyn there were few Bolshie planes in the air; probably they had been moved to the other fronts – Astrakhan and Kursk – where the Reds were having even worse luck at the moment.

But there were some, there were always some, and the black Fokker was one of them.

Tommy and I had gone out to escort an A Flight RE-8 on photographic reconnaissance over Kamyshin. We were approaching the bend of the Volga at Tsaritsyn when the two red stars jumped us. Glancing up, I saw my old arrogant friend, the Fokker with the ace of clubs tail, hovering with all the confidence of a vulture who had dined well on his main course and now looked forward to dessert. We were his dessert, if his comrades should cripple us.

The Bolshies' dive carried them past us without damage, and I got one of them, a Nieup, in my sights. A long burst and I had flamed him. That left even odds. I signaled the RE-8 to head for home on a path the Fokker could not cross unless he reckoned with me, and when the RE-8 had lumbered off and Tommy was occupied with the other Nieup, I waggled my wings at the ace of clubs, taunting him to come down and fight.

He dived, firing, and I turned sharply right. As he passed I dived in turn, giving him a short burst that missed his upper wing by inches. We closed, and he was even better than I had thought, spinning neatly out of turns tight as I could make them and presenting nothing vulnerable to my sights. Once, outguessing me, he put a burst in my tail. Since neither of us was giving the other a chance to break off and climb, we were losing height rapidly; my altimeter showed one thousand feet, a four thousand-foot loss in the last few minutes.

The Bolshie tried an Immelman, a manoeuvre which the Camel could accomplish only at the price of a considerable loss in altitude. As he went into his upward corkscrew turn I gave him a long range burst and dove below him. The tracers passed his nose close enough to smell, and I saw his right aileron flapping in the breeze. I had cut his control wire.

Steadily and dangerously we were losing height. I knew my ammunition was running low, and at five hundred feet decided upon a manoeuvre I had once used successfully against a two-seater fighter on the Western Front. To avoid the rear gunner's fire I had dived beneath the two-seater, come up under its blind spot, and raked its belly from tail to prop from below.

The Fokker pilot, having lost me, had leveled out. I got below him while his eyes were still searching the skies above. Standing on my tail and hanging on my prop, I gave him my last burst, emptying my guns into the black coffin of fuselage at twenty yards.

I had to get him. If I failed, his guns would be on me before Tommy, a thousand yards away, even noticed.

The pilot slumped forward onto his joy stick and the Fokker went into a straight dive. It crossed over the vertical, and was going into a loop upside down when it crashed on its back with terrific force into the river.[2]

Tommy had just sent down his damaged Nieup, and we flew together back to the drome.

That night Wrangel wired his congratulations from Ekat, where he was meeting with the Ataman of the Kuban Cossacks. It seemed the black Fokker had been top ace on White bombers, having downed more than a dozen in all sectors of the southwestern front.

In celebration we gave Clarence the Pig his first bowl of Bass ale. Discriminating pig that he was, he loved it.

★

On my next flight I was forced down with pump trouble near Kotluban, one hundred miles from Tsaritsyn.

A pitchfork-wielding peasant, a dead ringer for Leo Tolstoy, ran up to me with the evident intention of forking this Red marauder, and for a moment I was afraid I'd have to use my revolver on him.

'*Nyet, nyet*,' I said. '*Angliski*.' I pointed to the Camel's Allied insignia. '*Angliski* pilot.'

He looked at me suspiciously, his small eyes glittering, and it occurred to me that if he had never seen a plane before his caution was justified.

'*Angliski*.' I repeated, and made flying motions with my arms.

His face darkened, and he rattled off some Russian, the gist of which was, I assumed: How can there be such a thing as an English bird which flies like a man?

That stumped me. Fortunately I had brought some money, and I pulled out a roll of rubles and English pound notes. I offered him some rubles, and he shook his head. Then I held out a ten shilling note with the King's face on it, and he beamed.

'Ah, *anglichanin*,' he said, and pocketed it with satisfaction.

Tolstoy pointed to a thatched hut a hundred yards away and invited me for tea, but I thanked him and inquired in my very stiff Russian for the location of the nearest telegraph. He pointed across the field to what must have been a road and then jerked his thumb to the right.

I left him fondling the ten shilling note, and set off across the field.[3]

Coming to the road, I turned right, and followed it about two miles to a railroad siding. On the siding was parked a hospital train of twenty or so cars, each with a red cross on its side. The smell, half disinfectant and half putrefaction, was strong enough to bring tears to the eyes.

Outside of one of the cars stood a white-smocked orderly, smoking. When I asked him where I could find a telegraph, he shrugged his lack of comprehension and stepped back into the train. I stood there for a moment, fuming. Then I swung up the steps into the car.

It was packed with wounded in double bunks against both walls. For the most part the men lay comatose, or staring up at the ceiling. A few groaned and one silently wept into his coverlet; several moaned in delirium. Except for the Russian that the mumbler spoke I might have been in any hospital train I had ever seen in France or Belgium; the sheets were clean and the black uniformed nurse coming down the aisle toward me smiled brightly.

I asked her my question, and shaking her head, she smilingly pointed to the next car. There was someone there, I gathered, who spoke English.

The next car was dark, with its shades drawn against the late afternoon sun. I suppose there was little possibility that I could have avoided running into the young nurse I encountered,[4] and probably less that she could have managed not to spill part of the bottle of carbolic she was carrying on my leg.

'Oi! *prostite!*' she cried.

I scowled, and moved back into the half-light of the vestibule to determine the damage.

Fortunately, since I was wearing my flying suit, it was minor; the leather was only slightly burned. The nurse, who had followed me out into the vestibule, put down the bottle and applied a rag. I kept my eyes sourly on the top of her black headdress, resentful but curious to see what she looked like once she lifted her head.

The job done, she got to her feet.

'What is the matter?' she said in strongly Russian-accented English. 'Why do you stare?'

I swallowed. 'Was I staring?'

She took off her headdress and touched her shining chestnut hair. There was no coquetry in the gesture, only feminine concern for good grooming. 'I would say you were staring. There is something wrong in the way I look?'

'No, nothing,' I fumbled. 'It's just that I didn't expect to see so beautiful a nurse in Russia.'

She laughed. 'Oh, we have many beautiful nurses. But you are repaired now?'

'Yes, I am repaired.'

She stooped for the bottle and I moved quickly to pick it up for her. Our heads bumped, but she managed to hold on to the carbolic.

'Better luck this time,' I said inanely.

'If you will let me pass?'

I wasn't going to let her pass. Quickly I introduced myself. 'I am Captain Aten of 47 Squadron, at Beketofka. I was forced to land nearby and I must get in touch with my squadron. Can you tell me how far it is to Kotluban station, if we're near Kotluban at all? I can send a wire from there.'

'We are near Kotluban, but it is five miles, too far to walk. If you must get there immediately, I will speak to our commandant, Dr. Major Alexandrovsky, and he can arrange transportation for you.'

'Oh, it isn't at all urgent,' I said, grinning in what I hoped was a boyishly charming way. 'I thought you might be kind enough to offer me a glass of tea.'

'Certainly. I am just going off duty. Please follow me.'

I would have followed her to the Kremlin gates and back. She took me through eight cars of wounded and dying, and the typhus ward, and though it may have been heartless, all I saw was the girl before me, small and lissome, gliding along so gracefully that she hardly seemed to touch the floor. And all I heard was her lovely voice that greeted the men, and replied to their greetings in a Russian that made me realize I had never really heard the language, in all the beauty of its plaintive cadences, before.

'*Tsaritsa moevo serdtsa*,' I said, repeating the words the wounded had called out most often to her. 'What does that mean?'

'Tsarina of my heart,' she said over her shoulder, blushing. 'They are great flirts, the ones who are not so badly wounded; it keeps their spirits up.'

Suddenly it occurred to me that being so desirable to other men she was no doubt married or engaged, and I glanced at her left hand. It was ringless.

'The dining coach is not much further,' she told me. 'I am sorry to have shown you so many melancholy things.'

We came into the dining car. At its end, on a white-clothed table, stood a huge samovar, with glasses ranged before it.

I sat down, and she brought two glasses of tea, lemon and sugar.

'My name is Nina Dmitrievna Anohina,' she said. 'Would you have met my brother Alexei? He is a lieutenant on the staff of General Denikin.'

I was afraid I hadn't, I told her. There were thousands of men on the southern front. Then I dropped my sugar into my tea, and she laughed.

'No, it is Russian to put the sugar in your teeth and drink your tea through it.'

She showed me, but I proved a dud at it. First I dropped the sugar and then I swallowed half the cube. Nina had to pound me on the back before I got it up again. Not only that: the glass was too hot to pick up in the ordinary way, and I spilled quite a bit of tea before I got hold of the glass properly with thumb and extended forefinger.

'You will never be Russian,' she said, rather sadly. 'No, you are angliski forever. It is bad, no, that they have locked your King George up in the Tower of London?'

'Hold on,' I said. 'First, I am *amerikanski*, not *angliski*. Secondly, King George is not locked up. Where on earth did you get that information?'

'The Reds have said so. Olga, she is my friend and a nurse also; she told me she saw it in a Bolshevik propaganda leaflet.'

'What else did they say?'

'They say, how you call it, an MP has formed a provisional government in London. Also, that the British Navy is flying the hammer and sickle flag and is on its way up the Canadian River to help the Soviets of Canada.'

'Lenin may be a genius, Nina,' I said, 'but that isn't true.'

She seemed distressed by the familiarity of my address, and turned her head away.

'You mustn't believe all this Bolshevik propaganda,' I told her hastily.

'I shall not in future. It is good to meet an *amerikanets* from the outside world who can correct these false impressions. Do you know, Captain, I have never before met an American? Tell me about

Chicago. It is a very great city?' It seemed she thought all Americans came from Chicago.

I told her about Chicago for a while, and then I managed to switch the conversation around to Nina herself. She was twenty, she told me, and came from Rostov, near Ivanovo, in the north. Her father was a merchant. She had attended the university in Ivanovo, where she had studied English and become interested in English literature. At seventeen she had joined the nurses' corps, and served through the last months of the European war. When the civil war had broken out she had joined the White hospital at Velikoknyazheskoye as a nurse's aide.

Last spring the Reds had captured the hospital, removed the medical staff, and burned it down with five hundred wounded still inside. A cordon of Red guards had been drawn around the hospital to shoot anyone who managed to crawl out of the building.

'You saw all this?' I asked her.

'They made us watch, Captain. They told us the same thing would happen to anyone who refused to co-operate.'

'So you were with the Reds for how long?'

'Six months, until I was sentenced to be shot,' she said, quite conversationally.

I set down my glass. 'And how did that happen?'

'After the burning of the hospital, the Reds assigned me to a hospital train near Saratov. A Red commissar, one of the few who became wounded, was brought aboard the train. They made me his private nurse. He recovered after a few weeks of convalescence, and then he forced himself upon me.'[5]

She pulled back her shoulder cape, undid the buttons of her blouse, and slipped down the top of her shift. From her left breast a piece of flesh had been bitten. The wound was still black and blue and the whole breast discoloured. I wasn't shocked; what she had done had been too natural for that. But it surprised me that she could show me her body and yet be embarrassed when I called her by her first name.

I watched her button up her blouse again.

'I gave him poison,' she said, 'and stood there while he died. It did not take too long. When they discovered the body they told me I would be shot in the morning. They would have done it that night, except that the soldiers were in the village, drinking. The Cossacks took the village and the railway yards at dawn.'

The dining-car door opened, and a big man with a handle-bar mustache and wearing a blood-stained white smock, came in and joined us at the table. He drooped with exhaustion; sitting there, hunched forward, he was like a beached whale. Nina introduced him to me as Major Alexandrovsky, the commandant of the hospital train, and went to the samovar to get him a glass of tea.

Alexandrovsky said he would be glad to arrange transportation for me to Kotluban station, and Nina left the car to get a lorry. The major, in passable English, asked if it looked to us *pilotts* as though Wrangel were going to evacuate Tsaritsyn. I said I didn't know.

He closed his eyes for a moment, and then took up his glass. 'We have shortage of men all over. Wrangel cannot defend Tsaritsyn without more men, and I cannot run my train without more doctors, nurses and orderlies. Now we have but one nurse to fifty wounded, and I am afraid it will get worse.

'Nina must work like a dog,' I said, 'yet she looks fresh as a daisy.'
'Daisy?'
'Like a flower. She is fresh like a flower though she must work very hard.'

He smiled. 'Nina is like an angel from heaven above. The men, they worship her. If I did not have her many more would die.'

Nina came back with word that the lorry was waiting outside, and I shook the major's hand and said goodbye.

The *plenny* seated in the lorry driver seat wore the same black fatigues as did our own POWs. In the middle of his back was a yellow half moon, an aid to the marksmanship of any guard who caught him trying to escape.

I felt suddenly shy with Nina, but I managed to ask her if there was much chance of the hospital train coming down to Tsaritsyn.

'Only if there is a retreat.'
'Will you be getting any leave, perhaps?'
She shook her head. 'There is too much work and too few nurses.'
'We might be moving up toward Saratov,' I said.
'I would enjoy seeing you again, Captain.' She smiled. 'We can talk about Chicago, though I think you are a tease, and do not really live there in – what is the state of Chicago? — Michigan.'

'You're right. I don't come from Michigan, but California, which is right next door to Chicago. We can talk about that.'

'I will try to find out something about California, Captain; we have one or two American books aboard the train. So that I might discuss it with you intelligently.'

'Fine… Nina – may I call you Nina, or is it too soon for that?'

'It is soon, but you may call me by the name. And now, Captain, *do svidaniya*,' she said, and turned inside the train.

There was no road along the track, but the steppe was as flat as Cowderdrill's feet, and we were at Kotluban station in a few minutes. I asked the *plenny* to wait for me, and went into the station.

Like all the others I had seen it was square and made of stone. In the centre of the waiting room was a big pot-bellied stove with wooden benches around it. Sunflower seed hulls littered the floor like chaff from a threshing machine. It was stifling; with typical Russian horror of fresh air, the windows were all closed and bolted. A *muzhik* looked up at me, smiled like a saint, and returned to the contemplation of his manure-caked boots.

I had trouble getting across to the stationmaster that I wanted to send a message on the telegraph; he kept pointing the way to the outside privy. Finally he took me into his littered office and at the operating table I dot-dashed a message to Kink at the drome. He wired back within minutes. He had seen me go down and would have already dispatched a DH-9 with mechanic, had I the sense to wire him my exact location immediately.

The *plenny* drove me back to Tolstoy's field. An hour and a quarter later the DH-9 landed with mechanic and new pump. We were back at the drome in time for dinner. Kink asked why I had taken so long to wire in. He had to ask me twice.

'I was talking to a girl,' I said, ' a nurse, an angel. She's on the hospital train at Kotluban.'

Kink's sharp eyes probed into mine. What he saw there disturbed him. 'God, Bunny,' he groaned, 'we're fighting a war, man. This is no damn time to fall in love.'

All at once it came to me in terror that he had correctly diagnosed my condition. Maybe it was the war and maybe it was Russia, but I doubted it; had I met Nina walking down Main Street in El Centro I would have followed her home and knocked down any man who tried to stop me.

Kink looked at me with that kind of respectful pity that new lovers inspire in all of us. 'Bunny,' he said, 'you better have a drink. Have several.'

★

Russky and Eddie were having one of their debates on modern Russian history. Russky had begun with a salute to the halcyon years of 1906 to 1914, with their balanced budget and booming trade, their foreign investments and records in production. Russia, he told us, was giving democracy a chance to work. He insisted, against Eddie's objections, that because Russian democracy had failed it had been bound to fail; when Eddie brought up the immense backwardness of Mother Russia, Russky replied that the experiment proved at least that his country could be governed by other means than those of the *Okhrana*, the secret police. And Stolypin's land reforms: could Eddie deny that the Russian premier, perhaps the greatest of them all, had set up a new class of peasant land-owners that numbered at least six million? In 1917 the Bolsheviks were shouting their slogan 'All Land to the Peasants', but Stolypin had already given the peasants three-quarters of what the Reds demanded.

Eddie countered by asking who had proved Stolypin's most dangerous enemy, and Russky had been forced to answer: the Empress Alix, wife of the Tsar, who fawned upon Rasputin and showed Stolypin the door. He didn't deny Eddie's charges that Russia in the last war had been criminally unprepared. He admitted that military discipline was brutal and that men in the ranks had been treated like cattle. We listened in amazement to his admissions of flogging, to the rule that forbade enlisted men to travel in street cars or eat in public restaurants.

But Russky couldn't understand Eddie's indignation over the fact that no one could rise to be an officer from the ranks of the Tsarist army. 'That natural,' he said, 'the best officers, they come from the military academies. Like the Grand Duke Nikolai.'

'Do you mean to say,' Eddie protested, 'that the Grand Duke was a good soldier? He lost nearly four million men.' Waving away Russky's expostulations, he went on: 'If he wasn't a good soldier, then maybe he was better as a statesman. But how do you explain the million Jews he drove out of Poland and sent on the roads to wander and die?'

'The Grand Duke thought they were spies for the Germans,' Russky answered.

'But he was wrong, wasn't he?' Eddie insisted, and finally Russky had to admit the Grand Duke had been wrong about the Jews.

He somehow got on the subject of Rasputin, and Prince Yusapov's murder of the false but mesmeric prophet who had held the Empress of all the Russias in the palm of his hand. Eddie let him finish, and said; 'And how did the Tsar react after Rasputin's death? Here was his chance to break out of his shell of apathy and indifference. And what happened? He was more apathetic and indifferent than before. Do you know what he said to one of the Allied ambassadors? He said, 'Do you mean that I am to regain the confidence of my people, or do you mean that they are to regain mine?'

'So he was stubborn man,' Russky said angrily. 'That I do not deny. But he could rise to greatness, too. Listen. I read you the Imperial Declaration of Abdication, and you tell me no.' He took a well-thumbed piece of paper from his pocket.

Lighting a Gold Flake, I saw the scene before me as Russky had once before described it: the parade ground with its regimental standards limp in the windless air, the chaplain adjusting his stole, the Bible and the silver cross on the altar, the standard bearers of each regiment taking up their positions to hear their Colonels say the words that changed 300 years of Russian history.

Russky read, and his poor English somehow did not spoil the drama of the words; it made them, in fact, more affecting:

We, Nikolai the Second, by the Grace of God Emperor of all the Russias, King of Poland, Grand Duke of Finland … Let it be known to all our faithful subjects that in these days of heroic struggle against an external enemy which has for three years attempted to enslave our country, it has pleased God to send Russia a new and terrible trial. Internal troubles threaten to have fatal repercussions on the further conduct of the war. The destiny of Russia, the honour of our people, the whole future of our beloved country, demand that by all costs the war be continued to a victorious end. The enemy is making his last stubborn stand and the hour is near when our valiant army together with our glorious allies will utterly defeat him.

In these grave days for the future of Russia, our conscience commands us to facilitate for our people the unification and organization of all its forces in order to obtain a speedy victory. For this reason we, in agreement with the Duma of the Empire, have decided to abdicate the throne of Russia and to lay aside our supreme power…

As we do not wish to be separated from our beloved son, we make over our inheritance to our brother, the Grand Duke Mikhail Alexandrovich, whom we bless at his accession to the throne… We appeal to all faithful sons of our country and call upon them to do their duty… May the Lord help Russia. Nicholai.

Russky took out his handkerchief and blew into it. 'We weep,' he said. 'We are soldiers, and tears are for children, but we weep as though it is our father who has died.'

In the silence Eddie knocked his pipe against the fireplace. The rest of us cleared our throats and shuffled our feet, or looked away out the windows. It was hard not to be moved at the death of an Idea and the passing of an Empire, even if they weren't your own.

'Time for a drink,' Kink said, breaking the spell, and rang the bell that summoned Cowderdrill.

There was no answering 'Yes, Sir, right away, Sir,' from the pantry. Instead Clarence the Pig wandered out and rooted in Bill's hand. I noticed he was growing by leaps and bounds.

'Where in the devil has that idiot gone?' Kink said. 'Tommy, go and take a look, will you?'

Tommy came back shaking with laughter. 'Cowderdrill's fallen between two cars up the line. Half of A Flight's trying to get him out.'

We ran to the scene of the disaster. Five cars down, the centre of an uproarious group of off-duty A and B Flight mechanics, our messman was wedged in between two freights, snug as a trapped mouse and twice as frightened.

When he saw Kink, Cowderdrill brightened. 'Please Sir, you'll get me out? The trains might move.'

'If they moved, which they won't, you'll deserve it,' Kink said sternly. 'I've told you a hundred times that those damn samovars of yours are safe and yet you've got to keep on coming down here to check on them.'

'Yes Sir, I disobeyed your orders. But Cor, Sir, and the Lud love you, if you don't do something about getting me out of here, I'll never be able to disobey an order of yours again!'

Laughter. Kink stilled it with an upraised hand. 'Does any of the audience have a suggestion as to how to get this man out?' he asked the enlisted men sarcastically.

One A Flight man grinned and said, "is every wiggle wedges 'im in deeper, Major. We thought we might use a little explosives to kind of *blow* 'im out.'

As Cowderdrill groaned, his great eyeballs swiveling in panic, the laughter swelled. Again Kink cut it off, this time more sharply.

'You there, Cross, get the block and tackle. Hammond, Bradley and Swanson, go along to help.'

Tommy and I offered Cowderdrill encouragement while the A Flight man went for the means to extricate him, but it was no use, the messman's imagination had created fresh terrors. 'Sir,' he asked me, 'won't I be pulled apart, like a piece of chicken? What if my top comes along but my legs stay put?'

We told him that was nonsense, but he was gibbering with fear when the men came with the block and tackle and set it up. Under Kink's direction a loop of rope was passed over Cowderdrill's head and under his armpits, and the two men on the windlass ordered to crank away.

'It's all right, Clarence,' one of his tormentors yelled, 'if the thing don't work, yer sister gets yer pension!'

'If you feel yer arms coming off, just yell!' shouted another.

And another: 'If the rope don't get ye then the Bolshies will!'

The winch squealed and the rope around the messman tightened. A Flight men were making the inevitable bets, most of them loudly convinced that while Cowderdrill might finally escape from his prison, he was bound to leave at least one limb behind.

The first effort was unsuccessful; he didn't budge a centimeter. Kink pushed back his cap and scratched his forehead.

'Again, Cross. This time a little slower.'

The men grunted at the windlass. There was a sound of ripping cloth, but Kink motioned for Cross and company to continue. Cowderdrill groaned, bellowed, then yelped in pain. A cheer went up as he lifted a couple of inches.

'We're getting there,' Kink encouraged him.

'Major, we might be getting there, but you're leaving my ruddy skin behind!'

'Cross,' Kink ordered, 'slow down!'

Cowderdrill began to emerge, a little of him at a time. Soon his shoulders and trunk were clear, and then, as a shout rose from the men, the whole of the messman dangled in the air. He had, however, left behind his breeches and underwear, and was naked from tunic to leggings and shoes. To loud huzzahs and laughter he was lowered to the ground and deposited trackside. The rope was untied. Bets were paid off while Cowderdrill accepted Kink's garrison hat as a fig leaf and gratefully swigged from a flask of brandy.

Kink sent a B Flight man to get a blanket. Before the man moved off I heard him mutter, 'Bloody fool. If 'e'd only stayed there over night I would 'ave 'ad myself a neat five quid, and nobody the worse for it.'

★

Slowly and skillfully, Wrangel retreated from Kamyshin to the gates of Tsaritsyn. We had three and four patrols a day, harassing the Reds streaming down the roads to the city. They were smarter now, taking cover in the roadside ditches at our approach, and their fighter planes were on the scene more often, though for the most part the opposition they gave us was second-rate. During the first two weeks of August we bagged ten red stars.[6] Most of the victories went to Kink and Colly, who came up to the front lines for a 'little vacation' from paper work in Taganrog, to which base headquarters had now been transferred from Ekat.

Wrangel, awaiting reinforcements he was none too sure would arrive in time, ordered the gradual evacuation of Tsaritsyn. Despite his orders that arms and munitions were to leave first, the civil and military administration second, and the civilians last, word got to him that the departing trains were packed with civilians and their household goods. Russky happened to be at the station one afternoon when the general descended upon it in all his wrath.

'It was like typhoon had struck the place. Pianos, mirrors, furniture was all smashed on the platform. Then Wrangel come across locked carriages whose documents say they carry munitions. He break them open, and they filled with passengers have bribed the stationmaster. The general, he court martial stationmaster and hang him on spot. He swing from top of station house now.'

By the 18th the town was completely evacuated,[7] including telephone and telegraph equipment, and our Camels were loaded on the flatcars, ready to start south at a moment's notice. Two days later they were in the hangers again; a Cossack cavalry division had arrived to take up positions within and outside of the city. A few Kuban regiments were in control of Kotluban and the surrounding area; that accounted for the fact that Nina's hospital train was still a hundred miles to the north. But if Tsaritsyn fell there would be only isolated pockets of White resistance between Tsaritsyn and Saratov, and the Reds would certainly capture her train. The thought made me shudder.

It also made me a more efficient fighting machine in the three days of ferocious battle between August 22nd and 25th,[8] when the Tenth and Eleventh Soviet Armies attacked the city. I came back from sorties with my thumbs aching from pressing the gun trips, and when Kink called us out again after an hour's rest, there were no complaints from compartment nine.

B Flight suffered some casualties. While we were away on patrol a Red flight from Urbakb came over Beketofka for the first time, bombing and strafing, and two mechanics and four men were killed. Hoskins, manning a machine gun on the runway, brought down a Bolshie Pfalz. Cowderdrill and Feodor grabbed rifles and blasted away from the kitchen window. Russky got a Nieup into the air, but too late.

When Trotsky's attack was over the Reds had lost eighteen thousand prisoners and considerable *matériel*. The rest of their troops staggered back to Saratov. Again 47 Squadron was commended for the part it had played in Wrangel's victory.

In the cafes of Tsaritsyn *Na Moskvu!* was heard again. Now Moscow by Christmas was a reasonable assumption, and even Eddie ceased to scoff. On the Tsaritsyn front the Reds had drawn back in confusion. Over the summer months Denikin had taken two hundred and fifty thousand prisoners and gained a vast stretch of territory. Now his lines stretched from Poltava in the west, through Kharkov and Pavlosk toward Kamyshin. He was only three hundred and seventy-five miles from Moscow. It looked as though Yudenich, in the northwest, would be attacking Petrograd soon. Even Kolchak's armies had rallied in the east.

If all that was good news, for me, at least, the news we got in the first week of September was even better. We were moving up to Kotluban. And not to the town itself, but outside it, to siding 'N.' The flat fields along siding 'N' would be our temporary landing field.

Unless I was mistaken, siding 'N' was precisely where Nina's hospital train sat.

★

As we came into Kotluban station Kink eyed me nastily. 'Good Lord, Bunny, if you don't quit cracking those knuckles of yours I'll put your hands in splints. Why in hell are you so nervous?'

'Wonder if we'll bump into any *parushki* nurses?' Tommy said too innocently. 'I hear there's a lot of hospital trains between here and Kamyshin.'

Eddie, who was writing a letter home to his girl, looked up from his pad. 'Leave the swain alone, why don't you? I think he's lucky to be interested in a nice, plain girl. Those fancy countesses gave me a pain in the neck. Grabbing with their little greedy hands.' He looked down at his naked wrist. 'Next time we encounter the nobility, I'm wearing my watch to bed.'

Russky drew himself up as haughtily as a man can when he is sitting down. 'With all respects, you give insult to women of the nobility. They do not steal from foreign soldier.'

'Not having met a real one yet,' Bill said, 'I'm not qualified to say. But it so happens I left Beketofka without the twenty quid I had tucked under my mattress.'

'Maybe the *plenny* take,' Russky said, but with faltering conviction.

'Horse apples,' Bill replied. 'My batman would die for me, and you know it.'

Russky buried his head in a copy of *La Vie Parisienne*. His reading knowledge of French was poor, but the risqué illustrations, he said, had 'the intrinsic interest'.

'Getting back to the real issue,' Kink said, 'when a man joins the RAF it should be part of the articles he signs that the bloke guarantees not to fall in love. Love ruins more men than drink. Look at poor Boyce-Porter, fell in love with a French girl in Dunkirk and deserted; the MPs found him upstairs in a bistro, shot through the head. Then there was Dicky Farquar, as good a man who ever flew a Camel. This woman's husband caught Dicky and the Jezebel in a Bayswater flat, and Dicky was named co-respondent. He had to resign, and now he's selling autos. And what about Monk Harvey? You remember Monk Harvey. He – '

'Kinkead,' I said, 'there's ice water in those veins of yours. That's what makes it so easy for you to play the cynic.'

Kink lifted his untrimmed eyebrows. 'Play? My dear boy, I am a cynic. And that's what's going to bring me alive and happy through this mess. While one day up there in the sky you'll be mooning over a pair of eyes or a bustle and a rude Bolshie bullet will get you in your mooning head.'

'But he'll have lived and loved,' Eddie came to my defense. 'He'll have felt the softer passions that make a brute a man. And what will you have survived for? I'll tell you. A mess in Cairo, Aden or Kuwait. Sweating out the sun, the bugs, the filth and the wogs. Getting drunk every day because you've forgotten how not to. Sneaking into corners with the Colonel's wife while the old man's playing a chucker of polo. You call that being alive? You fellows with the cast-irons hearts simplify life to its inessentials, and then crow about it, forgetting that you're standing on a dung-heap.'

'And what's your future, Fulford?' Kink sneered. 'Leading the vanguard of the Canadian Revolution for the eight-hour day, the women's vote and compulsory arbitration? What makes you think that after we take Moscow you're going to quit the service, any more than the rest of us will, with the possible exception of Bunny? You've got flying in your blood and it's crippled you for normal living like every-other man Jack in this car. And all the books you read won't take it out of you. If you don't cop your pocket in a crash, you'll sweat with me in that mess in Kuwait, and you'll get blind drunk with me at Shepheard's, and you'll go running after the Colonel's wife. Except that you won't get her. She'll turn up her none too Grecian nose at all your sickly talk about the poor, downtrodden natives. And what will you end up with, you poor cheese? A wog mistress who doesn't wash her feet!'

Silence. For once Eddie, bested, had nothing to say. Tommy reached for the Clerget bell to call Cowderdrill for refreshments, but Kink held up his hand. 'Not now, Tommy. We're coming in.'

We came to the siding, and there was a hospital train parked toward the front of the first track, but it wasn't Nina's. Her train was numbered 242, wasn't it; or was it 424? It was almost half an hour before the switchman took us off the main track, and then, going down the number two siding we passed only refugee coaches stranded and waiting for engines, a long string of box cars, coal drags and flats, and several armed locomotives, the *broneviks*.

Then we stopped, and looking out the window, through the empty space between the end of one freight and the cowcatcher of a burned out engine, I saw it: number 242. It was at the end of the first siding, about thirty yards away.

'Bunny, where the devil do you think you're going?' Kink said as I bolted for the door.

He didn't wait for my answer. 'We've got work to do,' he barked at me. You're off duty at six o'clock!'

First B Flight was called to formation. Then, under the officers' direction, the men unloaded the Camels and wheeled them into the field beside the roadbed.[9] A maintenance tent was set up, and small individual tent hangars. It took over two hours, and afterwards I was too sweaty and grimy to go calling on Nina without a shower and a change.

I was first out of the shower, and dashed back to my compartment.

Feodor had anticipated me. Laid out on the berth was a complete change of uniform. Resting on the pocket of my khaki tunic was my Order of St. Vladimir.[10] The decoration was new since I had seen Nina last, but I rejected it as too flashy. Cowderdrill's dinner bell rang as I was combing my hair.

Dinner could wait, and so could the comments of my flight-mates. Rather than pass through the lounge car I went out by the Pullman's back door.

I stopped first at the hospital train dining car, but it was empty, though lit. I asked a nurse in the next car for Nina, and she directed me to the administration car toward the head of the train. In the administration car an orderly sat on duty at the table, cracking sun-flower seeds.

It took a while, and involved much pantomime, but he finally got across to me that Nina was at present in car seventeen, assisting Major Alexandrovsky in an operation.

At car seventeen, the surgical ward, a nurse sat on the steps smok-ing a cigarette.

'Nina Dmitrievna Anohina?' I asked hopefully.

She nodded and smiled and held up ten fingers. Then she put her hands down and held all ten fingers up once and twice again.

Thirty minutes, I gathered. I had a half hour's wait.

I tried talking to the nurse, but it was difficult, and she went inside after a few minutes. It occurred to me, sitting there, that I was very hungry.

'Captain?'

I turned. There she stood in the vestibule, tired and smudged, with her hair a mess. She was not so lovely as I remembered.

'Nina, I'm here,' I said foolishly.

'I am glad.'

She could have, I thought, sounded gladder.

'It took a while,' I said, 'for me to come.'

'Sometime, in a war, time goes slowly. Others, fast.'

There was a pause. I said: 'You, you're not going to invite me aboard?'

'I cannot. I have only this moment. There is another operation. We have many wounded from the fighting around Saratov.'

'You're working too hard,' I said, selfishly annoyed.

'*Nichevo*,' she said, shrugging, and my resentment vanished; I wanted her only to be less tired; I felt a compulsion to wipe off the smudge that was high on her right cheekbone.

But I didn't. 'Look,' I said. 'It's seven o'clock. We're having a *prazdnik* tonight about nine. Can you come?'

'Yes, Captain. That would be nice. I am tired, but I will have a little time to take a nap and freshen up for your *prazdnik*.'

'Yes, take a nap. And bring some nurses. The pretty ones.'

'There is only one, Olga, who is really pretty. But we have two others who are – how do you say? – attracting.'

'Fine. Bring them.' I retreated along the cinder roadbed. 'Nine o'clock. At 47 Squadron's train. We're two sidings over and to the right. Ask if you get lost.'

'At nine, Captain.'

As she disappeared back into the train, I backed into a Russian colonel of artillery. He bristled, and spat '*chto takoe!*' I brushed past him, not bothering to salute.

The boys were on their vanilla pudding. As I came in Kink paused, spoon halfway to his mouth.

'Did you find her?'

'She's here.' I kicked away Clarence the Pig and started in on my Bovril.

'This *baryshnia* of yours – does she have any friends?' Tommy asked, bright-eyed as a fox and twice as predatory.

'She's bringing a couple over to the *prazdnik* tonight.'

'Who said anything about a *prazdnik*?' Kink said. 'I've scheduled a dawn reconnaissance for tomorrow.'

There was a general groan of disappointment, and Kink growled, 'All right, but we turn in early. Why I cater to you frivolous types I just don't know. One day General Holman's going to drop by at the wrong time and tear off my pips. A *squadron*! Good Lord, this is a *boîte de nuit* on wheels!'

Nina arrived with three other nurses at half past nine. Her nap had done her good, and my flight-mates whistled in admiration. Tommy quickly appropriated Olga, a slender, pretty brunette, and Bill, Claudia, a nice looking *blondinka*. Eddie sat down with Sonia, a rather hefty but appealing girl with wide brown eyes who seemed awed by the splendor of our lounge car.

Kink and Russky had one drink and then excused themselves. They returned in an incredibly short time with two refugee women. One, a stunning Circassian redhead with cold eyes, was introduced to us as a princess; the other, her travelling companion, was only a garden variety countess. They had been stalled overnight in Kotluban, the engine of their train having been appropriated by a colonel of infantry who had orders from Wrangel to be in Tsaritsyn with his regiment by midnight tonight. Kink, of course, paired off with the princess.

Shy with Nina, as she was with me, I was glad for the *prazdnik*; it took the strain off our reacquaintance. Our self-consciousness dissolved in the laughter and conversation, and I held her close, dancing the foxtrot to the Victrola Tommy had contributed to the mess. The *angliski* music had drawn a crowd outside our windows, and the refugees peered wistfully in. Kink told Cowderdrill to lower the shades, and then, conscience-stricken, sent him outside to distribute tins of bully beef.

'*Spasibo, kunak, spasibo*,' the refugees called through the windows, and then shuffled away.

'Your comrades, they are nice,' Nina said, sipping the Scotch and soda I had mixed for her. 'Especially Major Kink. He tries to be the brutal soldier, but does not succeed.'

'Don't tell me you think Kink's the cat's pajamas?'

She frowned. 'The cat's pajamas?'

'Attractive. Sympathetic. Someone you, ah, wouldn't mind spooning with.'

'Spooning? What is it to spooning?'

'What Kink and the princess there were just doing.'

'Princess?' Nina curled her lip. 'To me she looks like actress in the provincial theatre some officer – how you say it? – has thrown over the side. As to Kink,' she said in her candid way, 'I think he is attracting for his type, which is short and dark, but that you are more attracting than he.'

The Circassian, who, during Kink's temporary absence, had been staring at me under heavy eyelids, came over and held out her hand. I rose.

Ignoring Nina, she said something to me in Russian I couldn't understand. Nina was smiling in a curious, tight way. 'The princess is asking you to dance,' she told me. 'Do you wish to dance with the princess?'

'I will dance with the princess,' I said obligingly, and took her in my arms. She danced very close, gluing the length of her body against mine, breathing Slavic intimacies into my ear. I wasn't conscious of her leading me, though she must have; in another minute we were at the passageway that led to the compartments, and with a beringed hand she was reaching to open the door.

It happened quickly. Nina rushed up and grabbed the Circassian's arm, pulled her away from me, and threw the last of her drink into the princess' face. While the girl stood wiping Scotch and soda from her eyes Nina sprang at her, spitting Russian invective.

I got between them and shoved. The Circassian went reeling to one lounge and Nina to the other on the opposite side of the car. She sat down with a thud.

Tommy turned up the Victrola volume and grabbed for Olga. As the princess' girl friend hurried to her side, Russky intercepted and whirled her into the dance. Bill and Eddie did the same with the two nurses.

Kink, who had just come back into the car, took in the situation at a glance. With a look of mock disgust in my and Nina's direction he led the Circassian out of the car and to his compartment, nodding his head to her every word, not one of which he understood.

'I'm sorry,' I said. 'I should have known better. I'd had a bit to drink.'

She avoided my eyes. 'I must go now.'

'Nonsense,' I said. 'The party's just begun.'

'I am embarrassed. I have a bad temper, a Russian temper. I also come from a very jealous family.'

'I don't think it's so bad to be jealous. It shows spirit, fire. Why, I'm the jealous type myself.'

Nina was ready to change the subject. She fluffed her hair. 'I am very disarranged?'

'No, you look lovely.'

'I must be disarranged. Is there a mirror?'

'We have one in the lav.'

When she came back fifteen minutes later, I was alone in the lounge except for Cowderdrill, who was cleaning up.

'Where is everybody?' Nina asked naively.

'Oh, they've all gone on a – tour of the train.'

Cowderdrill snickered, and I glared at him.

'They will be back soon?' Nina asked.

'Yes, soon.'

Cowderdrill turned off most of the lights and went to bed. I lit a Gold Flake and reached for Nina's hand.

'Your English cigarettes smell pleasantly,' she said.

'Actually I like them better than American cigarettes.'

'American cigarettes, they are made in Chicago?'

'You and your Chicago,' I laughed. 'No, they're made in our southern states.'

'Tell me about your southern states. You have people like the Cossacks there?'

'Not quite. But I can't tell you much about the south except for Texas. I was born and grew up there. At least till I was ten, when we moved to California.'

'I would like to know about Texas.'

I started in on Texas, but she interrupted me. 'They call you by a funny name, Bunny. That means rabbit in English, does it not?'

'Yes, but they're not exactly calling me a rabbit. Bunny's more of a nickname.'

She looked me over carefully. 'You do not have long ears, nor does your nose twitch. I will not call you by that name but by another. Sasha. It was the name of my pet pony, and I loved him very much. Do you like it?'

'I like it fine. But what shall I call you. You must have a nickname too. Would it be – let me guess – Ninita?'

'Certain ones have called me Ninusha. But it is very familiar,' she said gravely.

'Then it's familar enough for me.'

Tommy came into the car, barefooted, in his blue silk robe.

He started at the sight of Nina. 'Any whisky around?' he asked apologetically.

'No,' I said, 'and Cowderdrill's locked up the bar.'

He left, mumbling.

Bill, wearing only a pair of khaki pants, came in a minute later. I delivered the same information. As the door closed after him we heard from the Pullman car, a trill of definitely feminine laughter.

Nina, blushing, got to her feet. She had finally understood what high points the 'tour' of the train included. 'I must get back,' she said. 'You will accompany me to the train?'

At the hospital train I asked if she would come tomorrow night for dinner.

'Do you have the food?' she asked, surprised.

'We have the food. It's more a matter of your standing Cowderdrill's cooking.'

She smiled. 'He is droll, your Cowderdrill. Like a rag-doll which has life. All right, I shall come. And now, *Spokoinoi nochi*, Sasha.'

I reached for her in the darkness of the vestibule. Our kiss was long and gentle, and she trembled.

'*Spokoinoi nochi*, Ninusha,' I said, and then she slipped away.

I walked back to B Flight train, whistling.

BOOK THREE

*

Nina

Chapter Six

*

One hundred... ninety... fifty. The altimeter needle dipped to twenty-five feet and my engine gave a last resentful cough and conked out. The greyish-brown steppe rushed up to meet my wheels and I landed on the level ground as smoothly as if it had been an asphalt runway.

I snapped up my triplex goggles and swung out of the cockpit to the ground.

There were three neat bullet holes in the gas tank, and as I watched the last drops of petrol trickled down into the hard sun-baked earth. The *bronevik* machine-gunner had caught me as I came down in the cartwheel behind Eddie Fulford. I hadn't known I was hit, and I was coming in again on the armoured train when I saw Eddie pointing at my tank. Looking down, I had seen the petrol spraying back into my slipstream. Immediately I had cut away from the action and headed for home.

B Flight must have knocked out the train and continued further up the line toward Saratov, hoping to flush more game. Otherwise, by this time, they would have passed me on the return trip to Kotluban.

It was afternoon on the steppe, a lonely time. The plain stretched vast and treeless to the horizon, and I could understand the melancholy of the southern Russian; this immense, unrelieved flatness overwhelmed the soul and stultified the emotions. Distance, I thought; it was the Russian's greatest enemy.

Had any human being ever stood where I stood now? A Tartar horseman? A Turkish janizary strayed from his mercenary band? A Cossack fleeing his boyar for the adventurer's freedom, women and loot?

Over the centuries how many nations had established their homes in this Scythian wilderness, and how many had survived? Only those who had been able to defend a given area at any moment in hand-to-hand encounter with the enemy. We were fighting the enemy precisely as the Cossacks had fought their enemies for hundreds of years; from a shifting base, ready to move forward or back at the note of a bugle, the glitter of an upraised sword. Our planes were the Cossack's horses, their bivouacs our train and coaches.

This time no pitchfork-wielding Tolstoy came running toward me across the field. I missed him. I missed everybody. It was goddam lonely here. I slapped my flying gloves against my thigh and wondered, what to do?

I took a hard look at the surrounding country. About two miles straight due south was a slash of earth lighter than the steppe around it. A road? Perhaps, though there was no road on my map of the general area.

I decided to investigate.

Distances on the steppe are deceptive; I walked for forty minutes, and still the road seemed no nearer than before. Though my throat was dryish I felt no great thirst, and it occurred to me suddenly that I had no need of water because it wasn't hot. The weather had changed abruptly, as Russky had predicted. In the air, still faint but there, was the exciting tingle, the bite of fall. Summer was over.

After another twenty minutes of walking I came to the road. It was a real road; no mistake about it; wheel ruts led both ways into infinity, and they were fairly fresh. I lit a fag and sat down cross-legged on the ground. Somebody would be coming along. They had to. Nina was expected at the train tonight for dinner.

The muted drone of engines, high. I looked up: five or six miles to the west B Flight passed at twelve thousand feet. Flying at such a height they had undoubtedly missed my downed ship, the bastards; now I was stuck for fair. Unless someone came down the road I would spend the night on the steppe, huddled in my cockpit. And what if I was never found? I would die here, and Wrangel would enter Moscow without me, and in the year 1961, a patrol of motorized Cossacks would stumble across my bleaching bones, and report my death to the President of the Autonomous Republic of the Don. What would have become of Nina, I wondered. Whom would she have wed? For of course she would have married, after grieving for a decent interval of, say, four or five years.

I waited and I waited. An hour, another half. The sheer illimitability of the steppe made my eyes ache. I rested them against my palm and tried to doze, but they kept snapping open again to scan the horizon right and left. I couldn't afford to fall asleep. Some stupid *muzhik*, musing on his millet crop, would pass me by.

And then I saw a speck coming down the road. It was another thirty minutes before I could make it out; an ox-cart drawn by two bullocks. In the back caged chickens squawked and fretted.

The cart came swaying towards me, axles squeaking. On the seat sat a farmer in sheepskin *kaftan* and dusty boots. His head nodded; he was asleep.

'*Kunak! Stoi!*' I yelled, and leapt into the middle of the road.

He jumped two feet. I have never seen such terror on a man's face before or since, '*Chort! Chort!*' he gasped. He thought I was the devil.

'*Nye chort*,' I said. '*Angliski* pilot.'

The bullocks regarded me with bovine skepticism. '*Chort!*' the farmer gasped again, and tumbling off the seat, fell on his knees in the dust before me, pleading for his life. I could make out most of what he said. He was definitely not the most godly man in his village. Last Sunday, in fact, he had not gone to church. He would be worse in future. He would beat his wife when she did not deserve it. He would soak his soul in vodka. He would enter into an adulterous affair with Katya, the wife of Vatkin, who had been after him these last two years. He would sin in a regular manner if I would only let him go.

I offered him a Gold Flake and tried to explain, speaking slowly and clearly, trying to remember what Nina had taught me. Gradually he began to understand, though it wasn't my Russian but the cigarette that did it. The devil in Russia would not be smoking a short *angliski* cigarette; he would be smoking one of those long Russian ones that he, Vasili, had once seen in Kamyshin. I lit the cigarette for him, and watched him pull on it gingerly. He nodded in satisfaction. Not even the *chort rossi* would be smoking such excellent tobacco.

It was a mystery to Vasili why I should want him to take the team off the road and across the steppe into nowhere, but when I offered him the rest of the cigarettes he agreed with a shrug. Obviously he had never before seen an aeroplane. He thought the Camel was some monstrous bird of prey, and wouldn't go near it till I had rapped my knuckles against the fuselage to prove that what I was striking was not flesh but wood, fabric and glue.

We settled on a price for hauling me home, which he said was not so far away, perhaps ten miles. I got out some heavy rope I was lucky enough to have with me, and Vasili helped tie the under-carriage wheel axle to the back of his cart. I climbed into the cockpit and we were off, the chickens objecting querulously to this unaccustomed object bobbing along in their wake.

Actually, had I walked due east from my downed Camel I would have run into the railway tracks. They led, of course, straight to the siding, and all Vasili had to do was to follow them south toward Kotluban.

The oxen, however, lumbered more slowly than a man could walk, and it took another two hours to cover the eight or ten miles to the siding. Twilight was falling when we bumped up to B Flight train.[1]

Outside the lounge car Kink and Tommy were taking the early evening air.

'*Bozhe moi!*' Kink said. 'Look at him, sitting up there like a damn king! Bill, Russky, Eddie! Come and see the prodigal's return!'

My other flight-mates were in time to see me clambering down from the cockpit. I failed to see the joke, and stood scowling at them while they slapped their thighs and doubled over in malicious mirth. A number of grinning enlisted men had gathered down the track.

'The least you could have done,' I told Kink accusingly, 'was keep your eyes peeled for me on the steppe. If Vasili here hadn't come down the road I'd be halfway to the Ukraine by now.'

'Sorry, Bunny,' Kink said, wiping his eyes. 'As a matter of fact I was going to send out a search plane as soon as I'd finished my gasper.'

'You could have done that three hours ago,' I grumbled. My feelings were definitely hurt.

'Strewth,' Bill got out, still sputtering with laughter. 'It's the first damn time I've ever seen an RAF-type with a chauffeur. How was the ride, just a little bumpy?' He doubled over again.

'Swear to God,' Tommy said, 'Kink had a feeling you'd make it back on your own. And he was right, wasn't he? You've got to admit Kink's psychic.'

'He is also a number of other things,' I said coldly. 'Will somebody give Vasili twenty rubles and get my Camel tucked away? I'm going in to wash.'

'Hold on,' Eddie stopped me. 'You'd better go see Nina right away. She's worried.'

'Worried?'

'Cossack headquarters got report that aircraft shot down and she think you it,' Russky told me. 'We tell her it White plane in nearby sector but she believe we try to save her from the terrible truth.'

'She thinks you may have been the White plane,' Kink explained. 'She's been over here twice in the last half-hour, and before that she had orderlies running a shuttle service between the train and the hospital vans, making desperate inquiries.'

'Somebody could have told me,' I said, and hightailed it over to the Red Cross train.

I met her a few yards from our observation coach, coming down the tracks toward B Flight train.

She rushed into my arms, sobbing.

'Ninusha,' I said softly, comforting her, 'Ninusha, nothing's happened. I'm here.'

She lifted her tear-stained face and smiled. 'Oh, I am so glad, Sasha. I thought you were dead. I was sure of it.'

'But Kink must have told you. It was some White plane shot down in the area. You needn't have worried so.'

'I am a worrier,' she said, as I wiped away the tears. 'My mind, it is very imaginary. It becomes filled with pictures that are so very terrible, my Sasha. Do you understand?'

I understood, and I knew why, all of a sudden, I was so outrageously happy. She loved me. She had thought I was dead and it had taught her that she loved me.

She pulled away. 'I must go. I am on duty and the Major would be very angry if he knew I had left the train. I came to tell you I would not be able to come to dinner. Sonia is ill and I must share her shift with Claudia.'

'Then I won't be seeing you tonight?'

She looked down at her shoes. 'You may see me later, if you wish. I will be off at midnight.'

I caught my breath. She was offering to come to my compartment. For a week and a half now I had been after her, night and day, to be alone with me, but it had been like talking to the wind. She would come to our *prazdniks*, she would give me Russian lessons in the lounge car; she had even said she would go overnight to Tsaritsyn when we both got leave. But she would not come to my compartment.

A week and a half in wartime seems like many days, especially when we had no idea how soon we'd be leaving Kotluban, and I had been resentful. Kink and the boys had quickly established relationships with the other nurses; why not I, the only one among them who really cared? It seemed unfair.

God, what a fool a young man could be. He should learn to wait. To wait was to win.

'Till midnight, then, Ninusha. I'll be waiting.' I was afraid to say anything more.

She touched my cheek, and hurried away.

A few minutes after midnight she rapped lightly on my door. Rushing to it, I almost knocked over the bottle of champagne that Kink thought he had buried successfully at the bottom of his closet.

Nina stood there, her eyes shining.

'Good evening, Sasha. Do I not say that like an American girl?'

'You don't, for which I am glad. I'm tired of American girls now that I'm crazy about a Russian.' I kissed the soft hair at her temple, and drew her inside.

'Champagne!' she cried, and clapped her hands like a child. 'Oh, but we are very gay!'

I took her and her head-dress and tossed them on the berth. Holding her at arms length I said, very seriously, 'We are gay and yet we are not gay. I want you to know that this for me is not just a *prazdnik*. I have been to many parties and they are forgotten quickly, the next morning. But with you – '

She put her finger on my lips. Here eyes were still shining. 'Sasha, we do not need to talk, no? I am here and I am joyous. I have no fear.'

I held her to me so fiercely that she broke away with a little laughing cry.

I watched her as she sat at the edge of the berth and took the pins from her hair.

She laughed. 'Sasha, do not stare at me so. It is embarrassing; it is like my Uncle Leonid, who suspected me of meeting young officers when I was late coming home from the gymnasium. Of course he was right. Can you not pour the champagne?'

I poured the champagne.

★

Two days later Colly came up from Taganrog on a surprise visit. He hadn't come alone; with him was Brigadier General Maund.[2]

Maund was a temporary acting-general elevated from three ranks below. For a while he had been one of General Holman's staff officers in Ekaterinodar; then, for some reason, probably at Holman's request when White headquarters had moved up to Taganrog, London had given Maund the job of roving information officer. He now travelled around to the various British units at the southern front, inspecting and giving brief talks on the military and political situation.

To those, that is, who wanted to listen. The British Military Mission was somewhat ambivalent about telling the troops in Russia what was going on. It was an attitude that reflected that of Lloyd George and the government itself. Officer personnel might attend these lectures if they wished; if not, no pressure was brought to bear upon them. It was as if the government hadn't quite decided whether keeping the men informed was really necessary or if – and this was more to the point – whether such a course of action was actually desirable at all. The same old story: muddle in the interests of an amiable vacillation. How expertly led and superbly performing military units could result from such a policy I could never understand.

Maund's talk was held in the lounge car. Hoskins had scrounged an easel from somewhere for his maps and charts, and Cowderdrill had set out bottles of Bass all around. Colly sat at the back of the lounge with his collar open, winking at each of us in turn as he caught our eye. We knew what he thought of Maund's information program: a bloody waste of time. We should be up in the skies against the Bolshies, or shooting up the Red troops; with winter coming on there was precious little flying weather left.

Maund was medium-sized with a pink face, patent-leather hair and a uniform cut on Saville Row. Russky had evidently recognized him from somewhere; with knitted brows he stared at Maund as he fussed around the easel, setting up his exhibits with Cowderdrill's fumbling assistance.

'Know him, Russky?' I asked.

'From somewhere but I cannot place. Will come to me later on.'

Maund began to speak, his high-pitched voice sounding, in the upper registers, too much like the squeak of chalk on blackboard. 'We are engaged,' he said, 'in a vast conflict on three fronts which has engaged many thousands of men. We here on the southern front see only part of that conflict, large-scale though it may be. It is the purpose of these talks, which we hope to give from time to time, to broaden your perspective on a total picture which, perhaps, no man can view in its entirety or hope to describe in all its aspects. So,' he said with a conciliatory smile, 'we shall hope only for the middling best.'

Here we go a-middling again, I thought.

'Obviously in a brief talk I cannot cover as much ground as I would like. I plan to discuss mostly the more current events: you are all more or less familiar with the pattern of Allied intervention which began in Russia in the summer of last year. Today I propose to discuss the difficulties of Cossack Separatism that currently plague General Denikin, and that are giving the British Mission some cause for alarm.' He took a deep breath; in the pause I heard Colly belch distinctly.

'During the Tsarist regimes,' Maund went on, 'the Don, Kuban and Terek Cossacks had enjoyed a large degree of self-government under their military chiefs, the Atamans. As privileged landowners of the steppes they paid few or no taxes, instead serving long periods of military service, in which they provided their own horses and men. Now in all the Cossack territories there was an almost equal number of *Inogorodtsy*, people from other towns who had entered the Cossack country as settlers, or who had been there when the Imperial ukases gave possession of it to the Cossacks. The outlanders bitterly resented the privileges of the Cossacks, and the conflict between the two explains a good deal of the present difficulties of the Volunteer Army on the steppe.

'After the revolution of March 1917 the Cossack territories turned toward democracy. The Cossacks formed councils to discuss their affairs, and the outlanders pressed for their share of control. When the Bolsheviks came, the outlanders and a few of the younger Cossacks took sides with them. But with the approach of the Volunteer Army, the Cossacks became definitely anti-Red. However, separatist sentiment of the Kuban Cossacks grew as anti-Bolshevik forces came to depend upon them increasingly for food and men. In December, 1918, as soon as the Reds had been driven out of the Kuban, the Kuban council, the Rada, sent a deputation to the Paris Peace Conference to set out their position and their claims. They demanded recognition of the Kuban as a separate and independent state. This was plainly ludicrous, and the conference made it clear that no such ambition could be entertained.

'However, still aiming at separatism, the Kuban thereafter joined with the so-called "Republic of Mountain Peoples", who claimed to represent the tribes of Daghestan and the Caucasus mountains. Agreement between the two bound them to respect one another's independence and integrity and in effect eventually to withdraw assistance from the White armies in the interests of neutrality. Separatism among the Cossacks became critical during the past summer months, and General Wrangel was sent by General Denikin to the Kuban to pursuade them to remain loyal to the White cause and to send reinforcements and supplies for the Kuban troops who were fighting with him at Tsaritsyn. He succeeded, but only at the threat of dissolving the Rada. The situation for the future is not precisely an encouraging one. The Rada is becoming more self-willed and demagogic, and is fiercely opposing General Denikin. His rallying cry, "Russia, One and Indivisible" is looked upon by the Cossacks with disfavour. There will be more problems to solve before our Cossack allies will band together in amity for the decisive destruction of the Bolshevik threat.'[3]

As Maund put down the pointer with which he had been taking desultory stabs at the easel, Cowderdrill began to applaud. Kink's glare made him stop abruptly. Smiling blandly, Maund asked if we had any questions.

'I'd like to ask him about the French loans and the British big money interests,' Eddie muttered, 'but I wouldn't want to be a 2nd Lieutenant again.'

There were no questions.

Colly came forward to join us in another round before the general went on his inspection of the squadron.

'So, Sir,' Colly said, 'you still think it's definitely Moscow by Christmas? Some of us are beginning to wonder.'

'Absolutely, Colonel,' Maund said. 'I have no doubts at all.'

I asked the general if he had ever been in Moscow.

'Oh, yes, before the war, in 1912. I've seen quite a bit of Russia, as a matter of fact. I even survived a trip on the Trans-Siberian to Vladivostock. It's a good thing we'll have won the war by New Year's; you have no idea how cold the Russian winters can get. Why, in Vladivostock it was ninety degrees below zero. One side of the locomotive froze solid, and there was a full fire in the box. The passengers kept warm by beating one another.'

We smiled politely.

'However, gentlemen,' Maund went on, 'the winter never gets too cold for a good flying man. I've flown in weather that froze the oil in the tank.'

I doubted that; not even General Maund could fly with a chunk of ice in his oil tank. From the look on the faces of my flight-mates, I knew they were just as dubious.

'No, gentlemen,' Maund shook his head. 'If you think this is an honest-to-goodness war you're mistaken. Before the Revolution I was with a French squadron flying with the Tsar's troops in Poland. When the Austrians broke through – '

Russky's face lighted with sudden, delighted recognition. 'Now, Sir, I remember. I was liaison officer between French and Russian squadrons. You then captain. When Hun sweep through you ride away in lorries at night, leave aeroplanes behind. Many Spads, Sopwiths, DeHavillands. We have to fly aeroplanes away for you when the Austrians a mile from the drome.'

Maund's pink face darkened to red. 'Lieutenant, you must be mistaken. Um, yes, quite.' He took a long swallow of Bass. 'You're confusing me with someone else.'

'Am not mistaken,' Russky said stubbornly. 'After we save aeroplanes from capture you take them back and sign for them.' He turned to Kink, who was staring up at the ceiling with vast interest. 'True, Kink, is true. I know, was there.'

In the silence General Maund spooned up caviar and spread it on a cracker. Then he began to chatter. Wasn't it wonderful, all this fresh caviar? Better than the Crillon bar in Paris. Where had we managed to find a jewel like Cowderdrill? The fireplace was a definite inspiration. 47 Squadron was writing an imperishable record across the Bolshie skies; he wouldn't be surprised if General Holman had a few more decorations in his bag for us. If we needed any extra rations, he'd be delighted to send them along as soon as he returned to Taganrog.

Kink made the most of it, and said we were short of rum. The general promised a dozen gallons.

Colly asked Cowderdrill for another ale. 'General,' he said innocently, 'did you ever recover that Ford van those brigands got away with in Ekat?'

B Flight cleared their throats in unison. Early in the year, while

Colly was outfitting the squadron in Ekaterinodar, the boys had filched the van he spoke of from a warehouse siding. They had painted red crosses on its sides and hidden it in a brothel alley. Nobody ever questioned Red Cross markings, Kink had said. He was right. The van had come in very handy.

Maund shook his head sadly. 'I'm still quite upset about it. Mind you, it's not the loss of the van that bothers me so bally much. It's the fact that someone in my command had the audacity to steal His Majesty's property right from under my nose.'

'Strewth, Sir,' Bill said, 'maybe Makhno's got it.'[4] He was referring to the renegade bandit whose black-flagged Green Guards fought to the death every army and government – Red, White, and the Forces of the Ukrainian Directory.

'I think not,' Maund said decisively. 'The *plennys* told me it was some of my own men. If I ever find out who's responsible, I'll trundle them back to Blighty under arrest.'

During the eight hours he was with us, General Maund spent five of them riding around in his pilfered van. He made a special point of commending Hoskins upon the Ford's excellent condition.

Colly stayed on another day, taking part in three patrols in which he traded two Bolshie planes and fifty Red infantrymen for a couple of bullet holes in his rudder.[5]

He landed from the last patrol with a bad headache and an upset stomach. Kink insisted upon putting him to bed, and asked Major Alexandrovsky to drop over for a diagnosis.

'It looks like typhus,' the Doctor told us. 'I am not quite sure.[6] We will know tomorrow.'

'But we were all innoculated against typhus,' Kink protested.

The doctor shrugged. 'The Russian bacillus may be too hardy for your angliski vaccine. But do not be too anxious. The Colonel may be better tomorrow.' He grinned at me. 'It may have been some of your execrable bully beef that was tinned in the days of Queen Victoria. I will send Nina Dmitrievna over with a purgative.'

Next morning Colly woke thoroughly nauseated and shaking with chills, and Alexandrovsky told us it was definitely typhus.

'Damn it all, doctor,' Colly told the big man, 'I've got to get back to Taganrog. Kink, get a plane ready.'

The doctor motioned for Nina to give him a combination analgesic and sedative. 'My dear Colonel, resign yourself to at least a week in Kotluban. You are in no condition to be flown back to Tsar-itsyn, and so far as I know there are no hospital trains due through Kotluban for the south for at least ten days. Consider yourself fortunate. Nina Dmitrievna will act as your nurse, when I can spare her.'

Colly lay back on his pillow, groaning. 'I should consider myself fortunate. Thirty-seven crashes and I wind up dying of a foul disease transmitted by a louse or a flea. Aten here's the only one who's getting the clean end of the stick – a chance to see his girl. And I hate him for it.'

'You can monopolize her, Colly,' I told him. 'I promise.'

'Oh, get the hell out,' Colly said. 'All of you except Nina. And Nina, I want you to bring me a Scotch and soda right away. I'm thirsty as the devil.'

'For you there is no Scotch and there is no soda,' Nina said firmly. 'For you are the liquids which are non-alcoholic, such as water and tea and broth.'

'He should have broth immediately,' the doctor said. 'Preferably beef.'

Kink said, 'We're out of Bovril and we don't have a steer in the house.' He turned to me. 'Bunny, you're forage officer this week. Go out and buy a steer or a bullock.' He handed me a hundred rubles of squadron funds. 'Pay the *muzhik* what he wants, and bring Russky along as interpreter.'

I found Russky in the lounge, lost in a copy of *La Vie Parisienne*. We took the van and followed the cart tracks to a farm about two miles from the village. Two broad-beamed peasant women were plowing a field for winter wheat with a stick-like affair that might have been novel in the days of Peter the Great. I pulled the van into a farmyard that was full of thin pigs and scrawny chickens. A little sad-eyed boy, raggedly dressed, sat near the house, singing to himself and desultorily mending a harness.

Russky gave him a few kopecks and asked that he repeat the song for my benefit. Shyly he sang:

Ekh, sharaban, da, sharaban,
Ne budet deneg – tebya prodam!
Ekh, sharaban,
Da, trogai, trogai!

A ya poidu,
Svoey dorogoi!

(*Ah, charabanc, yes, charabanc*
If all my money goes, I must sell you!
Ah, charabanc,
Get along with you, giddap!
And as for me,
I'll go my own road!)

A middle-aged peasant in blouse, boots and military cap came out of the mud and clay farmhouse. As he saw our uniforms his eyes lit with cupidity.

I looked around the farmyard while Russky palavered with the peasant and a hen pecked curiously at my boots. On a lean-to wall hung farming implements so primitive that the average American farmer would have been hard pressed to identify them. A steer looked out at us stupidly from his stall adjoining the house. On cold winter nights he slept with the *muzhik* and his family.

Russky told me the farmer wanted eighty rubles for his 'magnificent beast', and though it was a third too much, I approved the deal. We went into the house to seal it with a glass of vodka.

Inside were a table, chairs, and the inevitable Russian stove, a Dutch oven six or eight feet long. All the furniture was painted brightly in cheerful red, yellows and reds. There were ikons on all four walls. A big samovar sat on the middle of the stove. Off in one corner, lying on a heap of dirty cloths, was the grandfather of the house, a squat and powerful man. To my amazement I saw that he was smoothing out his shroud, made of a number of pieces of linen sewed together.

'Is nothing the matter with old man,' Russky whispered as we sat down at the table, 'but he has decided he is going to die.'

'Why should he die if there's nothing the matter with him?' I wanted to know.

Russky shrugged. 'Is Russian peasant. He will die.'

The peasant's wife smilingly served us small glasses of vodka, and withdrew to the other side of the room. Russky and the peasant talked. The latter had heard many rumours which he wanted verified.

Was it true that the Whites had taken Moscow, and that Lenin had been hanged from the top of the Kremlin? Would the English and the Americans now come to put the American President on the throne? Or would the Pope take over? Would Russia give up farming for the making of the motor car? If it did that would not be good for him, Nicolai, who knew nothing about the making of motor cars and would not enjoy working in the cities.

Russky made no effort to set Nicolai right but merely nodded his head at every question, a method of response which seemed to satisfy the peasant.

The amenities concluded, we went outside to get the steer, and tied him to the rear of the van bumper with a length of rope for which the farmer demanded another two rubles. As we started off down the road the little boy waved a melancholy farewell.

Our progress was slow and painful. The steer, who was either lazy or sensed his fate, began to balk, and we had to drag him along at two miles an hour. That would have been all right, except that the rope began to fray. Russky got out and prodded the beast from behind with a letter opener he improbably yet typically had on his person.

A mixed crowd of B Flight enlisted men, hospital train orderlies and refugees greeted our appearance with expectant grins. Some of the British and hospital train personnel had already seen me in action with the oxen of the week before, and they were clearly looking forward to a second act of the bovine follies. When Russky untied the steer, he took the opportunity to make his break, and lumbered clumsily toward the tent hangars set up thirty yards or so trackside.

'After him!' I yelled, 'He'll tear down the hangars!'

We were too late to prevent the steer from invading one of the tents, knocking it down, and smashing the aileron of a parked Camel, but five or six B Flight men succeeded in heading him off from the tool tent. Bewildered by all these foreign faces, the steer allowed me to slip a noose over his head and lead him back to the train.

Cowderdrill was waiting with a huge butcher knife and a bungstarter. 'Right, Sir, fine, Sir,' Cowderdrill said. 'Now if you'll just pick three or four of these loafers to assist me in the slaughter, we'll have broth for the Colonel tonight.'

'Stevenson, Plummer, Oliver, Templeton!' I bawled at four enlisted men who were melting away. There's work to be done! Hop to it!'

From the lav, wiping away the dirt and grime of the chase, I could hear the steer's loud and dramatic end.[7] I was toweling off when I heard Kink growling from the open doorway: 'Bunny, do you realize the mechanics can't get that damaged bus into the sky until tomorrow afternoon? That means we'll be one plane short on morning patrol. Another C.O. would have you up for court martial.'

'I'm sorry, Kink. The dumb ox got away from me.'

He tapped his head significantly. 'You're not thinking. I warned you. I told you not to get barmy over a foreign female.'

'Yes, Sir. Is there anything else, Sir?'

He left, muttering, 'It's not a goddam squadron I'm running. It's a goddam *circus*.'

★

The broth perked Colly up a little, but in the early morning hours I heard his moans coming from the compartment adjoining mine. I got up, slipped into my khakis, and went next door.

He was lying spread-eagled on the bunk, sweating profusely and slightly delirious. His full-modeled, almost girlishly-shaped lips were bloodless, and the only colour in his face were the two faint spots of red high up on his cheeks.

The wet cloth for his forehead I got from the lav seemed to help a little, but after a few minutes he was off again, muttering disjointedly of his training days in England, of air battles on the Western Front; of comrades, famous and unsung, who had been buried in squadron cemeteries long before I arrived at the front.

'Petrol on! Switch off! Suck in, Sir… Turning home, back to Ochey, and we haven't lost a man… Coming into Burbach watch the Archie; when the Boche bracket you, you dive!… The fool, he's hanging his own *crêpe* up…! Six Halberstadts north of St. Julien, high in the sun. And Allmenröeder's bright red Albatross… Sandy Alexander copped his packet; whose next for an empty chair? My God, they're blowing up the ridge!'

He started up from the bunk, his eyes staring, back now in the day the British blew up the Messines-Wytschaete ridge in the greatest explosion ever made by man. I had heard of how, early in the morning of June 7, 1917, the entire German defensive position, two years in the building, had gone up in a roar of dirt and steel and

German flesh, and of how, after the British guns had opened fire, the Tommy battalions had swept up the hill. Going over to do battle with the Huns, Colly's l0th Squadron had seen craters as much as four hundred fifty feet across.

'It's all right, Colly,' I told him. 'It's over. You're here; you're safe.' I wished I could have been speaking the entire truth.

But it made no difference; he didn't recognize me, he didn't know I was there. His head lolled back on the pillow, and twisted from side to side.

'Lowenhardt's the best, and Lothar, Manfred's kid brother… And don't tangle with Udet… Put death from your mind and you're the last to die… At Operations Tent you study silhouettes from every angle; they're your passport to the girls back home… Two Pfalz and a Fokker in one afternoon that's shooting… It's spring, Charley boy; you can tell when the dunghills start to smoke in the sun… Dammit, Jones, I tell you it's a sooty sparkplug… Have a care, boys, when you criss-cross on the turns… Today we're over Zeebrugge, so wear your woollies…'

His voice faded.

I was reaching for the sedative when Nina came into the compartment. She took the bottle from my hand. 'You should call me, Sasha,' she reproved me, 'before you give medicine to the Colonel. He does not need this now. The worst of it is over.'

'You mean the fever's breaking?'

'No, but for now he will sleep. See, his eyes are closed.'

As I watched the redness left Colly's cheeks and his breathing became less laboured. When Nina smoothed his forehead he didn't stir.

'Come,' she said, and led me next door into my compartment.

She kissed me lightly and took off her cape.

'Hey,' I said. 'What if the Doctor sees that your little white bunk hasn't been slept in?'

'Claudia has taken care of any contingencies, my Sasha, by rumpling up the sheets. Tomorrow night I will do the same for her.'

I took her in my arms. 'You're a shameless hussy.'

'Would you wish me any different? Do I not please you this way? I am as forthright as I am shy; it runs in my family. When we Anohinas love a man we show it. But you must remember that we do not love so easily.'

'I know that. And I like you shameless.'

'Then kiss me, and do not talk so, Sasha. It is getting cold. Like most men you are a regular chatterbox always at the wrong moment.'

★

Tsaritsyn was a different town from the looted husk we had last seen in July. The shops were open and the market place filled with shrewd women bargainers. Nina pointed to a *molodka* threatening to hit a stall-keeper with a frying pan. 'The price will accordingly come down a ruble,' she told me.

'Not two or three?'

'No, for that she would have to hit him with it.'

We passed a cinema that was featuring a Western, and I asked her if she would like to go in.

She shuddered. 'No, there is too much shooting and death. Your Indians, they frighten me.'

I smiled. She, who was surrounded night and day by the wounded and the dying, was afraid of Indians. It was another example of Russian logic, or the lack of it.

We did some shopping. I bought her a heavy shawl for the cold weather and was about to pay an unreasonable price for a bowl of Yardley's shaving soap when Nina snatched it out of my hand and began to haggle furiously with the proprietor. We came away, having paid half what the man asked for.

'You must be firmer with these brigands,' Nina lectured me gently. 'What will you do when I am no longer here to save you from being cheated?'

The sky seemed to darken and the light to fail. I had put out of my mind the knowledge that some day soon, perhaps tomorrow, when we returned to Kotluban from our overnight leave, the hospital train would have received orders to leave or B Flight would have been moved elsewhere. It was best not to think of the future. More, it was imperative.

'Ninusha,' I said, 'you mustn't talk like that.'

She squeezed my hand. 'I am sorry. I would prefer to think we will never be parted. But my mind does not work in that fashion.'

'I know,' I said bitterly, 'you're a hell of a lot more realistic than I.' For some reason, perhaps because we were passing a hotel whose architecture reminded me of the Pera Plaza in Constantinople, I thought of Mr. Poulas. I wondered if he'd found a promising young man to manage his business and marry his hairy daughter.

'Do you resent my realism?' Nina asked me.

'No. You can take care of the family finances. I can't balance a chequebook to save my life, and I'd rather fight a Bolshie circus single-handed than figure out the small print in an insurance policy.'

'Well,' she said comfortably, 'that is because you are a soldier. You have no patience for the mundane things.' She smiled up at me. 'But you will stop your frowning and be happy for me today, no? You will not make me sad?'

'I will devote the day and the night both to making you happy. If I frown you may slap me. If I scowl you may slap me twice. And if I laugh you may kiss me, oh, three or four times.'

'Then laugh, Sasha, for I would very much prefer to kiss than slap you.'

We walked about the town, had tea in a cabaret, and then sat in the park watching the *droshkeys* go by and tossing cracker crumbs to the pigeons. The pigeons, sleek, aldermanic birds, looked better fed than the people. When the sun went down we took an *izvozchik* to the Black Cat, where I had arranged for Kink and Russky to meet us for dinner.

The Black Cat was a basement restaurant with hand-woven tapestries, royal Bokhara rugs, and gleaming silverware on table cloths of a startling whiteness. The past months had made us unaccustomed to the colour white, and Nina's breath caught with pleasure. The place was filled with Cossack officers, civilians, and more elegant women that I had imagined had escaped ravishment by the Reds. An orchestra was playing the wild, heart-tingling music of the Don.

The head waiter took us to a table near that of a high-ranking officer I saw was General Restigiev, of Shkura's Wolves. Kink and Russky arrived a moment later, and some of Restigiev's Cossacks recognized our squadron leader as he came into the room.

'Captain Kinky! Captain Kinky! *Za vashe zdorovye!*' They shouted to him.

Kink waved his arms good-humouredly like a fighter responding to applause as he enters the ring.

I had forgotten that it was the Russian custom, when either soldier or officer entered a public place, for him to approach the highest-ranking officer present, salute, and ask permission to be seated. The three of us excused ourselves to Nina, went over to the general's table, and made our request.

Restigiev, a fierce-looking man with ice-blue eyes like Wrangel's, replied that he would grant his permission only on the condition that we join him and his party of two officers and three women guests. We said we would be delighted.

One of the officers named Korgonovsky, a tall, hollow-chested captain with a sweeping mustache, impressed us with more than his hirsute adornment. The nails of his little fingers were at least two inches long. He had, we learned, sworn to let them grow till Shkura's Wolves entered Moscow.

That might well be soon, Korgonovsky told us happily. In a moment the general would rise and tell the entire room a piece of very good news.

I saw the captain exchange a look with his superior. Then, casually, Korgonovsky took a pistol from his belt and fired it at the ceiling. Nina and the other women shrieked; then there was absolute silence as Restigiev rose and cleared his throat.

Russky translated what he said after the bedlam stilled. The White Army had scored a major victory. This afternoon Denikin had taken Kursk, two hundred and eighty miles south of Moscow.

The orchestra struck up the 'Bozhe Tsarya Khrani', the national anthem. At its conclusion there was a moment of silence, and then the dancing began. Nina and I went out on the floor.

It was rough going. The Cossacks moved among the more conventional dancers with razor-sharp *kinzhals* held in hands and teeth, and whenever the fancy to do a dagger dance seized one of them, he called for more *kinzhals* from his companions, and bristling with knives, launched into his own fiercely individualistic version.

There were as many as half a dozen doing the dagger dance. It was all clean fun, of course, but I found it rather alarming. When I said as much to Nina she only smiled and shrugged and said 'Nichevo'.

A shower of daggers from the final leap of a *kinzhal* dancer convinced me finally that we had better retreat to our table.

Kink got up as we sat down. Korgonovsky had persuaded him to try the knife dance. One blade held in each hand and the point of a third held between his teeth were all that he could manage. Someone slapped a wolf-hair *shapka* on his head, and we watched him charge onto the polished floor to spirited Cossack applause.

'He'll kill himself,' I told Nina.

'He is more likely to wound one of the bystanders.'

Nina, as usual, was right. When it was over Kink had suffered nothing worse than a slightly cut lip, though a huge Cossack sergeant got a dagger through his toe. The big fellow bellowed with pain and then shouted with laughter, giving Kink a slap on the back that sent him half way across the dance floor.

Kink sat down dabbing at his lip with a handkerchief. 'God, I was a fool to do that.' He scowled at me. 'Why did you let me, Aten? You call yourself a friend?'

At that moment the lights went down. A pale spot was thrown on the dance floor, and a plump diva from the Moscow Opera got up to sing. She was followed in turn by a young contralto of the St Petersburg Opera, who was followed by a tall basso. The basso, with a voice that shook the wine glasses, sang 'Chorniye Gusary', the song of the Black Hussars. The Cossacks, men who were sensitive to music for all their arrant masculinity, gave the refugee artists an ovation, though you couldn't help thinking that these singers would have done still better on the opera stage or that of a concert hall. The atmosphere of civil war was hardly conducive to their best performance.

As if she had read my thoughts and extended them to include those other artists, the lovers of the world, Nina's hand reached beneath the table and clasped mine.

'You are frowning again my Sasha,' she whispered. 'Remember, you promised to be gay.'

Kink's eyes, with their combination of skepticism and sympathy, met mine for an instant. Then he looked away.

An aide from another table came to whisper something in Restigiev's ear. The general pushed aside his *zrazy s kashoy* and called for the waiter. He had unfortunately been called to a staff meeting, he told us. Settling the bill, he took out a sheaf of paper rubles that could have choked a mule. The money was in perforated squares, like sheets of postage stamps. He detached the amount of the check in twenty ruble notes like a postmaster tearing off stamps in lots of hundreds.

We had become accustomed to devalued currency: the exchange

value of the ruble had fallen from fifty cents to one cent at the time. But it was astonishing to see such a quantity of rubles in virgin sheets, fresh from the engravers.

'Do you print your own money, General?' I asked Restigiev, through Russky, jokingly.

He laughed. 'No, Captain, that is harder work than fighting for it.'

It was, I thought, entirely possible that Restigiev's money had been looted three times: first from the Bolshies, then from the Whites by the Bolshies, and then back from the Bolshies again by Shkura's Wolves. The Cossacks might have been poor speculators – few of them had any sense of money – but they nonetheless knew how to get their hands on it in unconventional ways.

The general raised his glass in a last toast. 'To Christmas dinner in Moscow! You shall all be my guests.'

We drank to it.

Korgonovsky moved his glass away and extended his long, surprisingly graceful hands on the table. He looked down at the overgrown nails of his little fingers. 'At that dinner I shall cut off these nails with Lenin's scissors, after cutting out his heart.'

Russky shook his head dolefully. 'Is not possible. Lenin has no heart. Trotsky maybe but not the evil Little Father, the anti-Christ.'

Kink sighed. 'Here we go again, getting serious, and I'm to bunk tonight with this lugubrious type.'

We left the café with the indefatigable Cossacks shouting out their twentieth reprise of 'Chorniye Gusary'. Kink and Russky discreetly parted from us at the corner. It was understood that we would meet at the station tomorrow morning for the return trip to Kotluban.

I hailed an *izvozchik* and gave the name of Tsaritsyn's best hotel. (Kink and Russky, we had agreed, would be staying elsewhere.) The driver let us off at the hotel we had passed by that afternoon.

Inside it in no way resembled the Pera Plaza. Though the lobby decorations were faintly Byzantine the walls were cracked and chipped, and a dusty rubber plant drooped disconsolately in front of the window. The lights were so dim that I took Nina's hand, crossing the threadbare carpet to the desk.

'It is not so bad,' she said cheerfully. 'At least we will have a nice big room to ourselves.'

I rang the call bell on the desk, but no one came. When I rang it again, impatiently, Nina put her hand on my arm.

'Sasha, you are not in Chicago. They will take a while to come.'

'Does this happen in all Russian hotels?'

She nodded. 'The best even. The desk clerk is probably having a glass of tea. He would not come if your President Wilson himself were ringing.'

'Suppose I was the Tsar?'

She wrinkled her nose. 'Ah, in that case he would finish his tea quickly.'

After another ten minutes a wiry old man, dressed in western style, shuffled through the door behind the desk and greeted us with a *dobry vecher*. I asked for a room in my execrable Russian. Cupping his hand behind his ear, he heard me through, then signified his lack of understanding.

'Sasha,' Nina said, 'let me talk to him. It is necessary.'

The desk clerk heard her out and without a word shuffled out the door again.

'Where the devil is he going?' I asked Nina.

'To get the manager.'

'Oh, Lord. Why do we need the manager?'

'Sasha, it is the way things are done in Russian hotels.'

Disgustedly I sank down into a shabby armchair and closed my eyes. What a fine beginning to the beautiful romantic interlude I had planned so carefully.

In another quarter of an hour the manager emerged. He was a bald, clean-shaven man in his fifties, wearing a celluloid collar and high button shoes. He spoke English, and with a vengeance. Ignoring Nina, he drew up a chair beside me and began to chatter away.

'You are not Englishman but *amerikanski*, I am right? I can always tell the amerikanski; it is for me the talent. I love America. For seven years I live in New York City and have many relatives in the United States. I remember the Singer Building, the Voolvorth Tower, Central Park. The first time I see the elewated I cry, it is so beautiful. You have traweled the elewated much?'

'Sir,' I said. 'We're a little tired. We'd like a room. If you'd be good enough to – '

'I am in hotel business seven years in New York City, but my wife, she prefers to return Russia.' He spat into a potted plant. '"For what?" I asked her, "for rewolution?" You understand, I see it coming. I know blood will run in the streets. "For blood," I ask her, "you will give up all the blessings of America? The food, the freedom, the air you can breathe?" Listen, I tell you what life in America, it means to me.'

He told me. Nina took the chair next to mine and sat listening with her chin in her hand, lost wistfully in some dream of fabulous America.

Finally the manager, whose name was Mr. Termitsky, ran down like the buzzer of an alarm clock, and with great courtesy invited me to sign the register. Mr. Termitsky himself took us up in the wheezing elevator to our first-floor room.

'Is bridal suite,' he said, opening the door. 'Not so beautiful as my hotel in New York but comfortable, no?'

I didn't answer. I had been foolish to expect anything better, but the place appalled me. Shrapnel had torn through the window, now boarded up, and buried itself into one of the walls; broken glass still littered the floor, along with little heaps of lathe and plaster. A section of the ugly fretwork mantel had been gouged out, though the mirror was still intact, and a brick propped up the broken fourth leg of a table.

'Mr. Termitsky,' I said, 'haven't you another room that hasn't been damaged in the bombardment?'

He nodded enthusiastically. 'We have several, but they are not the bridal suite. Moreover, they are small.'

'Sasha,' Nina said, 'we have not seen the bedroom,' and she pulled me through the archway into a small room dominated by a huge double bed. Shoved up against one wall was a scarred armoire; against the other, near a window, shattered at the top, stood a small table with a beaded lamp that was bulbless. The bed was unapproachable from either side; to get into it you would have to vault over the headboard.

'Is comfortable,' Mr. Termitsky said. 'You would sink into it like a cloud. Try.'

Nina shook her head at me in warning and assured Mr. Termitsky, in Russian, that the rooms would be fine. The door closed behind him.

She erased my frown with her cool fingers. 'Sasha, be practical. This is the best hotel in Tsaritsyn. And the bed is comfortable. See?'

'It's just occurred to me,' I told her, 'that we don't have a bathroom. I'm ashamed to take you to a place like this.'

'The bath is down the hall.' She put her arms around me. 'Come, try the bed.'

'I would, if I knew how to get into it.'

She giggled. 'I will show you.' Pressing her length against me, she pushed me back till we had both toppled over the headboard and onto the coverlet. We lay there wrestling and laughing till it came to me that kissing would be more fun.

Mr. Termitsky was right. It was a very soft bed...

The clatter of dishes awakened me.

Nina stirred, and I said, 'What's that?'

'Dishes, Sasha,' she murmured, and snuggled her head on my shoulder.

'Of course they're dishes. But where would they be washing dishes at this time of night?'

'In the kitchen. We are over the kitchen. Go back to sleep.'

I groaned. 'How can I go back to sleep when they keep rattling those dishes? It's intolerable.'

Nina didn't answer; she had dozed off again.

The dishwashing lasted for two hours. Fortunately my Gold Flakes and matches were on the table next to the bed. Mr. Termitsky had neglected to supply us with an ashtray, so as I finished each cigarette I tossed the butt out the broken pane of the window to the alley outside.

If Mr. Termitsky had a fire in his damn hotel it would serve him right.

Chapter Seven

*

We came back to Kotluban to find Colly intermittently delirious and broken out in dark red spots scattered over his chest, arms and legs. In his less lucid moments the only one of us he recognized was Kink. Alexandrovsky said that Colly's case was approaching the critical stage; if there was no south-bound hospital train through Kotluban in the next few days he would recommend that we bring him to Tsaritsyn by ordinary coach. Though such a trip had its dangers, it was necessary; the hospital train was running out of typhus drugs.

The next day, to our relief, a south-bound Red Cross train from Saratov stopped at the siding. Alexandrovsky went aboard to make arrangements for Colly and to transfer some of the Saratov wounded to his own vans. The train from the front was at least thirty cars in length, the longest I had seen. Bandaged men stared through the windows with bitter or indifferent eyes. Some asked for cigarettes, and we handed up what gaspers we had on us. The stench was as bad as the Chicago stockyards with a favouring wind. A crazed soldier made a break from one of the vans and was captured when he tripped over some points down the track. In the scuffle his bandages came off and I had to turn away from the ruin of his face; half of it had been sheared away as by the stroke of a meat cleaver, and his left eye hung by a viscous thread.

My God, I thought, sickened; in the past few weeks we've forgotten what war is like.

One of Wrangel's staff officers, a cavalry captain with a shattered elbow, gave us some news. While Wrangel was holding his own before Saratov, at the moment there was no chance of his taking the town.[1] He had too few men and General Erdeli, on his right flank in the Astrakhan area, was retreating. Wrangel had asked Headquarters for new orders countermanding those issued for the advance on Moscow, and when Romanovsky, Denikin's chief of staff, had insisted that he resume the attack on Saratov, Wrangel had gone to see him in Taganrog.

In Taganrog Wrangel had desperately repeated all his arguments against the Moscow advance. But Romanovsky was adamant. Wrangel told him he was through and demanded that the chief of staff replace him. Romanovsky's reply was characteristic: without Wrangel, he said, Denikin's plan could never be achieved.

Bleakly pessimistic, Wrangel had returned to the Saratov front. Not only was Saratov impregnable, but at the junction of the volunteer armies the Reds outnumbered Denikin three to one. Only a miracle could save the commander-in-chief from a terrible defeat. To make things worse, conditions behind the lines were more chaotic than ever. Makhno was looting trains and depots with impunity, and White officialdom was losing what little control over the civilian population it had. When you paid a man too little to live, what course had he but to be corrupt? The peasants were crying for land and getting a stone in answer. There had been no improvement in relations between Denikin and the Kuban Rada.

'On the surface it looks as though we are winning,' the captain said, 'but there are those of us who know better. God save Russia.'

We took Colly aboard the hospital train on a stretcher and found him a fairly clean bunk in the officers' typhus ward. Most of the men in the car were in more serious condition than he; the reddishbrown rash covered their entire bodies and they had completely lost their grip on reality. What worried me most was the lack of doctors and nurses. How could Colly get the attention he needed when there was only one nurse to every two hundred men and one doctor to every five hundred? And what if he got worse? I solaced myself with Alexandrovsky's promise that Colly would be all right unless Makhno's Green Guards attacked the train, or if there was some other unforeseen disaster. And somehow I couldn't see Colly fading out that way; he was the kind of man who would die not from a bandit's bullet but in bed, old and full of honours. Besides, Feodor was going along with him.

Colly, lucid at the moment, made an effort to smile. His voice came in a dry whisper. 'So long, you blokes. Sorry I've been such a mess of trouble. And thanks, Bunny, for the loan of your batman.'

'Stop feeling sorry for yourself,' Kink said. 'There's a hospital room waiting for you in Tsaritsyn with the prettiest nurse in south Russia. I arranged it personally.'

'Kink,' Colly whispered, 'you have some morphine?'

We looked at one another.

'I'm not the type – for suicide,' Colly said. 'May need – to get a little sleep. These fellows, they're going to be noisy. Promise I'll give it to the Doc... promise.'

From his pocket Kink took the vial of morphine all of us carried in case of capture by the enemy. He shook out half the grains, capped the vial, and slid it under Colly's pillow. He hadn't given him enough for a lethal dose.

The train lurched forward.

'Wire us as soon as you get to the hospital, Colly,' I reminded him.

He nodded, closed his eyes and said, so low that we could hardly hear, 'We'll fox 'em.'

We watched as the train got under way. Feodor, dressed in a pair of Tommy's fatigues, waved from Colly's window.

The train gathered speed and disappeared toward Tsaritsyn.

'God, I'm sick of trains and train farewells.' Kink muttered. 'There's so much death in them. And one of us should have gone along with him. I know it.'

He was probably right, but Colly would have pulled his rank and forbade it. We had already broken regulations by allowing Feodor, a POW, to accompany him.[2]

A packed refugee train had pulled into the space just vacated by the hospital train. Already the Kotluban peasants were bartering and selling food and produce at its windows.

There were suddenly shouts and screams from one of the coaches, and as we watched three big leather portmanteaus and an expensive *polushubok*, a winter fur coat, were hurled from a window to the roadbed below. Their owner, heaved from the vestibule, as abruptly followed, landing on her bottom on the cinderbed and setting up a terrible howl. She was answered by a flood of invective from a woman who had pushed her way to the window. Evidently the issue had to do with *amour*; after spitting in the direction of the *baryshnia*, the woman on the train turned to pummel the shamefaced man behind her.

The peasants, peddling their pancakes and boiled beef, paid no attention. They found such an event commonplace, as indeed it was. But we were fascinated. The girl who had been so unceremoniously ejected from the carriage was lush and lovely.

'*Bozhe moi*,' Tommy said admiringly, 'that's what I call a woman. Do we toss for her?'

Kink squared his shoulders and straightened his tie. 'Gentlemen, in Cossack country the spoils of war, when they're indivisible, belong to the Ataman. Step aside.'

'Think a moment,' Eddie warned him. 'She may be a perfect hellion. She was pretty unpopular on that train. You don't know what you're getting into.'

Kink looked at him blandly. 'Oh, don't I?' He stalked away toward the fallen angel.

As the train pulled out the young woman struggled to her feet and shook her fist after the departing refugees. We watched as Kink offered her his handkerchief and put on the charm. He bent to kiss her hand. Then he whistled, and Ivan charged upon the scene, to dust off the *polushubok* and pick up the portmanteaus. He lugged them away toward the B Flight Pullmans.

Kink brought his spoils of war over to where we stood and introduced us to the Countess Nona Beresofsky.

She was still indignant. 'They have throwed me out,' she complained in a husky contralto that sent shivers down even my own thoroughly committed spine. 'But the dirty pigs do not take my ticket to Novorossiisk where my husband waits. I will catch next train.'

'No more trains today or tomorrow, Countess, as I told you,' Kink said smoothly. 'You'll have to accept the poor hospitality of the Royal Air Force.'

She looked about her with haughty distaste. 'You have here no hotel?'

'Kotluban's just a village,' Kink said. 'We have only a vodka house, a grain merchant, a blacksmith and a tax collector.'

We nodded in corroboration.

'Oh, *quelle douleur*,' the countess wailed, dabbing at her eyes with Kink's handkerchief. '*Je suis perdue*.' Her distress seemed real enough, but on the other hand I noticed that the handkerchief was dry as an empty glass.

'Not at all,' Kink said. 'You have an invitation to B Flight train. Our private compartments are quite comfortable.'

The countess smiled. 'Major, you and the desolation of Kotluban have persuaded me. If there is hot water I will be more than content.'

The countess caused a sensation among 47 Squadron enlisted

men. It was as if all the sophistication and glamour of Nevsky Prospect had come to our little provincial chicken scratch in the dirt of the steppe. The mechanics and maintenance men paused at their football to stare with reverence at the way Nona's hips moved beneath her travelling suit. Cowderill, watching from the kitchen, stepped on Clarence, who was underfoot, and knocked over a pot of stew. Even the invulnerable Hoskins swallowed.

Kink and I accompanied Countess Nona to her compartment, which she surveyed with satisfaction. 'Is so much better than refugee train,' she shuddered elegantly. 'Even in first class is vermin and smells and dirty bodies. I must pay twenty rubles for hot water when we stop at station! Was never this way even during war with the Hun. And we move like turtle does. Four hours once it took to go three versts! I leave Koslov two weeks already, and today I am here only. Perhaps I will get to Novorossiisk never.'

'Countess, one must not despair,' Kink said. 'That's a rule we have here. And now we will leave you to your *toilette*. The lav is to your right. Tea will be served in the lounge car in thirty minutes.'

Kink hustled me down the corridor with his finger to his lips. In the vestibule he did a little jig of victory and anticipation. Then he put his hand on my shoulder and gave me his somber look. I sighed, knowing there was a 'little request' coming.

'Bunny, old man,' he said. 'I want your assistance in a certain delicate matter. You owe me a favour – remember that destructive steer of yours. Now there's a south-bound coach scheduled to pass through tomorrow afternoon. I'd prefer that the Countess didn't catch it.'

'Why?' I asked.

It was his turn to sigh. 'Oh, come now. Try to be cynical for a moment. What possible motive could I have?'

'Oh,' I said.

'Precisely.'

'But Kink,' I said, 'what if she decides to stay on for a while? You might not be able to get rid of her so easily.'

'She's got a husband waiting for her in Novorossiisk, hasn't she? What makes you think she'll want to stay on for more than a couple of days?'

'I don't know. Maybe she hasn't got a husband waiting for her. Maybe she does and she's not all that anxious to see him. Kink, you better be careful. There's something about this *baryshnia* I just don't like. And suppose Olga finds out? These Russian girls will scratch your eyes out if they catch you cheating.'

'Am I married to Olga? Listen, leave it to me. Are you going to help a friend out or not?'

I told him I would, and he gave me instructions. Tomorrow afternoon I was to take the countess on a picnic on the steppe. Cowderill would pack a hamper and I could take the van. I was to return no sooner than three o'clock; by that time, allowing for delays, the train scheduled to arrive in Kotluban at one o'clock would have come and gone.

'But Kink,' I protested. 'Who ever goes for a picnic on the steppe? What if it rains? And what about the afternoon patrol?'

'It's not going to rain and Charley tells me your spark plugs need overhauling. In any case, you're excused from patrol.'

'But why me? Why not Tommy, or Eddie, or Bill?'

'Bunny, you're in love. You're the only one I can trust with Nona.' He left me, whistling 'The Pilot's Lament'.

Nina was on duty that night and didn't come to dinner; nor did I see her later on in the evening. That made it easier. Over dessert I broached the picnic to Nona, and after a curious look at Kink, she accepted my invitation. At noon the next day Cowderill had ready a hamper of cold fowl, hard-boiled eggs, and a bottle of Crimean wine. It was a beautiful, cloudless day with that peculiarly golden light that falls over the steppe in the week or two before winter arrives in earnest. It was cool, but not too cool. I had to admit it was a fine day for a picnic.

We got back a few minutes after three. Cowderill was outside with Clarence, who greeted Nona effusively, pushing his snout up her skirts. She kicked him away and hurried up the steps into the Pullman. I gave Clarence a neckrub and he grunted with pleasure.

'Tsaritsyn train's been and gone, Sir,' Cowderill said, 'though beggin' your indulgence, I wish the lady'd caught it. I don't like them that mistreats an affectionate animal.'

'Neither do I, Sergeant,' I said, and as the sergeant and the pig disappeared into the train, sat down on a packing case and lit a gasper. I let smoke and breath out in a long sigh: it had been quite a picnic.

Nona had polished off most of the chicken and half of the wine. Then, acting on an impression that Kink, having lost interest in her, had turned her over to me, she had made it clear that any advances I might make would not be rejected. When I made it clear in my turn that I intended to make no advances, she had lost her temper and demanded to be taken back to the train. Only by inventing engine trouble could I manage to get back after the Tsaritsyn train had left, and Nona's complaints, while I poked around under the bonnet, had not made pleasant listening.

I finished my cigarette and went to look for my girl.

Claudia was in the headquarters car. When I asked for Nina she said she was on duty.

I glanced at the peg board. 'The board says she's off. Are you sure?'

She looked at me, I thought, strangely. 'Wait,' she said. 'I will see.'

She came back alone. Nina had a headache and was lying down. She wouldn't be able to see me.

I was puzzled. Nina had the constitution of a horse – a thoroughbred horse. She had never been indisposed in all the time I had known her, except for, as she put it, 'the month that is my time'.

'It's nothing serious?' I asked.

'Is headache,' Claudia said, turning to her paperwork. 'Will be better later on.'

I asked her to tell Nina I'd be back again after dinner, and went to my compartment. It was a mess, had been a mess since Feodor had left me yesterday. I thought of Colly and wondered if he were safely settled in the hospital at Tsaritsyn. We would be getting word of his safe arrival any moment now. Feodor should be back tomorrow, on the early morning train.

I dozed off and was awakened a few minutes later by the Flight's return. I got up and went out to the landing field.

Kink and Bill were helping Eddie across the field, with Tommy following behind.

I ran towards them. God, had Eddie been hit?

When I reached them Eddie lifted his head and grinned at me palely. 'I'm all right, Bunny. Just got my shoulder creased by a Bolshie bullet and lost a little blood. Kink shot the bastard down.'

Kink met my eyes, but with an effort. 'We ran into a flight of seven Red Spads.[3] They ganged up on Eddie. His bus is a sieve.'

As we walked on to the hospital train, I didn't have to remind Kink that had I been along today the odds against us would have been more even. He'd never make the same mistake again.

Alexandrovsky examined the bullet crease, bandaged it, and recommended that Eddie stay out of action for a couple of days. Kink, Eddie and Tommy went back to B Flight train to see if there was any news from Colly, and I went on looking for Nina.

I found her in the surgical ward, drying her hands on a piece of waste. 'Yes, Sasha?' she said coolly.

I moved to take her in my arms, but she pushed me away.

'Ninusha, *Malenkaya Ustritsa*, Little Oyster, what have I done?'

Her lips were tight. 'Please do not play the worldly one with me. Have you no shame, to come looking for me after what has occurred?'

'Nina, stop this nonsense. If you're speaking of the picnic, and I assume you are, I was doing Kink a favour. He didn't want the Countess to catch this afternoon's train. Does that explain it?'

I could see that she was wavering, but she had suffered too much to let me off as easily as all that. 'You were away three hours,' she said. 'Much can happen between a man and a wanton slut in three hours, especially when they are in the middle of the steppe.'

'You know nothing happened. Now stop it.'

One of the doctors called to her from the ward.

'I must go now,' she said.

'Will you come to dinner tonight?'

'I cannot, but thank you. I am taking Claudia's duty.'

'I happen to know you're not. Claudia's on duty now.'

She smiled. 'All right, Sasha. I will come.'

I reached for her, and one of her tears wet my cheek.

'You're a silly *ustritsa*,' I told her. 'I adore you and could touch no other woman. Do you believe that?'

She nodded doubtfully. The doctor called again. I whacked her on the fanny and left the train.

When I came into the lounge car I knew something was wrong; the boys had no drinks before them. The face Kink raised to me was strained.

'Colly isn't in Tsaritsyn, and the hospital doesn't know if his train got in or not.'

'Damned incompetents!' barked Eddie.

'Strewth, I'll bet the Green Guards got the train,' said Bill.

'Bull turds!' Kink snapped at him. 'Makhno doesn't put trains under his arm and carry them off. He loots, he rapes, he takes a few *paruski* prisoners to fight for him. If Makhno had stopped the train he would let it go on again, and Colly would have made it to Tsaritsyn.'

'Maybe he's holding him for ransom?' Tommy put in.

'Is not probable,' Russky said. 'Would not take sick man who might die. British would accuse Makhno of killing him. And Makhno fears British more than Whites and Reds put together.'

I asked Russky what he thought had happened.

'Is three main possibilities,' he said. 'One, train went through Tsaritsyn before Feodor could get Colly off, and is now on way to Ekat. Two, train has not yet got to Tsaritsyn because of delays or Makhno. Three, Feodor has taken Colly off.'

'Why should he do that?' I asked.

'Maybe doctors all taken by Makhno and Feodor thinks Colly has more chance off train in village. Kink gave him money so he can pay. Maybe so many die in typhus ward that Feodor frightened Colly would die there too.'

Kink got up and began to pace the floor. 'Colly in the hands of that ignorant *plenny* who the Whites might jail any minute; it makes me sick! God damn it, one of us should have gone along with him!'

'Feodor may not have much education,' I said, 'but he's smart as paint and he's loyal to the death. You know that, Kink.'

He made a gesture of apology and sat down again. 'Sorry, Bunny, you're right. Feodor's a jewel. It's just that this Colly business has shot my nerves. And being cheek to jowl with the hospital train's beginning to get me down. The death, the suffering, the corpses! Do you know how many bodies the Red Cross crew carted off into the steppe this morning? Over forty. They were stacked like cordwood. And the morning before it was thirty-five. Typhus, most of them. I used to love Russia and the *paruskies*, now I'm beginning to hate everything about the place and the people. They're either beastly cruel like the Bolshies, or they're so weak-livered, self-pitying and incompetent that you can understand somebody like Ivan the Terrible or Lenin coming along and cracking the whip to make them jump. They crave the whip; that's the trouble. And these inhuman steppes; they're so vast, so endless; they dwarf the personality and make you feel like a bloody cipher. You get swallowed up and vanish without a trace. Like Colly. I'll tell you this: if Colly's dead I'm going to resign my commission and go back home.'

We knew he was only letting off steam; none of us could resign our commissions. But we didn't dispute him, it was good for him to get his frustrations off his chest. And I thought of Nina; if it was tough for us, how difficult was it for a young girl sheltered for all her life in the drawing rooms and conservatories of upper-middle-class Russian life? How could she stand the filth, the pain, the death? For her it was never ending; no sooner would a bunk be empty than a train from the front would bring more wounded to scream and suppurate and die. That blankness in her eyes when she came from a day or night of nursing and assisting in the surgical ward – was it her defense against death and the terrible cheapness of it? It must be so, I thought, though I had never discussed it with her. She never spoke of her work, much as a soldier never speaks of the men he has killed in battle.

Kink rang the Clerget bell and Cowderill scrambled out of the pantry with Clarence at his heels.

'I understand that General Maund's conscience rum has arrived,' Kink said. 'Break it out, Cowderill, and make us some hot toddies. It's chilly. We might as well be drunk and warm at the same time.' He glanced toward the fireplace. 'And get some coal from the tender and a batch of those Denikin communiqués we use as lav paper. We'll start a fire.'

'Yes, Sir, right away, Sir,' Cowderill swallowed, 'And, um, Sir, the Countess Nona has been asking for you. She'd like you to come to her compartment.'

Kink replied with an obscenity.

The toddies were excellent and the fireplace drew very nicely; not a wisp of smoke escaped into the lounge. But we were all too grim to feel the rum and after a while, one by one, we made excuses and left for our compartments, except for Russky, who had picked up a copy of *La Vie Parisienne* and was reading it with his usual absorption.

'My God, Russky,' I said, 'don't you ever get tired of sex?'

He smiled sadly. 'When my heart is melancholy it gives me – how you say it? – the uppick. I think if I live through the war of how many beautiful *baryshnias* I will meet and it makes me feel better.'

'I thought you had a pretty fiancée and were going to marry her after we take Moscow?'

'Oh, but I will. Is only that your comrades they have corrupted me' – he tapped his blond head – 'in the intellect. In the body I do not intend to do much bad but the mind it is lustful. You have read the *Confessions* of Rousseau? He speaks of same phenomenon. In Chapter Five – '

'Russky,' I interrupted him hastily, 'we'll talk about it later.'

I just didn't feel like an intellectual conversation.

*

After dinner the gloom was still thick in the lounge. Nona retired early, with a headache, and was followed shortly by Kink, who complained that Cowderill's beef Stroganoff had upset his stomach. Nina and I were next to go, taking the droughts-board with us to my compartment.

We didn't play long: as soon as Nina saw she was losing, she threw all her counters away in typical Russian fashion, in a series of wild, desperate moves.

'It is boring to lose always,' she said, and knocking the board aside, sat down in my lap.

When I tried to kiss her she put her fingers to my lips. 'Shush,' she whispered, 'I am listening.'

From Kink's next door compartment came a giggle and the rustle of shed clothing.

'Don't be indecent,' I told her. 'Kink deserves his privacy. Would you like him to listen to us?'

'But Sasha, of course he listens. And if he does, why should I not listen to him?'

'You're not supposed to be interested in Sam Kinkead.'

She kissed me swiftly. 'I am not. I am interested in you, my shy soldier. And I hate that woman,' she said without transition, 'she who has taken him away from Olga, who now is miserable.'

'Olga shouldn't have fallen for him. Kink told her not to, he doesn't owe her a thing. And anyway, as soon as Nona leaves he'll take up with Olga again. Nona's just for the scented moment.'

She laughed. 'Oh, you men, you are so stupid! Do you think he will get rid of her so easily? No, the trollop will be with Kink for the rest of the war, unless she finds someone better. A colonel, or a general, with a private coach.'

'Nona says she's got a rich man wating for her in Novorossiisk.'

'That is *kavardak*.' Her grey eyes were wistful. 'But I envy her. She will be seeing you when I am gone. Soon, *skoro budet*, will be our parting, Sasha. I know it.'

'*Seychas budet* will be our parting,' I said. *Seychas budet* in Russian meant instantaneoulsy, but we of B Flight used it in our own ironical, private sense to mean never. It was one of our comments on Russia and the Russian character.

She squeezed my hand so hard it hurt. 'No, Sasha, do not joke. I have the certainty that we will be separated soon. Last night I woke up with the most terrible dream.'

'It must have been indigestion.'

'No, it was the truth. In the dream our trains were on the same track, going to the same destination, and then you were switched off to another track and went off in the opposite direction, so fast that we did not have a chance to say good-bye.'

'Ninusha, dreams are only an expression of our fears. They don't necessarily tell us our futures.'

'I believe that they do.'

It suited me at the moment to be above such superstition *kavardak*. 'My little oyster,' I said, 'you are half Russian, half Christian, half Tartar and half saint. And I don't know which half of you I adore the most.'

She gripped my tunic lapels tightly. 'Do you love me really, Sasha? If I was sure of that I would have more hope.'

'I love you beyond description.'

'With you it is not like Kink? If a *volupté baryshnia* came along you would not forget me?'

'You are everything voluptuous to me, *tsaritsa moevo serdtsa*. You are passion and sweetness and goodness and all my hope. My present and my future both. How could I forget?'

'Then prove it to me, Sasha,' she said. 'Take away my fear.'

If I had known that now was the only time we were to have for love and loving I could not have proved it to her better.

Three days later General Holman, and one of his staff officers, Major Bingham, arrived in Kotluban with two pieces of news.

One was very good news. Colly was safe at the hospital in Novocherkassk. Feodor hadn't taken him off at Tsaritsyn; there had been a pitched battle going on in the trainyards between a band of Bolshie saboteurs and a *sotnia* of Cossacks, and the engineer had gone on through with his throttle wide open. When he stopped ten miles outside the city to let his Tsaritsyn passengers off there had been no stretchers available for the wounded and the ill, and Feodor had decided to take Colly on to Novorcherkassk.

It had been a lucky decision, Holman told us. The Tsaritsyn hospital was jammed with wounded and typhus-stricken and for several days had been out of drugs. It was unlikely that Colly would have survived there. But the journey to Novocherkassk had been no picnic, and Colly had told Feodor that he could stand the filthy, stench-ridden typhus ward no longer. Feodor had taken him off the train at a small station stop while the orderlies were dragging out the corpses of the typhus victims who had died the night before.

Standing on the station platform was a Russian woman who had met Colly in Ekat. She brought Colly and Feodor to her house in the village and nursed Colly through the worst of the disease.[4] When he was able to be moved, Feodor had taken him to the Novocherkassk hospital. The doctors said he would be up and around in a week or two. Feodor, Holman added, was on his way back to Kotluban now.

'Good man, that little *plenny*.' the general said. 'If the Whites had more like him they'd win the war hands down.'

We were still beaming when Holman dropped his heavy bomb. The RAF's war in South Russia was over. An air ministry order had come through ordering all British combat units to leave; only the instructional mission would remain with Denikin's armies.[5]

Kink broke the stunned silence. 'Sir, do you happen to know why?'

'The War Office gave no reasons, Major, it never does,' said Holman, 'but I can guess. Public opinion in Britain is thoroughly against this war, and now that the French have pulled out the government is more reluctant than ever to pursue it. That Sherwood-Kellogg letter in the *Daily Express* against the war didn't help much, either. Winston Churchill's the only man who seems to see the Bolshevik threat, and Lloyd George keeps shouting him down.'

'But we're doing so well at the moment,' Kink said. 'Kolchak's just reoccupied Tobolsk, and the Poles are pushing into Red territory; Denikin's knocking at the gates of Voronezh. And Yudenitch is about to attack Petrograd. Why, the Whites have almost a third of European Russia within their lines!'

'There's a possibility,' the general said, 'that a continued White advance would change the War Office's mind; the fact that we've been ordered to evacuate gradually rather than immediately seems to indicate that. But meanwhile these are our orders.' He grinned.

'However, gentlemen, they are not necessarily your orders. Major Bingham, will you describe the volunteer plan?'

Bingham, a quiet man with fine eyes, put down his tumbler of Scotch. 'Gentlemen, Colonel Collishaw pleaded so hard from his hospital bed that 47 Squadron be kept at the front, that General Holman has arranged to attach it as a unit to Wrangel's Army, provided enough men volunteer for continued service. Several men in A and C Flights elected to go home, but if B Flight is unanimous to stay, Wrangel will have a close-to-strength squadron.'

'I know all of us want to see the war through, General,' Kink told Holman. 'I don't need to poll the officers. But if you'll excuse me, I'll call the enlisted men to formation and get their votes.'

Not a single one of B Flight's ninety-odd enlisted men failed to volunteer. Kink's voice broke as he gave the results to Holman before he and Bingham boarded their private train for the return trip to Taganrog. We knew the news of B Flight's loyalty would be good medicine for Colly.

That night we had a special *prazdnik* to celebrate Colly's recovery and our narrow escape from recall. With us was a special guest, the female leader of a Cossack *sotnia* on its way to join Wrangel at the Saratov front. Katrina Kovich and her men had fought with us against Budenny in the ravines beyond Tsaritsyn.

When I told Nina that 47 Squadron had almost been sent home she burst into tears and simultaneously hugged me, overjoyed.

'I am sad because you are not out of danger and happy because we are together still. Is that selfish, Sasha? Are you disgusted with me?'

'I'm used to your Russian extremes. Now dry those eyes and come over and meet Kitty of the Kuban, our guest of honour.'

Nina made a face. 'The woman who is dressed like a Cossack man?'

I tried to frown. 'Don't be jealous of a pretty girl who's fighting for her country. Besides, she's no competition. She and Tommy are already a duet.' On the lounge opposite us Kitty, a good looking, dark and extremely vital young girl, sat *tête-à-tête* with an enraptured Tommy, while Russky acted as interpreter.

'Yes,' Nina said, mollified, 'she is attracting. You will introduce us, Sasha?'

Kitty's soft voice and agreeable femininity made it almost impossible to believe she was a soldier, but this was a strange country which bred even stranger women. Once in Tsaritsyn a slip of a Cossack girl had been pointed out to me as a veteran of one of the Don cavalry brigades. I couldn't believe that Denikin had awarded her the St George Cross for sabering three Red machine gunners, pistolling two more, and then, under heavy fire, binding the wounds of her squad.

Through Russky Kitty told me that she knew all of us from that day on the steppe when we had routed Budenny and saved the Cossacks from encirclement and annihilation. Was it not Kink who wore the little flag on his aeroplane? I told her that the little flag she referred to was Kink's flight commander's streamers which flew from either wing strut of his ship.

Kink left Nona and came over to propose a toast to our charming visitor. Nona, temporarily in the background, poutingly cranked up the Victrola and put on a turkey trot.

I turned to see Sergeant Hoskins in the doorway, trying to get Kink's attention, and went over to see what he had on his mind.

'Pardon, Sir, for disturbing you, but one of the freights has caught fire.'

I alerted Kink, and we of B Flight piled out after him down the track. The crisis was real. Our terminal boxcar was blazing. It was empty except for crates and boxes, and constituted no great danger in itself. The trouble was that it was next to one of the ammunition cars, and the coupling was badly jammed.

While Hoskins and his men tried to put out the boxcar fire, Kink and I set to work with a sledge and a crowbar to get the link and pin coupling unjammed. Russky, Tommy and Bill held back the crowd of refugees, who had no idea of the seriousness of the situation and were frankly enjoying the whole business. It was a relief from the boredom that plagued them worse than hunger.

Sparks rained down as we worked at the coupling; Hoskins wasn't having much luck with the fire. We had too little water to fight it effectively.

'*Bozhe moi*,' Kink said, his face streaming with sweat, 'if we don't do the job in the next five minutes the heat's going to drive us away. And if that happens at least ten cars are going to go up in the blast. All our liquor, food and winter clothes. Holman will reduce me to the bloody ranks. Put some muscle on that crowbar, man!'

'I'm with you, *kunak*. Let's try the sledge again.'

It took us another ten minutes, and the heat seared our faces and necks like a dragon's breath, but under the hammer blows the coupling finally shattered. Kink yelled for Hoskins and his men to join us, and together we pushed the burning freight a hundred yards down the tracks. More than one of us singed our hands doing it.

We were walking away from the blazing car when Tommy suddenly clapped his hand to his forehead. 'Lord, Kink, I forgot to tell you! There's a hundred and twelve pound bomb aboard that freight! I planned on unloading it tomorrow. Run! Run for your bloody lives!'

We ran. We were seventy-five yards away when the bomb exploded, and the concussion knocked us flat on the ground. Flaming debris fell and floated down around us. Kink was the last to get up; he lay on the cinderbed for quite some time, drumming his fingers on the ground.

I offered him a Gold Flake. He looked at all of us in turn, except Tommy. Then he said, very quietly, 'Anybody got a match?'

*

Later that night Nina suddenly stopped rubbing ointment into the superficial burns I had sustained from the blazing freight and sat bolt upright on the bunk.

'What's the matter?' I asked her.

She frowned. 'I am thinking that I would not fit as the wife of a – how do you call it? – rancher,' she said. 'I am almost positive.'

I was both amused and relieved; relieved it wasn't gloom and doom she was talking, but of our future, in however perverse a way. I knew she was only waiting for me to reassure her our life together, after the war, would be all California sunshine, oranges, and love.

I frowned too. 'Why are you so positive?' I said, going along with it.

'For one thing, you have no Russian Orthodox Church in the Chocolate Mountains.'

'Nina,' I reminded her. 'I don't live in the Chocolate Mountains. The town of El Centro is below the Chocolates, in the Imperial Valley.'

'*Khorosho*, then in your village of El Centro.'

I let the insult pass. 'It's true there's no Russian church in El Centro, but every Sunday I'll fly you to Los Angeles in my private plane. I promise. There's bound to be a Russian church in Los Angeles.'

'Sasha, do not joke, I am serious. From what you have told me of the ranch, I know there are no luxuries. Now I wish to warn you. I come from a bourgeois family of much solidity and this perhaps may be a source of friction between us.'

'You mean the inconvenience of an outhouse?'

She blushed, being at the moment not a nurse but a prospective bride. 'Yes. Is it not very uncomfortable to live on a ranch which does not have the conveniences? Especially in the cold weather?'

I sat up on the bunk and pretended anger. 'Now look here, Ninusha. A rancher needs an honest to goodness wife who doesn't mind getting her hands dirty, not a choosy, complaining aristocrat who spends all her time at the hairdresser's and at church.'

She bridled. 'Ekh, you are doing me a favour? Remember, the Anohinas are important people in Rostov. They are not peasants but people of means. My father was a Councillor, and once he met the Tsar!'

'Well, damn it, the Atens aren't peasants either!' I tried to keep my face straight. 'We're good Dutch and Scotch-Irish stock,[6] and you won't find a book on Texas history that doesn't have my father in it.'

Her face was white. 'Sasha, do not swear at me.'

'Dammit, I'm not swearing!' I laughed and reached for her. 'You little foolish oyster, don't you know I'm kidding?'

She held away from me a little. 'What is kidding?'

'The great American occupation. Chaffing you along, teasing.'

She looked at me gravely. 'Then you do not mean what you said? You would not mistreat me on the ranch? I would be a lady?'

'I'd beat you very seldom, and you'd always be a lady, yes.'

She kissed my shoulder, near the burn, and turned her earnest face to me. 'Sasha, I do not mean to make demands, to be difficult. It is only that I think that if we talk about certain things they will come true. It makes them more real. Do you understand?'

'I understand.'

'So. How is it where you are burned?'

'Better. Your touch healed it.'

I tried to take her in my arms, but she eluded me. 'No, you must sleep now.'

'Ninusha, I'm perfectly all right, believe me.'

She kissed me on the forehead and moved to the door. 'I must start now being a lady. Goodnight, Sasha.' The door closed behind her.

Russian temperament, I thought, sighing, and turned out the light.

*

Next morning, when I came into the mess car for breakfast, Kitty and Tommy were holding hands on the lounge. Beside them sat Russky, his hair disheveled and his eyes gummed with sleep. Good Lord, I thought, they'd gotten him out of bed to interpret for them. I wondered if he had been on call during the night.

Tommy looked up at me glumly. 'I keep telling her – I mean Russky does for me – that war isn't for women, and she keeps telling me to give up flying and come along with her *sotnia* for much adventure.'

I got myself a cup of tea at the buffet. 'Why don't you offer to teach her how to fly? There's no reason why a woman can't join this crazy outfit. Tell her that a Vickers on a Camel can mow down more Bolshies in five minutes than a Cossack sabre can account for in a week.'

Russky duly translated, stifling a yawn, and Kitty smiled and answered back in Russian. Russky translated for her: 'I will make bargain with Tommy. When we are in Moscow and the war is won, he will teach me how to fly. Until then is better he fly aeroplanes and I with my Cossacks ride.'

'Tommy,' I told him, 'you've got a reasonable woman here, besides a looker. She'll keep you on the straight and narrow. Better marry her before you explode another freight and Kink ships you back to Blighty.'

'I've already proposed to her,' Tommy said. He shook his head. 'She wants to wait till the war's over.'

'And a damn good thing!' Kink shouted from the doorway. 'Burns Thomson, if you complicate my life again I'll drop you in the middle of Moscow and watch you bounce! I mean it!' He stalked to the buffet, and I could hear him muttering, 'Damn pipsqueak lovers. Sex is for the mature. Youngsters can't handle it worth a damn…'

His entrance speech had awakened Russky abruptly. 'What to translate next?' he asked Tommy anxiously. 'There is something that I miss?'

Kitty got up from the settee. She must go, she said; her troop was waiting. She thanked us for our hospitality. We would meet again in Moscow, God willing, and until then, *do svidaniya*.

She kissed Kink, Russky and I, and we kissed her back with enthusiasm, not just because this was a kissing country but because she was such a good-looking girl. Then she and Tommy disappeared into the vestibule for their private good-bye.

Through the window we could see Kitty's *sotnia* lined up outside on the steppe in four rows of twenty-five horsemen each. The Cossacks cracked their *nagaikas* as their animals neighed in the icy air; a few of the men, from sheer excess of good spirits, fired pistols.

'Is very fine specimens of men,' said Russky. 'Did you know that first Cossacks would plunge their new male babies into snowdrifts? All survived, became fighting Cossacks. All who did not... ' He didn't have to finish the sentence.

'I'd hate to marry a girl who flew better than I did,' Kink said. 'If Tommy does latch up with that female Cossack after this war, which I don't anticipate for a second, mind you, he'll have to be the best damn soldier in his wing. Which, of course, I don't anticipate either.'

Kitty emerged from the vestibule, blew Tommy a farewell kiss, and leapt up gracefully into the saddle of her mare. With a wave of her hand she signalled the *sotnia* forward. Shouting '*Na Moskvu! Na Moskvu!*' they swept over the frost-whitened steppe toward Saratov. It was a stirring sight.

Tommy slumped back into the settee. 'The first girl I've ever really loved, and she has to be a *soldier*. You know, chaps, that hardly makes you feel like a man.'

'You felt like one last night,' Kink snapped at him. 'Those sounds from your compartment proved it... And that's enough sentiment before breakfast. Get snapping on those eggs of yours. We've got a patrol this morning, and I'm going to get you bastards back before it snows. Where's Daly and Fulford? Still sleeping? Dammit, they bribe their batmen to let them get an extra forty winks. This isn't a squadron, it's a damn hotel!' Cursing, he left the lounge to rout out Eddie and Bill.

It was a fairly eventful patrol. We bombed out a bridge above Balashov, and then sighted an armoured train a mile or so beyond the bridge, running for safety at full throttle.

Coming in on the *bronevik* we noticed that their guns lacked sufficient declination to get us in their sights if we flew level with the train. We dove, and leveling out close to the fleeing engine and the turreted cars, slowed down to their speed and chased them along the road bed.

The firemen shoveled coal frantically, the engineer's head popped turtlelike in and out of his window. We played with them, slowing down and letting the train run ahead, then catching up again. Kink waved in friendly fashion to the engineer, but the man must have been a fanatic Bolshie: he made an indecent gesture and spat.

Then the game was over. Kink signaled for us to form a line, and climbing above the explosive range of our bombs, we laid our sights along the train. Wiggling his wings, Kink went in against a hail of lead and dropped his eggs. His accuracy was, as usual, phenomenal. We followed in close order, scoring several hits. The train rolled off the rails and lay on its side, smoking.

We reformed and headed for home. Flying right wing, I was first to see the convoy of red-starred lorries crawling over the rough road that led from Balashov to Rtishevo.

I signaled to Kink, climbed to get a longer interval of fire in my dive, and then went down in leisurely fashion, Vickers chattering.

My guns were raking the convoy and doing a nice bit of damage, but when I tried to pull out of the dive I couldn't; my metal map case had fallen off its hooks and jammed the stick. I had about eight seconds to think of where I would crash the plane, and, if I came out of the crash alive, whether I could get the contents of my morphine vial down before the Bolshies arrived and put a gun in my back.

A tarpaulin peeled off and a heavy machine gun opened up at point blank range. A bullet sang through the bottom wing and nicked my main spar. Another tore a jagged hole in the starboard aileron. A cut fuselage bracing wire set up a hum that tickled my spihe like an electric vibrator. All in five seconds, or six.

I thought of Nina, absurdly of how she lost at checkers, and it seemed to give me strength and luck. The stick came free when I kicked at it a last, desperate time, and I zoomed up and over the lorries. Three machine guns and fifty rifles threw lead in search of my guts. Men in heavy brown wool uniforms ducked as I passed over them at a dozen feet.

And then Flight B was on my tail, scattering the column, and I was homeward bound. Back at the field Charley counted thirteen bullet holes in my fuselage.

Kink came over, scowling, 'Dammit, Bunny, I told you to have those map hooks fixed and you didn't.'

My mouth dropped open foolishly; though his X-ray eyes had seen through my plane to other operating deficiencies in the past, Kink's talent for diagnosis never failed to amaze me. He always knew what had gone wrong, sometimes before you did. This time his omniscience annoyed me, and I was still a little peeved at the way he had spoken to Tommy this morning, so I said: 'It wasn't the map case. It was the stick itself that jammed.'

Kink looked at me steadily and said, 'You know, Bunny, if you weren't my friend, I'd say you were a liar.' Then he walked away.

'Call me a liar, Charley,' I said to my mechanic.

Charley sighed. 'I know, Sir, ain't it a caution? Sometimes I wonder if that man ain't God.'

*

On the morning we turned out for Russky's flying début on Camels the steppe was white as far as we could see; last night the first snow had fallen, not in quantity, but enough to let us know we had left only a few weeks at most of regular flying weather. With the advent of the heavy snows there would be no more Bolshie planes spinning downward like tops whipped by our ingenuity and craft; no more dropping of our deadly eggs on the skillets of the *broneviks*; no more winging back at twilight with the knowledge of a job worth doing well done on a bridge, a crossroads, an ant-like pullulation of brown-uniformed men blindly and obscenely bound on our destruction.

When Feodor brought in my tea that morning and I lifted the shade to glance outside, a desolation had settled over me, as white and shroudlike as the snow. Somehow I had known that we would never fly again, white eagles in a red dawn; the part we had played was done, and our guns were muted. Come next spring the war would be over, for good or ill. And with the war our adventure, and with our adventure, our youth.

'Strewth, but you're pensive, Bunny,' Bill Daly said. 'Didn't you hear what I said?'

'Sorry, Bill. I was thinking winter thoughts.'

'I asked if you thought Russky was going to make it.'

'He will, but I don't see what difference it makes, except to Russky. We've had about our last patrol for the winter, and Kink knows it. If Russky crashes it won't be from a Bolshie bullet.'

'You think Kink warned him about the right hand turn?' Bill fretted as Kink and Eddie strapped Russky into the cockpit. 'Or about the throttle and adjustment levers? Russky ought to watch the gun butts on landing, or otherwise he'll bash in that perfect Roman nose.'

'Don't worry your head,' I assured him. But I was more than a little apprehensive myself. Kink had surely read Russky the book on flying a Camel, but that didn't mean Russky had listened to him carefully. A Camel was a tricky machine, less nervous than a Nieup and more solid on frozen ground, but it had a whole set of neurotic symptoms of its own. It was more stable on its back than in normal flying position. In the right-hand turn, unless you were quick on opposing rudder, the nose dropped with incredible speed and pulled the ship into a power spin. If you manipulated your throttle and adjustment levers improperly you stalled the engine. There was a definite art to 'blipping' the engine, switching it on and off to control your average speed.[7] On landing, if you had a nose-in crash, you were thrown forward and bashed your nose against the gun-butts. Such facial damage was usually permanent, and before the afternoon was over Russky stood a good chance of ending up with a disfiguring 'Camel Face'.

Kink and Eddie joined us at the field's edge as two mechanics kicked chocks under the wheels of Russky's undercarriage. Charley, the third mechanic, his hands on the prop, called out, 'Petrol on! Switch off! Suck in, Sir!'

Russky moved his throttle forward and repeated, 'Petrol on! Switch off!'

Charley swung the prop to 'suck in' the fuel mixture. Then he called out, 'Contact!'

'Contact!' Russky repeated, and the air was filled with the bittersweet stench of half-burned castor oil.

The rotary engine roared, then idled into a mutter that lasted for about a minute. Russky opened the throttle gradually until the engine roared again steadily, whereupon he throttled it down again.

He waved his arm from right to left, in the signal that meant 'Cast off the chocks'.

The two mechanics removed the chocks, and Russky, his nose pointing into the wind, leapt forward, rising smoothly and well to meet the morning.

All was well until he made a turn over our heads, leveling with such a jerk that the ship turned in the opposite direction.

But the mistake wasn't fatal. Russky's pilot instinct got him out of it, and he came in on a steep glide to land.

'Oh Lord, he isn't changing his angle of descent,' Kink groaned. He signaled to Russky wildly, but if he was looking he paid no attention; his undercarriage hit the ground at too sharp an angle and he bounced once, twice, up into the air, sending the frost and dirt flying. Pulling on his stick he was off again, going five miles in a straight line before he turned around and came back to land.

This time he made the same kind of landing, only a little worse. His left wheel wobbled off as he came to a stop, and we rushed up to the plane to see the total damage.

Russky lifted his goggles gaily. 'Kink,' he said, 'what is the matter with altimeter? I watch closely like you said and when I come down very close to ground it say one hundred feet.'

Kink paled. 'Do you mean to say you landed by looking at your altimeter instead of at the ground?'

Russky looked at him, puzzled. 'Of course, I watch all the time and it say one hundred feet. Altimeter no bloody good.'

'Russky,' Kink said very slowly, 'for your information the altimeter doesn't register under one hundred feet. I thought you knew that.'

Russky ignored the implied criticism. He smiled beatifically. 'I forget. Now I go with you and boys on patrol?'

The look Kink gave him was full of sorrow. 'No, you're officially grounded. I can't trust that literal mind of yours. If you got Bill's red Camel in your sights you'd shoot it down because red's the Bolshie colour. Now isn't that true?'

'Oh, no,' Russky protested. 'I know Bill flies Camel with red wingtips and I would look at his face very careful to make sure before I shoot. Oh, *very* careful, indeed.'

*

Next morning I woke to hear Nina arguing with Feodor in the passageway outside my compartment door about who was to serve the captain's tea. There was something about her voice, not precisely lack of animation, not precisely stubborn quietness, that alarmed me, and I shouted for Feodor to give her the mug and go about his business.

She came in, her eyes not meeting mine, and I knew what had happened. The hospital train was moving; she was going away.

She gave me the tea and sat down on the edge of the bunk. I gave the mug back to her and she set it on the floor.

I said, 'When?'

'Now. I have only minutes.'

'So soon?'

'We would have left two days ago, except that the Major could not get a locomotive engineer.'

'Where are you going? To the Astrakhan front?'

She shook her head. 'To Orel, to receive the wounded from Kutepov's army.'

I felt numb. She was getting into the thick of it.

'Do you know how long you'll be there?'

'No. The doctor's orders merely say that we should proceed as soon as possible toward Kharkov.'

I took her hand, which was very cold. 'It won't be too long, Ninusha. This war can't last more than another five or six months.'

She smiled faintly. 'And then we will meet in Moscow?'

'Then we will meet in Moscow, for a victory celebration. And we will stay at the best hotel, the National, on Gorky Street, not over the kitchen, and take *droshkey* rides and go to see the animals at the zoo and have every hour and every minute to ourselves.'

'Oh, Sasha,' she said, and the tears came, and I held her close.

'All isn't lost, Ninusha,' I said. 'We're both alive. Our flying operations are about finished for the winter. Who knows what can happen?'

'Yes, that is the trouble. Who knows?'

'You mustn't be a pessimist.'

'I think we are parted, Sasha. For all time.'

'*Kavardak*, and you know it. A good-bye isn't a parting but a good-bye.'

'Please kiss me, Sasha, very hard. So that I can take with me the taste of your kisses. And handle me, roughly, so that I can bring with me the feel of your hands.'

After a moment I got up and began to get dressed. 'I'll see you off,' I told her, but in that instant the whistle blew from the hospital train. Nina said, 'There is no time. You must watch from the window.'

She came back into my arms and pressed her cheek against mine, and then she rustled swiftly from the compartment.

Soot belched from the smokestack; the hospital train was already switched onto the main, southbound track to Tsaritsyn, and about to start. I watched through the window as Alexandrovsky helped Nina up the steps to one of the vestibule platforms. She turned and waved, and then the train gathered speed slowly and took her away.

I looked up to see Feodor standing in the doorway with another mug of tea.

'*Spasibo*, Feodor,' I said, and took it from him.

It was strong and bitter.

Feodor shut the door behind him. I sat there in pajamas and socks, staring at the carpet where it was fraying slightly in the middle of the floor.

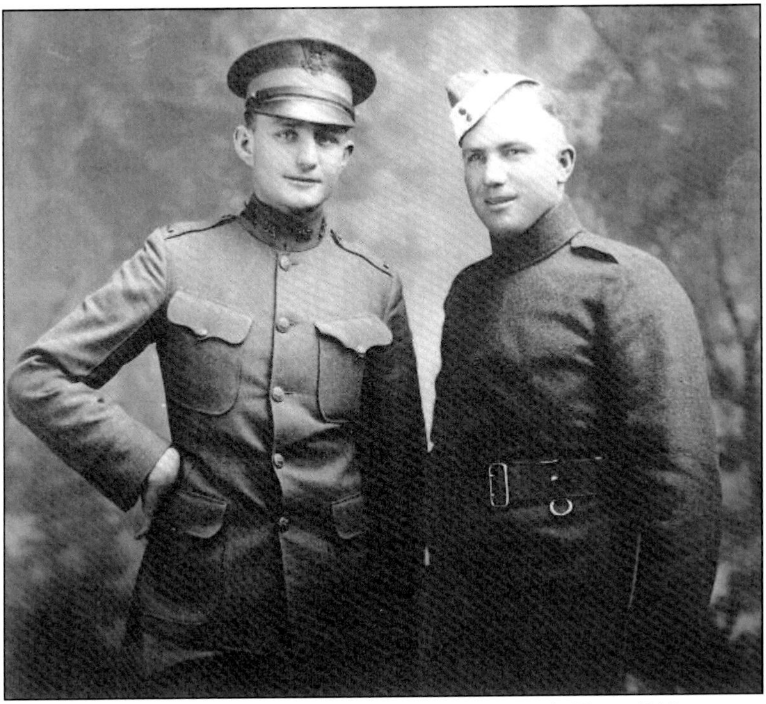

ATEN FAMILY

Boyce (left) and Marion Aten. Photo taken in Fort Worth, Texas, 1918.

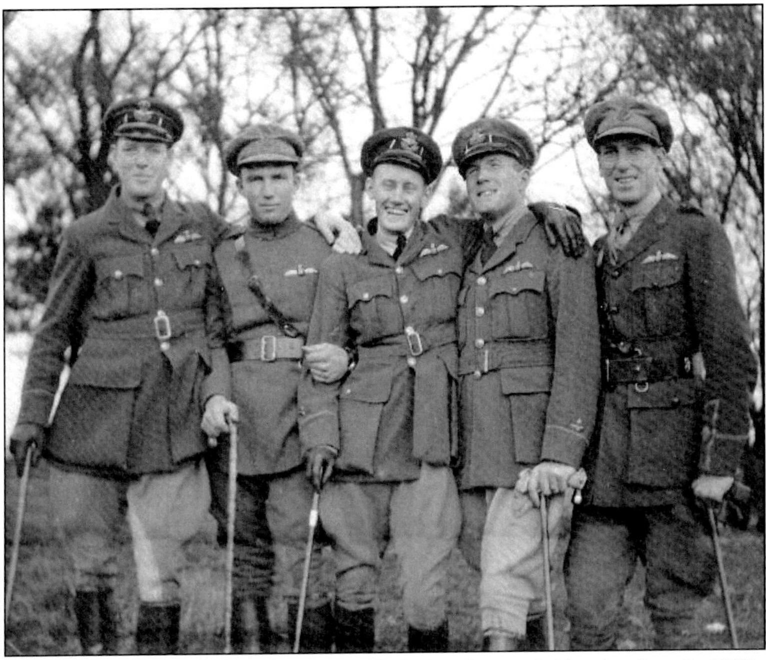

ATEN FAMILY

Raymond Collishaw (left) with arm around Marion Aten, probably taken in early 1919.

ATEN FAMILY

ATEN FAMILY

Two photos from the 1918 crash in which Marion Aten sustained a shoulder injury.
Marion wrote on the back on one of the photos: 'I did it!'

The B Flight Train.
(l to r): Bill Daly, Grigoriev (Russky), Tommy Burns Thomson, Marion Aten.

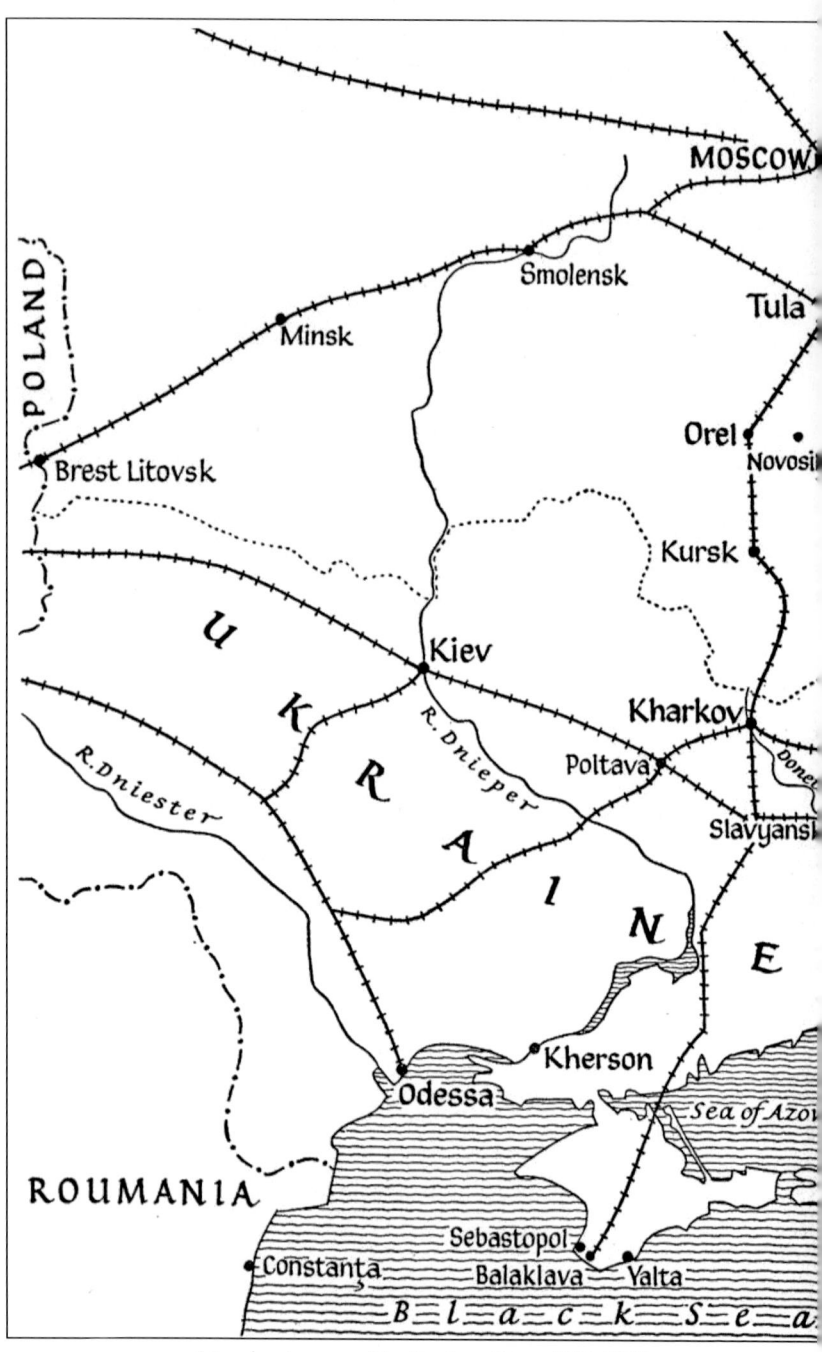

Map showing area of the Southern Front, 1919-1920.

The arrows show the route of B Flight, 1919.

Samuel 'Kink' Kinkead. Photo taken during WWI.

Katrina Kovich (Kitty), standing, with left hand on hip.

Seated (l to r): Generals Romanovsky, Denikin and KN Sokolov.
Standing (l to r): NI Astrov, NN Savitch.

General Mai-Maievsky (left) reviewing the 2nd Kornilov Regiment.

General Peter Wrangel.

General Holman in the gunner's seat of a RE-8.

Eddie Fulford (standing by machine gun) and his RE-8 after a forced landing on the steppe.

Civilians preparing to evacuate Kharkov, December 1919. British officer in foreground.

Stacked frozen corpses in South Russia.

White Russian Calvary or Horse Artillery.

Sopwith Camels in Novorossiisk, late 1919.

ATEN FAMILY

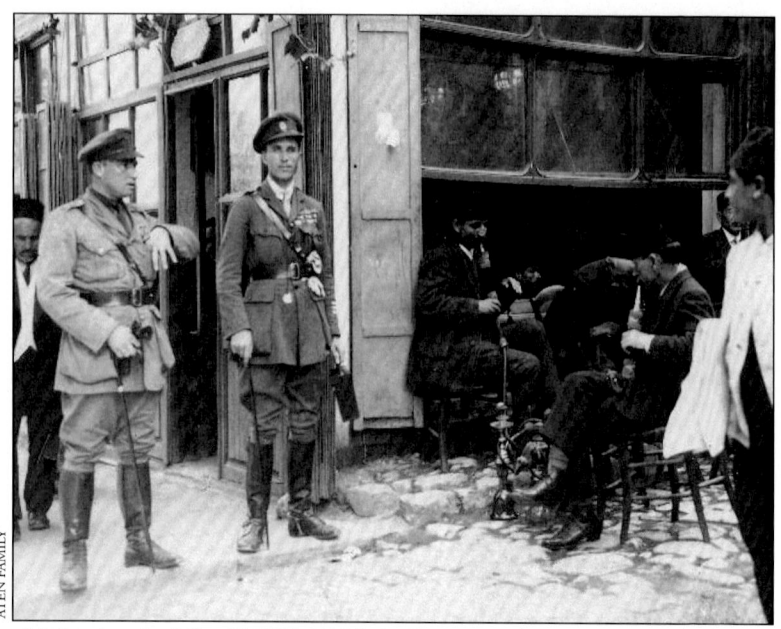

Marion Aten (on left) with Wally D'Adix in Constantinople's native quarter, mid-1920.

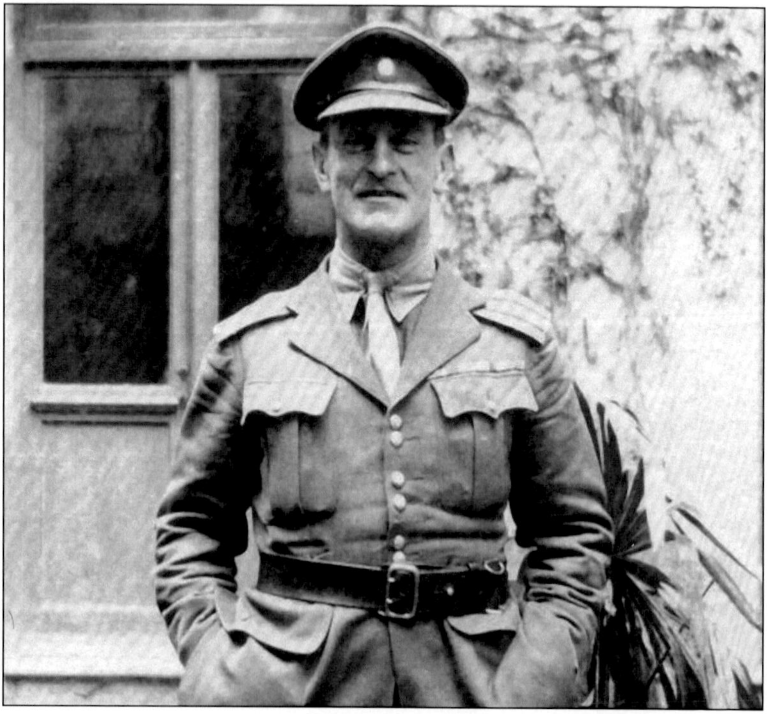
ARCHIVE OF COLONEL GEORGE D TRELOAR

Colonel George D Treloar in Constantinople, late 1920, after evacuation from Sevastopol.

The last parade of White Russian troops, in front of the Hotel Kist in Sevastopol, mid-November 1920: General Skalon (on right) with raised sabre; General Wrangel, saluting.

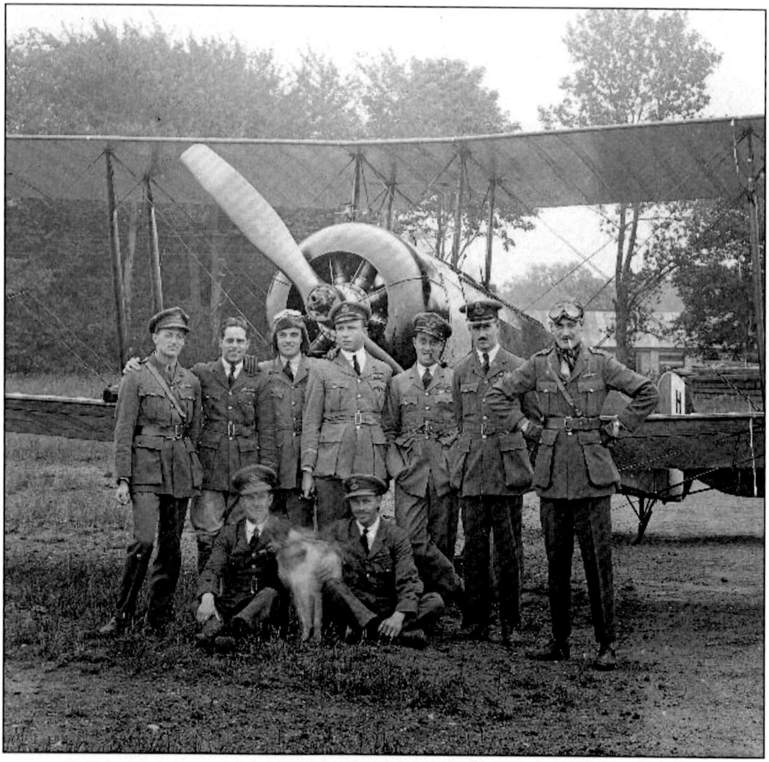

ATEN FAMILY

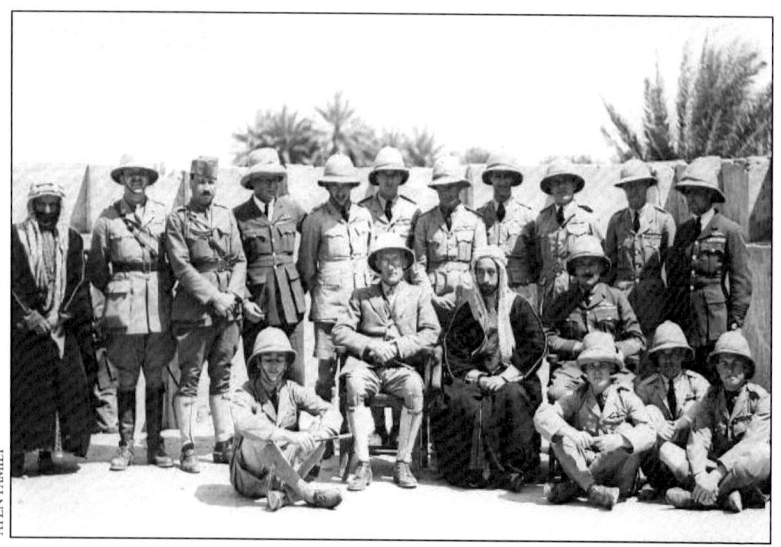

Marion Aten (standing, centre) at flight instructors course, England, mid-1921. The airplane is an Avro 504.

ATEN FAMILY

Sir Percy Cox, British High Commissioner of Iraq, (seated, centre) with King Faisal of Iraq (seated, next to Cox). Marion Aten is standing, fourth from left.

Marion Aten DFC.

ATEN FAMILY

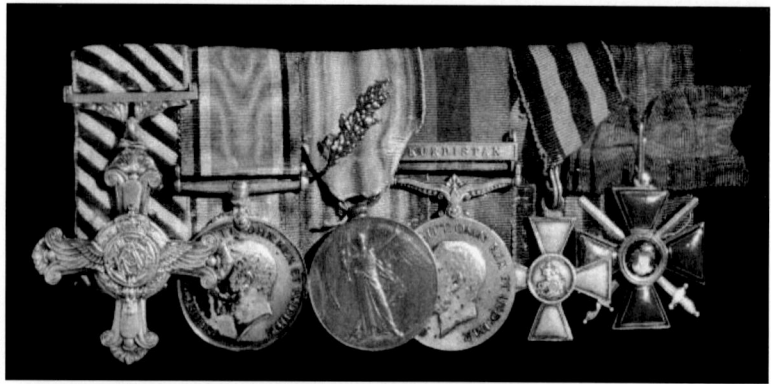

Marion Aten's medals (l to r): Distinguished Flying Cross (UK); War Medal (UK); Victory Medal with Mention in Despatches emblem (UK); General Service Medal with Kurdistan clasp (UK); Order of St George (Russia); Order of St Vladimir (Russia).

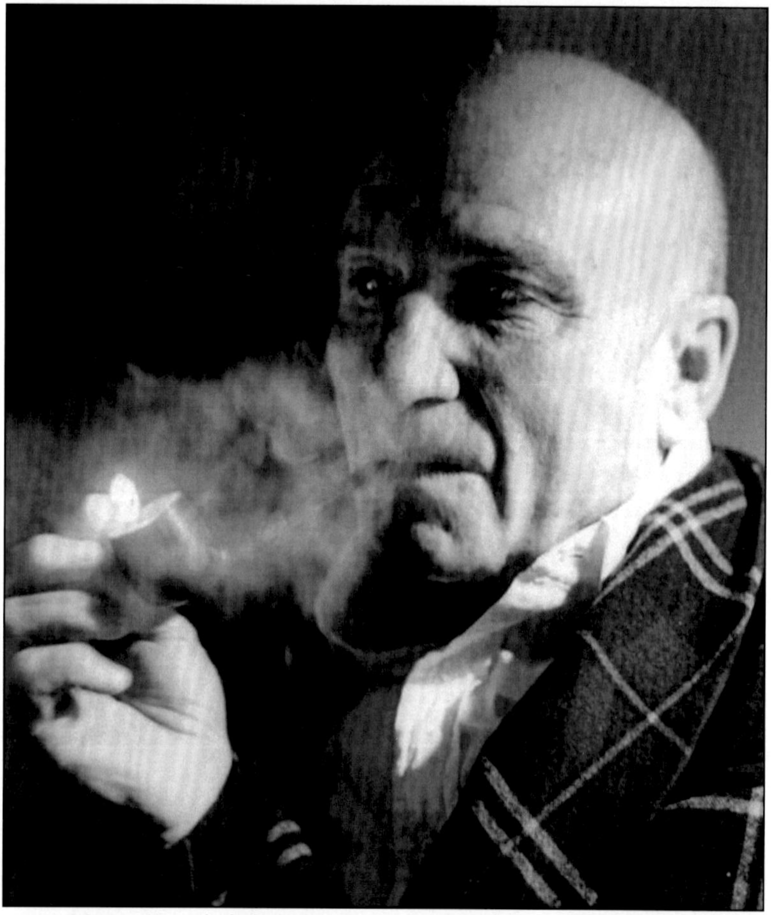

ATEN FAMILY

Marion Aten as he looked when working on the book with Arthur Orrmont.

BOOK FOUR

✱

The Retreat

Chapter Eight

＊

It was as if, with Nina's departure, mercy left us and the sky fell in.

There had been signs of the approaching disaster; though Denikin took Orel and Novosil, only two hundred miles south of Moscow, on October 13th, the Reds occupied Kiev two days later, and for some days previous troop trains from Saratov had been passing Kotluban on their way to Tsaritsyn. It was obvious the Saratov front was pulling back, and Colly wired Kink from Taganrog to get ready to withdraw with it. Trotsky, he said, was battering at the junction between Sidorin's Army of the Don and the Voronezh-Lisky front of the Volunteer Army, and now B Flight would probably be attached, along with units of Wrangel's troops, to Mai-Maievsky's Volunteers. B Flight would be more valuable in the open field, assuming the heavy snows held off, than in defending Tsaritsyn.

We went to work dismantling the Camels and the hangars and loading them onto the flats.

There was more bad news on the 19th.[1] Trotsky, with an overwhelming numerical advantage in men, had split open the Don-Volunteer junction. The Whites were evacuating Kursk and Orel in a hurry.

'The chickens are coming home to roost,' Kink said, 'except that they look more like buzzards. If Denikin had taken Wrangel's advice and concentrated heavy cavalry strength around Kharkov, as an army of manoeuvre, we wouldn't be in this pickle today.'

'When Yudenitch take Petrograd,' Russky said hopefully, 'situation changes.'

'Not enough,' Kink told him. 'Denikin's spread his lines too thin. It's like holding a broken dyke. You can stop a leak at one point, but the water's going to come through at a dozen other places. Do you realize how badly we're outnumbered by the Reds? The effective White forces, including the Cossacks, are about a hundred thirty thousand men. The Reds have one hundred eighty thousand, and huge reserves. On Mai-Maievsky's front it's twenty thousand men against fifty.'

Russky had no answer to that.

A few days later Kink came into the lounge car with a Red communiqué dated October 22nd. Russky translated and handed his pencil scrawl around:

> *On all fronts our enemies are retreating. Kolchak's rout is near.*
> *Archangel will be ours in the course of a few weeks. Our aim is no*
> *longer to defend Petrograd, but definitely to crush Yudenitch. In two*
> *or three more weeks we shall have finished with him.*
> *On the southern front we have learned the art of fighting against the*
> *enemy's methods. Denikin's position is hopeless.*
> *Our forces and our reserves have increased to such an extent that*
> *victory is certain.*

'Is merely propaganda,' Russky said contemptuously. 'Yudenitch will take Petrograd. We will rally, the morale will improve. Is still chance Moscow by Christmas.'

Eddie finished his rum toddy. 'I've only one thing to say to that, Russky. Those fingernails of that Shkura Wolf you met in Tsaritsyn last month must be growing as long as regret.'

On the 28th, the day that Yudenitch suffered an overwhelming defeat at Petrograd, Colly wired orders for B Flight to proceed immediately to Kharkov. There we would join the Volunteer Army under Mai-Maievsky. Four of Wrangel's Kuban cavalry divisions, Colly said, were being shifted from the Caucasian Army's right flank to help the hard-pressed Volunteers.

Though we hated leaving Wrangel's command, we welcomed the promise of action; and there was no doubt that we would be more valuable to an offensive force than to an army in retreat. For me the news was at least half wonderful. I might be seeing Nina, and much sooner than I'd expected.

'What's our route?' I asked Kink quickly.

'From Tsaritsyn east on the lateral route to Debaltsevo,' Kink answered my question, 'and from there to Rostov and Taganrog. At Taganrog we'll go north again, to Kharkov, by way of Kupyansk.'

If Alexandrovsky's train hadn't already left the Kharkov front, I thought, we might be running into it on the leg from Debaltsevo to Kharkov.

'All right, Bunny,' Kink said, 'Get that ineffable look off your face. It sickens the soldier in me.'

We left Kotluban at noon of October 29th,[2] on the express track with official right of way through to Rostov. It was a seven-day trip that in ordinary times would have been no more than two, but even with a clear track there were delays; the refugee exodus had begun from north to south, and when we came to a siding or a junction, refugees waiting for a southbound train would beseech us for a place on the boxcars, on the flats, for a handhold on the roofs. The terror and desperation of these people, most of them with infants or children in arms, was pitiful, and it upset Kink to refuse them. For most of the trip he was in a vile mood, snapping at us and ignoring Nona. He had even moved her to another compartment.

In retaliation the countess threatened to leave at the first opportunity. That was all right with Kink; he wanted nothing better than to get rid of her. He was back at war in earnest and a woman was superfluous, especially one who complained about the food and expected Ivan to do her less personal laundry.

'Dammit,' I heard him shouting at her, 'when I look at you I can understand the Bolshies! Don't you understand that people weren't put on this earth merely for your conveience?'

'*Chart evo poberi*!' she shouted back, telling him to go to hell. 'You are nothing but a stupid bourgeois! A mere Major! Sometime I will find a man who appreciates beautiful woman and treats her well.'

'Madam,' Kink told her coldly, 'your conversation implies a certain assumption of permanence aboard this train. Let it be understood that you're going no farther than Rostov, and you're perfectly free to get off before then if you choose. And if a General's coach should come by I'll be delighted to flag it down and recommend you in the highest terms. If I weren't a gentleman, I'd throw you out now, bag and baggage.'

Though we stopped briefly at Tsaritsyn, Nona made no effort to get off there, and we guessed we were stuck with her till we hit the Black Sea ports.

The news we heard en route to Rostov was all bad. Kolchak had evacuated Omsk and, except around Kharkov, Denikin's armies were in full retreat; the Hampshires had sailed from Vladivostock for home. There were a number of wild rumours: the Reds had slaughtered the entire population of Kotluban because the *angliski* airmen had had their base there; there had been a revolution in the United States, and President Wilson had joined forces with the Bolsheviks and was about to declare war on Britain, Poland and the Ukraine.

I kept peering out the window for Nina's train. Though she was probably still at Kharkov, I had become obsessed with the thought that one day we would pass Alexandrovsky's vans on the local track. Tommy, our other starcrossed lover, was equally convinced that he would run into Kitty.

'Quit that mooning, Bunny,' Kink snapped. 'Your *baryshnia* isn't within five hundred miles of this sector. Anyway, you better get cracking. You're taking over the guard in fifteen minutes.'

'May I remind you that I had guard duty last night?'

Kink spread margarine on his toast. 'You might,' he growled, 'but I wouldn't advise it. Eddie, I'm giving you inspection this morning. Rout out that sluggard Daly and our braw Scot lover and take them both along. I want you to crack down on the Ac Emmas; the mechanics' bunks are in disgraceful shape. You and the rankers both have got to learn this isn't a damn sightseeing trip I'm wet-nursing; it's Collishaw's squadron, and that means the best.'

That day we made pretty fair time, and Kink was cheered enough by our progress to allow a little entertainment after dinner.

It was a nostalgic evening; now that it looked as though the war was ending in defeat, our thoughts turned to another war that had ended in victory. We sang all the old songs, glass in hand, booming them out to the accompaniment of the clicking wheels as B Flight train ran on through the Russian night and the cold rain fell and the fog closed in like the ghosts of Makhno's raiders.

We sang, in bad French:

La Madelon vient de nous servir à boire
Sous la tonnelle au flanc de son jupon
Et chacun lui raconte une histoire;
Une histoire à sa façon.

La Madelon pour nous n'est pas sévère
Quand on lui prend la taille ou le menton,
Elle rit y c'est tout le mal qu'elle sait faire,
Madelon, Madelon, Madelon.

And we sang:

The young aviator went stunting,
An 'neath the wreckage he lay,
To the mechanics assembled around him,
These last parting words did he say:

'Two valve-springs you'll find in my stomach.
Three spark plugs are safe in my lung,
The prop is in splinters inside me,
To my fingers the joy stick has clung.

'Take the cylinders out of my kidneys,
The connecting rods out of my brain;
From the small of my back take the crankshaft,
And assemble the engine again.

And we sang:

Stand to your glasses, steady!
The world is a world of lies;
A cup to the dead already
And here's to the next that dies.

And we remembered. About oatmeal and Karo, and the afternoons over Amiens, hot and full of pockets, and the trenches like ringworm below on the scabrous dun face of the earth, and making yourself small as the Archie crumped up and a piece of steel singed your linen. About how your eyelids were sandy on dawn patrol and how the gun flashes winked over the landscape in little points of bluish light; about singing 'Madelon' in the *estaminets* and fighting over the affections of a trollop and better, more aristocratic love in London on clean sheets in a borrowed flat. About out-racing a Pfalz in a Spad on the level and how it felt in cloudy weather to knife through the clinging wet and leave the ragged wisps trailing out behind.

We remembered these and a hundred other stoicisms, griefs and triumphs.

We remembered, and sometimes we did not.

'Kink, you got first kill – a Fokker over Merville. Colly made the second kill that afternoon. A Halberstadt.'

'Little Benny Bates was the best Ac Emma. Dammit, I say he was! Fixed my bus in half an hour, and my rudder shot full of holes.'

'Allmenröeder got Hank Henry, not the Baron. Look it up in the record books if you don't believe me.'

'My girl was Mignonette. You had Celeste. Now come off it, Tommy, don't you remember that crazy night? You thought the police were the fire department, and you jumped into the garden without a damn stitch on.'

The party began to break up when Nona came *en negligée* and complained about the noise. Kink told her we would damn well make as much noise as we wanted, but we began to whisper anyway, and then Clarence wandered in sleepily and did a mess on Kink's highly polished boots. When Kink came back from the lav Tommy had passed out and Bill and Eddie were snoring.

Kink staggered to one of the lounges and sat down heavily. 'Hell,' he said, 'I thought you types could drink. This isn't a squadron I'm running, it's a goddam kindergarten.'

He passed out himself a moment later, and Russky and I had the job of hauling him back to his compartment.

★

Approaching Rostov we were stopped at every station by bands of Wrangel's military police, who had full powers to search all trains returning from the front for stolen goods, deserters and marauders. Once we had established our credentials we were quickly waved on, but the delays were time consuming. Though our Russian engineer had promised Kink he would get us to Rostov no later than the morning of the 7th, we didn't pull into the Rostov yards till after twilight of the next day.

The stationmaster told us there was no possibility of getting out till tomorrow morning; the heavy traffic east had put the switches to the Taganrog tracks out of order and they were being repaired. Kink wired Colly in Taganrog to expect us tomorrow morning, posted a guard on the train, and gave the rest of the squadron leave till one a.m.

We left the yards and went into the town. The war maps in the shop windows showed ever-narrowing circles of red around Omsk, Kursk and Kharkov, and half the cafés in the main streets had been requisitioned for the troops, but aside from that you wouldn't have known a losing war was on. The trams were running, the parks were open, the theatres and restaurants doing a good business. At the kiosks there was a choice of half a dozen newspapers. We had dinner at what seemed the best café, and later sampled a few of the others that offered entertainment.

We met a cavalry captain who told us some harrowing stories of the Caucasian Army's retreat. In one town the last hospital train had been about to leave in the evening when, in the dim light of the station lamps, he had seen some strange figures crawling along the platform. They were White officers ill with typhus, wearing grey hospital gowns. Rather than be left behind to be tortured and murdered by the Reds, they had crawled through the slush from the hospital to the station. The doctor in charge of the train had refused to allow them on, claiming that his cars were full. But there was still room: in one compartment he found a civilian and three ladies busy manicuring their nails. They had bribed the doctor to get the places. The captain had thrown the four of them out on the platform and put the doctor under arrest.[3]

In an action behind Red lines the captain and his company had come upon a house the Reds had set afire with a hundred villagers inside. There had been only one thing to do, since the house was blazing: unlimber a light artillery piece and shell the walls so as to bring them down, allowing those who were still alive inside to escape. Twenty-five men, women and children had gotten away; the rest had perished.

'You cannot imagine the cruelty of these Bolshevik beasts,' he told us. 'They rival Tamerlane. They wish to make a river of blood on which they can float down to the sea; the Don isn't good enough for them. One million, seven hundred thousand died in the Red Terror of last year. I have lost my wife and two children, also my home. Now all I wish to do is die fighting against the bastards with a sabre in my hand.'

'Do you think anything can stop them from sweeping down to the sea, Captain?' Eddie asked.

'It is perhaps not good to say this,' the major said, 'but I do not think anything will stop them now. I would advise you can get a ship at Novorossiisk as soon as possible and leave for home. This is your war no longer. It is not even ours anymore. It is between the Reds and God, and I think that God is going to throw in the towel.'

Wrangel, the captain told us, was currently in Rostov, waiting for

Denikin's arrival for a crucial meeting. The talk was all against the commander-in-chief, and no one had any confidence in Mai-Maievsky and his Volunteer Army; people went up to Wrangel in restaurants and asked when he was taking over Mai-Maievsky's command. Though the burly general was popular with his troops and tough as nails, his drinking bouts and orgies were a scandal and had affected the morale of his men.

We looked at one another hopefully. Not that we had anything against Mai-Maievsky, but we much preferred to serve under Wrangel.

Coming out of the café we saw a group of mounted Cossacks bringing in a batch of prisoners. Their captives, bound by the ankles and wrists at the end of lariats attached to saddle trees, were forced to keep pace with the trotting horsemen. One prisoner slipped and fell, and I sucked in my breath as the Cossacks, refusing to stop, dragged him along the cobblestones until he staggered upright again, torn and bleeding. But then I thought of the villagers stumbling out of the burning house, and turned away.

When we got to the train Hoskins had a surprise waiting for us: the tarpaulin-covered body of a Bolshie the guard had caught trying to dynamite one of the ammunition cars. 'The bugger slipped in as cool as could be,' Hoskins told us, 'and was setting the charge. Carstairs of C platoon got him with a knife before he finished with the wiring. Sir,' he asked Kink, 'I know we'll be tangling with Makhno's brigands, but are we likely to be running into much more of this?'

Kink bit down on his lip. 'A lot more, Sergeant. When the Reds are on the march the local Bolshies make trouble in the towns and cities. Get rid of the body and double the guard. These saboteurs are too smart for comfort. I don't like the way this one figured out where the ammo was.'

That night the snow came down heavily, muffling the sounds of shunting trains in the yard, but none of us slept too soundly. Once I woke, sweating, from a dream in which a Red Commissar, laughing madly, carried Nina away on a sledge loaded with high explosive, mocking me with the lit match in his hand.

Waking the next morning, I rolled up the shade and looked outside at the snow-covered yards. Five feet away on the next track was parked one of the White infantry's regimental trains, and I had a clear view into its diner. In the lavishly upholstered coach sat two people having breakfast. One of them was a fat colonel with a white handlebar moustache, the other was Nona. Two waiters in privates' uniforms and white jackets, napkins on arm, hovered deferentially in the background. The colonel lifted Nona's hand and kissed it; Nona laughed and playfully waggled her fingers against his thick lips.

As I watched, Nona and the colonel began silently to drift away, and for a moment I wasn't sure which train was moving, Nona's or mine. Then, by fixing my eyes upon a signal box on the snowcovered ground, I could tell it was Nona's. I waved, but she wasn't looking in the direction of B Flight train, she was busy with her omelet now, and couldn't have cared less.[4]

When I told Kink that his bird had flown he grinned in relief. 'Bunny, if we have any more time for hanky-panky before the roof caves in, I'm going to choose myself a peasant girl with thick ankles and a bum the size of a barn. They're flattered to death that a dashing *angliski* looks at them, and they *tickle*.' He looked at me thoughtfully. 'Olga tickled. Do you know that Nona never tickled; absolutely insensitive. If a girl can be tickled that shows she's got a soul.'

He might be right, I thought. Nina tickled.

We left Rostov half an hour later for the short trip to Taganrog. The approach to the yards was jammed with trains – armoured, hospital, regimental and refugee – and Colly, anticipating the jam, was waiting for us at the signal-box at the entrance to the yards. He swung aboard looking fit and handsome; it seemed incredible that only a few weeks ago he had almost died from typhus.

He refused a drink. 'General Holman wants me to get you chaps Kharkov-bound as soon as possible, so we don't have much time for a reunion. Where's the imcomparable Feodor? I've got a present for him.'

I called Feodor, who came shyly in, and Colly shook his hand and presented him with a gold wristwatch. On the back was the engraved inscription: 'To my friend Feodor Anikin, who saved my life, in eternal gratitude and admiration. Raymond Collishaw.'

Russky translated Feodor's reply. 'He say he is overwhelmed. He has always wanted wrist-watch but does not deserve a gold one.'

Feodor was crying, the tears streaming down his cheeks, and in embarrassment at this *paruski* display of emotion we turned our eyes away.

'All right, Feodor, you better go now,' I told the batman in my halting Russian, 'or we'll all be blubbering.'

'*Spasibo! Spasibo! Spasibo!*' Feodor said, and turning, rushed from the lounge.

'There goes a man,' said Colly, and blowing his nose, returned to business. He didn't like to be the bearer of ill tidings, but there was more bad news. A few days ago Lloyd George had made a speech at Mansion House in which he said that the British Government considered the civil war in Russia over.[5] Denikin's rout was continuing, and there was already heavy fighting around Kharkov. It was no longer possible to concentrate the Cossack cavalry around Kharkov as Wrangel had advised Denikin to do, and if the Reds took the city, the Whites' chief strategic position would have been irretrievably lost.

'I'm not even sure you chaps can get to Kharkov, the congestion on the line is so bad,' Colly went on. 'But go as far as you can, unlimber the planes, and wait for orders. If we're lucky, the snow and the weather won't be so bad for a while that you can't help Mai-Maievsky. I'll be coming up the line with A Flight train as soon as they get to Taganrog. C Flight's out of it, I'm afraid;[6] Holman doesn't think there's room for more than one bomber flight at the front, especially with winter on the march. Kink, I assume you've got something to keep the engines warm?'

Kink nodded. 'Kerosene lamps covered with asbestos.'

'Colly,' Russky said hopefully, 'I fly Camels now?'

'You can count on it,' Colly laughed. 'We're going to need every scout we can get into the air to tangle with the Bolshies.'

'What about Wrangel taking over Mai-Maievsky's command?' asked Eddie.

'We understand in Taganrog that it's only a matter of time. I hope he takes on the job before things get much worse. When he does, at least you'll be flying for the best there is.' Colly glanced at his watch. 'Meeting at Mission HQ in fifteen minutes. In typical British fashion, we're setting a time for consideration of when to burn headquarters' documents and papers.'[7] He shrugged. 'Sorry I've got to buzz off; I've got a lot more to say to you intrepid types, but it'll have to wait till we meet again on the way to Kharkov.'

'How long is that likely to be, Colly?' Kink asked.

'A week or so, most likely. So long, chaps, and let's fox 'em.'

We watched him go, reluctantly, and it seemed so suddenly dark in the lounge car that Kink asked Tommy to turn on the lights.

We sat outside the Taganrog yards for three hours, and then the congestion let up enough for us to get through to the northbound tracks. As the switchman put us on Kink noticed that Cowderdrill was missing.

'Just like the bloody clown to hold us up! God knows what he's up to. Bunny, go tell the switchman we won't be moving out for a while. Bill, ask Hoskins to organize a search. And Russky, put down that dirty magazine!'

Hoskins returned with Cowderdrill twenty minutes later. The messman carried two huge samovars under either arm, and two of Hoskins' men were dragging a cardboard box which held five others. On Cowderdrills' homely face was the unholy light of commercial triumph.

Kink sent Hoskins to tell the switchman we were ready to leave, and turned his furious attention to the errant Cowderdrill.

'Sergeant, absence from your post in wartime is an offense punishable by death. Do you realize that?'

'Yes, Sir, quite, Sir, but I wasn't exactly absent from my post, Sir. I was just in the station, buying up samovars. Oh, it's terrible with them refugees, Sir. They're sleepin' on the benches and on the floor, and they're so discouraged that when you step on them they just grunt and roll over.'

'The station is not your post, Sergeant. Now haven't I told you a hundred times that these samovars are worthless? Dammit, man, put the goddam things down!'

Cowderdrill set the samovars down on the carpet and hung his head. 'Yes, Sir. You have that, Sir.'

'And you still don't believe me?'

'Well, I don't think you're completely right, Sir,' the messman said. 'Now for instance, when this here war is over, the Russians are going to need their samovars again, Sir. And I'll be one of the few that can sell them back to them.'

Kink put his face in his hands and groaned. '*Bozhe moi*, I can't take much more of this. Back to the pantry with you, Cowderdrill. Just stay out of my sight.'

Cowderdrill picked up his samovars, frowned, and set them down again. 'Yes, Sir, quite, Sir, but permit me to ask, if I'm to stay out of your sight, how am I going to serve you dinner?'

Kink got to his feet and left the car, carrying himself very tightly. As he went out the door we could hear him muttering, 'I didn't hear that. I didn't hear that. I didn't...'

★

There were few trains going north, and the line was fairly clear till we arrived at Debaltsevo, the junction between Taganrog and Kharkov. But then the trouble began, with another two hundred miles to go. There was a terrific, monumental jam in the Debaltsevo yards. The stalled southbound trains extended as far back as we could see, and when we got out to inquire about getting on a north-bound track, we discovered that the stationmaster and his assistants, overwhelmed by the magnitude of their task and the clamor of com-plainants, had simply disappeared.

But there was worse to come. When we got back to B Flight train we learned that our Russsian train crew had struck for higher wages. They wanted ten rubles more a day per man, or they would take us no further. After all, they had their wives and children to think of. Not only were we heading into enemy country while everybody else was fleeing from it, but we were in Makhno country, too. It was a wonder that we hadn't been attacked yet by the fierce brigands of the Green Guards.

Patiently Kink explained through Russky that he had no power to raise salaries. The engineer then suggested that he call or wire the British Mission at Taganrog and get authorization for an in-crease. Kink agreed, but in attempting it discovered that the tele-phone and telegraph wires were down, cut by Red saboteurs, Makhno's band, or by one of the several less identifiable outlaw groups that roamed the country.

The engineer was leaving the cab when Kink pulled his revolver on him. He and his crew, Kink said, were staying whether they liked it or not, at least till we reached Kharkov. He had better get used to the idea. A guard would be posted on the engine and tender, and any man trying to get away would be shot as a deserter.

Back in the lounge car Kink tossed his greatcoat down in disgust. 'You can't fight a war when somebody's sticking a knife in your back. Dammit, things are really getting scratchy.'

In the end, we organized a search party for the stationmaster and his men, and with the help of some cavalrymen, found them in a tavern in the village. We rubbed their faces in the snow to sober them up, and dragged them to the station house, where, after a while, they came back to their senses.

Gradually the chaos of the yards returned to normal disorder, though it wasn't till the afternoon of the next day that B Flight train got out of Debaltsevo.

Even then it was like swimming upstream against a powerful current. The endless southbound trains, packed to the platforms with white-faced refugees, overflowed every junction big and small, and it would take hours, and sometimes whole mornings and afternoons, to get past the tangles and the snarls. We bribed more than one stationmaster with food and clothing; we knocked down more than one and threatened him with a rifle slug till he threw the switch that let us through.

It was a hell, a nightmare of traffic, and it frayed our nerves to the breaking point. We would have welcomed a bandit raid, but there was no relief from the stopping, the starting and the crawling; only the stream of refugees – frightened, apathetic, stunned and humble. Too humble.

Kink was a perfect ogre, and we tried to stay out of his way. Even good-natured Russky growled when you asked him a reasonable question, and nobody at all could talk to me; I had grown so irritable looking for Nina's train that I threw a punch at Eddie when he tried to kid me about it.

For three days we made our way from station to station as the line momentarily cleared and opportunity arose, through the beautiful Donets Basin with its winding little streams frozen solid, its great groves of pines capped with snow. There had been no trees worth speaking of back on the steppe, and the pines were the first things I noticed in the changing scenery. They made me think of Christmas, soon approaching, and they made me think of it bitterly. *Na Moskvu!* I wouldn't be spending Christmas with Nina in Moscow or anywhere else. The odds were ten to one she had already passed me on her way south.

We came finally to Kupyansk station. The village itself, a few versts to the east in a valley, was one of the many south Rusian communities that had refused to pay blackmail to its original builders, and the railroad, accordingly, had detoured around it.

We could go no farther; the double track ahead was blocked with southbound trains, following one another so closely that they seemed coupled together. In fog and mist we pulled into a siding, the only train in that vast assortment of rolling stock that was headed north towards the Kharkov front a hundred miles away.

The bearded stationmaster, the fur of his *shuba* up to his ears, appeared through the fog to tell us that a body of roving cavalry under Momontov had raided through the Red lines as far north as Tula, only a hundred and twenty miles from Moscow. He added casually that the Bolshies had captured Omsk and split Denikin's centre. Swayed by hunger, defeat and Lenin's skillful propaganda, Volunteers were deserting to the Reds by the thousands.

Kink had the ground crews unload two Camels and rig them for flying. They sat in a field alongside the track with asbestos-wrapped kerosene lamps under their engines, ready for action when the fog lifted. Cowderdrill broke out the rum and we sat drinking hot toddies while the whole world fled past in an unbroken stream of hospital vans and refugee trains. I had never known there were so many people in Russia. Hopefully, unrealistically, I kept peering out the fog-shrouded window for Red Cross train 242, until my eyes blurred and I got a raging headache.

'Christmas in Moscow,' Tommy kept repeating aggrievedly. 'What bloody rot.'

Finally Russky squared his shoulders and replied, 'All respects, tide may yet turn. We must not give up the hope.'

Eddie snuffed out his half-smoked gasper, making a face; we had run out of Gold Flakes and were now reduced to Woodbines. 'Come now, Russky,' he said, 'let's be realistic. The army has ceased to exist as a fighting force. We've got less than half the men the Reds have. The railway workers are leaving their jobs. Makhno and dozens of other guerillas are raiding the interior with nobody to stop them. The Bolshies have practically won the goddam war, and none of your crazy optimism is going to change things an iota.'

'If we pray,' Russky insisted, 'is possible things improve. Denikin will shortly put railroads under better control. He will fortify bases behind the lines and organize police. We must despair not, is un-Christian.'

'If Wrangel could only get Denikin to agree with him on something,' Bill Daly said, 'or the other way around, I might see some sense in what you're saying. But strewth, Russky, the dice are cast, and it's come out just plain craps.'

'What is "crap"?' asked Russky.

Kink fixed his eyes upon him more sadly than sourly. 'Crap, Russky, in this context is a number of different things. It's White poverty of money and equipment, inefficiency, old regime bureau-cracy, and disorganization. It's separatism, the landed gentry, crooked officialdom and profiteering. It's Denikin's inflexible 'Russia, One and Indivisible.' It's the Bolshies' slick lies of Land and Freedom. It's British policy, which helps the Whites with one hand and knocks them down with the other. It's the Americans and the French and everybody else who've just about lost this war because they were never sure they wanted to fight it. It's a score of other things, from bad strategy to typhus, from staff intrigues to a lack of an *esprit de corps*. And the worst crap of all is this: that we're losing a war that we could have won.'

We were silent. The logs blazed in the fireplace and outside the tightly sealed windows the snow came down in huge soft wet flakes, snowflakes that here, in Russia, the biggest country in the world, were bigger and softer and wetter than anywhere else. The trains inched and shuttled and rocketed by. We sat warm and cozy and full of hot buttered rum – and ashamed.

Chapter Nine

*

On our second day at Kupyansk the passing trains contained a sprinkling of uniformed men. On the third day there were quite a few. On the fourth we saw about as many men in uniform as refugees, and thereafter the trains came by loaded with infantrymen, cavalrymen and artillerymen packed solid inside and out. Despite the cold and the intermittent snowfall, soldiers and Cossacks sat and lay on the tops of the coaches, clung to the steps, hung out of the open windows. A good many had flasks of vodka from which they drank continuously and uproariously. If it hadn't been for the hospital trains, endless, funeral and stinking of iodoform, I would have been reminded of students and alumni returning from some glorious gridiron victory.

Kursk had fallen to the Reds,[1] the men shouted at us, and laughed, asking why we sat there on the siding like *duraki*. '*Skoro budet Bolshies!*' they shouted, their breaths frosting in the cold, sharp air. Some pantomimed a sharp knife and a slit throat. None of them would stop, not even for a drink. That, more than anything else, told us how serious the situation was.

The stationmaster developed a fondness for the fireplace and Cowderdrill's rum toddies, and regularly visited B Flight train. We liked the man for his sad eyes and enormous moustaches, but every time he took off his *shuba* we came to expect more bad news.

'He say Mai-Maievsky so drunk last week he not answer dispatches,' Russky translated.

'Stationmaster say many Don Cossacks desert. Kuban Cossacks, he say, do not feel like the fight when their headman say there is no way to stop Bolshies. Many White officers are leaving front to sell loot in Ekaterinoslav Province. We have seen the many luggage vans. One regiment carry behind it over a hundred carriages.[2]

'In Slavynsk they are starving. Denikin has sent armed force to Kuban, arrested dozen members of Rada, and hanged one of them. When Wrangel force new Constitution on Rada, many Kubans very mad.'

The trains kept passing and the snow kept coming down. On November 25th we heard that Wrangel had assumed command of the Volunteer Army on the day before, choosing Chatilov as his chief of staff. But by the 27th we had still received no orders.

Even if we had, it wouldn't have made much difference. During the night someone had stolen our engine. Kink, not dreaming that thieves would have any use for a locomotive in all that niagara of rolling stock, had neglected to put a guard on it.

On the tenth day the trains stopped coming and the track was clear. We were alone with the stationmaster, two hungry mongrels, and a lame ox. There was nothing else alive on that dreary knoll; even the villagers had fled southward.

The snow stopped and the fog finally lifted enough for flying weather of a sort. Kink and Tommy took off to investigate. They were gone for an hour and a half and came back with enough bullet holes in wings and fuselage to discourage any further sorties of the kind.

'Both wings of the Volunteers are falling back,' Kink told us, 'and Budenny's outflanking them. If we're lucky, the Red cavalry vanguard should be at Kupyansk within forty-eight hours. If we're not, they should be on our tails in another twenty-four. Chaps, I'm sorry about that damn engine.'

'What the hell,' Bill said. 'We couldn't have run it ourselves anyway.'

'If you've lost your morphine vial, Cowderdrill,' Eddie said to the mess sergeant cheerfully, 'I'll loan you mine.'

Cowderdrill shook his head. 'Oh no, Sir. I think drugs is immoral. I'll take my rifle and put a bullet through my head.'

'After you've killed a few Bolshies, Cowderdrill,' I said sternly. 'Remember that.'

'Must I, Sir?' the messman pleaded. 'I'd hate to kill a man face to face like. If I shot myself as soon as the Bolshies attacked, would that be all right, Sir? Then you wouldn't have to be angry at me for not fighting.'

While I was figuring that out Kink said, 'Break out the Lee-Enfield .303s, Bunny, and distribute them to the men. We can pot at the bastards from the windows.'

'The *plennys* too?' I asked.

'The *plennys*. We can count on their loyalty a hundred percent. The only food within a hundred miles is on this train.'

To my surprise, the POWs accepted the rifles with an enthusiasm that far exceeded that of the enlisted men, most of whom were quietly fed up with our situation. Feodor, especially, was overjoyed.

'Is prettier much than Red rifle,' he said admiringly of the well-oiled Lee-Enfield. 'Will boom-boom many Reds!'

'You bet,' I said, and handed a rifle to Ivan. The shaggy giant, laughing delightedly, swung it around his head like a war club, and I ducked just in time.

'No, Ivan, you shoot it,' I said, and showed him how. But I had an idea that come a fight, Ivan would revert to the primordial and use the rifle like a shillelagh.

We had two welcome visitors next day at noontime: Colly and General Holman,[3] who emerged from the fog in the cab of a lone engine and tender. They were, we told them, just in time for lunch. Coming into the lounge car, Holman had to bend his head to keep from striking the lintel of the door.

Except for the weather and the menu – caviar, bully beef and rum toddies – it might have been a social occasion, for all the anxiety that Holman showed. In the best tradition of the British officer, for whom imperturbability is as *de rigeur* as courage, he spoke, for a solid hour, of anything and everything other than the predicament that we were in. We discussed London, Paris, the little bar at the Savoy, the Long Bar at the Trocadero; when we ran out of bars we discussed women. There were no names mentioned; in a British officers' mess it was tradition that, favourably or otherwise, a woman's name must never pass a gentleman's lips. Should it do so, the offending officer is obliged to stand a round to all present.

Tommy made sure the general's hot toddy mug was kept brimming, and Colly rebuked him for it. 'For God's sake, Tommy, the General's got a reputation to keep up. You've only got to keep your rum down!'

Holman lidded his eyes and grinned. 'Correction, Colly. I have my spirits to think of as well as my reputation. Burns Thomson, pour away!'

Our laughter broke the tension, and leaning forward, Holman said, 'Of course you want to know our present situation. Gentlemen, I intend to hide nothing from you. The Reds should be in Kharkov within a matter of days. Only a miracle will prevent them from retaking Kiev. Denikin's centre and both wings are falling back.

Mai-Maievsky's already left the army and Wrangel's taken over, but there's nothing he can do with disorganized, completely outnumbered troops. There's nothing you can do. The White's next line of defense will undoubtedly be the Tananrog-Rostov area, and if Denikin doesn't stop the Bolshies there, the war is lost. So far as your own immediate situation is concerned, only a short length of destroyed track north of Kupyansk has prevented Red *broneviks* from being in your midst at the moment. Budenny's advance scouts are only about twenty miles away.'

From the pantry we heard a crash. Cowderdrill had dropped a tray of glasses.

Holman cleared his throat. 'I notice you have no engine. I'll pull you into Debaltsevo and you can get a locomotive, engineer and firemen there. Colly was farsighted enough to arrange for a pool of train crews at the junction. It's going to cost Lloyd George a couple of pounds, but maybe Winston can calm him down about it.'

Hoskins knocked and came in to report rifle fire from the north. When we opened a window we heard it – a faint sound like the popping of firecrackers in the far distance.

We went to work dismantling the two Camels and loading them onto the flats. Minutes later, with Colly at the engine controls, we were under way. We waved our *do svidaniyas* to the stationmaster from the lounge car windows. He and his two mongrels dwindled into black specks against the white of snow and disappeared.

★

It was a four-day trip to Debaltsevo. Hundreds of trains had joined the hegira from stations along the way; on long stretches of track the trains were piled up cowcatcher to caboose. Guerrilla bands began raiding on the second day out, and Kink inaugurated a system of standbys and alerts that kept us in uniform around the clock.

The outlaw bands would most often attack at night, riding in close to the coaches on their fast ponies, sending up an assortment of vari-coloured flares they had captured in their depot raids, and trying to pick us off through the windows. The Greens were superb horsemen, and they had learned the Cossack method of shooting in full gallop from beneath the bellies of their mounts. But if the flares allowed them to see us they allowed us to see them too, and even with their fancy equestrian tricks they made better targets than we did.

Tommy suggested that we start a pool, the winner of which would have potted the most Green Guards by the time we reached Debaltsevo. Holman and Colly joined in with enthusiasm, and Colly, with his incomparable shooting eye, left all of us far behind. It was characteristic of him that the shooting match should engage all his energies, now that for the moment he had nothing more important to do, and time after time I would be sleeping soundly in my bunk after a spell of guard duty when he would come in to rouse me for another event in the competition.

'Bunny, didn't you see that flare behind the snow bank?' he would say, excited as a kid at a shooting gallery. 'Come out and join the fun. You're right behind Kink in the standings; maybe tonight you'll pass him. Make believe it's cowboys and Indians and the varmints are after your sweetheart's scalp.'

In the lounge car I would take my usual place beside the general, and with an open box of cartridges at my feet, bang away at the lines of horsemen that would appear suddenly over the brow of a snowbank or hill, and then sweep in on the slow-moving train and around it to the other side, concentrating their fire on the machine-gunners in the vestibules and then, as their charge carried them past the Lewis men, aiming for us through the windows of the coaches.

'Nice shot there, Captain,' Holman would say, 'you got number three, line two.'

'Was that your shot toppled number eight, line three, Sir?' I would ask the general.

'Not sure. Might have been Gregoriev.'

'No, Sir,' Russky would reply at the next window, 'I missed big fellow. Was you.'

Russky, of course, had gotten the guerrilla, but as I had learned, a Russian considered it more important to please a guest than to tell the truth.

'Dammit, Tommy,' Colly would complain from the other side of the lounge, 'I told you I was aiming for the big one! Why did you have to go and take my man?'

'Sorry, Skipper. Sometimes the bastards don't give you a chance to think.'

The raids lasted from about twenty to thirty minutes, never more. If by this time the Green Guards had failed to knock out most of the defenders, they gave up the attack as a bad job. Usually, after a skirmish, we would count ten to fifteen bodies on the snow; our own casulaties would be nil or at the most one or two superficially wounded, from ricochets. When we came into Debaltsevo junction we had four *plennys* and five enlisted men in bandages. The lounge car walls were badly chewed up, the fireplace chipped in a dozen places, Russky had two bullet holes through his garrison cap, and Cowderdrill was a nervous wreck. But there were no serious casualties and we had travelled roughly half the distance to Taganrog.

Others, though, were less fortunate. We passed several trains tipped over, looted and burned, with only a few charred corpses to show that refugees had met their death there. What had happened to the hundreds of men, women and children who had been on these trains we never found out; either the guerillas had herded them out into open country and slaughtered them there, or they had been picked up by other trains that had come along later on. Stationmasters along the way were reluctant to discuss the question; they had enough trouble on their hands just getting the flood of trains through, and as long as the authorities were too busy to make inquiries – *Nichevo*!

At the junction Colly collected his shooting match winnings, got an engine and crew for us from one of the pools, and switched the engine that had hauled us to Debaltsevo over to A Flight train, waiting for him on one of the sidings. General Holman, who had promised to catch up with us in Taganrog, dashed off on a spur line to find some lost tankmen. The stationmaster told us it would be a couple of hours before he could get us through to the southbound track, and we went over to A Flight train for a reunion. The boys were grim, and we stayed for only a while.

Cowderdrill was waiting for us outside the train. 'Sir,' he said to Kink, 'I hope you won't be angry, but there's some refugees I let into the lounge. They was such well-spoken and fine-looking people I didn't have the heart to turn 'em away.'

'What did they bribe you with, Sergeant,' Eddie asked, 'money or samovars?'

Cowderdrill blinked respectfully, but didn't answer the question.

'Sergeant,' Kink snapped, 'if we take one we have to take as many as we can. You know that.'

'Yes, Sir, quite, Sir, but them back there are real aristocrats, the cream of the *paruski* nobility. They even acted royal to the pig. Sir, you'll see what I mean when you talk to 'em.'

'You're just a disgusting snob, like all the British,' Kink said and pushed past him into the car.

Perched on one of the lounges was a couple which, had it not been for the overcoats and furs they wore, might have been posing for a picture. The man, tall, pince-nezed and scholarly looking, sat straightbacked and faintly smiling; he wore a *shapka*, a stone marten greatcoat and highly polished leather boots. The woman, her eyes slightly downcast but still looking at the imaginary photographer, was slavically dark and handsome, and swathed to the ears in the most luxurious mink I had ever seen. I had the feeling that under the mink she wore a fortune in jewels and diamonds.

They were certainly aristocrats; for all we knew they might have belonged to the Imperial Circle at St. Petersburg and been related to the Tsar himself. Considering the way they were dressed, I wondered how they had gotten this far without having been murdered and stripped for their clothes.

The man rose, clicked his heels and introduced himself and his wife in perfect English. They were, he said, Count and Countess Orloff of Novgorod. They hoped to make their escape to Paris, where their children were waiting for them. The count hoped we would forgive his intrusion, but he had his wife to think of and a drowning man clutched at every straw. If we were bound for Rostov, as he assumed we were, would it be possible for us to take them along?

Kink sat down and rubbed his jaw. 'Count,' he said, 'I appreciate your predicament, but I have strict orders against carrying any refugees. There are at least twenty refugee trains on these sidings; what's to prevent you from taking one of them?'

The Count smiled. 'I might say typhus, Major, but I would be lying to you. There is only one thing that prevents us from taking a refugee train: the Orloff diamond. We are well known in this part of the country, Major, and so is the diamond. We would be murdered for it very quickly.'

'Kink,' Russky broke in excitedly, 'the Count speaks truth. The Orloff diamond is one of the great stones of the world.[4] Like the Koh-i-nor, the Hope, the Porter Rhodes or the Stuart. It weighs over one hundred ninety carats, and has great history – it was stolen by French soldier from the eye of idol in Brahmin temple, and after that stolen from the soldier by captain of a ship. From ship's captain Prince Orloff bought it for one hundred thousand pounds.'

The count bowed in Russky 's direction. 'Lieutenant,' he said, 'I must congratulate you on your knowledge of the great stones. I would, however, make one correction. The Orloff diamond cost my ancestor only ninety thousand pounds.'

'*Bozhe moi*,' Kink groaned, 'We haven't got trouble enough.' He squinted up at Orloff. 'Tell me, does this diamond have a jinx attached to it? So many of the great stones do.'

The countess spoke up then. 'No, Major, there is no jinx.' She smiled sadly. 'We do not feel it has brought us bad luck, since we are still alive. We hope you will not prove us wrong.'

Eddie tossed his Woodbine stub out of one of the bullet-shattered windows. 'Kink, you're not asking for my opinion, but I can see you're weakening. If we've got orders against taking on refugees, I don't see why we should make any exception for the Count and Countess here. The Orloff diamond is about as neat a symbol of the old régime as you could find. We haven't been fighting this war to save the nobility, or have we?'

I looked at the elegant couple. You had to admire them; they didn't turn a hair.

Eddie's objection had precisely the opposite effect he had intended. 'Dammit, Fulford!' Kink yelled, 'I'm in command here and nobody, especially no parlour pink, is going to tell me what to do! I'm sick and tired of all your talk about the British cornering the oil fields, and the goddam Morgan-Baker-Stillman interests, and Wilson cramming the jails!' He turned back to the Orloffs. 'Count, you're welcome to a compartment in our Pullman car. I make only these conditions: that you take your meals there, keep your shades down, and stay out of sight.' He waved away their thanks. 'Bunny, will you show the Count and Countess to compartment twelve?'

The Orloffs, I noticed, had only two pieces of luggage, the countess' vanity case, and a leather briefcase with a double lock. In it, I was somehow sure, was the fabulous diamond.

While the count was washing up in the lav the countess hung up her mink in the closet and took off her babushka. When she turned around I had to catch my breath. There was a fortune in jewellery around her neck and arms, and in her hair she wore a tiara, in each of whose seven points there was a diamond. She positively glittered with diamonds, emeralds and other precious stones I wasn't lapidary enough to identify.

As I watched she began to take them off.

'Forgive me for saying so, Countess,' I said, 'but wasn't it rather foolish for you to wear your jewels on the trip? And the clothes you travelled in were hardly suitable for a flight from the Bolshies.'

'Oh, we had no chance to change, Captain,' she said. 'It is hard to believe, but the Reds came in the front door of our Kharkov château as we went out the back. We had to leave everything except what we had on and what I could snatch from my jewel box. Fortunately my husband had just returned from the city and the sleigh was in the drive. Otherwise we would never have escaped. As we left the house the Reds began to shoot the servants.'

'You came by sleigh all the way to Debaltsevo?'

She nodded. 'Once a peasant took us in, and another time a village doctor, but the rest of the nights we slept in the sleigh under the fur robes. My husband bought food in the villages. Once he had to shoot a man who would have informed upon us. Our horses dropped from exhaustion just outside the junction. We had to leave them with the sleigh on the road.'

'And you are hungry now?' I asked her.

She sat down weakly on the edge of the bunk. 'We have not eaten for a day and a half. But we do not wish to bother you. The Major has already been so kind.'

'It's no bother,' I said, and brought tea and biscuits. They were the last of the biscuits, I noticed; from now on the food situation was going to be increasingly tight. We had nothing left but Bovril, hardtack and bully beef, and the retreating Dobrievolsky army had already requisitioned whatever food had been available along the railroad. In the light of that Kink had been doubly generous in taking the Orloffs aboard the train.

The count, carrying the briefcase, came back from the lav as I was leaving the compartment. When he saw the tea and biscuits his eyes lit up but the rest of his face remained politely expressionless. I left after accepting his repeated thanks.

For a moment I listened at the compartment door. The Orloffs may have been starving, but they were the Russian nobility, not animals, and they intended to observe the amenities until the end. Slowly, deliberately, they poured the tea, and slowly, deliberately, they munched on the biscuits. They would rather have died than bolted their food down, even before one another.

I wondered if it was upon such shoals of stubborn pride that the Romanovs themselves had foundered.

★

Finally a junction official switched us through, and we came from the siding onto the main tracks and a place among a line of coaches that extended forward and back for miles in both directions. Alongside was another track as closely packed as the one on which we travelled. It was another hell of traffic, worse than that between Debaltsevo and Kupyansk, and we were doomed to suffer it for all the one hundred forty miles from Debaltsevo to Taganrog. We were lucky to make ten miles a day, moving forward a few yards at a time as the train before us moved forward, followed behind by another coach which usually bumped us when we stopped. And sometimes we would even have to move back to let in another train from a siding along the way.

Our engine driver developed a bad case of nerves and began drinking heavily. We could hardly blame the man, but then Kink caught him trying to sneak away with his bundle of belongings, and had to double the guard on engine and tender.

As we came into Makeeva, the train on the track alongside burned out its boiler. With stolid disgust, indifferent to insults and blows alike, the occupants of the train behind it piled out of their coaches and pried the offending engine and coaches off the train with jacks. It took them six hours to do it, and they never once stopped to rest. The passengers of the junked train fought their way into others and the fleeing line crawled on.

The crowded and unsanitary living conditions caused hundreds of new typhus cases daily, and the refugee death rate climbed to fantastic heights. Every station had its rows of frozen, unburied bodies, and mornings at seven we would wake to women's lamentations over a son, a husband, a brother found dead.

There were no doctors except the desperately overworked medical men on an occasional hospital train, and drugs had long been non-existent. If we fared better than the civilians it was only because we had an official RAF medicine chest.

Since all of us were medical illiterates, we drew lots to determine who should be train doctor. I won, or rather lost, the draw.

Kink and I unlocked the big straw pannier with its baffling array of bottles, boxes, little nippers and knives. There were no instructions other than the admonition: 'Keep this chest dry'. Finally I found a gallon tin, labeled powdered quinine, that held no mystery for me.

When Hoskins reported three men sick I gave them a tablespoon of quinine in half a glass of water. The next morning, when I called with the gallon tin, all three were out of bed and playing cards on the top of a packing crate.

Private Simpson eyed the quinine with loathing. 'I'm all right, Sir. That rotten stuff brought me around in a twinkle.'

'You, Beasley?' I asked the man on his right.

'Fine, Sir. Won't be needin' any more of *that*.'

'And how about you, Costigan?'

'Sir, I never felt better in all me life.'

I kept the can of quinine in the bar. When anyone reported sick I gave them a quinine cocktail first and inquired into their symptoms afterward. Cowderdrill got a dose for his chilblains and Clarence, for a runny nose. Both recovered promptly.

But there was one enlisted man for whom the pannier held no cure. He developed pneumonia quickly, and one silent, snowy afternoon outside Gorlovo, he died. We buried him as best we could in the frozen ground with Kink reading the service from the Bible. Behind us, in one of the refugee coach vestibules, a little girl aired her doll as we shoveled dirt over Private Samuel Brown, who next to my own Charley Lamston, had been the best damn Ac Emma in 47 Squadron.

The next morning Russky was absent from the breakfast table. I thought he might be talking to the Orloffs, but the countess told me she hadn't seen him that morning.

When I knocked on his compartment door he called weakly, 'Do not come in. The health is badly.'

I found him shivering with a chill. He had a splitting headache and his pulse beat was rapid; his tongue was coated white. My heart sank. I knew the symptoms all too well: Russky had the *tif*.

Through chattering teeth he said: 'I will be well for Christmas? Bunnuski, you will recover me for Christmas, yes?'

'Hell,' I said, 'Christmas is a week and a half off. I should have you up and around in a jiffy, and if it's anything half-way serious, don't worry – in another two or three days we'll be in Taganrog, and they've got the best hospital south of the Donets River.'

He clutched my hand. 'I have same symptoms as Colly. It is the *tif*, I know. Do not leave me in the hospital. *Pozhaluista*, Bunnuski. I will die there.'

Now was no time to talk sense. 'Stay where you are,' I kidded him. 'I'll get some quinine and blankets.'

He couldn't keep the quinine down. When he begged the boys to take their long faces out of the doorway and let him get some sleep, I motioned them back and shut the door behind me.

'The bug?' Kink asked.

I nodded. 'We ought to get him to Taganrog as soon as possible.'

Kink looked out the window at the snarl of motionless trains and smashed his fist against the wall. We hadn't moved twenty yards since reveille.

'Attend to him, Bunny, will you?' he said in his tight, dangerous voice, and we watched him continue on down the passageway to the enlisted men's cars for his regular morning inspection. Woe to the Tommy who hadn't oiled his rifle or polished his shoes.

★

The approaches to Taganrog were hopelessly blocked with a sea of trains. Two miles out Kink unloaded the Red Cross van and the two of us went into the town to find a doctor for Russky. He was worse; sooner than usual the mulberry rash had broken out over his chest and legs, and most of last night he had been in delirium.

The hospital was a madhouse. The line of stretchered wounded and sick waiting at the receiving ward was three blocks long, and one glance inside the chaotic entrance hall convinced us that there was no possibility of snaring a staff doctor. We took an *izuozchik* on runners to the better part of town, and, on the off chance, cruised around looking for a man with a small black bag leaving one of the houses. Luck was with us; within half an hour we found a doctor, and he was willing to take a look at Russky on the train.

The doctor told us Russky had both typhus and smallpox. His chances were poor unless he was moved immediately to the hospital, bad as conditions there were. Patients at Taganrog would be moved to Rostov when Taganrog was evacuated in the next few weeks, but the doctor wouldn't advise that we take Russky on to Rostov now; the delays en route and the lack of drugs would probably prove fatal. The doctor had a certain amount of influence with the staff doctors at Taganrog hospital and could get Russky a bed in the typhus ward. But we must hurry.

We took Russky into the van on a stretcher and brought him to the hospital. The doctor hadn't exaggerated his influence; orderlies took Russky directly into the typhus ward and put him in a bed near a window. He smiled up at us from his slipless pillow.

'It is all right you bring me to hospital; I know it would be bad for me on train. I will get well, I promise, though not in time for Christmas.'

'I brought along a stack of *Vie Parisiennes*,' I told him. 'They're under the bed.'

'Colly and Major Bingham will be looking in on you,' Kink said. 'You'll have the complete resources of the British Empire at your beck and call.'

Rusky closed his eyes for a moment. 'Kink, I am sorry we did not fly together with the Camels. It would have been much fun.'

Kink's fists were clenched tightly. 'When this war is over we'll fly together, *kunak*, and you can take up a Camel any damn time you please. Now you just hold on.'

'I will hold on, Kink,' he said in a dry whisper. 'You and me and all the boys, we fox 'em.'

A nurse came over with a sedative, and indicated that it was time for us to go.

'*Do svidaniya*, Russky,' we said.

'*Do svidaniya*, Kink, Bunnuski. We fox 'em, you and me.'

Outside the ward Kink said, 'God dammit, I should have let him fly with us at least once. You sod, why didn't you talk me into it?'

As we drove away from the hospital the snow began to come down in thicker flurries. Halfway to the yards Kink got out and took a rag to the windshield. I think he welcomed the opportunity to blow his nose in private. And it gave me a chance to blow mine.

★

Back at the yards there was such a scurrying and commotion that we were sure for a moment that the Bolshies had attacked the town. Hundreds of refugees, impatient of the stalled trains, were taking their valuables off and piling them into carts with starving horses or oxen drooping in the traces. In these carts they planned to ride to Rostov, thirty-seven miles away by rail, in the snow and cold. I saw a grande dame exchange a diamond ring for a cart with a broken axle, and a *chinovnik* in a furlined overcoat gave a gimlet-eyed townsman a suitcase stuffed with rubles for a pram at least fifteen years old.

At B Flight train another group of refugees, put off a string of coaches by some Cossacks who had commandeered it, were besieging Eddie, Bill and Tommy for a place on our boxcars and flats, offering them anything from jewellery to their daughters and wives. At the back of the vestibule crouched Cowderdrill, a butcher knife in his trembling hands.

We pushed through the crowd to the vestibule steps. The hope that Kink's rank and natural authority inspired on dozens of upturned faces was a pitiful thing to see. I found myself looking into the fevered eyes of a typhus-stricken child, and as a snowflake made her blink, I had to turn away.

From the steps Kink made a speech in broken Russian to the effect that B Flight train was the property of the British Air Force and that we were forbidden to take on refugees. 'Nye refuganski poyezd!' he shouted. 'Nye refuganski!'

I hoped none of the more desperate of the crowd had peeked into the Orloff compartment; if they had, they might have torn us to pieces.

But as Kink spoke, the hope faded, the faces crumpled, the people turned away. And then, as if it were a sign from heaven, the train ahead jerked forward. Slowly, painfully, only a yard or two or three, but the train was moving, and so was the train ahead of it, and in a mad dash and scramble the refugees rushed to try and find places in the jam-packed cars.

Kink sighed and shook his head. 'If we move more than twenty yards tonight it'll be a miracle. Boys, let's go inside and get a drink. I'm due at the British Mission, but if I got any more bad news today I think I'd sit down on my fanny and burst into tears.'

Later that afternoon Colly and Major Bingham brought the bad news with them. The Reds had taken Poltava and Novo Nikolaivsk and recaptured Kiev. Kolchak's troops had fought their last battle in Siberia, and revolutionaries were bound to overthrow his government in Irkutsk. Daily, the cities and villages of the Ukraine were falling into the hands of the Reds. The Bolshies were consolidating their gains in the Donets Basin, and it looked as if nothing could stop them from splitting Denikin's forces in two. If that happened the Red Army, outnumbering Denikin's troops by almost nine to one,[5] would be pitted against them at the commander-in-chief's line of defense at Rostov.

Kink made a face. 'And our orders, Sir?' he asked Bingham.

'To establish a base a short distance south of Rostov from which you can operate as soon as the line holds firm. God knows if you'll be able to get any planes into the air in this weather, but we'll hope so. So far we've seen as little Bolshie aircraft as we've seen Bolshie artillery, but if they should get cracking with either one I hesitate to think of the slaughter.'

'Colonel,' Eddie asked. 'Do Denikin and Wrangel finally agree on how to fight this war?'

Bingham smiled his brief but warming smile; this time it was touched with disappointment. 'No, Captain, I'm afraid not. Wrangel thinks the Whites should evacuate Taganrog and Rostov immediately, and retreat to the Crimea, where they'll have good protection. Denikin refuses to desert the Cossacks and lose touch with their surviving fighting organizations. In the Taganrog-Rostov area he hopes to reform his troops and hold the crossing of the Don.'

Kink asked which strategy the colonel thought was the better one.

'Only time will tell, but I'm inclined to go along with Denikin. He's an excellent military man, you know. Anyone who could rise from the ranks as spectacularly as Denikin has must have ability of a rare order. He might not be as brilliant as Wrangel, but he's not as proud and imperious either. Denikin's been blamed for mistakes that aren't his fault at all: lack of discipline among his officers, the breakdown of morale, corruption, brutality and incompetence. I doubt if any other man could have done better, considering the in-consistency of Allied aid and the lack of co-ordination among Russian forces in the field.'

Kink shifted in his chair uneasily. 'Yet, Sir, it looks as if Wrangel was right in thinking the Whites wouldn't be able to hold Taganrog. They'll be evacuating it any day now.'

'I don't deny that,' Bingham said, 'but if you'll permit me a little irony, at least we have Denikin's promise that he won't leave Tagan-rog without taking the Mission staff and archives along.'[6]

We told the colonel and Colly about Russky, and they promised to look in on him as soon as they could. Bingham told us he was sending over what food supplies the Mission could spare – a few dozen cans of bully beef and some hardtack. The unappetizing stuff arrived shortly before dinner.

That evening, around eight o'clock, we heard firing south of us in the yards. 'Must be some Cossacks putting refugees off trains,' Bill said, and settled back comfortably to relight his pipe. The lounge was cozy and warm again; Hoskins, through some miracle, had found a glazier to put in new windows for those that had been broken in our skirmishes with the Greens.

The firing became heavier and closer, and Kink put on his great-coat and went outside. I went along.

A fairly heavy fog had descended upon the train yards, though it had stopped snowing. As we stepped to the ground a bullet hit the coach three feet above Kink's head and ricocheted away. At that moment Hoskins loomed up before us in the fog.

He saluted. 'Major, I hear the Bolshies have timed an infiltration with the approach of some Red cavalry. The cavalry hasn't showed yet, but it looks like the infiltraters have.'

'All right, Flight. Alert the men and order half of them out with rifles; post the rest to guard the train. The captain and I'll do some reconnoitering.'

Unholstering our revolvers, we moved toward the sound of firing, keeping to the cover of the trains and watching out carefully for the spaces in between; from one of these a Bolshie could shoot before we saw him. A few refugees threw open their coach windows to ask startled questions, but by now most of them were used to night attacks, and at the sound of rifle fire they automatically stretched out full-length on the filthy floors.

We had gone about sixty yards down the track when a man emerged suddenly from behind a box car, put a rifle to his shoulder, and sent two shots off to our right. Kink and I dropped to our knees and pulled our triggers almost simultaneously. The man stumbled and pitched forward onto his face.

We went up to the body and turned it over. One of our bullets had passed through his neck. The man was dressed in civilian clothes and wore a red-starred military cap.

Another shot to our left kicked up dirt and snow, and we retreated to the shelter of the train.

The gunfire was concentrated two hundred yards ahead of us,

around the station and behind us, a mile distant at the entrance to the yards, where there was a small Cossack guard. 'Pretty obvious what they're after,' Kink said. 'They're trying to knock out the Cossack *sotnia* guarding the station, and then fan back to wipe out any scattering of opposition from the trains. Soon as they've done that they'll send up a flare and the cavalry on the outskirts of the town will know it's safe to ride in.'

'What if they don't knock out the guard at the station?'

'Good question. Then they'll fall back here in strength, hoping to draw the station Cossacks out after them. Go back to A and B Flights and get all the men, except for a handful to guard the trains with the boys. Send forty to me, and take the rest around the outside tracks to outflank the Bolshies. If it works, we'll catch the bulk of them between us.'

Bully beef had upset my stomach and I didn't particularly like the idea of a special mission in fog that was thickening so badly you couldn't tell friend from foe, but I did as I was told.

Halfway to B Flight train an infiltrator lurched at me from between a cowcatcher and a caboose. I sidestepped and he slipped and fell, and then I lost him in the fog as he scrambled up and away. I sent a few shots in his general direction, but they missed, whining off the side of the train.

Eddie met me at the steps of the lounge, and together we rounded up the men of the flight. After the boredom of the last few days they were anxious for a fight.

The gunfire at the north of the yards slackened as I led the men around the outside tracks toward the station. It looked as though Kink was right; the infiltrators were withdrawing from the station and coming down the yards.

We took positions behind a string of boxcars at a siding and waited for the Reds to come. 'Tell the men to be absolutely quiet,' I told Hoskins. 'And remember, they're not to follow after the Bolshies till I give the word.'

Hoskins nodded and limped down the line to deliver the order. A few minutes later we saw the first of the Bolshies drifting back through the yards. They had, I saw, been well trained; they kept to cover, and they carried their rifles before them, so that they shouldn't knock against obstacles only dimly glimpsed in the fog. From the station the rifle fire was only desultory now.

I counted over a hundred men; beyond them, along other tracks, there must have been a couple of hundred more making their way toward the yard entrance.

When the first pursuing Cossacks filtered through the gloom I gave Hoskins the signal and we rose to follow.

We had barely taken cover behind another string of flats when Kink and his men, stationed at four different points, opened with their first volley. Reloading as fast as we could, my group pumped bullets into the knots of astonished men. Caught in the murderous crossfire, the Bolshies went down in droves, and those who had escaped scrambled for the undersides of the nearest trains.

'Let's get the bastards! Watch their knives!' I yelled, and leapt from cover.

For the next three-quarters of an hour it was a deadly game of hide and seek, of peeking around corners and behind wheels to see if the man lurking in the shadows wore a *shapka*, a garrison cap or the military type hat worn by the Bolshies, and pulling or not pulling your trigger accordingly. Bullets hit the train sides, producing the sound of struck gongs; they smashed the windows of refugee cars and sang and whistled overhead. Rifle flashes lit the yards like sparklers on the fourth of July. The fog was lifting, but it was still the most dangerous kind of close combat.

The *plennys* were fighting along with the rest of us. I saw Feodor blazing away from a box car window, and the huge, bear-like Ivan searching for infiltrators with his rifle held like a club. Something glistened on the end of the polished stock: Bolshevik blood.

The Red cavalry vanguard never entered Taganrog yards.[7] Though many infiltraters had managed to escape, to betray their city another day, we counted next morning over a hundred Bolshie dead. The Cossacks had suffered twenty-odd fatal casualties; B Flight had gotten away with knife wounds and a bullet through the bugler's arm. A Flight had two Tommies dead and a couple of others wounded. It was nonetheless a decisive victory, and we had Kink's strategy to thank for it. Had the Red cavalry been able to come in from the outskirts of the town, the Cossack station guards would have been no match for the combined infiltrators and cavalry, and not many people in the yards, including A and B Flights, would have survived.

Chapter Ten

*

We got out of Taganrog at one o'clock the next afternoon loaded down with the refugees Kink had finally decided to take aboard the train. Colly had gone to see Russky at the hospital that morning, and was due back around noon with a report, but at lunchtime the switchman got us on the east-bound local track, and Kink decided we had better take advantage of it. We pulled out of the yards with a Cossack regimental band playing a tuba-heavy version of 'Rule, Britannia!' in appreciation of the part we had played in last night's little unpleasantness.

The roadbed was only double track, with the express track kept clear for headquarters' trains. Two *broneviks* patrolled the thirty-seven mile stretch twenty-four hours a day. If a refugee train sneaked into the stretch of open track it was confronted by the turreted guns of an armoured train and forced off onto a siding.

The trip to Rostov was another exercise in Jobian patience. The line crept forward, a mile an hour, sometimes only two or three miles in a morning, an afternoon. When we passed a station it was necessary to keep our engine jammed tight against the rear of the train ahead; otherwise refugee coaches, waiting for a box-car length of space to pounce on, would cut into the line. Kink had sympathy for the refugees, but our orders were to get to Rostov as soon as we could.

Seaward, three hundred yards at this point, lay the Azov, cold and bleak and fog-shrouded. The wagon road on the landward side of the tracks was black with refugees, soldiers, and mounted Cossacks on patrol. The civilians and military travelled in carts, sleighs, on horse and on foot. Both were typhus-ridden, and bodies, some stripped of their outer clothing, dotted the landscape.

'Strewth,' Bill said, 'this is a race precious few of those poor sods are going to win.'

'We might not get through ourselves, you know,' said Eddie. 'We're in a bottleneck, and something's bound to get left as dregs.'

'Never thought of that,' said Tommy.

'It's that monolithic British chauvinism of yours,' Eddie chided him. 'You just can't admit you can be worsted by anybody on earth.'

'Don't call me an Englishman,' Tommy said coldly. 'I'm a Scot. And I don't know what chauvinism means, but it sounds like an insult. Take it back.'

'Suppose we compromise and I take back 'monolithic' instead?' Eddie said innocently 'Will that do?'

Tommy hesitated. 'I guess so.'

Later in the day we stopped at one of the many way stations to take on water, and a few seconds afterward Kink slammed into the lounge. 'Everybody out with buckets, pans and tins. The water tank's frozen solid and we've got to get the tender filled with snow. Bill and Tommy, rout out the refugees and the Tommies. You too, Cowderdrill. Nobody's excused but the Orloffs.'

Everybody capable of standing on their feet turned to, except for the count and countess. But there was one unapproved exception: an arrogant baron from Slavyansk who had appropriated a corner of one of the freights and rode with a cologne-soaked handkerchief pressed to his very long nose.

When we hauled him out trackside he began a speech in Russian to the effect that manual labour was demeaning and that his family hadn't soiled its hands with work in five hundred years.

'The Rewalution comes, you vork,' Kink mocked him. He motioned over a couple of enlisted men. 'Roll this cove in the snow till he gets the spirit of co-operation.'

With the refugees looking on blankly, the Tommies rolled the baron in the snow. He got to his feet screaming and spitting with rage.

'Roll him a bit more,' Kink said.

They rolled him till he arose groggy and gasping. Floundering dazedly, he started for another train.

'Head him off!' Kink shouted. When the baron was brought before him again, Kink said he wasn't getting off that easily. It was either work or get rolled. The baron finally gave in.

A bucket of snow melts into only a few cupfuls of water, and it took us half a day of dumping snow into the tender to raise enough steam to get under way.

In one way I was glad that we moved so slowly. It gave me a chance to look for Nina's train among the many hospital vans sidetracked by burned out boilers and frozen points. Though the stationmaster at Taganrog hadn't remembered Nina's train, I was sure Alexandrovsky had passed through Taganrog toward Rostov before we had.

On our third day out the staff cars began passing on the open track. Drawn-faced officers stood looking dully out of the windows of the coaches clicking by at express train speed. Obviously Taganrog was being evacuated. One string of trains had a palatial dining car in which an orchestra and jugglers entertained a fat general with white, close-cropped hair. In cinema dramas to come of the Civil War, I thought, such a scene would undoubtedly figure.

'Look at that,' Kink said disgustedly. 'There's one reason why we're losing the goddam war.'

'If Russky was here,' Eddie said, 'he'd remind us that Denikin's wife has only one dress made from the lining of her husband's dress uniform, and that the Wrangels don't have a penny to their name.'

Kink chewed on his lip moodily. 'Denikin's clearing out of Taganrog sooner than I thought. And when he goes the Mission will be going with him. I hope Russky's being taken care of.'

'Colly will see to it that he gets to Rostov hospital,' I told him. 'Don't worry.'

'On the contrary,' Kink said. 'I've got to keep worrying. Not only about Russky but about every goddam refugee we've got on this train, even the Baron. If I quit, I might stop being human.' He closed his eyes for a moment. 'Alenka, that little black-eyed girl in freight sixteen, she died last night. When I went in there she was still holding onto that pitiful doll. And what's-his-name, that unpronounceable lawyer from Gorlovo – not one of his family's going to last the trip. If we only had some quinine left!'

'We're feeding them, Kink,' Eddie reminded him. 'What more can we do?'

Kink looked at him. 'Eddie, I wish I knew.'

Hospital expresses and staff trains from Taganrog continued to flash by at intervals through the night and into the next day. Aboard one of them were undoubtedly Holman, Bingham, Colly, and other officers of the British Mission.[1] General Maund's train, improbably, came last. It passed us while we had stopped again to snow the engine, and though Maund's engineer was making faster time than had any of the others, the brigadier rose a few notches in our estimation for bringing up the rear. After Maund had passed the patrolling *broneviks* allowed the express track to be put into use, though there was still so much rolling stock that it seemed to make no difference in the general rate of progress.

And then, all of a sudden, it was Christmas Eve.[2]

Kink introduced the intimately related subjects of Clarence and our Christmas dinner.

'I don't like to bring this up,' he said, 'but Clarence isn't a piglet any more, and if we have bully beef and hardtack for tomorrow's dinner I'm going to be utterly depressed.'

Tommy, who was fond of the pig, looked distressed. In the pantry we could hear Cowderdrill agitatedly slamming doors.

'I agree with Kink,' I said. 'We can't keep Clarence forever, and he's better off in our stomachs than in the Bolshies'.' I was very hungry, and there were refugee children who were hungrier than I.

'Strewth,' Bill protested, 'eating that pig would be an act of cannibalism. Why he's practically a human being.'

'I say an end to this sentimentalism,' Eddie said. 'Clarence isn't a human being but a hog, and hogs are meant to be ate.'

'In these brutal times,' Bill went on with an air of injured dignity, 'we have a goddam obligation to observe the goddam finer sentiments. I know Russky would have been against turning Clarence into a loin of pork. If we put him to the knife we'll only be lowering ourselves to the level of the Bolshies.'

'We'll take a referendum on it,' Kink said. 'Since Cowderdrill's taken care of the animal, it's only fair to give him a double vote. Sergeant!' he yelled.

The messman stumbled into the lounge, his face as grey as one of his ill-laundered napkins. Clarence waddled after him. 'Yes, Sir, you called, Sir? Rum toddies? A spot of Bovril?'

'Don't pretend,' Kink told him. 'You heard every word. Now what's your vote on Clarence?'

Cowderdrill swallowed. 'Well, Sir, you put me in a hard spot there.'

'Your two votes, Sergeant,' Kink said grimly.

The mess sergeant scratched his head. 'Well, Sir, I'm attached to the creature, and I keep remembering when you picked him up in Tsaritsyn and he wasn't no bigger than a quart of Gordon's. I'd miss his company, but when I see refugee children coming round with their hands out and their eyes like saucers, it breaks my heart. And a pig is a pig, and the way things is going, he ain't never going to get any fatter than he is right now.' He paused. 'There's only one thing, Sir.'

Kink waited.

'I couldn't bear to slaughter him myself, Sir. Could Ivan do the job?'

Kink looked away from Clarence who was rooting at his boots and grunting affectionately. 'All right, Sergeant. Call Ivan now. Let's get it over with.'

Christmas dinner was hardly a gala affair. None of us had much appetite for loin of Clarence, and Bill and Tommy couldn't eat it at all. While Cowderdrill distributed the cooked ham, sides and butt to the refugees and *plennys* at the kitchen door, we concentrated on the rum and reminisced about other, better Christmas dinners at home.

'My mother made a fine haggis,' Tommy said. 'I used to eat myself sick. And the good Scotch whisky! We had gallons of it – Uncle John was in the spirits business.'

'Dad never allowed liquor at home,' I told them, 'but mother's Christmas dinners were wonderful. A twenty-five pound turkey, five kinds of potatoes; mince, apple and pumpkin pie.'

'We'd have a set of beef ribs it took two farmhands to carry in the kitchen door,' Kink said, 'and roast new potatoes the size of big peas, and a Yorkshire pudding that would melt in your mouth.'

'Please, boys,' Bill implored us, 'My old lady wasn't so bad a cook herself.'

'It was a stuffed goose on the Fulford's groaning board,' said Eddie, 'and when we'd picked one clean my mother would bring in another.'

Tommy pushed roast pork around on his plate. 'I wonder what they're feeding Russky at the hospital. Bones-of-chicken broth, if he's lucky. And Kitty's probably having the last of the hardtack we gave her.'

Nina, I thought for the tenth time that day; what was Nina having for her Christmas dinner? Was she having anything at all? And where was she having it? Five, ten miles down the track, on some siding quiet with the terrible stillness of typhus and death? Was she at Rostov hospital? Or had Alexandrovsky's train crossed Rostov Bridge on its way to Ekat?

I looked out the window to see if the coaches on the express track were moving.

'Come on, Bunny,' Kink said. 'Quit that woolgathering and join us in a toast.'

'I didn't know there was anything to drink to.'

Kink grinned sardonically, arching his Mephistophelian brows. 'To Christmas in Moscow, Captain. The toast that Napoleon's Generals drank in Vilna. The toast we drank with Wrangel and Restigiev at Tsaritsyn.'

We rose and extended our toddy mugs.

'Gentlemen!' Kink shouted, 'To Christmas in Moscow!'

We had drunk the toast to its bitter dregs when we turned to see Hoskins standing in the doorway.

'Don't like to disturb you, Sir,' he said to Kink, 'but there's trouble at the engine.'

'What trouble, Flight?' Kirk said wearily.

'The engineer and the fireman tried to escape, Sir. The guards had to club them about a little till they settled down. Now they won't run the engine.'

Kink sat down. He didn't seem terribly concerned. 'Chain them to their places, Hoskins. Tell them they won't get fed until they realize their responsibilities to General Denikin, General Wrangel and His Majesty the King.'

'Right, Sir. Then can I relieve the engine guards for their Christmas dinner?'

'Yes, Flight. Merry Christmas!'

'Merry Christmas, Major. Merry Christmas, Captain Aten, Captain Daly, Captain Fulford, Captain Burns Thomson.'

Tommy and Bill wished Hoskins a Merry Christmas in return, but Eddie and I only nodded. We were fed up with the words and the hollow sound of them and we didn't have the heart.

★

The following night, at a station about twelve miles from Rostov, we unexpectedly drew alongside General Maund's train. Maund's boiler had burned out and his engine, tender and five coaches were blocking the line. The brigadier dropped over a few minutes later, pushing his way through a crowd of apathetic refugees who, used to such delays, merely had an academic interest in determining what or who had caused the latest inconvenience.

Maund explained that his train had been the last to leave Taganrog. Denikin and Russian headquarters, panicking at the approach of the

Bolsheviks, had abandoned the town without a word of warning to the British Mission. Holman, Bingham and Colly had already left for Rostov with half of the staff, but there were over a hundred men left and the bulk of the archives were still sitting on the station platform.[3] Wrangel, returning from the front, had learned of Maund's situation and sent a train from Rostov. It had been one of his last official acts before relinquishing command of the defeated Dobrievolsky Army.

Maund was pale and his face was deeply lined; some of the patent leather shine had gone out of his carefully groomed hair. He declined a drink and sat back with one hand shading his eyes.

'I've got a suggestion, Sir,' Kink said. 'I can drop part of my train and pick up yours.'

Maund shook his head. 'No, Major. I'll wire General Holman to try and send another engine. I wouldn't think of putting you out.'

'Then we'll stand by till your new engine arrives,' Kink told him. 'It seems the *broneviks* have stopped patrolling, and we have no idea of what might be coming down that track.'

'I won't have it,' Maund said definitely. 'Push along while you have the chance. In any case, I wouldn't leave here till I saw you safely away.' He smiled faintly. 'One of us has to make Rostov Bridge before the Bolshies.'

After the general had left Bill said, 'We misjudged old Maund, you know? A man can change. A losing war sometimes brings out the best in him.'

Twenty minutes later Maund's train pulled out with a swish of airbrakes, and we rushed to the windows to see what was going on.

'I'll be damned,' Eddie said. 'He got an engine. Now where in this God-forsaken hole would be find an engine? He might be a great soul, and all that, but he's certainly no miracle man.'

The corporal of the engine guard, Lewis gun on his shoulder, stepped into the lounge. 'Sir,' he blurted, 'the General took our locomotive and crew.'

'What?' Kink said, amazed.

''e said it was all right and 'e put 'is guard on in our place. It was a General talkin', Sir. I 'ad to obey 'im.'

'Are you sure it was General Maund, Mallows?'

'The General 'imself, Sir, and nobody with 'im but two 'eadquarters sentries, 'e even took the *paruski* train crew, Sir. 'e said they might come in 'andy.'

'All right, Corporal,' Kink said calmly, 'dismiss the engine guard. We don't have much use for it.'

Kink rested his forehead against the cold marble of the fireplace mantel. His fingers gripped his Woodbine so tightly that it broke in half. Straightening with a quick movement, he flung the broken gasper into the fireplace and laughed.

'Tommy,' he said, 'Go out and find some refugee girls that are typhus-free and who can dance. Tonight we're going to have a real *prazdnik*. It damn well might be our last.'

★

Our engineless state, so far as I was concerned, was not without its advantages; it gave me a chance to look for Nina. When I woke Kink at dawn and asked his permission for a half day's leave, he gave me his reluctant consent. 'But remember,' he told me, 'If we can find an engine before noon we're going on without you. And to save my neck I won't hesitate for a minute to report you dead. You know what that means in the RAF – you'll have a hell of a time proving you're alive.' He scowled, pulled the covers over his head, and turned over.

I would have taken the Red Cross van, except that the wagon road was too rutted and icy for the worn tires. I decided to go on foot, a more rapid method of transit than hitching a ride on one of the slow-moving trains on the local track.

A mile or so out I came across one of the many saddled but riderless horses we had been seeing from the train since leaving Taganrog. Vaulting into the saddle I noticed that the horn was caked with blood. Why one of the fleeing refugees hadn't appropriated the emaciated bay I didn't know; perhaps it was because a horse had to be fed, and if they had any food at all, the refugees had to save it for themselves.

The misery I had seen aboard the trains, heart-rending though it was, was nothing compared to that of the road. Singly and together, scores of refugees lay dying and dead from cold, starvation, typhus, smallpox or all of them combined. I passed a mother with two children huddled up against her, like animals, for the last warmth she could give; some passerby, taking pity, had tossed an Oriental rug over them and then gone on his way. A demented woman sat on the roadside counting and recounting her fingers. The weather had turned more sharply cold, and adults and children walked alongside or rode on the rough carts, the ancient buggies, the rusted sleighs, with frostbitten feet and fingers.

From none of them was there any sound of agony or complaint. It was as if they were conserving their energy for what still lay before them, or as though they had learned the futility of any reproach to man or God.

The next station, three or four miles away, was jammed with holed up trains. Refugees milled around the platforms, but at the top of every flight of steps stood men who were kicking out at the people trying to get on. They shouted at them, '*Zaniato! Zaniato!*'

The station house was crowded with refugees jostling for a place around the pot-bellied stove. A knot of people surrounded me, asking for news or information.

'*Nyet novy.*' I told them in my pidgin-Russian, and in English, for good measure, 'I have no news.'

A plump woman in a man's *shuba*, her face marked with the first lesions of smallpox, began to cry.

'*Prostite,*' I said, '*Prostite,*' and backed the bay away toward the siding. At its end there was parked a Red Cross train.

A middle-aged man followed me for a way, shouting violently and waving his arms. I imagined he was reproaching me for having the insolence to be sorry that I had no news, not even bad news, when people were dying like flies and God knew how close the Bolsheviks were to Rostov.

I rode up the siding to the hospital train. A shell had struck the side of the headquarters car, obliterating its number. The train looked familiar, and my heart gave a lurch. I tethered the horse to a tree branch, and swung up the steps.

There was nobody in the first car but those the *tif* had struck down: soldiers, frozen stiff, piled willy-nilly upon one another on the wooden bunks. They were part of a regiment of cadets, none of them older than twenty. Putting my handkerchief to my nose, I hurried through the car and into the next.

It was the same, as was the next, except that in the third car lay the wounded for whom the *tif* had been only a final complication. Panic-stricken now and unthinking, dreading that I would find Nina dead in the next car, I threw open the connecting door and stumbled through it.

It was the nurses' quarters, and four nurses lay dead on the bunks and on the floor. Like the girls of hospital train 242 they wore black Red Cross habits with red brassards and black kerchiefs, but they weren't Nina, Olga, Sonia and Claudia, and this wasn't hospital train 242.

I left the car.

A young man in an expensive *polushubok* was busy untethering my horse from the branch.

'*Von! Von!*' I shouted, and ran towards him, unholstering my revolver.

He dropped the bridle and sprinted away down the siding, glancing back over his shoulder frantically for the bullet he was sure was coming after him.

I returned the Smith & Wesson to its holster and took the bay back to the road. It was almost nine-thirty; I had to get a move on.

It took me an hour to get to the next station on the line. Midway I ran into a sotnia of Cossacks, dragging their typhus victims behind them in carts. They hogged the road, and when I tried to pass, three of them unsheathed their sabres and shouted at me to get back.

Their eyes glittered with fever, and I knew they were in no mood to be crossed. I fell back.

The next station was larger than the last, and its sidings and passing tracks were black with trains. I sought out the harassed stationmaster and asked him if he had seen Alexandrovsky's vans.

He took me into his office and consulted his scrawled work sheet. Then, loosing a torrent of Russian, he pointed east, toward Rostov. He had definitely mentioned hospital train 242.

Not bothering to wipe his spittle from my cheek, I took him by the lapels. 'Do you mean the Red Cross train was here, but it left yesterday?'

'The day before yesterday,' he told me.

I asked him how far it was to the next stop, and he said it was three miles.

'*Spasibo*,' I said, and gave him twenty rubles. He glanced around furtively for the military guard, and stuffed the notes in his pocket as I went out the door.

The bay pulled up lame half a mile down the road. I left him in the hands of a local peasant, and continued the rest of the way on foot. The plodding refugees thought I was a madman for hurrying so fast. *Zamedlite!* Slow!' they shouted at me, and one wit yelled that the speed limit was forty kilometers an hour; I would be arrested by the Cossacks for going too fast.

I hardly heard them. Head down I ploughed forward through the slush, and if someone got in my way – man or woman – I pushed him aside. I was unconscious of the effort involved until I reached the station. There, exhausted, I collapsed on the side of the road.

After a while I got up and went toward the siding. I doubted that Nina's train was here; in two days time her train should have been able to cover more than three miles, even in this molasses of rolling stock. Still, it was possible the engine had been stolen or commandeered or that the boiler had burned out from lack of water.

I cursed myself for my selfishness. How could I wish that Nina hadn't reached Rostov and crossed the bridge? To be stuck somewhere in the eight or ten mile stretch between here and the bridge might mean the difference between survival and a Bolshie bullet.

I went down the siding, looking at the numbers on the hospital vans. There were two trains, one behind the other. The boiler of the first was burned out; that meant that the same was true of the second train, otherwise it would have been ahead on the siding.

A big man in a rumpled major's uniform passed me, and then turned around. 'Captain, *pozhaluista*, it is you?'

It was Alexandrovsky, but so thin and haggard I hadn't recognized him. I gripped his hand. For a moment I couldn't speak.

He saw my heart in my eyes. 'I know after whom you have come,' he said, 'so I will not waste the time in conversation. Captain, *kak zhal*, Nina is ill. She is very ill.'

I looked at him.

'Five days ago she was struck in the shoulder by a sniper. The bullet was a dum dum; it shattered the shoulder bone and made a terrible wound.'

He reached out and steadied me with his hand under my arm. I couldn't bear to ask it, but I had to. 'Major, will she live?'

'If the tetanus does not set in, she might recover, Captain. But we had for her only one dose of serum, and even if we had more I could not make to you the absolute promise.'

I asked him if I could see her now.

'Certainly, though I would prefer that you do not stay too long: she should not have too much excitement.'

He led me to the nurses' quarters. Entering the car it was as if I had dreamed the hospital train of earlier this morning in preparation for this, the reality. It was the same car, with the same furnishings, the same pearly light of a clouded winter day coming in through the curtained windows, the same odor of stale camomile. Only two things were different: the ikon on the wall was of the crucifixion, not the resurrection, and only one of the four bunks was occupied.

In that bunk lay Nina.

I fought to disbelieve it, to stay in the borderline of ambiguity between a future I had prefigured and a present that I could not accept. Alexandrovsky coughed in the doorway and then closed the door behind him.

I had no choice but to accept.

The blanket was pulled up to her armpits. She wore a grey hospital robe under which I could see the bloodstained bandage. Her head was turned away from me, her long hair spread out on the pillow.

I went over to her and knelt by the side of the bunk. She turned her head and opened her eyes and smiled. In the pallor of her face they were enormous and bright.

'Zdravstvuite, Ninusha,' I said, and kissed her on the forehead. It was warm and slightly flushed; she was running a low fever.

'Zdravstvuite, Sasha,' she said, in a voice that was half-whisper but not weak, not the voice of a dying girl, and I was suddenly drunk with hope.'

'I knew you would come,' she said. 'It was a very strong feeling.'

'I would have come looking for you before, Ninusha, if I'd been able to get away.'

'You have lost weight,' she said. 'You are thinner.'

'Don't talk about me. We haven't the time; the Major says I mustn't stay too long. Listen to me now. The boiler of your train's burned out and there's no way for the hospital train to get to Rostov. In a very short time, perhaps tonight, perhaps tomorrow, I'll come by and take you off. I'm sure Alexandrovsky won't mind.'

I had forgotten that we had no engine; yet, had someone reminded me of the fact, I would have told them, with perfect certainty, that we would get one.

'No, he will not mind if you take me. That would be very nice, Sasha. We would be together for a while.' She stiffened in a sudden spasm of pain. 'But I would not want to be a burden.'

'Stop your *kavardak*, Ninusha. We'll be together for more than just a while. It's almost two hundred miles to the hospital in Ekat, once we've crossed the bridge, and you can imagine how long that's going to take with conditions on the railroads as bad as they are just now.'

She smiled. 'Yes, they are very bad. I know your impatience, Sasha. Have you been very bored?'

'No. I had you to think of.'

She closed her eyes. 'I am glad, Sasha.'

Alexandrovsky knocked lightly.

I leaned forward and kissed her on the lips. 'I must go now.'

Lifting her good arm she reached up and brushed the back of her hand against my cheek. She was crying. 'Sasha, say you will take me to California and that we will live on the ranch with your dog and all the animals, even though it is not true. Say we will be together and again lovers, even though you lie. Lie to me, Sasha, so that I may have some hope. *Pozhaluista*, my beloved, please.'

I wiped her tears. Somehow I managed to keep my voice flat and level. 'It would be no lie if I told you that, Ninusha. Trust me. I'll come for you soon, and we'll spend New Year's Eve together. That I promise.'

I went to the door and opened it and closed it behind me without looking back. Alexandrovsky was waiting in the passageway. 'Captain,' he said, 'there is a patrolling *bronevik* on the express track heading east in a few minutes. They will take you back,'

I thanked him and asked if I could take Nina off the hospital train when we came past the station. He nodded. 'If you can get her to a hospital sooner than I can, I have no objection. If it is later a case of tetanus we would be equally helpless.'

I tried to put my mind on something else. 'And Olga and the other nurses, they are well?'

'They are well except for Claudia, who has the smallpox.' He looked at his watch and told me the armoured train was about to leave.

A platform guard pulled me aboard as the *bronevik* was pulling out of the station. He pointed the way toward the headquarters' car, and I entered it to find a major and his adjutant sitting at a table. They spoke very little English, but I managed to piece out the latest bad news: Lihaya, seventy-five miles from Rostov, had fallen, and the Reds were advancing on Alex-Grush and Novocherkaask with very little to stop them. When they took Novocherkaask the Bolshies would be able to flank Rostov from the north and east, and cut off the southbound line to Ekat.

'*Ochen plokho*, very bad,' they said, and went on to tell me of the latest difficulties between Denikin and Wrangel. Wrangel recently had gone to Ekaterinodar to raise troops among the Kuban and the Terek Cossacks. Arriving there he was furious to discover that Denikin had dispatched General Shkura on the same mission. Among Shkura's staff were two Intelligence Department agents sent by Romanovsky to inform headquarters of Wrangel's actions and movements. To add injury to insult, these agents had spent their time in Ekat fomenting rumours that Wrangel planned a *coup d'état* to re-establish the monarchy.

Wrangel had arrived in Rostov planning on a showdown with the commander-in-chief.[4] There he had delivered his report to Denikin, refused command of the Kuban troops and stated his opinion that Novorossiisk should be fortified immediately. Denikin had disagreed, saying that to fortify the city would be to admit the possibility of disaster and would result in hopeless panic. At that point, holding out his hand, Denikin had signified that the interview was over. Wrangel had saluted, ignoring his outstretched hand, and left the room. But later in the day, having changed his mind, the commander-in-chief had given Wrangel the job of turning Novorossiisk into an armed camp.

'*Ochen plokho*,' the major said, and shook his head.

The *bronevik* had been going along at a steady clip, and looking out the slit I saw we were approaching our station. It occurred to me that the major seemed to have no definite orders, and if such were the case, he might be able to tow us into Rostov. It could be managed easily enough if we left some of our freights behind, bitter news as that would be to the refugees.

I put the question to the major, and he agreed. He would, in fact, be delighted to pick us up tomorrow morning on the return leg of his Rostov-Taganrog patrol. I was feeling halfway alive again when I swung off the train and took the news of our deliverance to Kink and the boys.

★

The *bronevik* didn't show the next morning, or even that afternoon. There was only the endless drag of refugee trains past the siding, and at twilight Kink, worn out by his vigil, called it a day, and asked Cowderdrill for a double toddy.

'They probably got ate up by some Red tanks outside of Taganrog,' he said. 'Or Makhno's torn up the tracks. We're right back where we started.'

'I can feel the Bolshies' horrid breath on the back of my neck,' said Eddie.

I couldn't afford to believe the armoured train wasn't coming. 'How do we know what happened?' I said. 'Maybe they stopped off for a *prazdnik* with some live-for-the-day *baryshnias*. Or maybe they discovered a vodka warehouse along the way. Anyway, we're forgetting the chance that Maund might send back the engine.'

Eddie's disgusted look showed me what he thought of that possibility. He took a long swallow of toddy. 'I'm thinking the *bronevik* deserted to the Reds.'

Bill glanced out the window. 'Do you know what these bastards are doing? They've switched the points behind us and they're moving off the trains without even bothering to shunt us to another siding!'

Kink closed his eyes and leaned back in his chair. 'I find it hard to summon up any indignation. Though such an attitude hardly befits a leader of men, I just don't give a ruddy damn.'

Tommy came in from the Pullman car with a cheering bit of information. The Orloffs had quietly quit the train for a more reliable means of transportation. They had left a note on one of their neatly made up bunks thanking us for our hospitality and wishing us the best of luck.

'Don't say it,' Eddie said, anticipating the thought in all our minds. 'I'll say it for you: like rats deserting a sinking ship. Not that you can blame them. I've noticed that about the aristocrats; they're much more adaptable in the face of disaster than the lower orders. The Orloffs and their kind will be surviving grandly when we bourgeois are six feet underground.'

'They might have said *do svidaniya*,' Bill said a little ruefully. 'Them and their damn diamond.'

'I think it showed good taste that they didn't,' Kink said. 'They realized how much it would have depressed us.' He glanced up at Cowderdrill, who was standing there with a woebegone expression on his extraordinary face. 'What's the matter, Sergeant? Feeling fretful about the Bolshies?'

'Sir, I was rather hoping that if something happened to the Orloffs, not that I wished it, Sir, you understand; but if something *did* happen to them, why, we would have inherited the diamond. As spoils of war.' He sighed. 'That's why I'm sorry they left us, Sir.'

'I suppose you've already spent your share of it on those Riviera trollops that keep tripping through your imagination?' Kink asked, not benignly.

Cowderdrill blushed. 'Well, Sir, as a matter of fact, I did think a little of what I could do with my share. It rather took my mind off the Bolshies.'

Kink closed his eyes again. 'Well, I'm afraid you'll have to depend on the fortune you'll make from the samovars. Of course that should be more than sufficient. As it is, I can see you losing a thousand pounds at Monte Carlo without a quiver.'

The messman brightened. 'Now that you mention it, Sir, I believe you're right. You've made me feel much better, Sir. I'm grateful.'

'Don't mention it,' Kink said. 'Just repay me by showing a little imagination with that hardtack and bully beef we're going to have tonight for dinner. How about braising the bully, Sergeant? Have we had it braised yet?'

'Well, Sir, you can't braise bully beef. You see, Sir, braising is for them meats that ain't tender enough for roasting or broiling. Now as bully beef's just corned beef, you can't – '

'As you were, Sergeant,' Kink said wearily. 'I was just pulling your leg, but every time I do, it comes off in my hand. You may serve dinner.'

But we didn't have dinner till considerably later that evening. As Cowderdrill stumbled off toward the kitchen the guard knocked and came in to tell us that the *bronevik* was outside on the main track and ready for us to hitch on.

Chapter Eleven

*

The *bronevik* major gave us thirty minutes to detach six freights and couple B Flight train onto his terminal car. Mutely, the dispossessed refugees piled out with their belongings and mutely they transformed to other cars in the line behind us. With one exception, they expressed neither gratitude for past favours nor blame for present inconvenience. Only the baron from Slavyansk was on hand to object as we pulled out of the station; he stood in the middle of the track, shaking his fist and hurling maledictions at the perfidious *angliski*.

The major offered no explanation for the delay, but he had no need to; we saw several good-looking refugee girls, scantily clad for the cold weather, peering from the windows of the Pullman section.

When we came to Nina's station Eddie helped me carry the stretcher into Alexandrovsky's train. Kink came along to say hello – and good-bye – to Olga.

The doctor met us in the vestibule, looking at least no grimmer than he had on our last meeting, and I took that as a good omen: Nina must be improved.

That wasn't exactly true, he told me. She was no better, but at least she was no worse, and holding her own.

'You have sterile gauze?' he asked me.

'Yes, and cotton-wool.'

'Good. In a day or two put on a pressure dressing and change the dressings regularly thereafter. Avoid too much iodine and such; nature heals a wound best. If an abscess develops, open the wound and drain it; Nina Dmitrievna will direct you. And morphia, are you well supplied with that?'

I nodded, and asked him how I would recognize the signs of tetanus.

'They are very obvious, Captain. A stiffness in the back of the neck or in the muscles of the jaw and face. There is difficulty in opening the mouth and its corners are drawn downward and back; they become fixed in that position. The muscular contractions are very painful, and that is when you might need the morphia. Let us hope you do not.'

I shook his hand. ' 'Doctor, I'm very grateful. Look, there's still some room on our train. I know Kink wouldn't mind. Why don't you and the nurses– '

'My boy, the commanding officer of a hospital train is like the captain of a ship. There is no deserting it… Go now to your Nina. I will send in some orderlies to help.'

Nina was asleep, and so peacefully that I hated to wake her, but when Eddie and I closed the door behind us she woke with a happy little cry.

'Hush,' I said, 'save your strength. This is going to hurt a little.'

'I do not care. *Zdravstvuite*, Eddie.'

'Hello, yourself,' Eddie said. 'You're looking lovely.'

She smiled. 'I am looking terrible.'

'Please,' I told her. 'You mustn't talk.'

The orderlies came in then, and together we lifted her from the bunk to the stretcher. Hurting her badly was unavoidable, and twice she gasped with the pain and her face turned white. When she was on the stretcher I checked the gauze, but there was no sign of haemorrhage.

The *bronevik* blew its whistle as we came out to the platform. Olga and Sonia were there to say their farewells. Kink, I noticed, looked very uncomfortable.

The girls kissed Nina on both cheeks and then did the same with us. Both were weeping.

'Hey, this isn't a Chekhov play,' I tried to say gaily. 'We'll all meet in Ekat or Novorossiisk for a first class *prazdnik*. By that time she'll be bouncing around.'

'Of course,' Olga said. 'We must act like the grown-ups.'

Kink licked his lips. 'It's time to go, Bunny.'

Alexandrovsky came out and kissed Nina good-bye, and then we carried her to B Flight train. As we turned into the Pullman the *bronevik* started off. Kink waved to the doctor and the girls from the window.

He took off his garrison cap and wiped his brow. 'Whew! That was worse than the retreat from Moscow!'

Nina smiled faintly. 'It is all right, Kink. Olga is over you now. It was not so bad for her as you think.'

I didn't want her to get started talking and motioned to Kink not to reply. What she needed most was sleep.

Nina bled a little when we transferred her from stretcher to bunk, but examining the bandages herself, she told me it wasn't serious. Diffidently she asked if I could change the bandage in another hour or two. I pulled down the shade. 'Ninusha, let's get something straight – you're no bother. Now I'm going to bring you some Bovril, and then I want you to get some sleep. After that Feodor and I will change the bandage. You're going to be a good girl now, and listen very closely to papa.'

When I brought in the broth she had fallen asleep, and I tiptoed out again. Back in the lounge the boys were looking out the windows at the mouth of the icebound Don. It wasn't the same river we had seen only a short time ago, passing through Rostov to Taganrog and the front; then the Don, though flowing fairly swiftly, had been quiet, serene. Now, in a way I had never seen before, the ice, as though whipped from below by a gigantic eggbeater, was frozen into hillocks and ridges, some of them two feet high.

Bill shivered. 'Strewth, I wouldn't want to cross that ice with the Reds shooting at my tail. You'd slip and break your neck crossing the first mountain range to the second.'

'It's smoother and flatter near the bridge,' Kink said. 'This is where the river runs into the sea.'

By nightfall we were only half a mile out of Rostov, though the congestion ahead on both express and local tracks was so bad that it looked as though we would have to spend the night where we were sitting.

It had begun to snow again, and as though the first flakes of the new fall were a signal, a rattle of rifle fire broke out down the tracks around the refugee trains that were behind us and on the exposed right-hand line. There were shouts and screams; caught by surprise, some refugees had been shot at the windows.

The armoured train, on the express track, was blocked off from replying directly to the rifle fire by a refugee train on the local, but it nonetheless swung into action immediately, and began lobbing over incendiaries and four-inch shells. B Flight train shook from the recoil of its turreted guns.

'Lights out and rifle stations,' Kink said. 'That refugee train blocking us out is going to pull ahead.'

He was right, and in the next minutes the refugee coach on the local track moved forward, leaving us open to the Red attack.

Like the Green Guards the Red Cavalry used Verys, and as we waited with fingers on trigger guards, the night became brilliant with red and yellow and green flares. Three hundred yards over the level snowscape we could see two big tanks and about five hundred horsemen deploying in loose, irregular lines. By now what Cossack patrollers and refugees there had been on the wagon road had crossed the tracks to take shelter behind the trains on the express line. Red bullets had dropped a dozen of them.

As the tanks began to throw their shells the horsemen moved in fifty yards closer at a slow trot and recommenced their fire. It was concentrated on the refugee trains, and I wondered what possible motive the Reds could have for this slaughter of the innocent; certainly by now the lack of retaliatory fire from the refugee trains had told the Reds that they contained no soldiers. A tank shell hit a refugee coach fifteen or twenty cars down, and the cries and screams of the wounded carried clearly through the crisp, clear air.

Our Lewis guns were taking a heavy toll of the cavalry and a direct hit by one of the armoured train's shells put a Red tank out of commission. The Reds drew back out of range, and I got up from my place at one of the lounge windows and went into the Pullman section to see Nina.

In the darkness I took her hand. 'It's a Red attack,' I told her. 'We've beaten them off for the moment.'

'I am not afraid. We had many such raids coming down from Orel, from the Green Guards and Bolsheviks both. The Bolsheviks were the worst; they would shoot at the white of the men's bandages. Then, when an armoured train came up, they would run away.'

'They get bolder with success. Do you feel all right? How's the pain?'

'I am not too badly, Sasha. Feodor has been giving me aspirin.'

'Good.' I kissed her on the forehead and tugged the blankets up to her chin. 'Keep warm, Ninusha. I'll be back *skoro budet*.'

I had just picked up my Lee-Enfield again when the cavalry attacked for the second time, coming within two hundred yards of the tracks. The *bronevik* and Lewis fire was devastatingly accurate, and the Reds fell back again, without being able to carry off their wounded. The other tank sat on the lip of a snowbank, motionless and smoking.

Kink put his hand on my shoulder. 'Bunny, see if the men are *khorosho*, will you? That Red lead might have done some damage. And watch out for infiltrators; some may have come in around the back.

I left the train on the seaward side and went toward the rear, cocked rifle on my hip at the ready. As I came to the last car a figure rounded the end and we met head on. He fired his pistol point blank into my face.

I lunged forward into the blinding flash, and as I lunged the tip of my rifle muzzle sank into the pit of his stomach. I pulled the trigger. He slipped backward into the snow, and I fell across him.

Was I dead? I should be. I could be.

But if I'd been dead than I wouldn't have been listening to the death rattle in the Bolshie's throat.

The couplings crashed and the train moved forward. I got up unsteadily and felt my face and throat. No damage. Then I pulled at the stock of the rifle. It stuck. The muzzle, following the bullet, had gone through the cavalryman's body and caught between his ribs and his spine. I tugged again at the rifle and it came free.

Beside the dead man lay a package of dynamite sticks tied together. He had been sent to blow up the tracks.

I picked up the dynamite and trotted after the red tail-light of the train. As I ran I kept telling myself insanely that if I had had time to tie my pistol to the Red's rifle and stuck the muzzle forward into the snow, they would have formed a cross.

★

Early that morning we came into the Rostov yards and uncoupled from the *bronevik*; the major had orders to carry a general's train across the bridge and could take us no further.

The yards lay a quarter mile from the bridge on the flat north bank above the river. Bordering the bank rose an unbroken line of snow-covered bluffs. From our place on the siding we could see across the river to the low south bank, where the Don had overflowed and spread out onto the steppe in a vast, shallow, frozen lake.

The bridge itself was arch-supported, and about three hundred yards long and seventy feet wide. It had a double track, a foot path, and a crossing for vehicles. Now, and for the next five days we were in Rostov, it was covered, night and day, with refugees and the military in trains, in carts, on horse and on foot.

General Brough, the British Railway Transport Officer, came for breakfast from his office at the station.

He told us that Holman, Bingham and the rest of the Mission staff had already crossed the bridge and were southward bound; so was Colly, with A and C Flights. Colly had arrived in Rostov to find A Flight already there waiting for him.[1] The A Flight boys had gotten to Rostov from Tsaritsyn faster than we had made it from Kupyansk.

Brough said it was going to be a devil of a job getting an engine for us, but that he would do his best. Rostov station had no personnel remaining on duty and the railway organization itself had ceased to function. Manoeuvreing of the trains was now left entirely to the passengers. If he failed to get us a locomotive, the general said, we should be prepared to leave the train and walk across the bridge.

'Sir, what's the war news?' Eddie asked with a straight face, and we laughed.

Brough took a typed sheet of paper from his pocket. Explaining that he had translated it from a Red communiqué, he handed the sheet around. It read:

> As of this day of December 30th the Donets Coal Basin is in the hands of the Red Army. We have cut Denikin's forces in two. We are battering at the gates of Tsaritsyn and Krosnoyarsk, and will soon take both cities. The remainder of Kolchak's forces will shortly lay down their arms. Within a matter of days we shall have captured Taganrog. Rostov will fall soon thereafter.
>
> The year 1919 has been a year of victory for the working classes on the front and in the rear. It was a year of consolidation for the Soviet authority. The Red Army on the field of battle inflicted deadly decisive blows against the counter-revolution. Under the mighty blows of the Red Army the hordes of Tsarist generals have melted away. With red standards and a shout of victory we shall break into the New Year of 1920.
>
> In the next year we shall attain a victorious end to the civil war. In all Siberia, in the Ukraine, on the Don, in the Caucasus, they desire the Soviets.

'What's today's date?' asked Tommy.

'The 31st,' Bill answered him.

'Then it's New Year's Eve,' Tommy said, surprised. 'Since Christmas we've completely lost track of the time.'

'Sir,' Kink said. 'Would you care to join us tonight for a kind of conservative *prazdnik*? Perhaps our long faces could stand some shortening.'

Brough shook his head and got to his feet. 'No, thank you, Major. I must be on duty all night at the station. But if your messman will send over some of those celebrated rum toddies of his, I'd be delighted to drink with my adjutant to the New Year and to some better luck.'

When I went in to see Nina a few minutes later Feodor had just finished changing her bandages. 'Is better,' he said, beaming. 'Notice, more the colour in the cheek.'

'Cheeks, Feodor,' I corrected him, smiling. He was right. Nina had lost some of her deathly pallor and her eyes were brighter.

I smoothed her hair. 'I know it's going to be a happy New Year because you're getting better.'

'Yes. I hope so.'

She seemed to be in some doubt about it, and I said, 'I *know* so. None of that Asiatic pessimism of yours now. Do we promise?'

She smiled. '*Khorosho*, we promise. Sasha,' she began hesitantly, and stopped.

'*Tsaritsa moevo serdtsa*, I know you've got something unpleasant to say. Out with it.'

'It is not so unpleasant, Sasha. I know your comrades will want to have a *prazdnik* tonight and I do not wish you to spend the evening here, playing draughts. Especially since you will have to move my counters for me. It is so tedious for you.'

'Being with you is never tedious, and moving your counters is a joy.'

'You are laughing at me.'

'No, I'm not.'

'But I am serious. And I should sleep.'

'It's New Year's Eve and maybe if you sleep this afternoon you'll be able to stay up for a while tonight. Anyway, I'll be back early from seeing Russky at the hospital.'

'Is that so? I should have thought the hospital would by now have been evacuated.'

'From what we hear they're not going to move the wounded, but leave them there with some prisoners to arrange protection when the Reds come in.'

Nina looked at me in shocked surprise. 'Do you mean they are trusting the Reds to spare the sick and wounded? That is a fatal stupidity. They will murder them all.'

'Ninusha,' I said gently, 'the Reds are winning the war. They'll be inclined to be magnanimous. There are five thousand wounded and sick at Rostov hospital; they wouldn't kill that many people. Naturally you remember what happened at Velikoknyazheskoye, and I can understand why you're not able to forget. But it isn't likely to happen again.'

She turned her head away. 'Sasha, you do not understand the Bolsheviks.'

'We won't argue about it,' I said, and got up from my chair. 'Have you had your aspirin?'

She nodded.

'Then I'll leave you for a while. I promised to take Tommy's guard; he's out looking for Kitty again.'

'Sasha, if Russky is better, take him with you on the train, *pozhaluista*.'

'Try to get some sleep,' I said, and left the compartment.

After the evening meal the five of us took the van into the city to the hospital. Rostov was as deserted as a poor man's funeral. The shops were shuttered and the houses dark, except for an occasional glimmer of light through blinds behind which one was conscious people were peering apprehensively. The streets were empty save for a battery of field guns clattering through from the north and an exhausted troop of Don Cossacks drooping in their saddles. As we passed them one raised his sabre ironically and shouted, '*S novym godom! S novym schasteim!*'

'Happy New Year to you,' muttered Eddie.

We drove by seventeen lamp-posts from which seventeen men hung motionless in the windless air, the snowflakes gathering in the folds of their clothes. One victim, bare-chested, had been hung by a noose made from his shirt.

Kink whistled in a descending scale. 'That's a bad sign. Whenever the White Army starts hanging men wholesale it means they don't plan on being around too long.'

The hospital seemed infected by the same silent, protestless paralysis that gripped the town. It was as if doctors and nurses alike had

fled into dream to avoid the terror of reality. Kink had to speak twice
to the nurse at the desk before she looked up from her work, and
as we went down the corridor to Russky's room the doctors we
passed seemed like somnambulists, walking the night with unseeing
eyes. The call bells rang ceaselessly, but one felt that a private understanding existed between caller and called that no serious attention would be paid to them.

In the semi-private room Colly's influence had undoubtedly
wrangled for him, Russky lay in bed staring listlessly up at the ceiling. But it looked as though he were making a good recovery; the
mulberry rash had faded almost completely, and though he had lost
a great deal of weight, the eyes he turned to the door as we entered
were fairly bright.

'Don't expect any wildly enthusiastic greeting,' I told the boys.
'During convalescence typhus patients are pretty badly depressed.'

We got no wildly enthusiastic greeting, but clearly Russky was as
glad to see us as we were to see him. Leaving the hospital in Taganrog, Kink and I had been sure we would never see him alive again,
and that certainty had been symptomatic of our general feeling of
hopelessness and defeat; now that he was before our eyes again,
alive and on the mend, we could tell ourselves that omens were
false and only competence and luck mattered.

'You will excuse,' Russky said, smiling. 'I am weak and cannot
greet you as I would like. In a few days when I am better and back
on the train, will be different.'

We were careful not to exchange glances. Evidently they hadn't
told him there was to be no evacuation of Rostov hospital. Remembering what Nina had said I felt a chill; if the hospital authorities
thought there was no danger from the Reds, why should they be so
reluctant to tell the sick and wounded what their plans were?

We brought him up to date on our composite biography since
leaving Taganrog and listened to his. He had arrived in Rostov four
days ago on a Red Cross train with a thousand men packed into it;
at Rostov station more than half of them had been taken off dead.
'They put me near broken window and I think it save me, the fresh
air. Can you believe?'

We could believe. During the retreat we had observed that the
cold and open air had been more beneficial than not to the typhus-
stricken; the people who had travelled the wagon roads in open carts

had fared generally better than those carried in the closed hospital vans and refugee trains.

Kink was giving Russky an edited report on the latest military developments when a nurse came in to shoo us out. Visiting hours were over. We left, promising to look in again tomorrow if we could.

'It's a load off my mind to know Russky isn't going west,' Kink said, 'but that hospital gave me the willies. Let's get a drink.'

'Where do you get a drink in this graveyard of a town?' Bill said.

'We'll try the Hotel Rostov,' Kink told him. 'If it's closed we'll know there's no sense trying anywhere else.'

Though the Rostov's rococo lobby blazed with lights, there was no doorman on duty at the entrance. We stamped the snow off our boots and walked over Persian carpets to the ornate desk. Eddie pushed a bell, and it rang loudly in the silence, but no one came to answer it.

'Reminds me of the Crillon during a Zeppo raid,'[2] Eddie said. 'Once I dropped in while the bombs were falling, sat down at the writing desk, and wrote three letters to my girl.'

Kink moved off toward the glass-enclosed palm court with its fountain in the centre. The fountain was dry. In one of the delicate chairs sat a beefy porter with his dirty boots up on a table top. Before him was a bottle of sparkling wine and a brimming glass. He was smoking a long black cigar.

'The revolution comes to Rostov,' Eddie laughed.

Tommy grinned. 'Kink, ask him for a table for five near the fountain and away from the string quartet.'

'*Pozhaluista, ofitsiant,*' Kink said, asking the man to call a waiter.

He was ignored.

'*Daite nam viski!*' Kink snapped out.

The man spat on the floor.

Kink stepped forward to teach the lout better, but we restrained him. 'Forget it,' I said. 'The help's probably looted all the liquor anyway. Let's go back to the train.'

On our way back to the yards, the snow had drifted so heavily at the street corners that several times we had to get out, put down the boards we carried in the back, and use them to get the van across the worst of the snowdrifts. A wet and starving wolfhound watched us for a while from the shelter of a doorway and then, licking his chops, vanished down an alley.

When we got back to the train Kink and the boys settled down to some serious drinking. I excused myself, made a cup of Bovril for Nina, and brought it in.

She was dozing in the dim light Feodor had left on, but awoke as I came in the door.

I made her drink the hot broth though she didn't feel like it; the steam heat we were getting tonight was none too satisfactory.

She handed me the empty cup. 'You did not celebrate the New Year in the city?' she asked me.

'It wasn't very gay in Rostov,' I said.

'Do you not wish to join your comrades in the lounge? I can hear them singing.'

'Ninusha, for the last time, I'd much rather be here with you to collect my kiss at midnight.'

She looked at me, puzzled. 'But can you not kiss me any time?'

'This is a special kiss. In the United States it's the custom on New Year's Eve to kiss your girl on the stroke of twelve.'

'Why, Sasha?'

'Well, it's a kind of promise of love and devotion for the coming year. The sealing of a bond. The lover's recognition that he's the slave of time, and can never afford to forget it.'

'That is sad but nice. But is it not true that you do not kiss much in America except on special occasions?'

I laughed. 'Listen, we do quite a bit of kissing in America, even if we aren't as partial to it as the Russians.'

'You disapprove of all our kissing?'

'I didn't say that. Let's say it's going to take me a while to get used to it.' I pulled the blanket up. It was quite chilly in the compartment and getting colder.

Suddenly I sneezed, and sneezed again.

'You have a chill?' she asked me.

'I guess so. We were up to our knees in the snow tonight, getting the van through the drifts in town.'

'Take an aspirin.'

'I'll be all right.'

'Take some aspirin, Sasha. There is water in the carafe.'

I took two aspirin tablets, and then she insisted upon feeling my forehead for fever. I was running a slight temperature, though I felt perfectly well. I had to go on feeling perfectly well. Now was no time to come down with flu or pneumonia.

Someone knocked at the door, then opened it. It was Tommy, two sheets to the wind, with a glass in his hand. I could hear the boys roaring out 'Madelon' from the lounge.

'Two minutes to midnight,' Tommy announced. 'Kiss her for me, Bunny. Wish I had Kitty here to kiss. Wish Nina the 'app – the happiest Yew – New Year ever.' He saluted with drunken precision and closed the door.

'If I'm coming down with something,' I said, 'maybe I'd better not kiss you.'

'It is *khorosho*.'

I waited a few moments and then, whispering '*S novym Godom!*' bent and kissed her mouth. It was soft and sweet.

She looked up at me in the dimness. 'Happy New Year, my beloved,' she said. 'I love you much.'

Chapter Twelve

❋

By noon the next day Brough had found us an engine, but when we went to pick it up at one of the filthy train sheds, we discovered that the boiler had a life expectancy of two or three hours at the most. It would have taken us over the bridge and a few miles south and then noisily expired. Kink yielded the dying locomotive to an optimistic *chinovnik* who had taken over one of the stalled refugee trains. Then he went to Brough for further instructions.

He returned with orders to pack a minimum kit and stand by to walk away from B Flight train. Meanwhile the general would keep his eye out for an available engine.

'Strewth, he'd better,' Bill said darkly. 'If we don't leave Rostov alive, Ramrod Brough won't either.'

'That's enough,' Kink admonished him sharply. 'Let's stop this whining. The Tommies' morale is bad enough. I don't want to hear any of you criticizing a superior officer from now on in.'

I saw now that the odds were heavily against our finding a locomotive that worked. There was only one thing for me to do: find a place for Nina on one of the trains that had already gained the bridge.

I took a walk past the packed station and down to the entrance. It was jammed with stalled traffic, and the river to either side was black with crossing fugitives moving slowly across the slippery ice. Some had linked arms to minimize the spills and falls, but it was rough going; many of the aged lay groaning with broken hips and sprained ankles, waiting for a Good Samaritan to come along and drag them to the opposite bank. Few people had time for pity; they had their own families and relatives to think of. Most kept looking over their shoulders for signs of the Reds on the bluffs above the yards.

Midway on the bridge was a stalled hospital train. I swung aboard and asked an orderly for the commandant. He directed me to the headquarters' car. There I found a colonel of the medical corps, sitting at his desk and staring at the wall.

In my laboured Russian I asked if he would take Nina aboard.

'*Nyet*,' he said.

I took out a bundle of rubles and pound notes and put it down before him. It was quite a bit of money.

'*Vsio*,' I said, telling him to take it all.

'*Nyet, Nyet*,' he repeated. Had I any idea how crowded his train was? Last night he had had to force over a hundred refugees off the roofs and buffers at gun point. A healthy passenger would have been bad enough, but to make room for a stretcher he would have to put two or three soldiers off. He was sorry, but it was out of the question.

I turned and walked out of the car. He called me back and pointed to my money on the desk.

Beyond the string of hospital vans sat a combined military and refugee train with an infantry private on guard in every vestibule. In response to my question, one of them gave me the number of the commanding officer's compartment and jerked his thumb to the rear.

The commanding officer was a lieutenant-colonel of the quartermasters. Crowded into his compartment, meant for one, were his wife and three children. The youngest, an infant, lay in a basket on the floor.

He came out into the passageway and spoke to me in French.

'Captain, what can I do?' He shrugged helplessly. 'Even the lavatories have their passengers. You saw how my own family is travelling. I sleep in my office in a chair. Even if we had a spare inch of room we have no doctor, and I could not take the responsibility.'

I told him he need assume no responsibility.

'No, I am sorry,' he told me. 'And there is no use trying the trains ahead. They are as jammed as mine.'

I tried two or three more and discovered he was right. Going back to B Flight train a terrible feeling of fatigue and depression came over me. If we had to walk across the bridge how would I take Nina? On a stretcher of course, but could she survive the cold, the snow, the exposure if there was no train to take us on the other side? I didn't ask myself if taking her was fair to the Flight or if Kink, indeed, would allow it; the thought didn't cross my mind.

Back in my compartment I went over the greatcoats, furred and leather, my flying suits, uniforms, shirts and shoes, putting this aside, rejecting that. I picked over photographs, letters from home and souvenirs. A snapshot of Nina, standing in the vestibule of the hospital train, shielding her eyes from the Kotluban sun. Another of her, candid, bending over to empty a basin on the roadbed; what lovely hips she had, even in the shapeless Red Cross uniform. The negative of the print of myself she had in her locket. My aviator's certificate from the Fédération Aéronautique Internationale. A snapshot of Charley Lamston grinning beside my Camel on the steppe. Others of Colly, Kink and the rest of the boys at Kupyansk, standing in the snow. The cigarette case given to me by one of Shkura's Wolves. More pictures of Feodor, Ivan, Kitty, Nona, some of the casual *prazdnik* girls. An eighteen-inch bottle of blue liqueur. My medals: the Cross of St. George, the Order of St. Vladimir, the DFC.[1]

I replaced the rubber band around the snapshots and cigarette case and tossed the liqueur and the medals into the waste can. It was a gesture, but I knew my own hands would never fish out the decorations out again.

I decided I could part with the blue riding breeches with white leather facings, but for the life of me I couldn't throw away my old plaid dressing-gown; it had the scent of Nina on it. Nor could I abandon the stone marten *shuba* I had bought in Taganrog from a refugee. Three times I made a bundle and each time it was bigger. Finally I stuffed everything back into the trunk but the snapshots and the *shuba* and locked it. Then a wave of weakness hit and knocked me across the bunk.

'Bunny, where in the devil's your… What's the matter, man?' It was Kink, standing in the doorway.

'I don't know,' I told him. But I did know; I'd been hiding it from myself all morning. 'I must have the flu. I'm sorry.'

'Sorry, hell. Get into bed. You've got to pull out of this! You're the only medicine man we've got. And I'm damned if we'll carry you across that goddam bridge on our goddam backs!'

I gave him a sickly grin. 'Get the medical pannier, will you, Major? I'll start on an aspirin diet.'

For the next twenty-four hours Feodor was kept hopping between Nina's compartment and mine. Kink wouldn't let me get out of bed to see her, nor would he allow my flight-mates to come farther into the room than the door. Tommy insisted upon setting the Victrola in the corridor and posted his batman to change the records. Finally I convinced him I could take just so much of 'Smiles' and 'Dardanella', and machine and batman disappeared. Actually, more than the repetition of the dance tunes it was the contrast between their tinny gaiety and the snow-smothered silence from the yards outside that was getting me down.

I had a medium-bad case of the flu;[2] despite aches and pains and a hacking cough that developed quickly, my temperature went down to one-hundred-and-one degrees and the gastro-intestinal symptoms were minor. I tried to get as much sleep as I could, obsessed by the idea that the more rest I crammed in the more quickly I would recover.

The next afternoon I awoke, sweating, with the inescapable and terrible conviction that something had gone terribly wrong. 'Feodor!' I shouted, and after a moment he came running in.

'Nina Dmitrievna – she is *khorosho*?' I asked him.

His face told me what I was afraid was true.

I sat bolt upright in the bunk. 'Feodor, what's happened? Out with it, man!'

He struggled to tell me. I caught the words *ochen bolna*, very sick. Struggling out of the bunk, I got into my dressing gown and slippers and went down the passageway to Nina's room.

Her condition seemed no different than before. She lay resting, eyes closed, in the blind-drawn compartment; beside her were the familar water glass and aspirin. Feodor had covered her with the stone marten *shuba* as I had asked.

'Ninusha,' I whispered.

She turned her head to me. She spoke, and did so only with difficulty; it was hard for her to open her mouth. Tetanus had set in.

'Sasha,' she said, 'you are feeling better?'

'Don't talk.'

'It is the lockjaw.'

The few words had exhausted her, and her jaw trembled from the effort of speech. I said, 'Ninusha, don't talk. Just nod to my questions. You're in pain?'

She shrugged, and I took that to mean that the pain was slight. It would get worse, much worse, and I decided to wait with the morphia. As long as she didn't ask for it…

Desperately I tried to pretend cheerfulness. 'Listen, I know that if tetanus comes on immediately after a wound and you have nothing to fight it with, the prognosis is bad. But your symptoms didn't begin until after a week. So don't give up, Ninusha. Please don't give up.'

She tried to smile.

'We'll find some antitoxin. The boys will turn the damn town upside down. I'll be back soon. You sleep now.'

Kink was waiting for me in my compartment, smoking a Woodbine furiously. He waited till I had gotten back into bed.

'We thought we'd wait to tell you, Bunny. I thought you weren't in any condition to know.'

'Well, now I know.'

'She can recover. It's been known to happen.'

'Kink, I don't believe in miracles.'

'I sent Tommy and Eddie over to the hospital. They're going to make a last try there, and if that doesn't work they're going to hunt up that doctor who helped Russky.'

'Thanks, *kunak*.'

'I can see you want to be alone. I'll let you know when the boys get back.'

'What's new with the Bolshies?' I asked him.

'The Cossacks beat off a probing action to the northeast of town. You may have heard the rifle fire. The bastards left a lot of dead; they won't be back for a while.'

'Any news on an engine?'

'No, but Brough's still trying.'

'We've got to keep trying, don't we, Kink?'

'That's right, *kunak*. As soon as we stop we're dead men.'

'I feel dead already,' I said.

He left the compartment, not dignifying my unsoldierly self-pity with a reply.

★

There was no tetanus antitoxin to be had in Rostov. The hospital had none; the doctor who had put Russky in the hospital had none; the hospital trains in the yards had been out of it for months. There was no lack of morphia, but morphia was the one thing we had plenty of.

I didn't have to tell Nina the boys had returned without the serum; she had known they would never find any in the city. Through the long afternoon and the short twilight I sat beside her, swathed in a cocoon of blankets. Every half hour I took a couple of aspirins from the bottle that sat next to the small brown tube of morphia pills on the tray. When her muscle cramps began I would start giving her the pills.

From time to time I reminded her that the train would leave when we got an engine, and that if we did not, Feodor and another *plenny* would carry her across the bridge.

She didn't answer.

When Feodor came in with her beef tea we began to hear rifle fire from the outskirts of the city. Cossacks putting down hoodlums and looters, Feodor told me. The Red vanguard had yet to return for a second attack.

Nina had difficulty in swallowing the Bovril, and I gave her a morphine tablet, hoping it would relax the face and throat muscles enough for her to take the broth from Feodor's spoon a little later on. In a minute or so she had fallen asleep.

'Tell me if she wakes and has severe pain,' I told Feodor. 'Meanwhile I'm going to try to get some sleep myself.'

Feodor's knock woke me three hours later. 'Is pain,' he said. 'Captain, you come?'

She had agonizing cramps in both her legs, and I made her choke down another morphine tablet with water before pulling back the blankets and gently massaging her calves. Finally, whether by the quick action of the drug or my massage, the cramps disappeared and she sank back on the pillow, exhausted.

'I just change bandage, when pain it come,' said Feodor. 'Is now better?'

'Yes. *Spasibo*. I'll call you when I need you.'

I wiped her perspiring temples. Her eyes held both the memory of pain and shy apology, and both worked to break my heart. Her mouth began to strain for words and I put my finger on her lips. 'No, don't try to talk, Ninusha. Sleep. I'll be here with you.'

For a long time I watched her as she slept. Tomorrow she would be worse, I knew. The next day, or the day after, she might be dead.

★

At dawn the tin-pan rattle of one of our Lewis guns briefly broke the stillness of the crowded yards below the bluffs. Then there was silence. I got up and put on my uniform, fleece-lined boots and heavy greatcoat. I was still weak, but the fever was gone. It was as cold in the compartment as a butcher's freezer.

From the bluffs a Vickers started up, its tone measured and deeper than that of the Lewis, which now resumed its fire. The Reds were shooting at the trains from three hundred yards away; the bullets whined overhead with a rising inflection.

It had happened. The Reds had ringed the town.

I stuffed the packet of photos and souvenirs in my greatcoat pocket and closed the door behind me. Brough was coming down the passageway. Each of the boys stood, fully dressed, in his compartment doorway. Kink stepped out and saluted. The general looked as though he hadn't slept in a week, but he returned the salute precisely.

'Major,' Brough said, 'the White rearguard crossed the river last night and the Bolshies are entering the town now against token resistance. We've got an ice breaker on its way down the Don to forestall Red pursuit once we and the refugees have made our way to the other side. The bridge is set to be blown up in an hour. A mission train's waiting at the bridge entrance. There's room aboard it. Withdraw B Flight to the bridge immediately.'

Brough returned Kink's acknowledging salute, turned on his heel and left the car.

'That's the first definite order I've had since the retreat began,' Kink said with satisfaction. He turned to me. 'Bunny, you up to forming the Flight in marching order?'

'There's Nina,' I said. 'I've got to get her on a stretcher.'

I looked at him, willing a certain answer. He might refuse. He was a soldier and would probably refuse.

But he didn't. He said: 'Eddie, form the flight outside on the lee of the train. Tommy, get Ivan to help with a stretcher. We've got to get out of here as soon as we can. The Reds will be bringing more machine guns and maybe even artillery up on those bluffs. It won't be pleasant.'

I went into Nina's compartment.

Feodor slept soundly, slumped forward in his chair; not even the machine-gun fire had disturbed him. Nina lay with eyes closed, the blanket rising and falling with her regular breathing. On the carpet, touching the loosely extended fingers of her hand, was the vial of morphine tablets and an overturned water glass. The vial was empty.

'No,' I said, and rushed to her as Feodor woke with a start.

She was still conscious, but going fast; as soon as she had heard the Lewis gun open fire, she must have taken all the pills, by some superhuman effort forcing all of them past her clenched teeth and swallowing the lot down with a mouthful of water.

'Ninusha,' I asked her, 'why? We were going to take you on a stretcher. We were going to carry you across. I'd made plans for it. Why?'

I kept repeating my question though it was senseless. I knew why. She had known we would get no engine. She was a nurse and she had known she would never have survived even if I had gotten her across the bridge and into a train on the other side.

'I sleep,' Feodor said brokenly. 'She take while I sleep.'

'Leave us,' I said.

I took her hand and she turned her head toward me on the pillow. She was trying to speak. Her jaw and throat muscles stretched taut but she couldn't open her mouth; the corners of it were drawn downward and back and fixed in the *risus sardonicus*. I thought: she willed herself to take poison but she cannot will herself to speak.

She tried to speak one last time and then, as though a curtain had come down between her eyes and mine, I lost her to the dark.[3]

Someone knocked against the side of the train.

I don't know how long I sat there before I felt Bill's hand on my shoulder. 'Sorry, Bunny,' he said, 'but the Flight's outside. We're ready to move. I brought your kit, old man.'

I followed him out of the compartment and out to the lee of the train where Eddie had formed B Flight's ranks in the freezing rain. The men carried rations and a rifle, or a light machine-gun; their kits were at their feet. I noticed that Mallows' nose was dripping and that Walters, in shaving, had cut his cheek; that Cowderdrill stood at rigid attention though the formation was at ease. The pocket of his heavy overcoat was stuffed with his junk jewellery, but he had been forced to leave behind his samovars. I felt like shouting at Mallows to wipe his goddam nose and thought I had, but when I looked at him again I saw that his face showed no trace of embarrassment or emotion.

Hoskins and half a dozen men were still at the Lewis guns on the platform, shooting at the bluffs. The Reds had moved up more machine guns and the air above us hummed with lead; much of it was hitting the refugees on the tracks beyond us who were leaving the trains for the ice and the bridge in a panicked flood. Their cries and screams were drowned out by the noise of the firing.

From around the terminal coach on the adjoining siding stumbled a crazed woman who held her hands before her as if she were blind. She ran down the track toward the entrance to the bridge three hundred yards away, falling and getting up to run again, till she came to an open space on the line, where she fell for the last time and lay motionless.

I had an errant, though to me perfectly logical, thought. If all these hundreds and thousands of people were dying and would die, then Nina's death would in their light be less terrible. If five or ten thousand died than I could consider her one of the five or ten thousand and grieve for her the less.

In the growing daylight we could see the hordes of refugees crossing the river over the ice and the bridge and, beyond them, to the wide ice-covered flats on the other side where what units were left of the Dobrovolski Army were forming in some kind of order for a stand. The infantry in the foreground wheeled into position; the artillery massed for action in the rear. On the flanks the supporting cavalry swung into protective reserve. From the bluffs Red shrapnel burst over and among them, killing men and horses, staining the yellow ice with red. When a man fell the space filled; it was like a demented game of chess. The Bolshies were moving up more and more guns to shell the deploying Whites; evidently they considered machine-gun bullets good enough for those of us on the north flats who had not yet gained the bridge.

'My God, what a sight,' said Eddie. 'Like a huge canvas by David.'

'You arty bastard,' I said, 'men are dying out there.' My voice was curiously flat in my ears, as though they were stuffed with cotton.

Eddie gave me an understanding glance and looked away.

From beneath the wheels of the stalled coach on the next siding crawled a wounded Russian officer. Shot in both legs, he could raise only the upper part of his body, like a dog whose hindquarters had been crushed on the road by a passing auto. Fascinated, we watched him approach and beg hysterically that we take him with us.

'Not able,' Eddie said loudly, in the way we shout at someone who does not understand our language. 'No stretchers. Doubtful if we can get away ourselves. Understand? Sorry.'

The Russian may not have understood Eddie's words, but he comprehended the negative shake of his head. Quickly he shifted his weight to one arm, drew his revolver, and shot himself through the temple.

Kink came down the steps of the train with the machine gunners following after.

'Tommy, take four men and fire the Camels and the store-cars,' he said, but then, as Tommy picked out the first of the men, he changed his mind. 'Order countermanded. God knows how many paruskies would get it when the bombs went up.'

He called the Flight to attention. 'Form fours. Right turn. By your left. Quick march. We're bound for hell, men, but who dares to say we can't take it!'

A cheer went up from the marching Tommies. The column moved toward the bridge, Kink leading, the officers at intervals flanking the line of fours. A mob of refugees, almost all oldsters, trotted after us, carrying their pitiful bundles; most of the younger people had already crossed the bridge.

The freezing rain had stopped. Now the fire from the bluffs passed overhead in a horizontal hail, spraying everything in sight. The noise of the shrapnel bursting across the river was a continuous *crunch, crunch, crunch*. The Whites' unprotected artillery on the flats was beginning to bear on the bluffs, and we would have taken courage from the whining shells had we not known that the gunners' range might shorten any second. Ahead we could see where the lines of sidings began to converge into the double tracks that led to the bridge and over it.

We marched forward another forty yards. Then 'Flight, halt,' Kink ordered. 'Fall out, the officers.'

We gathered around him. We knew what the trouble was; between the last car of the train ahead of us and the tender of B Flight train was a gap about two freight cars in length. It was scattered with refugee dead. A nest of Red machine guns, half concealed on the brow of the bluff, swept that open space ceaselessly. Nothing that was alive could cross it.

We had a choice. We could double back thirty or forty yards and, under the cover of trains on another siding, make our way down to the river and start across the ice. That was the easier way, except that fewer than half the refugees who had crossed the ice since the Reds had gained the bluffs had made it to the other side. The ice was strewn with their dead and dying.

Our only other course was to cross the open space, at whatever cost, and make our way behind the cover of the trains to the station house and from there to the entrance of Rostov bridge. The Reds had no intention of shelling the bridge or its crawling traffic; they needed it as a means of coming into direct contact with the Volunteers.

'Look!' Tommy shouted, his voice barely carrying above the din. 'Coming toward us down the track!'

In the lee of the coach beyond the gap lurched and stumbled a colossus of a man. He wore the black *riasa* and carried the crozier of the Orthodox Church; the gold cross hung from a heavy chain on his massive torso. Guiding him were two young girls in shapeless convent uniforms. He was blind.

We yelled a warning for them to stay where they were, to advance no further. They paid no attention. With bowed heads the girls led the priest on. They were the first to fall, barely four paces out of the shelter of the boxcar; then the huge priest leapt up, clawing at the air, and fell across their bodies. The machine gunners on the bluff lowered their sights and poured bullets into the dead patriarch till chunks and fragments of him, like chippings from a woodblock, began flying through the air. Behind us, in the crowd of refugees, we could hear women retching into the snow.

'All right,' Kink said, 'what's it to be? The river or the bridge?'

It occurred to me that our situation was like something out of a nickelodeon melodrama. Like my flight-mates, I took another look out over the ice of the hundreds of wounded and dying refugees; and then I looked back at the priest. He had been cut in half, and still the machine-gun fire minced him into smaller pieces. The pool of blood in which he lay seemed fed by some inexhaustible spring.

Panicking, some of the refugees hurled themselves past us and into the open space. One jacknifed within a second of entering the line of fire; another was struck midway and fell sliding on his face. A shawled *molodyka*, with an infant in her arms, almost reached the safety of the freight before the gunners cut her down. As she pitched forward the baby rolled out of her arms to lie inches beyond the reach of her outstretched hands. It lay there kicking. The young woman made a feeble effort to rise and then was still. The infant squalled.

'Strewth, the baby wasn't touched,' Bill said, and dropped his rifle and kit to the ground. I grabbed one of his arms and Kink held on to the other.

'It's no use,' Kink said. 'They'll get the child too.'

As we watched the infant, as though pushed and prodded by an invisible hand, slid backward on the ice, leaving a widening blood-stain beneath it. It was quiet now.

The boys turned their faces aside but my own eyes continued to observe the horror. I was unshocked, completely drained of emotion. Nothing could touch me now.

Bill spoke in a monotone. 'If we're going to die, why don't we charge the bluffs and cop our packets fighting?'

'Unnecessary, Captain,' Kink said. 'Look at the bluffs now.'

The mist had turned to fog. The formidable bluff walls looming greyly over us were gradually disappearing. A thick rolling fog was sweeping in on everything – yards, flats, river. As though a single order had been given and instantly obeyed, the Red machine guns fell silent.

Kink took immediate advantage of the opportunity.

'Flight, attention,' he called to the men. 'Close column. By your left. Quick march.'

We quick-marched past the open space and down to the station. The place was in an uproar. Refugees fought for a place on train roofs and buffers, even on the fire boxes. Others were climbing up the water pipes outside the station to its roof, and trying to jump from there to the roofs of trains. The distance was too great: some missed, falling to the tracks where they squirmed in agony with broken arms, legs and backs; those who landed on the train roofs knocked off others. Women and children were screaming; men bellowed pointlessly like pole-axed steers. A young boy knocked down an old man trying to scramble inside an open coach window and tried to hoist himself up instead, but he failed to reach the sill. No hand reached down to help him.

Rounding a turn in the tracks we saw, half a mile up the river, the smoke of the approaching icebreaker.

We slogged on through the masses of refugees down to the bridge entrance. Waiting for us there was the Mission train. We scrambled aboard, packing ourselves into the three coaches, and the train got underway.

Slow as its progress was, it took us over the bridge faster than we would have made it in marching order. The footpath and vehicular road were mobbed with Volunteers and refugees. The soldiers observed good discipline, but the shells whistling over their heads had panicked the refugees. They pushed and shoved and trampled. An old woman fell and lay motionless; a pregnant girl, kicked aside, sank groaning to the macadam. A small dog, separated from its master, ran to and fro, barking up into faces. Some of the refugees tried to claw their way up the coach sides and into the windows. The Tommies clubbed them back.

We were strangely silent. During the twenty-minute trip none of us said a single word.

The train stopped fifteen yards from the other side, and we poked our heads out the windows. Ahead, on the embankment, was a long line of stalled and empty trains, abandoned by the refugees when the shelling had begun. Beyond these stretched, southward, an endless concatenation of other locomotives, coaches and freights. They were moving very slowly, if at all.

The fog was too dense to see the icebreaker, but now we could hear its horn. To our right ghostly groups of refugees still crossed the river ice.

Kink snapped a command, and we left the train for the footpath that led to the cart road. As I shouldered my kit I glanced behind me. A few refugees were still emerging from the fog, but the bridge tracks were clear of rolling stock.

We had been on the last train to cross Rostov bridge. In minutes the Volunteers would demolish it.

We walked another half-mile before Kink ordered the column to halt and fall out. As we unshouldered rifles and kits and sat down at the side of the road, we heard a series of hollow detonations from the direction of the bridge.

'They've blown it,' Tommy said. 'And that, gentlemen, ends the Battle of Rostov on the Don.'

In my mind I saw the first Red soldier enter compartment twelve. He wiped his nose on his sleeve and glanced at the dead young woman before him. He called back to his comrades searching the rest of the car, 'Dead, only one dead girl.'

And then slammed the door on silence.

★

We walked eleven miles along the wagon road till we came to a Mission train stalled on the local track. General Brough was in the headquarters' car, poring over military maps. He had caught up with his train only a few hours ago, after hitching a ride with his aide and batman on one of the refugee coaches. Anticipating we would find him eventually, he had coupled several empty refugee coaches and boxcars onto the Mission train.

Had Brough been less resourceful, there would have been no room either for us or for our hundred enlisted men.

The aide assigned the Tommies to the boxcars and us to one of the filthy day coaches. We cleaned up as well as we could and presented ourselves in the mess-car for dinner.

It wasn't an auspicious meal: a small slab of hardtack, a raw onion, marmalade and a cup of Bovril, but the Bovril was steaming hot and we gulped it all down, and bit our tongues so that we wouldn't ask for more.

Not a word was said about what had happened that morning. The Mission officers talked about Sandhurst, punting on the Thames, the Oxford-Cambridge cricket matches and the London theatre season of 1917. But I noticed that the hands of more than one of them were trembling, and one Guards' type relit his glowing Woodbine at least three times.

I excused myself and went to the lounge. One by one the boys came in after me. Kink took a chair five seats down, respecting my desire for privacy, and the others sat down near him.

Kink turned to no one in particular and said, 'Their goddam bar is empty.'

'No fireplace, either,' Bill said. 'Improvident of them, wouldn't you say?'

'The lav's filthy,' said Eddie. 'Ours was spanking clean up to the end.'

Tommy sighed. 'Good-bye to old B Flight train. Well never see its like again.'

'We will, by God,' Kink said fiercely. 'We'll get outfitted in Ekat – new train and new Camels. The Whites'll hold the Don at Rostov and in another month or less we'll come roaring back and fill the Bolshies' arses full of lead. Can you imagine a chap like Colly quitting; a man like Holman? Do you know what Brough told me about Holman? On the way from Taganrog to Rostov a Red cavalry patrol attacked his train. He got out in a hail of bullets, unshipped a light Lewis, and put the Reds to flight. Outside of Rostov he commandeered a tank and drove back two companies of Bolshies. They left over sixty dead.'

The boys were silent: they knew we were licked, beaten, through.

And I for one didn't give a lead soldier. I wanted to get out of Russia as soon as I could; if Lloyd George had a transport waiting in Novorossiisk harbour that was just dandy. The country was too much for me; it was like a pet bear that had turned against me and tried to claw my heart out.

Two Mission officers came into the car, and I got up and went back to the day-coach. As I passed the boys kept their eyes on their shoes.

Feodor was making up a bunk for me on two of the day-coach seats with boards and a couple of Lysol-smelling blankets he had appropriated somewhere. The floor beneath was swept neatly clean of its dirt and refuse.

'*Spasibo*,' I said, and stretched out on the boards. They were uncomfortable, but better than nothing, and I was so exhausted I could have slept on the floor.

He stood there, shifting from one foot to the other. Finally he said, 'Captain, I have put medals in your kit.[4] You do not mind, I hope. And, Captain, you do not blame me for the death of Nina Dmitrievna?'

I shook my head. 'Nobody's to blame, Feodor.'[15]

He nodded and, shoulders hunched, shuffled away to the *plennys'* boxcar and his bed of straw.

★

We covered three miles that night and two the next morning; there were roughly one hundred eighty more to go till we reached Ekat. A *muzhik* who had hitched a ride a few miles back and then, dismayed at our rate of progress, had dropped off to walk, overtook us on foot, waving a scrawny chicken. Carts, *troikas* and *brichkas* filled with civilians and a scattering of Kuban Cossacks passed unceasingly on the wagon road. Most of the Cossacks had the shifty look of deserters; there were few men in uniform who didn't belong with the thirty thousand Volunteers on the south bank of the Don.

Late in the afternoon we ran into some bad congestion at a fair-sized stop. We knew it would be a while before the train got under way again, and hearing shouts and sounds of revelry from near the station house, the boys left the lounge to investigate.

'Come on, Bunny, sounds like fun!' Kink yelled from the roadbed, and I put on my scarf and greatcoat and joined them.

The noise was coming from a square cement building thirty yards from the station. We passed through the gates into the yard, where the racket was almost deafening. Kink opened a big steel door and we entered the building.

It was a vodka factory. About fifty Cossacks and a mob of civilian men from the town were making the place a shambles. In the process they were also getting magnificently drunk.

Bill licked his lips. 'For a man who hasn't had a drink in over forty-eight hours, this place is a find. Where do we start?'

Kink shrugged. It was hard to know where to start. The Cossacks were firing at the cisterns with rifles, making holes from which they drank. Men stood by other holes and spigots with caps, pails and flasks. Some caught the vodka in the palms of their hands and drank it on the spot. One bucket-carrying Cossack, balancing high up on the side of cistern, fell in, and two of his comrades, roaring with laughter, scrambled up the ladder to pull him out. Vodka flooded the concrete floor; the peasants and a few ragged townsmen bent down to lap it up like dogs.

'What do we do?' Tommy asked. 'Line up at one of the spigots?'

'There should be a storeroom,' Kink said. 'Let's take a look.'

At the nearest door stood a circle of Cossacks, their arms linked fraternally, roaring out a drunken 'Chorniye Gusary'. As we pushed past them one cavalryman good-naturedly pressed upon us a dirty pail of the colourless, potent liquid. We refused with thanks.

We went through the door and into a passageway that led, evidently, to the manager's office. Passing the room we glanced inside. Two plump peasant women were playing the Russian equivalent of strip poker with a couple of Cossacks.

The women were losing; they were down to their shifts. One of the Cossacks was bootless.

Bill turned to Kink. 'You want to wait and see what happens?'

Kink shook his head, and we passed on.

At the end of the hall we ran into a drunken watchman who pocketed Kink's ten rubles and motioned us through another door. We went through the door and found ourselves outside again in the yard.

Tommy tried the door and found it locked. As he lifted his fist to pound on it the train whistle blew.

Kink laughed. 'Well, it's fate, chaps. We don't get a drink till Ekat.'

The line had cleared temporarily and the Mission train was pulling slowly out of the station. We sprinted for it through the slush and snow.

Midway Tommy slipped and fell. When he got to his feet he grimaced painfully; he had twisted an ankle.

We hoisted him on to Bill's wide shoulders and trotted on.

Kink slowed down to a walk. 'No need to rush. The damn train's stopped again.'

We climbed aboard laughing, and I realized it was the first time I had found anything to laugh about in days.

Chapter Thirteen

*

A week later, at Tikhoretskaya, we caught up with one of the Mission trains that had left Rostov shortly after Holman and A and C Flights had departed the city.[1] Holman, a Mission major told us, had arrived in Novorossiisk along with the rest of 47 Squadron, which had immediately been ordered to the Crimea. Conditions in Novorossiisk were very bad, the major had heard by wire; the town was fuelless and jammed with refugees, most of them typhus-ridden and without shelter. Wrangel was getting all too little co-operation in fortifying the town from the Denikin-appointed military governor and the commandant of the fort.

Trouble between Denikin and the Kuban Cossacks had reached another boiling point; the Rada had elected a new Ataman who was in open opposition to Supreme Headquarters. Now the White armies were in the Kuban on borrowed time. And news from the Crimea and southwestern Russia was none too good. General Slashchov, a confirmed drug addict, was suffering reverses on the Peninsula, while in New Russia General Schilling was losing what little authority he had over his discouraged troops. Public demand was increasing for his dismissal and the appointment of Wrangel in his place.

Brough asked the major what he had heard about the situation on the Rostov front.

'The Reds are drawing up heavy reserves, and General Holman understands the Volunteers can't hold out much longer. Of course the Whites were pretty fired up about what happened in Rostov when the Reds came in.'

Kink leaned forward tensely. 'What did happen, Major?'

'Well, a lot of slaughtering, you know, of what bourgeois elements still were left. And then there was the hospital. The Reds drenched it with petrol and burned the place down with over five thousand wounded inside.'

We sat there, stunned. Finally Kink said, 'The bastards. The bloody, murdering swine.'

Brough remembered Russky, and tried to make things easier by saying we would get a replacement for him in Ekat or Novorossiisk, but somehow that only made it worse. We excused ourselves and walked numbly back to the coach.

How guilty should I feel, I wondered. Should I have taken Nina's advice and talked Kink into taking Russky out of the hospital and on to the train?

Kink seemed to know what I was thinking.

'Let's not blame ourselves,' he said. 'Those are the fortunes of war. Russky wasn't meant to survive; I believe that. What kind of life could a man like him have had in a Bolshevized Russia, even if the Reds had let him live?'

'Some people are going to get away,' Eddie said. 'To Constantinople, to Europe. Maybe Russky could have been one of them.'

Kink shook his head. 'He would have gone back to Petrograd for the girl he was going to marry, and they would have caught him. Even if they hadn't, Russky's roots were too deep in Russia; he wouldn't have been able to get along abroad. I never saw a paruski who was more Russian than that crazy, lovable sod.'

And that had to suffice as his epitaph from us, his comrades; a Mission staff officer came into the car to rout us out to gather snow for the boiler. The engine's water supply was running low again.

The days passed, undifferentiated, routine, colourless, un-exacting. We slept, we shivered, we ate; we tried not to take offense at one another's dirt and smell. All we hoped for now was a hot bath and a change of socks and uniform. And then, just as boredom would have made us welcome even disaster, trains from the front began to come by loaded with men. The attempted stand on the south bank had failed and the Volunteer Army was retreating in a rear guard action to the Kuban.

Three weeks after we had crossed the bridge, we came into Ekaterinodar.

The remote, little provincial town was filling the role of the White capital with the embarrassed inadequacy of an understudy who had neglected to learn his lines. The station telephone was out of order and the telegraph wires to Novorossiisk were temporarily down. White headquarters had made no provision for our billeting, though Colly had left instructions when passing through weeks before.[2] We sat around the train for half a day, shivering in blankets, till a runner from headquarters came with word that accommodations had been found for us on the outskirts of town. But there was no transport till three hours later, when an ancient lorry drew up alongside the tracks and promptly stalled. It took Tommy, who had a way with cars, an hour to get it going again.

The refugees who had been flooding Ekat seemed to have vanished into the damp, heavy air. The streets were bare and empty, the shops denuded. The huge cathedral stood deserted in the great square in the middle of the town.

Our billet was a three-storey, brick mansion with more bedrooms than you could count, but the Mission staff officers had gotten there ahead of us, and we were assigned bunks on the dining room floor. The pipes had frozen solid and there was no water available for a bath. Kink, though, was equal to the occasion, and with the help of a few packets of Woodbines, persuaded the mess sergeant to let us melt snow in basins on the stove. We rigged up a kind of primitive bathhouse in the corner of the kitchen and made it do.

Bill, putting on clean socks and shoes, let out a bellow. 'Strewth, I took along two extra pairs of shoes, but they're all for the damn left foot!'

'Cheer up,' Eddie said. 'You may get a leg shot off before this mess is over.'

Daly stared at the shoes, made to order in London; he was a great one for expensive leather and had owned thirty pairs. 'If I do,' he said, 'it'll be the damn left leg, be sure of that.'

Tommy disappeared after we had bedded down in the dining room. He came back two hours later, and shook me awake from a sound sleep.

'Bunny,' he whispered. 'I've got to have twenty pounds.'

I was annoyed. 'What in hell do you need twenty pounds for?'

'I've been playing cards with a couple of quartermasters in the ballroom.'

'And you lost your money to those sharks?'

'Shush. Kink'll hear you.'

'Well, why come to me? Eddie's got a wad on him.'

'Yes, but you're more understanding. Loan me some notes. I'm sure to win it back, quadruple. I'll give you half my winnings.'

'How can you be sure of winning?'

'Well, you see, I didn't catch on the game was crooked till I lost my last quid. But now that I know, I can be crookeder than all those bastards put together. Come on, *kunak*, pony up.'

I gave him thirty pounds and went back to sleep. The next morning I awoke to find sixty pound-notes tucked in my tunic pocket. Beside me Tommy snored gently, his downy hair stirring in a draft from the window.

★

We ran into Holman's engine, tender and staff car fifteen miles out of Ekat. Kink went aboard and came back an hour later, his eyes shining.

'We're back in business, types. The General's got a new train and planes waiting for us at Novorossiisk. Fresh-glue Camels, right out of the packing cases! As soon as we're completely outfitted, we move up to Ekat. What do you think of that?

It was obvious what we thought, and Kink's grin faded.

'All right, do you sisters want to mince back to Blighty on the next boat? I can arrange it! Tomorrow!'

Eddie spoke for us. 'It's not that we want to quit, Kink. But it looks like the show's over. Even you can see that.'

'I don't see anything of the kind, Fulford. And let me say I'm disappointed in all of you chaps. Canadians! Americans! They're no damn good; shoot off their top feathers and they show you their tails! If I had two Afrikaaners and a couple of Russkys…'

He strode off, too angry to finish the sentence.

'He'll get over it,' Eddie said. 'As soon as he sees what things are like in Novorossiisk. From what I've heard the city's like a cemetery, just before the grave robbers come in.'

It was an accurate pre-vision of the seacoast city. We came through the high passes of the Caucasus into the straggling town with its mole on the eastern shore and its breakwater to the west, and though the new train and Camels were a lift, Novorossiisk itself was like a damp shroud tossed into our faces.

On the way from the yards to the British Mission we saw at least thirty bodies lying on the streets. Scavengers moved among them, stripping those dead of typhus of their shoes and outer garments. From the window of a single room a family of ten, wearing overcoats against the cold, stared out at us whitely. Half the restaurants of the town had closed down and the queues before the shops were blocks long. We saw a militiaman accost a citizen and demand that he hand over his overcoat. When Kink started toward him, the militiaman dropped the coat and hurried off, cursing under his breath.

'Strewth,' Bill said, 'if it's like this during the day, how bad can it get at night?'

At the Mission Major Bingham, looking worn and haggard, offered us a cup of beef tea.

'You saw the long lines of Russians outside the embarkation office,' he said. 'We've had them night and day, and there's no let-up. We had to fire most of the Russian officials because they almost immediately started taking bribes. And the refugees, though one can't really blame them, are as shameless. They forge medical certificates and make deals in evacuation tickets with absolutely no pretense of concealment. Practically everybody who isn't stunned into apathy is a speculator, and every shop in town is a money exchange. The biggest offenders are able to bribe their way out of any situation. British pounds and Kerensky rubles are the big thing now; Deniken money is practically worthless. I imagine you've heard the story about this Russian Lieutenant-Commander Kuprin, who had a twenty-five hundred-pound note and bought half the town with it for nothing – nobody had change.'

Kink smiled and asked him how Denikin and Wrangel were getting along.

'We hear Lukomsky, the Governor-General of the city, asked Wrangel if he'd take over Schilling's command in New Russia. Wrangel said yes, but Denikin refused to appoint him. Then Schilling wired Wrangel offering to make him his adjutant, and Wrangel accepted. It looks like he'll be leaving Novorossiisk for Odessa around the end of the month.'

'I hope we have a chance to see him before he goes,' Kink said.

'The General was asking for you chaps just the other day,' Bingham told us. 'I said I'd let him know when you arrived.'

An aide had come in to stand beside Bingham's desk, and seeing how busy the major was, Kink got up to leave, after asking him to drop by our new train when he got the chance. We walked back to the yards via the harbour.

'The Major doesn't look at all well,' Eddie said. 'Maybe his job's getting him down.'

'Your job would get you down too,' Kink said, 'if you had to pass on who's leaving this deathtrap on a British ship.'

Attracted by the crowd, we stopped outside the quayside office of the Italian Lloyd line to Batum and Constantinople. There were a dozen altercations going on both inside and out. One woman was weeping that the Lloyd officials refused to accept rubles in payment for tickets and was insisting upon foreign money on a gold basis, at the lira's pre-war value of exchange.

'It is brigandage!' she was crying to anyone who would listen. 'They are thieves, thieves! Now I will never leave the city, the Bolsheviks will cut my throat!'

An aging grande dame in a lavish mink, by the looks of her at least a duchess, was complaining to one of the embarkation clerks that the Italian Lloyd had put her in a different cabin from that of her woman companion. Thinking of Nina, I wanted to spit in her face, but I restrained myself. What was the use? It was the mean and the selfish of this world who continued to survive, and they would continue to survive whether or not I told them they had no right to.

We pushed up the eastern quay past long lines of carts piled high with the baggage of fugitives lucky enough to have passage on a ship scheduled for immediate departure. The carters were asking and getting extortionate rates. One of them accepted a topaz ring when his customer couldn't produce in White rubles the huge sum he demanded.

We arrived back at the train in a sober mood. The town was on the edge of hysteria. I shuddered to think what would happen if the Reds entered it before the evacuation was complete.

Coming into the lounge we heard the unmistakable sound of sobbing from the pantry.

'*Bozhe moi*,' Kink said, 'Cowderdrill's in tears. I'd better go and see what the trouble is.'

He came back shaking his head. 'The cove went to a jeweller in town to have that stuff of his appraised. He told him it was practically worthless. Now Cowderdrill says he'll be in the RAF till they pension him off. No women, no yachts, no Monte Carlo.'

The boys laughed, but I found Cowderdrills disillusionment less than amusing. It was my fault, in a way; I should have wised him up in Kotluban, when the foolishness started.

I got up and went into the pantry. To my surprise, Cowderdrill sat smiling gently out the window.

'Sergeant,' I said, 'I'm sorry. I should have told you about the jewels before. I hope this doesn't sour you on Russia for good.'

His homely face broke into a smile. 'No, Sir, it don't. I've thought it over and I'm thinking now I should be grateful for all the happiness I had, Sir, just imagining what I'd do with the money. Them expensive women on my arm, and me leaning over the balustrade at Monte Carlo, dressed in white tie and tails, like a blooming toff, looking down at the water with the lights playing over it and the yachts moored below. And violins in the background, and the smell of bougainvillaea and a bottle of champagne waiting for me back at the hotel. Very Ethel Dell, don't you know, Sir?[3] Well, I've just been telling myself that everything you get in life you pay for, and I guess the jewels paid for my dreams of that.'

★

In the next days, while the Mission quartermasters were completing the outfitting of our train, we got a replacement for Russky. He was Count Vladimir d'Adix, a dark-haired captain of infantry who had fourteen decorations and as many wounds. D'Adix was tall and well-built like almost all Russian aristocrats; he spoke six languages; he was, we had heard, though not from him, one of the best harpsichord players in Europe. We stood in awe of his dignity and perfect manners till he spilled a cup of Bovril over his impeccable uniform, whereupon we started calling him Wally in comfort.

Wally d'Alix could never replace Russky in our affections, but we found him very likeable all the same; competent, considerate, modest, and a first-class soldier. Moreover, as an ex-staff officer of Wrangel's he was privy to Headquarters intrigue, and wasn't averse to filling us in on its juicier aspects.

Wrangel sent us an invitation to dinner at his headquarters car across the bay. We spruced up and arrived unfashionably on time, at eight o'clock sharp.

It was a small group compared to that which had attended his triumphal banquet in Tsaritsyn: only the general, his wife, his chief of staff, and a Cossack bodyguard of three men who served the dinner. The meal itself, though well-prepared, was simple and meager; I couldn't help thinking back to the gargantuan feast of victory we had enjoyed in the city on the Volga less than five months before.

Wrangel showed no trace of his recent frustrations; he was warm and outgoing, a charming host. I was seated next to the baroness, a dark and handsome young woman, unaffected and intensely alive. She apologized for her dress, and told me it was one of the two she owned.

'It is perhaps just as well that we will not take Moscow,' she said in English, smiling ruefully. 'If we did, I would have nothing at all to wear.'

'Lenin says different in his propaganda leaflets,' I told her. 'In the last one I saw you're said to travel in a coach upholstered in ermine with a dozen handmaidens, all duchesses, to anticipate your every whim. They say your jewels rival those of the Empress herself.'

'It is interesting,' she said. 'The Bolsheviks do not have much imagination, and when they use it, they manage to tell only lies.'

That was the only reference made during the entire evening to either the Reds or the military situation, either by the baroness or the baron himself. During dessert he excused himself to read two telegrams which had just arrived. From his face there was no way of our guessing that it was bad news, but Kink received a signal from Wally, and we left a short time later.

Outside Wally said, 'The General showed me those telegrams. One was from Romanovsky, saying that the Reds have reoccupied Odessa, and canceling Wrangel's appointment as adjutant to Schilling. The other was from Denikin, canceling the General's nomination as commander of the Crimean troops. Denikin's reason for the latter is obvious: if the White Armies are forced to retreat into the peninsula, Denikin himself wants to be governor of the Crimea.'

'What's Wrangel's next move?' I asked Wally.

He will send in his resignation, and Denikin will accept it.'

Kink struck his thigh with his gloved hand. 'Doesn't Wrangel re-alize that if he just proclaimed himself commander-in-chief of the White Army, Denikin wouldn't have any choice but to step down?'

Wally nodded. 'Many of the most important men in the army have begged him to do just that, but he answers, "A soldier must obey".'

The next day we heard of the tragic second evacuation of Odessa. Schilling had quit the town hastily, leaving the civilians to their fate, and what happened thereafter was a nightmare. Refugees slaugh-tered one another trying to reach the boats; others drowned them-selves in the harbour or blew their brains out on the docks and quays. The shops and houses were looted by Reds and Whites alike, and the rats of the underworld had emerged from the slums and cellars to maraud and rape and break into the warehoused supplies.

The news left us with a chill; this was precisely what was in store for Novorossiisk if the Reds entered the city before the evacuation was complete.

Within seventy-two hours we had received orders from Mission Headquarters to proceed to Ekaterinodar. The track northward over the Caucasus was clear, except for an occasional snowplow, and we made the trip in a morning. Along the way we passed tons of rolling stock bound in the opposite direction.

Ekat was jammed with soldiers of the Caucasus and Dobrovolski armies who were rapidly retiring upon the overcrowded town and beyond. The Volga front was breaking; it was depressingly apparent that the Kuban couldn't be held.

We were directed to a siding at the deserted Chernomorskt aerodrome, a mile out of the city. 'Another Kupyansk,' Kink said bitterly. 'We'll be here a week or so and then we'll move back with the rest of them. We'll never get our new buses into the air.'

Kink posted a guard and we broke out the cards, the chess set, the draughts, and the rum. When we wearied of rum toddies and each other's company we went into the cabarets in town. They were wild; you could always count on a drunken Cossack or a half-savage Daghestan mountaineer, wearing the green star and crescent, to take out his revolver and shoot up the place. It passed the time.

A week after our arrival in Ekat, Kitty rode back into Tommy's life.

I was first to see her peering in through the lounge car windows. 'Tommy,' I told him, 'there's someone here to see you.'

'Tell the bastard I'll pay him next week,' he said, and went back to his inspection report.

I said, 'It isn't a man, it's a woman.'

'Bunny,' he groaned, 'don't ever pay a cigarette girl any serious attention unless you speak Russian fluently and can protect yourself from her advances.'

'Listen, it isn't your cigarette girl. It's a good-looking *chernushka* in Cossack's boots.'

He threw down his pencil and rushed to the window, and from the window to the door, upsetting Cowderdrill and a tray of Bovril. He didn't even look back to see the damage.

They came into the car with their arms around one another, chattering away. Kitty had a bullet hole in her overcoat and another through her *papakha*, but otherwise, except for having lost a little weight, she was the same as when we had seen her last at Kotluban: radiant, full of *joie de vivre*, emphatic as a cracked *nagaika*.

'Aeroplaniffs!' Kitty cried and kissed us all, including Wally.

She refused to tell us in detail what she'd been through in the past few months – it was 'horrible – death, *tif* and much, much blood'. She'd had little chance to practice her English. Two-thirds of her sotnia had been casualties; the remnant had been attached to another regiment, and she had been told to proceed to Novorossiisk at her leisure for further orders. Tommy beamed; that meant she could be our guest for a while.

The next afternoon she and Tommy came into my compartment, faces tingling and flushed from a fast sleigh ride. Her eyes were very bright.

'It's a secret,' Tommy said.

'Yes, a fine secret. When's the date?'

'When war *fini*,' she said. 'Tommy and me, we go to Paris and marry.'

'Happy landings,' I said. 'Can I be godfather?'

'You can be godfather all six time,' she assured me.

They kissed long and then left the compartment, giggling. Kitty blew me a kiss through the window as she got into the waiting sleigh.

I thought of Nina.

★

Kitty invited all of us to lunch on Pancake Sunday at the home of a friend of hers, a Kuban doctor of Ekaterinodar.

Pancake Sunday was evidently a pre-Easter celebration meant to compensate for the coming rigors of Lent. The first course was *blinochki*, pancakes stuffed with various ingredients. It was followed by *blinochki' s syrom*, Ukrainian pancakes stuffed with a mixture of cheeses and fried in butter. Then we had *bliny*, buckwheat-flour pancakes served with melted butter and caviar. There were baked pancakes stuffed with cream cheese and pancakes stuffed with chopped beef, and small pancakes served with preserves.

On the table was a huge punchbowl of vodka with coloured pebbles, anchovies and fillets of smoked herring lying at the bottom. You served yourself from it with a big silver ladle. The dining room was cheerful with its sparkling chandeliers and brightly coloured curtains.

I got talking to Dr. Vailofsky's daughter, a shy, sweet-looking girl of twenty or twenty-one. Her name was Katinka. She spoke English with an academic precision that showed she had learned it from books, and I found her charming.

After dinner Katinka played the piano in the music room and sang from Russian light opera. It was a respectable, home-like scene which we hadn't shared for quite a while.

I took Katinka into the conservatory for more conversation. She wanted to know about Paris and London and New York, and what the girls there were like. I told her as best as I could, but when I got to London she interrupted me.

'You are sad,' she said with a frankness I hadn't expected of her. 'Why is that?'

'It's the war,' I said.

'No, you have lost something in the war. I can recognize it. I do not have much experience of the world or of people, but about sadness I can tell.'

I wanted to tell her. I hadn't talked about Nina with the boys, but now I felt it would do me good.

I don't know how long I talked, but it must have been for quite some time, for when I looked up again the conservatory was almost dark.

'Thank you for listening,' I said. 'I feel much better.'

'You will suffer for a long time, I think. But at least you will have had something to suffer for, something beautiful. When the Bolsheviki come for me it will be different.' She looked down at her hands. 'You see, Captain, I have never loved.'

I was delicately silent for a moment. Then I said:

'You talk as though you expect to be killed by the Reds.'

'We do. My father is a member of the Rada, and he has spoken up for the Whites.'

'But why can't you leave the country?'

'We hear there are two hundred thousand people in Novorossiisk waiting to leave on the ships. How can we get on ahead of them?'

'Can't your father use his influence?'

'At such a time there are many people who have influence greater than his.'

'I can speak to General Holman about you and your family,' I said. 'It's worth a try.'

She smiled. 'If you would do that, Captain, we would be grateful. Now shall we join the others?'

Leaving the house the boys, Bill in particular, couldn't get over the hospitality of the Cossack doctor and his family.

'Strewth, but that's something,' Bill enthused. 'With death around the corner they break their necks to make us feel at home, even though we'll never meet again.'

Kitty snuggled against Tommy in the corner of the sleigh. 'They fine people, Bill. Why you not get interest in nice Cossack girl like Katinka?'

Bill grinned. 'She seemed more interested in Bunny here.'

Kink cleared his throat in the embarrassed silence. Daly's remark had made everybody think of Nina. The sleigh bells tinkled as the runners fled over the snow behind the two matched chestnut mares. I wanted to break the spell but I could find no way to do it.

★

In one of the cabarets we ran across Korgonovsky of the long fin-gernails, whom we had last seen in Tsaritsyn's Black Cat Café.

'Ho, Kinky!' he shouted, and came weaving over to our table. He was very drunk.

'Sit down and drink to Christmas in Moscow,' Kink said.

The Russian laughed and held out his hands. The nails were so long they had begun to corkscrew. He had difficulty picking up and holding a glass.

Korgonovsky put his finger to his lips and looked elaborately around. 'Do not tell anyone,' he said, 'but tomorrow I cut them off!'

'You're drunk,' Kink said. 'Tomorrow you'll change your mind.'

'No, I am getting drunk so I may face the facts,' he said. 'I will cut my nails tomorrow.'

Korgonovsky, we noticed, no longer wore the insignia of Shkura's regiment but the uniform of a Dobreovolski captain of artillery. Eddie asked him why he had left the dreaded Wolf's command.

'I have resign,' he said. 'Was too much thievery and corruption and I am honest man. You know Metropole Hotel and block of flats on Katerina Street?'

We knew of Ekat's Metropole Hotel, whose prices were outra-geous despite the bedbugs and vermin. For days now wild parties had been going on there; passing one evening we had seen a couple of drunken Cossack officers toss a *baryshnia* out of a first-story window. The girl had merely brushed the snow off her bottom and staggered back into the lobby of the hotel.

'Shkura bought hotel and flats with loot from raids,' the artilleryman said. 'He is millionaire several times. He has sent much money to Dutch and Swiss banks.'

We weren't a bit surprised. There were bound to be a thousand Shkuras for every Wrangel in the White Army.

At one of the nearby tables a Cossack drained his glass, crunching the fragments between his strong white teeth. He tossed what remained of the wine glass over his shoulder, and then blew the chewed bits out onto the red-checked tablecloth.

Bill stood up unsteadily. 'Come on, you types, let's get out of here. We've seen this act before.'

'I'm staying,' Kink said. 'I've got a kind of tentative appointment with a bogus princess. She said she might bring a couple of bogus countess friends along.'

''Well, I'm for an evening of quiet, sexless drinking.' Bill said. 'Anybody want to join me?'

Korgonovsky good-naturedly left with Bill. I departed a few minutes later, leaving Kink and Eddie at the table. Making conversation with a real princess and countesses who knew no English was hard enough, but a couple of bogus ones were too much!

Next morning Bill groped his way into the mess and with shaking hands took up his mug of scalding tea.

He gulped from the mug and set it down. 'I woke up in a room at five o'clock,' he began, but got no further.

'Out with it, Daly,' Kink said. 'You're still alive. We're listening sympathetically.'

'I woke up in a cold room at five o'clock this morning,' he began again, but shuddered violently and was unable to continue.

'I thought you were going drinking with Korgonovsky,' Eddie said.

'He disappeared, and I got feeling sorry for myself and decided I needed some company. Anyway, I woke up in this room, bleary-eyed, with my head in a vise, and the most God-awful racket, groans and whatnot, coming from somewhere. I hadn't the foggiest notion how I'd come to be there, and then I noticed this woman lying beside me in the damn bed. I turned to her and asked what-oh.'

'Was she the one making the racket?' asked Kink.

'No, the noise was coming from the other end of the room. My bedmate laughs and says *malenki*, baby.'

'"Where?" I asked, and she pointed and said "*Skoro budet.*" I sat up and looked to where she was pointing. There on a pallet in the corner was another woman – in labour and just about to pay her dues. Well, I rushed out without my cap, and it's a good thing I passed out with my clothes on, or else they'd still be there too.'

'You should have assisted at the birth,' Kink said. 'Good Allied relations.'

Bill shuddered. 'Now come off it, Kink. You know I can't stand the sight of blood.'

The marmalade jar on the mess table was empty, and I called out to Cowderdrill to bring in another. He didn't answer, and I got up and went into the pantry after him.

He was standing in the vestibule, counting a huge roll of Denikin rubles he had just taken from the hand of a shifty-eyed townsman in a moth-eaten *polushubok*. Profiteer was written all over the man's sallow face. Cowderdrill was selling good English pounds for worthless rubles.

The man left quickly, and Cowderdrill came back into the pantry, whistling.

'Sergeant,' I sighed, 'you're making a bad mistake.'

He looked at me in surprise. 'Mistake, Sir? I wasn't buying any jewellery, Sir. I was buying them rubles.' He looked down smugly at the wad of currency in his hand. 'Got a hundred thousand of 'em just now, I did, for just thirty pounds. Pretty good deal, Sir, wouldn't you say? Looks like I'm on the high-road again to Monte Carlo.'

'No, Cowderdrill,' I sighed. 'You're on the low road again to the poorhouse. Don't you realize that inflation only goes one way?'

He cocked a puzzled eyebrow at me. 'Begging your pardon, Sir, but I don't quite follow. Seems to me the rubles I've got now, over a hundred and fifty thousand of 'em, is worth an awful lot of English pounds.'

'They would be, Cowderdrill, if rubles were at par value. But they're not. This week they're seven hundred to the pound. Next week they'll be eight hundred or a thousand.'

He blinked at me. 'Par value, Sir?'

'Look, keep your English pounds, Cowderdrill. Just don't throw them away. Will you remember that?'

A canny expression came over his face. 'But Sir, if rubles go up to more than a thousand a pound, shouldn't I take advantage of it? Wouldn't that be a deal I couldn't afford to miss?'

I gave up, and very quietly asked for the jar of marmalade.

★

A few nights later, the midst of a demi-*prazdnik*, Bill suddenly looked up, grasped my arm and said hoarsely, 'That little redhead over there, talking to Kitty. That's the girl!'

'What girl?' I said.

'The girl who had the baby.'

He dragged me over to Kitty and the girl, who recognized him and laughed.

'Kitty,' Bill said, 'ask her what happened to the *malenki*.'

The girl guessed his question at the word *malenki*, and by way of answer held up a tightly doubled fist to indicate an infant's head. With the index finger of her other hand, representing a hatpin, she stabbed her fist. Then she rattled off some Russian.

'She say,' Kitty said, 'How can she feed *malenki* when half the time she starve herself? How can she keep *malenki* when she have no place warm to live, and the Bolshies soon coming?'

The little redhead was nodding eagerly, anxious for us to understand. Then, abruptly, she broke into hysterical tears. Kitty took her off to the lav, clucking sympathetically.

It wasn't much of a *prazdnik* after that.

At daybreak a sergeant's guard from Holman's headquarters awoke Kink to deliver special orders. B Flight was to leave the train immediately and report to British GHQ in full marching order. There was no further explanation.

Wally insisted upon remaining on the train with Kitty. 'If it is saboteurs, I will talk them out of dynamiting the train. If it is infiltrators, Kitty and I will kill them. Please, Kink, understand that my place is with Kitty here.'

'Take good care of her, Wally,' Tommy said and gripped his hand.

There was a faint crack of rifle fire windward as we marched through the frozen, silent streets to Headquarters in the centre of the city a mile away. We were the last to arrive at the crumbling courtyard of the big public building, with its three field guns poking through the battered walls. Here, in a hollow square, stood most of what was left of the British contingent in South Russia: staff, infantry Tommies, tankmen, gunners, airmen. Among them were officers and enlisted men from the Irish, Welsh, Grenadier and Coldstream Guards, the Seaforth Highlanders and the Black Watch, those proud and famous regiments which had fought to glory at Aisne, Mons and Le Cateau, on the Aisne, the Somme, at St. Quentin, and Ypres.

Altogether we numbered about nine hundred men.

We stood easy as the first tentative flakes of the early morning snowfall fluttered down. Then Holman emerged alone from the building. We snapped to attention. He walked to the centre of the square and gave the command to stand easy. I noticed how grey his hair was against his cap's scarlet band.

He began to speak:

'Ekaterinodar has been abandoned by the White Army, except for a few companies fighting delaying actions in the outskirts of the city. In Ekaterinodar are ten thousand women and children, the wives and families of Russian officers with whom we have fought side by side. In the surrounding country are five thousand more.

'I have information that a Red uprising within the city plans to seize the railway stations and the local government tonight. If we go now, these women and children will be at the mercy of the Bolsheviks.

'When the retreat began I was ordered by the War Office to concentrate all British personnel at the nearest Black Sea port. This I could not immediately do without serious consequences to our Russian Allies. I did not do it.

'I have given my word to the Russians in Ekaterinodar that I will not leave until they have been evacuated to Novorossiisk. I have no authority to command you to stay with me. If you remain, and the Reds take the railway, you will have to walk to Novorossiisk. You know what that means.

'An armoured train leaves in thirty minutes for Novorossiik. Any officer or enlisted man who wishes to take it, advance two steps forward.'

It was the simple, straightforward statement of a soldier. There had been no dramatics, no heroics; no demand for loyalty. A man had spoken whose compassion and humanity were his only guides. And in the same spirit Holman had left the decision – one of possible life or death – open to each individual conscience.

For the moment the sound of distant gunfire had ceased. The silence, broken only by the tramp of the sentry pacing the courtyard gates, was the most terrible I had ever known.

I thought of the number ninety. It was ninety miles to Novorossiisk. Ninety miles was no great distance by train or motor car. But on foot, in the Russian winter, through the frozen passes of the Caucasus with the north wind from the steppe at your back, it was something more than ninety miles. Makhno's Green Guards and the pursuing Reds would make it more than ninety miles. We would have to fight every step of the way, and there would be many among us who would not reach the sea.

The silence was broken as Weller, Maund's staff wireless officer, along with two privates of Maund's command, moved two paces forward.

'I've got sore feet, Sir,' Weller said. He might as well have told the General that he believed a man should live out his fourscore and ten, or that he didn't want to die. All of the men in that courtyard wanted to live out their fourscore and ten, and none of them wanted to die.

The two privates had no excuses.

Holman ordered a corporal's guard to take the three men down to the station in a lorry. A hundred others were assigned to defend headquarters; the rest, including B Flight, were posted to the defense of the railyards.

Marching back to the yards, we heard the clanging bell of the departing armoured train.

At B Flight siding Kink sent the men to their stations. I met Eddie at the rifle racks, taking down his Lee-Enfield. He said to me: 'You know, it took more courage for those men to leave and live with the thought of it for the rest of their lives, than it took to stay and die with Holman. I couldn't have taken those two steps to save my life.'

He had, I thought, expressed it perfectly.

BOOK FIVE

*

Journey's End

Chapter Fourteen

✳

The local Bolshies had bluffed on the British leaving Ekat in advance of the uprising, and the threatened *coup* failed to come off. A few scattered shots were fired at Mission Headquarters and at the station, but there was no full-scale attack.

Shortly after we had left for HQ a band of fifteen men wearing Red brassards appeared at B Flight train. Cocking his Lewis, Wally had called out and asked them what they wanted. The group had hesitated, then melted away.

'Was good Wally and me stay in train,' Kitty said. 'If nobody here they would have come aboard and much destroyed.'

Next morning we began to evacuate the families of the White officers to Novorossiisk. There were over fifteen thousand women and children, and it took over a week. Those for whom there was no room on the crowded trains were sent in carts and sleighs and *brichkas* over the southbound roads with an armed escort of Mission Tommies.

Holman, working night and day, seemed to be everywhere at once: in the yards, on the streets, at the station. His immense personal authority overwhelmed every problem and made it seem like child's play. After an eight-hour shift at his side we would return to the train exhausted, but the general would continue on for another four hours or more, signing papers, interviewing refugees with special problems, dashing out of the station house to dress down a refractory engine driver, fireman or self-appointed official.

I had a chance to speak to him about Katinka's family, and he found a place for them on a train, though he could promise nothing about transport to the Crimea or Constantinople once they had reached Novorossiisk.

'You might not believe it, Captain,' he told me, 'but if Trotsky himself turned traitor and appeared dockside, we'd have to sling up a hammock for him in one of the galleys, and we couldn't guarantee that he wouldn't fall into the soup.'

Holman and his staff were on the last train to leave Ekat; B Flight train got out the day before, packed with four hundred Tommies. The trip through the mountains was uneventful till we got to the mouth of the pass beyond which lay Novorossiisk harbour and the sea.

The train puffed slowly up the grade and came to a stop. Kink raised his eyebrows and we swung off for a look. A quarter mile down the track, beginning at the right hand spur of the mountain, a long assembly line of booted and overcoated figures were handing rocks and stones to the anchor men who stood at the track. From the distance they looked like children playing a malicious game. They ignored us completely.

'Green Guards blocking the track,' Kink said. 'Get the men to battle stations.' He ran ahead to the engineer's cab.

Snipers from the mountainside opened fire as I ducked back into the car.

Hoskins was putting a new ammunition drum into his Lewis on the lounge car platform. 'How many of them do you expect there are, Sir?' he asked me.

I poked my head out and pulled it back as a bullet pinged off the side of the train. 'It's hard to tell until they attack in force. Maybe five hundred or a thousand, maybe more.'

Hoskins began shooting as I went forward to check on the other cars. Our other machine guns opened fire.

Kink had the engineer bring the train to within a hundred yards of the barricade, and we traded shots with them from there. The Greens had good cover and were giving us trouble. Aiming for the windows, they systematically broke every pane of glass on the exposed side of the train, and the ricocheting slugs were doing damage. They might put enough of us out of action to make a charge on the train. Should the Greens manage to get in close enough to grenade our ammo cars, they might be able to take us over.

Kink came racing back from the cab and told Eddie to take a squad out to the rear. The guerrillas might be blocking our escape route. Eddie came back a few minutes later saying that the track was clear.

'All right,' Kink told him, 'take fifty men and post them behind the rear cars. We can't let them cut us off.'

The Greens were concentrating their fire on the vestibule platforms, and now we were beginning to suffer some casualties among the Lewis men. A corporal and a private down the line were killed. Hoskins got nicked in the shoulder, and another gunner took a ricochet in the calf of his leg.[1] One of the Tommies aboard had been a medical orderly in Ekat, and he bound their wounds. I took over Hoskins' place on the lounge car platform. The Lewis got so hot I had to borrow the heavier gloves of the private beside me.

I had underestimated the number of Greens against us. There were definitely more than a thousand. I wondered how many Reds there were among them; certainly by this time the Kremlin had seen the value of infiltrating Makhno's ranks with men whose eventual purpose it was to take over the outlaw bands.

The Greens began to move in, slipping and rolling down the mountainside to take cover behind rocks and boulders closer to the train. They were so close now that I could see the band of green ribbon most of them wore across their chests.

Shells began to explode on the mountainside, sending up huge gouts of snow, rock and dirt.

'What's that, Sir?' the private asked me.

I drew a long breath of relief. 'Four-inch guns. An armoured train's come up behind us.'[2]

We kept up our fire, though it was superfluous; the shells of the armoured train were massacring the Greens at point-blank range. Where before they had been inching down the mountain, now they were scrambling up again, and the shellfire was taking a terrific toll. For a good half hour men and muck came tumbling down in an avalanche.

When the four-inch guns fell silent Kink sent out a detail to clear the tracks and paid a call of thanks to the commander of the armoured train.

He came back carrying a quart of Scotch whisky. 'The blokes thanked us,' he said. 'They've been stuck up in Ekat and this is the first action they've seen in donkey's years.'

Coming through the pass above Novorossiisk we saw immediately the change a few weeks had meant in the complexion of ships in the harbour. Most of the steamers and passenger-carrying freighters were gone, and only a few transports, lighters and launches were at anchor; the slips and the deeper water beyond the mole were filled with cruisers, dreadnaughts, scout-cruisers and destroyers, from the looks of their lines mostly British. There must have been fifty of them. The big guns of the dreadnaughts were trained directly on the pass.

If the appearance of the harbour had changed, the weather had changed also, and much for the worse. A cold wind of implacable strength and Arctic bitterness blew down on the town from the mountains above, chilling the Kalmuk and Cossack encampments on the hills above the city, blowing down on the rickety boxcars in which the White officers and their families huddled. We hadn't really been conscious of this winter wind, the famous Russian *bora*, till we came down into the town and felt it at our backs.

HQ had quartered us in an abandoned cement factory on the bluffs outside of town. A siding ran directly to it. We moved in as quickly as possible, and got a fire going in the boiler room furnace with coal from the engine tender.

For a long time we sat in front of the furnace, thawing out. Finally Eddie said, 'I feel like I've gotten off at the end of the world and the railroad's discontinued return service.' He spoke for all of us.

★

Next morning we bundled up and went out to take a look around.

Lined up on the wharfs were rows of field guns and mountains of ammunition, supplies and equipment. As we watched, companies of ordnance men stripped the guns of their breech-blocks and pushed them over the sides into the icy water of the bay.

'Strewth,' Bill said. 'That's probably twice as much artillery as Napoleon ever had.'

'The hell with the artillery,' Kink said, shivering. 'What I'm worried about is our planes. Any day we'll be getting an order to drop them over the side.'

We walked on, leaning into the terrific wind. In almost every street of the town lay bodies, some of them coatless and bootless, all turned blue from the cold. They lay in doorways, in alleys, in the gutters. Turning a corner you had to be careful about ice and a possible corpse in your path.

Tommy side-stepped a body irritably; yesterday he had been separated from Kitty when they had quartered her with a regiment of Cossacks in an armory on the other side of town, and his mood had been stormy ever since. 'For Jesus' sake, can't they cart the bodies away?' he wanted to know. 'You'd think there'd be a pretense of sanitation.'

'There is,' Kink said. 'These are the people who went west last night and early this morning. They cart the dead bodies away every afternoon at five.'

Chilled to the marrow, we stopped into a cafe for a spot of tea. When we came out again a gust of wind knocked Tommy down, and he had to grab on to a railing to avoid being carried down the street. Kink hailed an icicle covered *izvozchik*, and, teeth chattering, we were driven back to the cement factory.

Major Bingham came to dinner that evening. The strain had told; he was as nervous as a white cat in the Kremlin and prefaced everything he said with a short, abrupt laugh. We had never seen him drink so heavily; within an hour he had polished off the last of the Scotch.

The evacuation, he told us, was getting completely out of hand. Yesterday a mob of refugees had massed before the evacuation office, and he had had to call out a squad of Grenadiers to disperse them at bayonet point. He had put up a camp bed in his office to avoid the pleading refugees; everywhere he went people begged him for a place aboard a British ship. Several of those he had been forced to refuse had committed suicide. By now it was common knowledge that the civilian ship lines had canceled their runs to Novorossiisk, and that the only way out of the city, aside from a few barges, launches and tugboats, was aboard a military transport or an Allied man-of-war.

'And yet people hope,' he said. 'Especially the young. And that's the cruelest part of it. There are countless young girls and women of education and breeding who are selling themselves to get money to feed their families and to bribe a barge or tugboat captain. The other day my adjutant discovered one strangled in her bed. The murderer had taken all the foreign currency she'd saved for her parents' passage. Of course we'll never catch him; how can you do police work at a time like this? Another young girl earned enough from prostitution to buy her sister and herself passage on the Italian Lloyd. When they went aboard they were told accommodations and food weren't included. They needed another fifty pounds to save their lives. The girl finally cut her wrists in a hotel bathroom.' He reached for the bottle and poured himself another drink.

'Major, what have you heard about General Wrangel?' Kink asked, trying to turn the conversation to something less unpleasant and depressing. 'Is he still in the Crimea? Is there any chance he might take over there?'

'No, he's left Yalta and gone on to Constantinople with his family.

When he got to Sebastopol from Novorossiisk General Schilling begged him to take over the military area, but Wrangel told Schilling he could assume no command without Denikin's authorization. Then this Captain Orlov, who's raised an insurrection against Denikin in the hills, published a proclamation saying that Wrangel was the only man with whom he would negotiate. Wrangel refused the honour and asked Orlov to submit to his superiors. Then Wrangel read in the official White newspapers that he and Chatilov had been cashiered at their own request. That was almost the last straw. A few days later he heard that Denikin, through Holman, was demanding his expulsion from Russian territory. He left for Constantinople on the next ship.'

'So he's out of it,' Eddie said. 'The best man the Whites have.'

'I don't know,' Bingham said wearily. 'A lot of people are openly advocating Wrangel as Denikin's successor. Denikin's being discredited more and more every day. I saw him the other afternoon at White headquarters, and he didn't look like a man who had much confidence in either himself or his command.'

'Major,' Kink said, 'can you answer me this? I know General Holman thinks highly of Wrangel. Why doesn't the Mission take a stand on one man or the other and use its influence to see him through?'

'In the first place, Kink,' Bingham answered, 'it's British policy not to "interfere", but to "suggest". At bottom I'd say the problem was this: Holman has had contradictory orders from pro- and anti-Denikin British authorities in the Near and Middle East, both of whom spend their time checkmating one another. He's trying to use his judgment and doing the best he can.'

Muddle, I thought; the good old British muddle. It had won an empire. It could do its best to lose one, too.

The next day he heard that no civilians or POWs were to be allowed military transport from Novorossiisk. Only Mission troops, soldiers of the Volunteer Army and their wives and families, and a certain number of Cossacks were to be evacuated aboard the Allied ships. Bingham had promised Tommy there would be room for Kitty, and assured me he would do everything in his power for the Vailofskys, but it looked as though most of the forty thousand Kuban Cossacks, the civilians and the *plennys*, would have to leave on foot. It was easier not to tell Feodar of the high command's decision; I knew he would hear about it on the grapevine anyway.

That night the searchlights of the British dreadnaught, the *Emperor of India*, began to patrol the pass and the neighboring hills. Early in the morning we heard intermittent fusillades from the city. Wally went into town and reported back that the Green Guards had rushed the civil prison and released everyone held in the building. Makhno's men were getting increasingly bold: now they were dropping into the rooms of Volunteer officers and openly urging them to join the Greens.

After lunch Tommy and I braved the *bora* and went into town. We parted at the top of the hill, Tommy bound for the armory and Kitty, I headed for the hotel where the Vailofskys were staying.

The cold lobby of the Nicholas II was jammed with refugees who had evidently paid for the privilege of sleeping on the floor. The lift was out of order, and I walked up four flights to the Cossack doctor's rooms. Every landing had its family of fugitives huddled together for a little warmth. Some chafed their hands at kerosene lamps. I didn't like to think what would happen if one of them tipped over and spread fire through the flimsy hotel.

Katinka answered the door in her overcoat. Smiling shyly, she let me into the small suite. The doctor and his wife rose to greet me, and then retired into the next room.

Katinka and I sat down on the sofa. It was the only piece of furniture in the room aside from two small cots that had been pushed up against the wall. In the corner of the room was the family ikon, surrounded by tapers, other holy pictures and a collection of family photographs. The Vailofskys had left everything else behind but these, their clothes, and their money.

'I'm sorry I haven't had a chance to drop by before this,' I told her. 'How have you and your parents been?'

'All right,' she said. 'Mother had a spell of nausea and we were afraid it was the typhus, but she was better the next morning. And you?'

'We shiver and we wait and hope that we don't catch the *tif*. Which is about all that you can do.'

'Besides wait on the queues for bread. Now we hear a rumour that beginning next week there will be a bread shortage.'

'Don't worry about it. We've got plenty of hardtack. I brought some with me. You won't starve as long as the British are in Novorossiisk.'

'And how long do you think that will be?'

'We've still got a lot of stores and equipment to destroy. I'd say another week or two, maybe more.'

She nodded. 'That is good to hear. As long as the English are in Novorossiisk the Reds will not try to occupy it.'

'Katinka, I still haven't heard from Major Bingham about passage for you and your family.' Her face fell, and I was quick to add: 'But that doesn't mean he can't talk some launch or tugboat captain into taking you aboard. You have the money, and that helps. I don't think it's hopeless.'

'Father says we can offer anything they want.'

'Yes, and it's going to take a fortune. I hear there are thousands of people who spent their last ruble to get across.'

We talked a while, and then she offered me a cup of tea. I declined, saying I was due back at the factory. I was, as a matter of fact, feeling particularly blue. Much as I liked Katinka and her family they depressed me. The hotel depressed me, and if I could avoid it, I had no intention of coming back again. If Bingham came through I would give Katinka the good news over the phone.

Only later, back at the cement factory, did the reason for my acute depression at the hotel occur to me. It was simple enough: Katinka, a girl for whom I felt only fondness, was alive and had a good chance to go on living. And Nina was dead.

★

In the teeth of a screaming wind, against which we could hardly stand, we hauled the Camels from the flatcars to the nearest dock. There a tank lumbered over them, reducing the fuselages to torn fabric, splintered spruce and tangled wires, and the engines to twisted scrap. Tommy and an ordnance man were blown into the water, and from the hill above, a freight car, blown off its tracks, came crashing down the slope to the quay. When the Camels were destroyed we were put to work rolling forty brand new DeHavilland-9s still in their warehouse packing cases to the end of the quay, where the tank pulverized them. Then the tank, in turn, with controls set and engine running, was sent waddling over the dock into the bay.

On the way back to the factory we saw a cloud of smoke rising from the centre of the city. 'Strewth,' Bill said, alarmed, 'is that the Bolshies?'

'Looks like a blaze,' Kink said. 'Probably one of those tinderbox rooming houses caught fire and set off the whole block.'

There was a message waiting for me from GHQ to call Captain Sampson, Bingham's Adjutant. Sampson had welcome news: he had arranged passage for Doctor Vailofsky and family on a launch leaving for Yalta early tomorrow morning. I thanked him, hung up, and called Katinka at the hotel.

The military operator answered and told me to hold on. Then we were disconnected. When, after five minutes of trying, I got him back, the operator told me the line to the Hotel Nicholas II was down.

I asked him why, and he said there had been a fire. He had no further information.

I decided I had better take a look and see. Wally drove me into town in a van we had recently borrowed without permission from the Mission car depot.

There were no militiamen to stop us from approaching close to the hotel, only the fire itself, which was considerable. Half the block was blazing, and the Nicholas II was almost completely destroyed. A few ancient fire engines were on the scene directing apathetic streams of water into those buildings which still had a chance of being saved. Icicles had already formed around the nozzles of the fire hoses.

In the next block a kind of refugee centre had been established for the fire victims in an empty market. I didn't see the Vailofskys as Wally and I pushed our way through the crowd. I recognized the ashen hotel manager and went up to him.

'Ask him where Dr Vailofsky and his family are,' I said to Wally.

When Wally turned back to me he avoided my eyes. 'Bunny, I am sorry but everybody on the top floor of the hotel died in the fire, so far as the manager knows. He hasn't seen any of the Vailofskys, so he assumes they're dead too.'

'Does he know how the fire started?' I asked automatically.

'He says that one of the refugees' kerosene lamps tipped over and ignited the rug in the hall.'

'Let's get out of here,' I said, and we pushed our way back through the crowd. At the door I stepped aside as stretchered victims, most of them terribly burned, were carried into the market. They were the last of the saved. The Vailofskys weren't among them.

★

Sir George Milne, commander-in-chief of the Army of the Black Sea, arrived in Novorossiisk to replace Holman – reason unknown.[3] Maund was demoted in rank and sent back home – reason unknown.

With the fall of Ekat on March 17th the destruction of stores and equipment was accelerated. The Mission assigned us to ten-hour shifts in the warehouses and on the quays. One of my jobs was to help an officer of the quartermasters smash over five hundred one-gallon stone jugs of rum. With his cooperation I saved about fifteen of them. We carried the jugs reverently into the factory storeroom and put them under lock and key.

Nightly the searchlights of the *Emperor of India* swept over the pass and the hills, and occasionally its ten-inch guns lobbed a shell over the city toward the pass. The Greens attacked the military prison and were driven off. Three car-loads of British military uniforms were stolen from Mission HQ. The bread supply ran out and the bakeries were mobbed and looted. Organized bands of criminals systematically attacked, robbed and killed well-heeled refugees whenever and wherever they found them. We heard that transports, meant to evacuate the civilians, were being held in foreign ports under quarantine.

Wally came in one afternoon from White Headquarters with the news that Denikin had dismissed Romanovsky and replaced him with General Makrov. Several other high-ranking officers had been cashiered at their own request, but Wally doubted that public resentment had been satisfied. Kutepov, in charge of the defense of the city, had admitted to his staff that morale was so bad among the Volunteers and Cossacks, some of whom were refusing to fight on in the Crimea, that to postpone the final evacuation much longer would result in total disaster.

Wally handed Kink a folded sheet of paper. 'This is a letter written from Wrangel to Denikin. An officer sympathetic to Wrangel made copies in English of certain extracts from it. It was suggested that I show it to as many British officers as possible.'

After he had read the letter, Kink handed it to me without comment. It read:

You saw that your prestige was melting and that power was slipping

from your hands. As you clung to it blindly, you began to imagine
sedition and rebellion around you… Poisoned by the venom of am-
bition, drunk with power, surrounded by low sycophants, you thought
not of saving the country, but of preserving your authority…

The Army, brought up on arbitrary rule, plunder, drunkenness,
under the leadership of men who demoralized the rank and file by
their example, such an Army could not recreate Russia…

The eyes of the public began to be opened… More and more
loudly were acclaimed the leaders whose names remained unsullied
among the general corruption… Both the Army and the citizenry…
saw in me the man capable of giving them what they longed for…

Kink waited till we had all read it in turn. Then he said: 'I know
whose side I'm on. I think the same is true of you all. But I don't
believe it's our place to help stir up trouble. I doubt very much that
Wrangel wanted that letter shown around. You agree, Wally?'

Wally nodded.

Kink slowly tore the letter into pieces and dropped them to the
floor.

A Tommy private appeared in the doorway. 'Sir,' he addressed
Kink bewilderedly, 'the Mess Sergeant says yer Petrograd Ponies are
jumpin' the 'urdles.'

Petrograd Ponies was our private code word for Cowderdrill's
cold weather hot toddies. We put on our greatcoats, caps and scarves
and went across the yard to the train.

Kink was on his second Pony when a call from Mission Headquarters came for him at the factory. He returned deathly pale.

'Bad news, chaps. Major Bingham's just shot himself through the
head in his billet on the hill.'

We stared at him.

'It was too much for the Major,' Kink said. 'He fell apart.'

He finally broke the silence. 'Listen, GHQ wants to know by tomorrow morning which of you intend to go home and which of
you want to continue on with Colly in the Crimea. I know this is a
hell of a time to ask, but that's the situation. I might as well tell you
– I'm for Blighty.'

I raised my hand for the Crimea. I really didn't know why. Eddie
raised his hand too. I was surprised; I would have thought he'd be
the first to choose home.

The *bora* shook the train. Cold pierced the windows. Our fag smoke gathered on the ceiling.

'Cowderdrill!' Kink bawled. 'Another round of ponies! And make them with a kick, man!' Under his breath he added gently, almost absently, 'We've got a lot to forget.'

★

Another few days of waiting and the order came from Mission GHQ: evacuate March 27th, tomorrow. B Flight was among four thousand eight hundred troops assigned to a captured German merchantman, the *Bremerhaven*, built to accommodate one thousand five hundred.

Denikin and his staff were already aboard the French destroyer *Capitaine Saken*. The previous night the *Emperor of India* and the *Waldeck-Rousseau* had begun to bombard the pass at regular intervals,[4] and the big guns boomed from the harbour with the monotony of a tolling bell. Beyond the pass our old friend Budenny, his horsemen, and the Red armoured trains waited. The hillsides were guarded sparsely by a few outposts of Volunteers. White Headquarters had asked General Sidorin to occupy the foothills with his Don Cossacks till the bulk of the troop transports returned from the Crimea, but Sidorin had refused, and marched off with a section of his troops toward Georgia. We didn't hear of his reason and we didn't much care.

From time to time we heard shots from the town – looters and infiltrators were out in broad daylight – but otherwise there was the same baneful silence that had fallen over Rostov yards the night before the crossing.

One good thing happened: the *bora* abated. The weather was still bitterly cold, but to be outside about your work was bearable.

Tommy came back from town walking like a man who had gotten a bad knock on the head. He disappeared into his compartment, and I went in after him.

He lay on his bunk, staring at the ceiling. 'Kitty won't come,' he told me tonelessly. 'She won't leave the regiment of Kubans she's with if they can't get passage too. She's going to wait with them till the transports get back from Sebastopol.'

'Well, that's not so bad,' I said. 'Aren't they expected momentarily?'

'We were expected to win the war. When we leave the Reds and Greens are going to swarm down from the mountains. I know it, you know it. It won't take Budenny more than an hour to finish the Cossacks off.'

'I'll go have a talk with her. Maybe she'll listen.'

'Bunny, it's no use. I offered to stay with her, but she wouldn't have it. She threatened to put me under arrest and turn me over as a deserter. And she would have done it too... *Kunak*, if you don't mind, I'd rather be alone now.'

That afternoon we moved back to the train from the factory and got ready for departure. Kink planned to take the train all the way down to the pier; it was the only way to get through the thousands of refugees who had descended upon the quayside. He had been down to the docks at noontime and seen the huge and threatening crowds. Heavy guards were posted on all the Allied warships to prevent the refugees from swarming aboard and sinking the ships by sheer weight of numbers. The fugitives were camped on the piers in the thousands, squatting on their belongings and warming themselves around bonfires. One of them had dived into the icy water and swum to a nearby French destroyer. The French had picked him out of the water, dried him off, and then returned him to the wharf in a launch.

'You should have seen the refugees' faces when he stepped ashore again,' Kink said. 'It was as though they'd all planned in a pinch to do the same, and now they knew that way – the last way – was closed to them.'

Around eight o'clock Hoskins came into the lounge and told us there was a crowd of refugees in the factory yard. 'They have a spokesman says he heard a rumour in town that the English pilots were taking refugees along with them. I told him it wasn't true, but he wants to speak to the Major.'

We went outside with Kink. Huddled in a corner of the yard, slapping their sides with their arms to keep warm, were a hundred or so men, women and children. The hope in their eyes as they saw us approach made me feel like a louse.

Wally told them in Russian that the *angliski* were sorry but, as they knew, the regulations were that only military personnel was to embark on the warships. The major felt the greatest sympathy for them but he could do nothing.

'*Nichevo*,' he repeated. '*Prostite*.'

Several of the women began to weep. The spokesman stepped forward with a bundle of rubles. A woman pushed her attractive young daughter into the lamplight. A child offered Kink her dirty doll.

'I can't stand this,' he said hoarsely. 'Get them out of here.' He turned on his boot-heel and began to move away toward the train. Then he stopped and turned around. 'Bunny,' he said, 'break out the rum and distribute it. Let the poor sods die drunk. It's the best I can do.'

After I had distributed the rum and the refugees had left the yard I called Feodor to my compartment. I gave him a roll of Kerensky rubles, what clothes our orders allowed me to spare, and a German Luger, with ammunition, which I had picked up during my travels.

'The money's for you to go into town, right now, and get yourself some civilian clothes. The trade marts must be open. If the Reds catch you in that POW uniform – '

'*Da*, Captain. *Spasibo*.'

'Feodor, what are your plans? Are you going to lie low till things are quieter and then try to get home? I know you don't intend rejoining the Bolshies, not that I'd blame you, if it means your neck.'

He ducked his head. 'I would like, Captain, to go with you to Crimea.'

'I'd like that too, but we both know you can't.'

'Then I hide for while and after I go home.'

'Yes, you ought to go home and grab yourself a girl – along with a piece of the proleterian heaven.' I looked at my watch. 'You'd better be off. Tell Private Crawford I asked him to give you a ride in the van. I'll see you tomorrow morning.'

He hesitated. 'Captain, there is no way I go with you to Crimea? I not eat much and polish shoes till shine. I …'

'Feodor, don't make it harder for me than it is. *Pozhaluista*.'

'*Da*, Captain. *Spokoinoi nochi*.'

'Goodnight, Feodor.'

I checked my kit for the third time and left the compartment for the lounge car. Kink was sitting there morosely with a Petrograd Pony.

'Feodor just came through looking like he lost his brother. Did you say your good-byes?'

'I'm saving them for the pier.'

'Me too. I'm afraid to say good-bye to Ivan. He might put a bullet through his head.'

'More likely he'd jump into the bay and swim out to the ship. You better be prepared for it.'

He nodded.

'What does Ivan say he's going to do? Go down fighting?'

'He wants to take Budenny with him. I gave the sod some money and told him to forget the heroics and try to get back to Minsk.'

Bill and Eddie came in and sat down gloomily.

'We know,' I told him. 'We've just been through it.'

Bill hit the side of the chair with his closed fist. 'And there's not a blessed thing you can do. Strewth, that's the worst of it. The Bolshies aren't going to say they understand, let bygones be bygones. Once they catch Mikhail they're going to put him up against the wall and shoot him. If they don't flay him alive first.'

'I asked the MLO again about Valentin,' Eddie said bitterly, 'but it's no damn use.'

'How's Tommy feeling?' I asked to change the subject.

'I think he's trying to grow up, poor kid,' said Eddie. 'There's a gallon jug of rum under his bunk but the seal is intact. He's just lying there, staring into the dark.'

The *Emperor of India* boomed a shell into the pass. We waited, listening. Ten, twenty, thirty seconds. Then the boom of the *Waldeck-Rousseau*'s starboard gun. Another thirty seconds and the *Emperor* poke again.

'I can just see the Red bastards up there,' Bill said. 'Thousands of men and horses, a sea of them. And miles of trains. Waiting. Waiting till the bombardment stops.'

'And down here we're waiting too,' I said. 'Maybe if we both wait long enough nothing will happen.'

'Yes,' Bill said. 'Maybe we can just stop the clock.'

'You can stop the clock,' Eddie said. 'You can even get a chance to stop history. But only one chance. And we've had it.'

The French gunners sent another shell booming into the pass. We waited, counting the seconds, for the *Emperor*'s next asterisk on the page of history.

★

B Flight train didn't move down to the quay till four o'clock; there were other Mission trains ahead of us stalled by the flood of refugees overflowing the approaches to the piers, and the Tommies had been forced to use their bayonets and rifle butts to get them off the tracks.

All that day we heard scattered rifle fire from the bay area. The big naval guns were still regularly, monotonously pounding the pass.

Kink finally got the word from Headquarters to leave for the harbour. He came back from the factory telephone walking with the stiff-legged stride that told us there was trouble. 'It's a madhouse down there,' he said. 'Those shots you hear are from Red snipers on nearby rooftops. The men who stole the Tommies' uniforms are trying to use them to get aboard. Refugees are putting pistols to their heads and jumping into the bay. It's Odessa all over again, but on a much bigger scale.'

The train set off slowly for the quay. Coming down the hill into the harbour we could see the whole fantastic scene in panorama. The waterfront was black with human beings. A solid mass of people covered the shore, the quay, the piers, the mole and the break-water. Most of the wharves were littered with stores and supplies there had been no time to destroy. Rifle flashes came from the rooftops; fire had broken out in a number of buildings at the edge of the town. On a hill near the pier where our ship was moored fluttered the red-and-blue striped flag of the Kubans. Around it clustered a brigade and a half of exhausted men and horses watching, with seeming impassivity, the chaos below. Kitty was undoubtedly among them.

These were all that remained of the forty thousand Kuban Cossacks who had already left Novorossiisk to push along the coast to Georgia. Behind them were six years of constant, bloody warfare, from the Masurian Lakes to the Carpathian passes, first against the Central Powers, then against the Reds. All that was left to them was that tattered standard. As we watched, stragglers from the outposts at the pass continued to swell their number.

'Strewth,' Bill said with passion, 'it isn't fair!'

Tommy grinned crookedly. 'What is fair in love and war? As a matter of fact, what's fair out of it?'

At the quay Hoskins and a sergeant's guard got off the train and cleared the track of refugees to the pier. The *Bremerhaven* was moored thirty yards away. In the slip to the left of it was a rusty Greek destroyer; in the slip to the right a small steamer taking aboard cavalrymen of the Volunteers. Machine guns on the main deck of the steamer were trained upon the hysterical crowd.

As we left the train and started toward the ship the refugees pressed around us, shrieking, begging, imploring. Some of them were Kalmuks from the south, holding on to the bridles of horses and camels they had driven here from as far away as Manytch and Sal. They stank of sheep fat. A few even had with them the portable wooden huts in which they had slept in the hills around the city.

'Don't argue with the paruskis!' Kink yelled to the men. 'It's not our fault we can't take them along! Just say *sozhaleyu* – I'm sorry!'

'*Radi Boga!*' the refugees screamed, '*Radi Boga!*' begging for God's sake not to be left behind. One *molodka* fell to her feet before me and tried to kiss my hand. I shook her off, feeling like a murderer.

'*Sozhaleyu! Sozhaleyu!*' the Tommies shouted to the crowd, and moved forward. From the next pier we heard screams as the sniper's bullets dropped a number of people in the crowd.

In the slips on both sides of us floated an incredible amount of jetsam – trunks, saddles, clothes and furniture. Pushed by the crowd, a woman tumbled in. She reached for one of the floating trunks, but her fingers slipped and she went under.

Feodor, dressed in cheap civilian suit and overcoat, was waiting for me at the gangplank. I could see the outline of the Luger in his overcoat pocket.

We had only a moment to say goodbye. I shook his hand. '*Do svidaniya*, Feodor, and good luck.'

'*Zhelayu schastiya*, Captain,' he said, and pressed my hand so hard it hurt. I couldn't see the tears in his eyes for those in mine.

I struggled to get at my billfold. 'I want to make sure you've got enough money,' I began, but I never finished what I wanted to say; a platoon of Welsh Guards swept me up the gangplank, and when I had pushed my way to the railing to look for him, Feodor was lost in the crowd.

I scrambled up the companionway to the top deck where B Flight was bivouacked. The deck was jammed with Mission officers and men, some of whom were returning the snipers' fire. I used my knees and elbows to find a place for myself at the rail.

Below me was the steamer loading White cavalry officers and men. Around it swam horses driven off the quay by departing cavalrymen who preferred to see them drown rather than fall into enemy hands. I loved horses and could understand the Russians' feeling, but it was heartbreaking to hear the animals whinnying in terror and watch them swimming frantically toward the shore. Most of them became overcome with cold and exhaustion and drowned halfway there.

A mob of desperate refugees suddenly rushed the steamer gang-plank, and machine guns on the main deck cut loose. Ten men and women fell, twenty, thirty, and I could watch no more. I left the railing and went up to the hurricane deck.

Kink was standing near a lifeboat davit looking through binoculars at the hill where the Cossacks still were gathering.

He put the glasses down. 'Kitty's up there and I'm going to see if there's any way I can talk her into sailing. Look around for Tommy and see that he doesn't do anything rash.'

'The ship's whistle just blew the thirty minute warning,' I told him.

'There's plenty of time,' he said, and started for the companion-way.

I found Tommy sitting against a bulkhead with his head in his hands. Evidently he didn't know Kitty was up on the hill. It was just as well. I watched him for a while, and then went back to the com-panionway.

Kink had just returned from the hill. He shook his head. I didn't have to ask him what Kitty had said.

The Greek destroyer in the slip to our right backed out with a pounding of screws; on its deck were two motor cars, lashed down securely. All over the harbour, in the falling dusk, the Allied cruisers, destroyers and battlewagons were leaving the piers. The crew of the *Bremerhaven* had unmoored on the dock below; now the big tub shuddered and churned out backwards into the bay. The refugees on the wharf stretched out their hands in wordless supplication. Behind them half the waterfront was ablaze.

Beyond the mole the *Emperor* and the *Waldeck-Rousseau* were still lobbing shells toward the pass, but in another few minutes the big dreadnaughts would have moved out of range. Then there would be nothing to prevent the Reds and Greens from streaming down the mountain and into the town.

Eddie tapped me on the shoulder. 'Bunny, look at this damn thing I picked up on the quay. It looks like a Red Army pass. The Bolshies must have slipped in some men to distribute them among the Vol-unteers.'

Wally took it from my hand. 'May I read it to you?'

'Go ahead, if you can,' I said. 'The light's going fast.'
Wally read from the soiled sheet of pulp paper:

DOWN WITH THE GOLD-BRAIDED OFFICERS
AND IDLERS

All soldiers of the White Army now have the right to repatriate
themselves with the exception of monarchists, landowners, kulaks,
manufacturers, merchants, speculators and all those parasites who
are being banished from Soviet Russia and are not allowed to return.
    If any passes are left over please give them to other units. Present
this pass to the political department of any of the Soviet Armies.

STICK YOUR BAYONET IN THE GROUND!
JOIN THE RED ARMY!
JOIN HISTORY!
A NEW DAY HAS DAWNED FOR MANKIND!

As we left the harbour for Yalta the darkness fell.

Epilogue

✳

No one knows how many civilians and military died in Novorossiisk after Budenny took the town that night. Estimates vary from a few thousand to more than a hundred thousand.

About sixty thousand Don and Kuban Cossacks and thousands of refugees fled eastward toward the mountains of Georgia, constantly harassed by Red cavalry. Some escaped, but not many.

On April 4th, Denikin appointed Baron Peter Wrangel Commander-in-Chief of the Armed Forces of South Russia and sailed from the Crimea to asylum in Britain.1 The British Government had already told the White High Command that unless it concluded the hopeless struggle, the British would renounce all responsibility for its actions and would withdraw all further aid and support.

Wrangel knew his position was hopeless, but he hoped to win better terms of amnesty from the Reds and more substantial aid from the Allies when the remnants of the White Army were forced to evacuate the peninsula. He began plans for an offensive with forty thousand men, his objective the possession of the territory lying between the Dneiper and the Sea of Azov. This move resulted in a final rupture with Britain and the recall of all British Mission troops and technical assistants from the Crimea.2 Eddie and I were among the men who left Sebastopol for London in the early spring.3

France, interested in a Polish victory over the Bolshevik Army and the diversion of Red forces from the Polish front, gave de facto recognition to Wrangel's government and offered a certain amount of aid. But by mid-November, 1920, despite brilliant victories in the field, Wrangel's badly outnumbered troops had been forced to evacuate the Crimea. With the one hundred thousand White troops fled forty-six thousand civilians.

The struggle was over and the exodus was on. After confinement in various camps, White military contingents settled in China, in the Balkans, in the Baltic States and Germany. Under Wrangel's command, and still operating as military units, the men of the defeated White Army built roads in the Balkans, dug coal in Bulgaria,

Belgium and France, worked in plantations in South America, took jobs as factory workers and field hands in countries all over the world. For individuals life was even more difficult. Generals shined shoes in Constantinople and opened cabaret doors in Paris; princesses waited on tables in Berlin and solicited in the streets of Belgrade. Counts became blacksmiths and colonels' wives did needlework to keep from starving. In the 1930s it was estimated that two million Russian exiles were dispersed over the globe. A few prospered; most suffered terribly.

Peter Wrangel died in Brussels in 1928; Anton Denikin in the University Hospital at Ann Arbor, Michigan, in 1947. Their widows live in the United States, Olga Wrangel in Glen Cove, Long Island, and Xenia Denikin in New York City.4 They are friendly and see one another from time to time. The White Russian community, in the United States and elsewhere, is extremely close-knit.

In 1921 Kink and I resumed active service with the RAF in Baghdad. Colly had left for Persia to fly against the Reds. From 1922–4 we fought with him in the Kurdistan campaign. He saw service in Palestine in 1929, and in World War II commanded the RAF on the El Alamein front. Full of honours, he retired from the RAF after World War II with the rank of Air Vice-Marshal, and today lives in his native British Columbia.

Tommy was killed at Kantara, Egypt, in 1921, stunting his Camel at low altitude. Kink crashed fatally off the Isle of Wight in 1928, after breaking the world speed record. Bill Daly met his death in an air collision near Northampton, England, in 1923. Eddie Fulford, bound for the African theatre, went down with a bombed transport outside of Southampton harbour in 1942.5 He left a wife; of the officers of 47 Squadron Eddie and Colly were the only ones to marry.

In 1927 I resigned from the RAF and went home to take over my father's 8 N Bar Ranch in the Imperial Valley. On the way I stopped off in Paris and looked up Wally d'Adix, who was working as a tourist guide and giving harpsichord lessons. I also saw Clarence Cowderdrill in the South Downs, where he was proprietor of a small but thriving pub called the Beggar's Roost. Over one of the ex-mess sergeant's celebrated Petrograd Ponies we had a long and pleasantly melancholy talk about the past. He had forgotten his dreams of the Riviera.

Glossary

*

amerikanets, American (noun)
amerikanski, American (adj.)
anglichanie, Englishmen
anglichanin, Englishman
angliski, English

baryshnia, young lady
blinochki, small pancakes
blinochki' s syrom, cheese pancakes
blondinka, blonde (noun)
bora, heavy gale (particularly on the
    Black Sea)
Bozhe moi!, My God!
Bozhe Tsarya Khrani, God save the
    Tsar (the Imperial national
    anthem)
brichka, britzka (horse-drawn
    carriage)
bronevik, armoured car

chernushka, brunette
chinovnik, government functionary
Chorniye Gusary, Black Hussars (also
a song of the same name).
chort, devil
chto takoe? what's this?
Cossack sotnia, a detachment of one
hundred Cossacks

da, yes
daite nam viski, give us whisky
dobroye utro, good morning
dobry vecher, good evening
do svidaniya, good-bye

duraki, fools
inogorodtsy, people from
    other towns; outlanders
izvozchik, cabman, taxi

kaftan, caftan
kak zhal, what a pity
kasha, porridge
kavardak, nonsense
kazachok, Cossack dance
khorosho! good!
kinzhal, dagger
kunak, friend (in Caucasus)

malenkaya ustritsa, little oys-
    ter
malenki, little, baby (masc.)
molodka, young married
    woman
muzhik, peasant

nagaika, whip
na Moskvu! [let us march]
    on to Moscow!
nichevo, nothing; it doesn't
    matter
nye, not
nye chort, not the devil
nye refuganski poyezd, not a
    refugee train
nyet, no

'Ochi chornie', 'Black Eyes'
    (song)

ofitsiant, waiter
oi!, oh!

papakha, Caucasian fur cap
pilott, pilot
plenny, prisoner of war
polushubok, sheepskin coat
pozhaluista, please
prazdnik, party
prostite, pardon me

radi Boga!, for God's sake!
riasa, cassock, frock

s novym godom, s novym schastiem,
   happy New Year
seychas budet, at once, immediately
shapka, cap
shuba, fur coat
skoro budet, it will soon be
spasibo, thanks
spokoinoi nochi, good night

tif, typhus
tsaritsa moevo serdtsa, queen of
   my heart

von! get away!
vsio, all, everything

zakuski, snacks, hors d'oeuvres
za vashe zdorovye, to your health
zaniato, occupied
zdravstvuite, hello
zhelayu schastiya, I wish you luck
zrazy s kashoy, Ukranian meat
   dish with kasha

Notes to the Text

Attributions are as follows:

MHA/AO/TI: taped interviews between Marion Hughes Aten and Arthur Orrmont; dating from January 11th 1960 through January 18th 1960.

MHA/AO: correspondence between Marion Hughes Aten and Arthur Orrmont; dating from November 22nd 1959 through May 5th 1961.

GT: notes made on the text of LTORB by Colonel George Treloar DSO MC, Assistant Military Secretary to General Officer Commanding the British Military Mission to South Russia.

RCA: Raymond Collishaw's autobiography, *Air Command*.

RC: Correspondence between Raymond Collishaw and the Aten family.

MA: Mike Aten, editor. (Unattributed entries are also by MA.)

Other attributions are as noted.

Chapter One

*

1   I planned merely to have a few drinks with the squadron mates I expected to find at the Royal Automobile Club bar… [p20]
The club, as described, still stands today (with the small bar intact) on Pall Mall.

2   It would be some time before I could hope to be discharged from the RAF hospital at Eastchurch… [p20]
Aten's RAF medical records list him in hospital for treatment of an infection several months prior to this, from August 15th through September 4th 1918, but not for a period covering the Armistice.

3   There was a wise man who said that young boys must join circuses, and he said it right. [p20]
Aten, in his suggestions to Orrmont for the blurb on the book, wrote: *At sixteen he joined Barnum and Bailey circus, to get worldly experience. He got it.* MHA/AO
Gary Radder recalled: *My aunt (Marion's sister, Imogen) told me that when he came home from the circus (with his tail between his legs, so to speak) his mother marched him*

right outside, made him take off all his clothes and burned them on the spot, they were so filthy! Gary Boyce Radder, Marion Aten's nephew

4   'Darling blueboy,' the Modigliani said, 'were you very badly wounded?' [p20]
    The blue RAF uniforms of the period were something of a short-term experiment, as Raymond Collishaw explained: *The general officer responsible for equipment in the Air Ministry was friendly with an English leading actress and he took her advice as to how to dress the R.A.F. officers. So we were all dressed in a light blue sky uniform… the open pit aeroplanes splashed a good deal of castor oil about and in a very short time, the beautiful uniforms were much marked and damaged. There was such an outcry … that it was not long before the comic opera uniforms were discarded.* MA. See Colllishaw letter number two, Appendix II.

5   In the bar, where I had known they would be, sat Colly, Kink, Bill Daly and Tommy Burns Thomson. [p21]
    These were: Colly, Raymond Collishaw CB, DSO, OBE, DSC, DFC; Kink, Samuel Marcus Kinkead DSO, DSC & Bar, DFC & Bar; Bill Daly, Rowan Heywood Daly DFC; Tommy Burns Thomson, William Burns Thomson DFC. Daly was spelled 'Daley' and Burns Thomson was given as 'Burns-Thompson' in the original US & UK editions of *LTORB*.

6   …a trick only Colly, and perhaps Kink, could have attempted with any prospect of success. [p22]
    Aten arrived in Great Britain in June,1918, so the accident must have occurred after that and prior to the Armistice. Three photographs (included here in the photo section) were taken of the wreck at different angles. On the back of one of the prints Aten wrote: *I did it!* Aten mentioned that the flying accident had occurred in France and that he had sustained a shoulder injury.
    MA & MHA/AO/TI

7   'No kills in the air.' [p22]
    Aten only received his 'wings' (pilot's license) on November 12, 1918, one day after the Armistice. He stated that he had less than ten hours combat flying time during a month or less with 203/4 Squadron in France and Belgium during WWI. MA & MHA/AO/TI

8   I would have made it to Camp Mohawk on foot. [p23]
    Aten began training at Camp Mohawk in 1917. He was then sent to Texas for further training and to offer initial instruction to American student pilots as part of the Reciprocal Training Program that had been set up between the Royal Flying Corps (RFC) and the US Army Signal Corps. The Texas flying fields offered year-round training to the RFC which was not possible in Canada.
    Aten, in his suggestions for the blurb on the book, wrote: *After exhausting all channels of opportunity to learn to fly he wrote a personal letter to President Woodrow Wilson begging the President to help him. He received a personal letter in reply from the President's private secretary, stating that applications were being taken by the Aviation Section of the US Signal Corp (which then incorporated the US Air Force) for qualified pilots with thirty hours solo flying. And adding that Curtis of Buffalo N.Y. was giving instruction at the rate of five dollars per minute. FIVE DOLLARS PER MINUTE! Five dollars per hour*

would have dented young Aten's budget. The problem of learning to fly solved itself when a Scotch recruiting sergeant told Aten the Canadians were taking Americans who had enough 'bloody sense to say they were Canadians'. MA & MHA/AO

Aten also related an incident at the camp: *On parade first morning in RFC at Camp Mohawk Sgt Major Bissett, a great bull of a man poked me in the chest with his forefinger and battled the question, Had [I] shaved that morning? I told him it was none of his d★★★ business. He bellowed like a wild bull and sent me doubling to the guardroom under two man escort.* MA & MHA/AO

9 'Then how would you like to fly against the Bolshies?' [p23]

This offer likely came some time after the Armistice, probably in April or early May, 1919. As detailed in his autobiography, Collishaw was offered command of 47 Squadron after he returned to England on April 6th 1919, from an extended leave in Canada. By then, 47 Squadron was already preparing to leave for southern Russia from its wartime location in Macedonia. It was transported to Russia and was prepared for operations under another RAF commander. Before Collishaw left England to take command of 47 Squadron, one of his duties was to recruit volunteer personnel for the Squadron to replace those who wanted to return home. In recruiting pilots for 47 Squadron, Collishaw put a premium on prior combat experience. MA & RCA

10 '…and a chap named Eddie Fulford.' [p24]

Eddie Fulford (Edgar Fulford, Mentioned in Dispatches) and Marion Aten accompanied each other in training from Canada to Texas and both were sent to 203 Squadron in England.

11 'Sorry you can't leave with us, Bunny; we're taking off in a couple of weeks, and I doubt if you'll be discharged by then from Eastchurch.' [p25]

47 Squadron would not be sent to southern Russia until April 16th 1919, arriving in Novorossiisk on April 24th, according to HA Jones in *Over the Balkans and South Russia - Being a History of 47 Squadron*.

12 I wished my brother Boyce hadn't died of a machine-gun bullet near Apromont in the Argonne Forest the previous September. [p29]

Boyce Aten, Marion's younger brother, was an infantry officer with the US Army and was killed on October 2nd 1918, just a few weeks prior to the armistice. Boyce had a promising future – he had interrupted his studies at Stanford University to enlist. Probably, he was killed by shrapnel.

Chapter Two

✻

1 I don't know when it occurred to me that I could simply walk out of Eastchurch by the back door, but one night in late January I did just that… [p32]

The date of Aten's departure from England is not known but probably it was around the middle of 1919. His RAF medical record places him in London on April 25th 1919.

2   The MLO was doubtful about getting passage for me on the *Princess Ina*, leaving
     for Constantinople in three days. [p38]
     The *Princess Ina* was later involved in evacuating White Russian refugees from
     Black Sea ports. It was a merchant vessel fitted with a boom assembly attached
     to the bow for minesweeping.

3   He had known of several people who had gone to Batum and never come back. [p40]
     Aten wrote of an experience while he was in Constantinople: *A pretty girl came to
     my table. Dressed in white, even a big white hat. She said her name was Kali – that she
     was Armenian and afraid to go home alone because the Turks would get her and do many
     bad things to her. Would I escort her home?*
     *We left the Garden of the Little Fields and shortly turned into a cobblestoned, narrow alley
     that twisted up a slight hill. On each side were 2&3 storey apartment buildings all with
     iron-grilled doors and windows. Soon, we stopped in front of one … She grabbed me by
     the arm, trying to pull me inside, saying, 'Come in. My family would love to meet you.'
     Suddenly, as she tried to pull me inside a heavy flower pot came hurtling from above. I
     hurled the girl roughly away from me and took off down the cobblestoned alley like a mus-
     tang…. After I recovered my wind I looked up an MP and told him about it. He said, ''ell
     you been in SKIN ALLEY. The Den of the Forty Thieves. Not all of 'em wot goes in
     there comes out, Sir. You're lucky.'* Writing some forty years after the incident, Aten
     observed: *Fancy a sucker falling for that line. But I did with great gusto.* MHA/AO

4   'I wish he, rather than Denikin, were in supreme command.' [p49]
     The Baron seems to be singularly well informed about the White Army and its
     strategies and not the least bit hesitant to tell a strange foreign soldier about it.
     This appears to be a literary device to outline the general military and civilian
     situation in South Russia during mid-1919 and there are further uses of this de-
     vice later in the book. However, it is clear from the taped interviews that such a
     character did exist and Aten described him as a: *grey-haired old Czarist officer who
     was too old to be in the army. Arrogant and aristocratic*. MA & MHA/AO/TI

5   The *Konslavtina* docked at Novorossiisk in early March in bitterly cold weather
     that pierced my overcoat. [p50]
     If such ship did dock at Novorossiisk during March 1919, Aten was not on board.
     He did not formally join 47 Squadron in Russia until August 19th 1919, accord-
     ing to the official squadron 'Daily Status' sheet of August 20th 1919. Collishaw
     arrived in the region in early June, officially taking command on June 13th. Aten
     stated on more than one occassion to Orrmont that he had arrived in Russia in
     June. MA & MHA/AO/TI

Chapter Three

*

1   As a Texas and California boy I had never seen such mountains; the Chocolate
     Mountains of the Imperial Valley were dwarfed in comparison. [p55]
     The Laguna Mountains of San Diego County define the western wall of the

Imperial Valley and are visible from the Aten Ranch. Their heights reach to 6000 feet and they rise up abruptly and steeply from the valley floor. Just a bit north, toward Palm Springs, the mountains rise to 10,000 feet. The Chocolate Mountains define the eastern side of the valley and, as described, are much lower.

2   In the aerodrome mess Colly was having a second breakfast… [p57]
     According to Jones in *Over the Balkans and South Russia*, the 'aerodrome' was located in a muddy field next to a racetrack just outside of Ekaterinodar.

3   'Acting-Major Kinkead, will you fill in Acting-Captain Aten…' [p58]
     Marion had been temporarily promoted to Captain, an old term used in the Royal Flying Corps (RFC) ranking system. Since the formation of the Royal Air Force (RAF) in 1918, the former RFC rank of Captain was changed to Flight Lieutenant. Aten preferred the older RFC term of Captain and used it for the rest of his life.

4   'B Flight train pulls out today for Beketofka at the Tsaritsyn front, and you boys fly up tomorrow morning. A Flight's already at Beketofka drome.' [p58]
     B Flight didn't leave Ekaterinodar for Beketofka until late September, 1919 and by then Tsaritsyn had been captured by White Forces. 47 Squadron had arrived in the region in April and performed its first flight operations against the Reds on June 23th 1919, during the siege of Tsaritsyn, when C Flight bombed the railway station and several boats. C Flight then moved to Beketofka, located just 12 miles south of Tsaritsyn, in early July.

5   The flatcars were for our planes, now in the hangars at Ekaterinodar drome. [p59]
     A, B and C Flights, as well as Collishaw's headquarters, each had their own special trains. Given the mobile nature of the war across the broad, flat region of southern Russia, these substantial trains – sometimes exceeding fifty units of rolling-stock – offered the best means of mobility for 47 Squadron and its logistical support.

6   'Cowderill's got all those samovars he bought piled up on his bunk, and I'm thinking that if General Maund came by for a last-minute inspection, they wouldn't look so very soldierlike.' [p62]
     Cowderill is undoubtedly AC2 Frank Victor Cowderill, who was a batman with 47 Squadron, although in the US & UK editions of *LTORB* his name was given as 'Cowderdrill' and he is designated as a sergeant. General Maund, in both editions of *LTORB*, was styled as 'General Mudd'. Both Aten and Ormont were well aware of the pun.

7   'The only trouble is that Russky – we call him that – is a terrible pest about flying a Camel. I keep telling him that the Russians flew Nieuports during the war and that they'll never get used to the Camel's right-hand turn.' [p60]
     The rotary engined Sopwith Camel could make unbelievably tight right-hand turns due to the torque effect of the spinning engine/propeller combination and the close-coupled location of the engine, pilot and wings relative to one another. Experienced Camel pilots soon learned to use this to their advantage during combat, though the touchy handling characteristics of the Camel could be dangerous, even deadly, to those learning to fly it.

8   Off in a corner sat eight DH-9 bombers, half of them with the red, white and black insignia of the White airforce, the rest with the red, white and blue emblem of the RAF. [p63]
Photographic evidence of the period shows similar mixed batches of aircraft. Apparently, some of these aircraft were slated to be used by the White Russians but were assigned to the RAF Training Mission instead, of which 47 Squadron was a part.

9   At dinner that evening Kink told us that Eddie Fulford, the Canadian who was joining B Flight, would be flying up from Ekaterinodar… [p65]
Although initially assigned to a different 47 Squadron Flight, Eddie Fulford appears to have been attached to B Flight during the autumn retreat.

10   'I didn't know the Greeks were in this too.' [p66]
The Greeks may have been natives of Odessa, where they owned and controlled most shipping trade and shops, supported by a small contingent of Greeks from Crete or Greece. GT

11   'Lloyd George thinks armed intervention on a scale large enough to beat the Bolshies is impossible.' [p66]
[T]he British Military Mission was not a fighting Mission; it was a supply mission. But the airforce section of it, consisting of volunteers from the British Royal Air Force did in fact form an active service command, at first mainly on the eastern section of the front, known as the Volga front. In collaboration with Wrangel's famous Cossack Army, along a line stretching from north of Rostov to the Volga (key centre Tsaritsyn), they performed magnificently, and played a great part in many amazing victories. GT

12   I saw the broad trench in which, Kink had told us, lay the bodies of twelve thousand civilians slaughtered by the Reds when they had taken the town. [p66]
This was commonplace. Communism rules by terrorism. To my knowledge it happened in place after place. GT

13   It went straight into the river bank, exploding with a terrific crash. [p67]
There is nothing in RAF records found to date concerning this aerial victory, so it appears to be fictional. The description of it is similar to Samuel Kinkead's first victory in southern Russia, which occurred months later, on Sept. 30th 1919. While escorting a group of DH-9As from C Flight, a pair of Bolshevik Nieuports attacked B Flight and Kinkead succeeded in shooting down DN Shchekin, a twenty-year-old Bolshevik pilot who had shot down two British DH-9s in the Astrakhan area earlier in the year. Shchekin's Nieuport crashed into the Volga River.

14   'And now, of course, it's only a matter of time before the French get out of Sebastopol.' [p68]
Many thousands, including those who serviced the French, swarmed down to the waterfront, expecting and then begging to be evacuated. All were forced back. Many killed themselves, as we were to learn later thousands were slaughtered when the Reds took over. GT

15   'If the French have given up on getting back their loans,' Eddie Fulford said, 'that means the situation's really hopeless.' [p68]
The French were playing their old, shabby, deceitful game of staging an outwardly fine show of loyalty and gallantry, while manoeuvring to be out of a battle, while pretending to be in

it; or pledging their word to be in it. So if there be a victory they will be in it at the end with few if any casualties, but claiming the major part of success, because they would have the most powerful force in the field; but if there be a defeat or failure, they are well and truly out of it – loudly condemning a British defeat. This disgraceful business can be and is traceable from the Crimean War to the present age [1968]. GT

16   'We hear there's a big conference of Red Commissars in Tsaritsyn.' [p68]
In late June, a 112 lb. bomb dropped from a 47 Squadron aircraft demolished a building in Tsaritsyn and killed a group of Red Commissars. Trotsky was not present. B Flight did not participate in the operation as it had not yet commenced operations.

17   Then Eddie had chased a Fokker triplane rather deep into Red territory… [p69]
There is no evidence of the use of Fokker Triplanes in Russia. There was a single Sopwith Triplane operated by the Reds but not in southern Russia. It was likely used as a trainer. This aircraft, still extant, is on display in the Central Air Museum in Monino, Russia, about 30 miles east of Moscow.
However, Aten wrote: *I told Kink about the Triplane breaking up when we got back to the drome. He had seen it happen before on the Western Front. Said that whenever he spotted one in the air he would sit on its tail in a dive until its wings came off. Never firing a shot…* MA & MHA/AO

18   'This war is basically between two groups of people, the haves and the have nots.' [p70]
Orrmont used Eddie Fulford as a mouthpiece for leftist political analysis. Aten wrote: *Eddie by the way was one of our gayest pilots even though you have made him into a quarrelsome Pinko.* MHA/AO

19   We caught the forty boat flotilla ten miles above Tsaritsyn and bombed them at one thousand feet, coming down from five thousand one at a time. [p70]
This mission occurred as written, but in mid-October and without the defending Red aircraft. All three Flights participated, with B Flight's Camels using 20 lb. bombs as well as their machine guns against the Red flotilla.
Aten stated: *He [Collishaw] had gotten word from Wrangel's headquarters there was a gunboat up the river and that Trotsky was on it. It was the headquarters. And we bombed it… Oh, it was 20 lb bombs. Can't do much damage. We hit it once or twice, and it took off up the river. We didn't see it again. It stayed out of our range! It had a balloon attached to it, and Kink shot the balloon down. It was pretty well armored with machine guns, so we didn't get too close to it.* MA & MHA/AO/TI

20   Toward mid-April we heard that the French had evacuated Sebastopol. [p72]
Leaving the Russian Black Sea base exposed. Only too true! As the direct result, the position looked hopeless. But again Wrangel saved the situation. In command of all the Cossack cavalry on the Eastern Russian flank he ordered a general assault on the Reds, east of Novorossiisk. After a terrific three-day battle, he defeated them – smashed them – and then began a power-drive towards Tsaritsyn on the Volga, about 400 miles to the north east. GT

21   Colly immediately ordered B Flight to step up its operations and destroy as many Red planes as possible in advance of Wrangel's arrival at Tsaritsyn. [p73]
At this time (late May), B Flight was not operational and would not be until late September.

22   Combined operations with the 'Wanderers'. [P75]
     47 Squadron's primary function – ostensibly – was to train White pilots in combat and navigation techniques. Obviously, 47 Squadron took more of an active operational role but it still provided training when it could and also escorted White aircraft during missions.

23   ...and slid into the Volga. [p76]
     This battle appears to be fictional.

Chapter Four

✱

1   Hoskins did his usual fine job and the fireplace was installed, flued and plastered snugly in place against the lounge car sidewall by late afternoon of the next day. [p81]
    The fireplace was installed, but not until late September or early October.

2   We did our part, strafing the trenches and rear areas in advance of the attack, shooting up a couple of field guns, and downing the three Bolshie fighters that objected. [p83]
    Collishaw described an incident that occurred on October 7th 1919, three months after Tsartisyn had been captured by the Whites. Two Red Nieuports attempted to attack a flight of DH9As that Kinkead and Thomson were escorting. The two B Flight pilots 'drove down' the Red Nieuports. The 'three Bolshie fighters' mentioned here is possibly a reference to this engagement, as nothing else similar to the downing of three Red fighters in a single action has been found in the various records. MA & RCA

3   We were diving five thousand feet at a speed of three hundred miles an hour. [p84]
    The top speed of the Camel was about 120 mph, and if exceeded by very much, structural failure would occur. The figure of 300mph here and in the following paragraph is incorrect.

4   We had been in the air for almost two hours, Kink told us when he landed at the drome. [p87]
    This B Flight strafing mission occurred as described, but later in the year than the text indicates. Strafing missions such as these, backed up by Cossack cavalry, were very effective against Red cavalry forces. Aten stated that his award of the Order of St Vladimir 4th Class by the White Russian Government was for his part in this attack. MA & MHA/AO/TI

5   That night we could see from the lounge to the A Flight headquarters train, where Major Anderson… [p90]
    This was probably Lt Walter F Anderson, who, along with Lt John Mitchell, rescued Captain William Elliot and Lt HS Laidlaw on July 30th, when Elliot and Laidlaw's DH-9 was brought down by Red fire. Anderson, along with gunner and observer Lt. Mitchell, landed their DH-9 and crammed both Elliot and

Laidlaw on board after they had set fire to the crippled DH-9. Anderson's over-loaded aircraft staggered into the air just as Red cavalry arrived. For this action, Anderson and Mitchell both received the Distinguished Service Order (DSO). Collishaw believed that they should have received Victoria Crosses, no doubt in part because the Reds had proclaimed that they would crucify any captured foreign pilots. MA & RCA

6   You thought: tell this man the truth – if you don't, no matter how good a liar you happen to be, he'll know it. [p92]

Aten wrote that he considered General Wrangel one of the greatest soldiers he had ever known. MA & MHA/AO

Chapter Five

✳

1   B Flight was in the air for most of the day… [p101]

B Flight did not become active until late September and therefore did not participate in this particular attack.

2   It crossed over the vertical, and was going into a loop upside down when it crashed on its back with terrific force into the river. [p103]

See Note 17, Chapter Three.

3   I left him fondling the ten shilling note, and set off across the field. [p103]

This story with the 'pitchfork-wielding peasant' is fictional. Aten had set down because he was lost near Kotluban. MA & MHA/AO/TI

4   I suppose there was little possibility that I could have avoided running into the young nurse I encountered… [p104]

This is a fictional encounter used as a device to lay the basis for the romance to follow. Aten had met this nurse, Nina Dmitrievna Anohina, when Eddie Fulford had brought her as a guest to B Flight's train. MA & MHA/AO/TI

5   '… and then he forced himself upon me.' [p107]

In discussing this incident, Aten forcefully stated: *Attempted* [*rape*]! *He didn't succeed.* MA & MHA/AO/TI

6   During the first two weeks of August we bagged ten red stars. [p114]

Though Collishaw, Kinkead and several others scored aerial victories in southern Russia, the ten brought down in the first half of August are fictional.

7   By the 18th the town was completely evacuated… [p114]

According to official RAF record, it was the day after this when Aten actually joined B Flight.

8   It also made me a more efficient fighting machine in the three days of ferocious battle between August 22nd and 25th… [p115]

B Flight did not participate in this battle.

9   Then, under the officers' direction, the men unloaded the Camels and wheeled them into the field beside the roadbed. [p118]

This gave A, B and C Flights unprecedented mobility for an RAF squadron.

10   Resting on the pocket of my khaki tunic was my Order of St. Vladimir. [p118]
     Marion received this order, and that of the Cross of St. George 4th class, from
     the White Russians, but later in the campaign.

Chapter Six

✳

1   Twilight was falling when we bumped up to B Flight train. [p130]
    This incident, with the peasant towing Aten and his plane, occurred later in the
    campaign. MA & MHA/AO/TI
2   He hadn't come alone; with him was Brigadier General Maund. [p132]
    Maund had enlisted in the 32nd Canadian Infantry in 1914 and in 1916 was at-
    tached to 8 Squadron, RFC, as a Flying Officer and observer. In 1918, he com-
    manded the RAF at Archangel, in northern Russia, as part of the support that
    Great Britain was giving to the White forces during the Russian Civil War. By
    1919, he was a (temporary) General, having been elevated three ranks from Cap-
    tain, in the RAF Training Mission in southern Russia.
3   'There will be more problems to solve before our Cossack allies will band to-
    gether...' [135]
    Most land-holding Kuban Cossacks allied themselves to the White cause, along
    with the neighboring Don and Terek Cossacks. These Cossack groups consid-
    ered themselves and their lands to be sovereign. They formed a large part of the
    White Army and their activities shaped its successes and eventual defeat. They
    were motivated to serve the Whites primarily by the Soviet Land Decree that
    nationalized all private land, hence threatening their sovereignity. The self-serv-
    ing interests of many Cossacks and their determination to protect their lands at
    the expense of all else made them unreliable allies.
4   'Strewth, Sir', Bill said, 'maybe Makhno's got it.' [p137]
    Nestor Mahkno was the leader of an anarchist group that operated primarily in
    the Ukraine, one of several such groups collectively known as the 'Greens'. The
    threat posed by Makhno's band, which numbered up to 40,000, diverted the
    White Army when it came under attack by the Red Army's Latvian Brigades
    during the battle for Orel and, one month later, at Kursk. The White losses to
    the Reds at Orel and Kursk turned the tide of the Civil War. According to
    Richard Pipes in *Russia Under the Bolshevik Regime*, one of Makhno's main ob-
    jectives was that of looting upper-class estates.
5   'Colly stayed on another day, taking part in three patrols in which he traded two
    Bolshie planes and fifty Red infantrymen for a couple of bullet holes in his rud-
    der.' [p137]
    A bit of an exaggeration. Collishaw flew many sorties with B and C Flights,
    bombing and strafing Red gunboats, trains and cavalry. On October 9th, he
    scored a single aerial victory against a Red Albatros D-V.
6   'It looks like typhus,' the Doctor told us. 'I am not quite sure.' [p137]

Collishaw came down with typhus in the second week of October, 1919. Typhus was widespread in Russia during the Civil War and it killed many, both military and civilian. Collishaw wrote: *It was not possible for the medical officer to diagnose the disease immediately but he certified me as unfit and I set off by rail to Ekaterinodar, as a potential typhus case accompanied by two walking-wounded airmen.* MA & RCA

7 ...I could hear the steer's loud and dramatic end. [p141]
In fact, it was Aten who did the dispatching. He wrote: *At Beketofka, Cowderill tried to kill the bullock with an axe. He was flailing about with it like a scythe. The bullock was winning, but Cowderill [was] still swinging bravely. When it became a toss-up whether we would have Cowderill or bullock for chow, I shot the animal...* MA & MHA/AO

Chapter Seven

✴

1 While Wrangel was holding his own before Saratov, at the moment there was no chance of his taking the town. [p151]
The city of Saratov was at the eastern-most flank of the White Volunteer Army. Baron Peter Wrangel, probably Denikin's most able commander, was ordered to advance on Saratov at the command of the Caucasian Army. Taking Saratov, he was then to swing left, advancing on Moscow from the east. VI Sidorin was to lead the White Army centre and advance toward Moscow, while VZ Mai-Maievsky was to lead the left flank and advance on Moscow through Kursk, Orel, and Tula, approaching the capital from the southwest. This was Denikin's grand plan as described by Pipes in *Russia Under the Bolshevik Regime*, issued under Order No. 08878, which became known as the 'Moscow Directive', a strategy to which Wrangel objected (he thought that the White forces should link up with Kolchak's forces to the northeast of them). Though successful at first, it is believed by most historians that this spreading of forces in the drive towards Moscow doomed the White effort to failure.

2 We had already broken regulations by allowing Feodor, a POW, to accompany him. [p153]
The use of prisoners-of-war was common during the Russian Civil War. In *Russia Under the Bolsheviks,* Pipes describes the White Army drive towards Moscow: *As the front enlarged, so did the need for troops, and in the fall, the ranks of the Southern Army were filled with conscripts and prisoners of war.*

3 'We ran into a flight of seven Red Spads.' [p157]
According to Kondratyev in *Aircraft of the Russian Civil War*, the Bolshevik 4th Fighter Detachment that was in the region possessed only two Spad VII aircraft at that time. The Bolsheviks didn't often fly the Spads because their Hispano-Suiza V8 water-cooled engines required high quality aircraft gasoline which was in very short supply. The Bolsheviks were forced into using various mixtures of alcohol, kerosene and gasoline, that only air-cooled rotary engines of the day could burn, albeit at the cost of decreased performance.

4   She brought Colly and Feodor to her house in the village and nursed Colly through the worst of the disease. [p163]

Collishaw described the experience: *I was lying on a bed that had been placed in a luggage van and the two airmen looked after me very well until they both came down with severe cases of dysentery. By this time the disease had developed and I was delirious, and although the train crew realized my condition they were not able to do much to help me. When the train stopped at a village on the line I was taken off and fortunately for me word of my condition reached an elderly Russian refugee countess who was living there. As it happened, she had been trained as a nurse and she gave orders for me to be carried to the small cottage in which she lived. Nursing a typhus victim is much more than a matter of wiping the hero's fevered brow and holding his hand as they do in the movies. It calls for a strong stomach and a good deal of moral fibre. I lay unconscious while that good woman nursed me through the crisis in what amounted to little more than a one room cabin.* See also Collishaw's second letter in Appendix Two. MA & RCA

5   …only the instructional mission would remain with Denikin's armies. [p163]

Britain became politically divided over support of the White effort in Russia (partly based on Kolchak's losses in the east to the Red Army), leading to the official withdrawal of 47 Squadron and attachment of its personnel as volunteers to the RAF Training Mission as instructors in 'A' Squadron. As Collishaw observed: *None of this, of course, made the slightest difference to any of us nor to the squadron's operations but I suppose that it permitted someone to stand up on the floor of the House of Commons in Westminster and solemnly state that No. 47 Squadron of the Royal Air Force was no longer employed as a combatant unit in support of General Denikin.* MA & RCA

George Treloar wrote: *…the British Military Mission was not a fighting Mission; it was a supply mission. But the airforce section of it, consisting of volunteers from the British Royal Air Force did in fact form an active service command, at first mainly on the eastern section of the front, known as the Volga front. … In collaboration with Wrangel's famous Cossack Army, along a line stretching from north of Rostov to the Volga (key centre Tsaritsyn), they performed magnificently, and played a great part in many amazing victories. They became so conspicuous that Red (Communist) Russian protests about them reached England, and Lloyd George's Government, through the British Air Ministry, ordered 'all combat units to leave Russia' – meaning, at once. My observation – they did not.* GT

6   'We're good Dutch and Scotch-Irish stock…' [p167]

Most of the the Aten family in America descended from Adrian Hendricks Aten, who arrived in New Amsterdam (later renamed New York City) in 1651 from the Hanseatic League city of Doesburg in Holland.

7   There was a definite art to 'blipping' the engine, switching it on and off to control your average speed. [p172]

Though most rotary engines of the day, with the propeller bolted to the engine and both spinning around a fixed crankshaft together, had rudimentary throttle control, an electrical cut-off switch could also be utilized to 'blip' the engine, turning engine power on and off. Rotary engines, with the engine and propeller spinning together as one unit, were often utilized on WW1 aircraft because they were lighter for the horsepower delivered than typical in-line water cooled engines of the day. The rotating engine design whirled through the air, allowing it to be cooled without an additional, heavy water-cooling system.

Chapter Eight

✳

1   'There was more bad news on the 19th.' [p179]
By October 18th, the White Russian front had advanced to the most northern position that it would ever attain. The city of Orel had been taken and the Volunteer Army threatened Tula, a major industrial city and last city of any significant size on the route to Moscow. The capture of Tula would have been a major blow to the existence of communism in Russia. The Bolsheviks were so alarmed by these advances that Lenin made secret plans to evacuate the government from Moscow to Perm. But it was not to be. On October 19th, a counter-attack by the Second and Third Latvian brigades of the Red Army, parts of which took up to 50% casualties, halted the White advance and drove them southward. On the same day, an attack on the White eastern flank by the Cavalry Corps of Red Army General Buddeny threatened to outflank the thinly stretched White Volunteer Army, which was forced to retreat. By October 20th, Orel had been recaptured by the Red Army and the long defeat of the Whites had begun.

2   We left Kotluban at noon of October 29th… [p181]
According to Collishaw, B Flight left Beketovka, which is 12 miles south of Tsaritsyn, on November 27th. This was the same day that he returned to the unit from the hospital. B Flight must have left Kotluban and stayed at Beketovka briefly before being sent to the Kharkov front. MA & RCA

3   The captain had thrown the four of them out on the platform and put the doctor under arrest. [p185]
This story is also told in *In Denikin's Russia and the Caucasus, 1919-1920* by CE Bechhofer, an English journalist who was an eyewitness to events in southern Russia during the Civil War. The book was first published in 1921.

4   …she was busy with her omelet now, and couldn't have cared less. [p187]
Marion wrote: *Nona – blond, pretty, average height, shapely and beautiful. Manners and reserve of a duchess. Slightly spoiled, at times haughty – but good company. Well educated. … She wore elegant clothes, jewels and furs. Thought first, last and always of Nona. Which is, after all, the best way to survive.*
She made her train – the luxury train which passed us stranded between Taganrog and Rostov. As it passed us there was Her Grace Nona waving to us from a picture window in the dining car. Beside her a dashing officer of the Therniya Hussari (Black Hussars). She blew a kiss to Kink. And it was, Good byee Nona, Nona Gooood byeeee. Sing to the tune of 'Goodnight Irene'. MHA/AO

5   A few days ago Lloyd George had made a speech at Mansion House in which he said that the British Government considered the civil war in Russia over. [p188]
In this speech, given on the November 8th 1919, Lloyd George called for the

cessation of British support for the Whites and a negotiated settlement with the Bolsheviks.

6   'C Flight's out of it, I'm afraid…' [p188]
     Collishaw observed that C Flight was left on the Volga front to support Wrangel's troops. MA & RCA

7   'In typical British fashion, we're setting a time for consideration of when to burn headquarters' documents and papers.' [p188]
     According to George Treloar: *This could only mean the Mission's documents at General Holman's HQ in Taganrog, which were under my direct control as a Staff Captain to General Holman. I heard no such thing.* GT

Chapter Nine

❋

1   Kursk had fallen to the Reds… [p195]
     This was on November 17th 1919.

2   'One regiment carry behind it over a hundred carriages.' [p195]
     General Wrangel wrote of the situation to General Denikin on December 9th 1919: *The continual advance has reduced the Army's effective force. The rear has become too vast. Disorganization is all the greater because of the re-equipment system which Supreme Headquarters have adopted; they have turned over this duty to the troops and take no share in it themselves.*
     The war is becoming to some a means of growing rich; re-equipment has degenerated into pillage and peculation. Each unit strives to secure as much as possible for itself, and seizes everything that comes to hand. What cannot be used on the spot is sent back to the interior and sold at a profit. The rolling-stock belonging to the troops has taken on enormous dimensions - some regiments have two hundred carriages in their wake. A considerable number of troops have retreated to the interior, and many officers are away on prolonged missions, busy selling and exchanging loot.
     The Army is absolutely demoralized, and is fast becoming a collection of tradesmen and profiteers. All those employed on re-equipment work – that is to say, nearly all the officers – have enormous sums of money in their possession; as a result, there has been an outbreak of debauchery, gambling and wild orgies.

3   We had two welcome visitors next day at noontime: Colly and General Holman… [p197]
     According to Collishaw, B Flight arrived in Peschanoe, north and east of Kharkov, on December 5. Collishaw's headquarters train and A Flight's train arrived several days later. Collishaw also states that the B Flight Camels were badly worn, so he sent the flight to Taganrog on December 11th to refit. MA & RCA

4   'The Orloff diamond is one of the great stones of the world.' [p201]
     This gem should not be confused with the Orloff (or, Orlov) Diamond, which is on display as part of the Diamond Fund collection in the Kremlin. Once owned by Catherine the Great, it weighs about 190 carats and is displayed

mounted in a scepter, as it has been since 1784. Aten and Orrmont are probably referring to the so-called Black Orloff Diamond, which weighs 67 carats and is currently privately owned. Its early provenance is murky. It is speculated to have once been owned by Russian Princess Nadezhda Petrovna Orloff, who was born in 1898 and fled Russia after the revolution, eventually passing away in France at the age of ninety in 1988. Further speculation has it that Princess Orloff sold the diamond while fleeing Russia, as many Russians who were fleeing the country did at the time. Collishaw mentioned a large diamond he had purchased while in Russia (not the Black Orloff Diamond) and how it was lost in a train car fire. See the third Collishaw letter in Appendix II. MA & RCA

5   If that happened the Red Army, outnumbering Denikin's troops by almost nine to one…' [p209]
     The ratio probably wasn't that high, but the Red Army definitely possessed numerical superiority. According to Pipes in *Russia Under the Bolshevik Regime*, by October, 1919, the Red Army commander of the southern front claimed 186,000 troops, while Denikin recorded that his own forces numbered 98,000. These numbers, of course, were quite fluid as the Red Army was being reinforced with troops from the eastern front due to Kolchack's capitulation and with both armies suffering from large numbers of desertions.

6   '…at least we have Denikin's promise that he won't leave Taganrog without taking the Mission staff and archives along.' [p209]
     George Treloar wrote: *That was a rotten promise. Denikin was not in Taganrog during those terribly anxious weeks, running into nearly a month. He did nothing whatever about us.* GT

7   The Red cavalry vanguard never entered Taganrog yards. [p212]
     George Treloar wrote: *It was the Cossacks under Wrangel who held the Reds back from the railway between Taganrog and Rostov. Had it not been for valiant Cossacks, in and around Taganrog, the Reds would have smashed their way in and massacred all caught there.* GT

Chapter Ten

✻

1   Aboard one of them were undoubtedly Holman, Bingham, Colly, and other officers of the British Mission. [p215]
     This supposition turns out not to have been correct. Collishaw described making it to Taganrog only a few days after Christmas, 1919, by which time B Flight was crossing the Don River at Rostov on its way to Ekaterinodar. Collishaw continued, *…the headquarters staff, with A and Z Flights, remained on the Kharkov front, falling back from point to point but continuing to operate as best we could.* Z Flight was a Squadron recently formed in Taganrog by the British, utilizing supplies that had been built up there in support of the advance on Moscow. MA & RCA

2   And then, all of a sudden, it was Christmas Eve. [p216]
Collishaw recorded that Christmas Day found the headquarters train, A and Z
Flights in the eastern Ukraine village of Krinichnaya, still on its way to Taganrog.
MA & RCA

3   Holman, Bingham and Colly had already left for Rostov with half of the staff,
but there were over a hundred men left and the bulk of the archives were still
sitting on the station platform. [p219]
George Treloar, who was present during the British evacuation of Taganrog, re-
calls it somewhat differently: *Maund's train was not the last to leave Taganrog. His
own statement contradicts itself. He admits that he, Holman, and Bingham had left Taganrog, obviously in a safe get-away, leaving over 100 of the British Mission staff behind, plus
the bulk of the British Mission archives which were by then sitting on the station platform.
And I was one of those left behind. I knew nothing of Holman being present in Taganrog,
nor of his stooge Maund being there. If Holman had been there, he merely passed thro. I
quite believe there had been panic: but not among those left behind, that I can vouch for.*
Treloar also observed: *We did not get out of Taganrog until some days after New Year's
Day.* MA & GT

4   'Wrangel had arrived in Rostov planning on a showdown with the commander-
in-chief.' [p226]
Some of Wrangel's additional activities when he arrived in the region noted by
Treloar: *General Wrangel, made aware of what had happened, personally took over the
running of the railways to and from Rostov. He personally directed that one train on the line
would go at once to Taganrog, and bring away some of the mission staff, and that another
should be assigned at once to follow in about ten hours time and bring away (save) the re-
mainder – that is the historic fact.* GT

Chapter Eleven

❋

1   Colly had arrived in Rostov to find A Flight already there waiting for him.
[p234]
Alan Brough (Major General, 1876–1956) was mistaken. Collishaw and A Flight
were just arriving in Taganrog at the time B Flight arrived at Rostov. Brough
may have confused A Flight and the headquarters train with Z Flight (or with
another unit altogether) since, according to Collishaw, Z Flight, along with General Holman, had been sent ahead of A Flight and had managed to cross the
bridge over the Don River at Rostov, presumably shortly ahead of B Flight.
Collishaw states that A Flight and the headquarters train had been combined
while they were on their way to Taganrog from the Kharkov front. They were
forced to head west for the Crimea after arriving in Taganrog because the Bolsheviks had cut off the east-bound railway line to Rostov. MA & RCA

2   'Reminds me of the Crillon during a Zeppo raid.' [p238]
Fulford is referring to a raid by a German Zeppelin on Paris during WWI. The

Hotel Crillon, a luxury hotel in Paris, was left empty with the lights blazing during the raid. The staff and guests had evacuated to an air raid shelter.

Chapter Twelve

✱

1 'My medals: the Cross of St. George, the Order of St. Vladimir, the DFC. [p243]
Aten probably had his Russian medals in his possession at this time, but possibly not the DFC as the award was not officially announced until early 1920. Aten wrote to Orrmont: *A soldier does not detail his decorations personally – A real soldier, that is. If asked about them he will reply and pass on to other topics. I have heard a few fourflushers try to throw their weight around with their medals. Other than that it just isn't done. If you mention mine do it in context – Not personal, please.* MA & MHA/AO

2 I had a medium-bad case of the flu… [p244]
The malady was malaria, and not the flu. Aten mentioned that he had first contacted it that past summer, and stated: *The malaria had knocked me for a loop again! Oh, I think I must have had a temperature of 101, seemed like 110.* MA & MHA/AO/TI

3 She tried to speak one last time and then, as though a curtain had come down between her eyes and mine, I lost her to the dark. [p248]
The actual circumstances of Nina's death were considered inappropriate for re-telling in the 1961 & 1962 editions of the book. Aten recalled: *[She] died like I said she did – she asked for the morphine and I gave it to her like I would hope a friend would do for me in similar circumstances … I held her hand tenderly and kissed her on the forehead. And said goodbye… We said 'Dos Vidanya'.* MA & MHA/AO & MHA/AO/TI

4 Finally he said, 'Captain, I have put medals in your kit. [p255]
Marion Aten's medals are still in the possession of the Aten family.

5 I shook my head. 'Nobody's to blame, Feodor.' [p255]
Aten recalled in his correspondence with Orrmont: *I was thinking – remembering – [Feodor] Anikin's tiptoeing into my cabin when I was helpless with malaria, back on the Volga and the Don. He would wipe my fevered brow and face with a cool damp cloth and sit by me for hours, watching me like a doctor. And I remembered too, how tenderly he helped take care of Nina when she was wounded – dying.* MHA/AO

Chapter Thirteen

✱

1 …we caught up with one of the Mission trains that had left Rostov shortly after Holman and A and C Flights had departed the city. [p259]
A Flight , whose train had been combined with the headquarters train, was with Collishaw in the Crimea. C Flight had stayed in the Volga River region, supporting the orderly fighting retreat of Wrangel and the Caucasian Army. Neither flight had passed through Rostov with Holman during the retreat. Aten could

be mistaking the flights for Z Flight, which had passed through Rostov with Holman. It was a confusing, constantly shifting period of the conflict.

2 …Colly had left instructions when passing through weeks before. [p260]
Collishaw had flown there from the Crimea to consult with Holman. Afterwards he returned to the Crimea to direct British flight operations until Great Britain withdrew all support of the Whites. B and C Flights were never operational in Russia again. They did not participate in operations in the Crimea because Collishaw didn't have enough aircraft. He had use of only the surviving DH-9As that he had brought with him from the Kharkov front, along with some badly worn early model DH-9s that the Whites had on hand, along with a single Nieuport fighter.

3 'Very Ethel Dell, don't you know, Sir?' [p265]
Ethel Dell was an English author of popular romance novels of the day, usually involving love and passion in exotic settings such as colonial India.

Chapter Fourteen

❋

1 Hoskins got nicked in the shoulder, and another gunner took a richochet in the calf of his leg. [p281]
Sergeant-Major John Hoskins was awarded the Meritorious Service Medal by the RAF for his service in Russia.

2 'Four-inch guns. An armoured train's come up behind us.' [p281]
See the Kurbas letter in Appendix II for another eyewitness account of this incident.

3 Sir George Milne, commander-in-chief of the Army of the Black Sea, arrived in Novorossiisk to replace Holman – reason unknown. [p288]
Aten stated: *I thought he [Milne] was more of an expert in evacuations, in coordinating or something. No, it was no reflection on Holman. I rather think they [the authorities in Britain] wanted a personal report from him … on the war.* MHA/AO/TI

4 The previous night the *Emperor of India* and the *Waldeck-Rousseau* had begun to bombard the pass at regular intervals… [p290]
Here, and also on page 293, the original US & UK editions of *LTORB* had *Empress of India*, undoubtedly an editing error as the ship is correctly named earlier in the text.

Epilogue

❋

1 On April 4th Denikin appointed Baron Peter Wrangel Commander-in-Chief of the Armed Forces of South Russia and sailed from the Crimea to asylum in Britain. [p299]

Denikin, under pressure by his generals, resigned the day that he arrived in the Crimea.

2   This move resulted in a final rupture with Britain and the recall of all British Mission troops and technical assistants from the Crimea. [p299]

George Treloar wrote: *This is incorrect. The whole of the British Mission was not recalled... The plain fact is, a small group of British officers, under Lt Col Walshe, was left there in an observer capacity. I know because when I joined Wrangel's White Army, I actually lived, boarded with them in the same house as we occupied when the Mission was in full swing. This remnant of the original British Mission was evacuated with me ... when Wrangel's small army was defeated, and the final evacuation from Russia was carried out.* GT

3   Eddie and I were among the men who left Sebastopol for London in the early spring. [p299]

B Flight never flew in the Crimea, as aircraft were not available.

4   Their widows live in the United States, Olga Wrangel in Glen Cove, Long Island, and Xenia Denikin in New York City. [p300]

Orrmont interviewed Olga Wrangel in February 1960 as part of the research for the book. Xenia Denikin declined an interview but wrote Orrmont in response to questions raised in his letter. Olga Wrangel died in 1968, Xenia Denikin in 1973.

5   Eddie Fulford, bound for the African theatre, went down with a bombed transport outside of Southampton harbour in 1942. [p300]

Aten and Fulford had been regular correspondents and when the text of Fulford's last letter describing his being under attack on a ship in Southampton harbour broke off abruptly, Aten had assumed the worst. In fact, Eddie Fulford survived the Second World War and retired in early 1947, having attained the rank of Squadron Commander. Aten passed away never knowing that his friend had survived the war.

Appendix One:

The Original and New Editions

✻

Cossacks of the Air was Marion Aten's title for the material he produced on his experiences in Russia during 1919–1920. This work was brought to the attention of the New York Publisher, Julian Messner, after a radio interview in which Aten recalled his fighting days there with the RAF. Previously, he had placed his work in the hands of screenwriter, Michael Wilson, but this arrangement proved unsatisfactory. Messner commissioned Arthur Orrmont, a well-established writer, to work with Aten on the text. A contract was signed and Orrmont began research in late November, 1959. He then recorded a series of taped interviews at Marion Aten's 8N Bar Ranch in El Centro, California, from January 11th through January 18th 1960. Subsequently, the two corresponded voluminously, with Marion's last letter dated May 5th 1961, five days before his death. Aten was able to correct the galley proofs and *Last Train Over Rostov Bridge*, a title which he thought gave character to the book, was published on September 19th 1961.

Arthur Orrmont was at pains to construct a narrative arc which he felt would capture the excitement, adventure and atmosphere experienced by the pilots of B Flight as well as one which would bring to life the heart-wrenching tragedy of the Russian Civil War itself. *LTORB* is an amalgam of historical fact and well-constructed (but constructed nevertheless) drama. The period of time that Aten spent in Russia was stretched and some liberties taken in the description of events (especially with regard to actual dates of occurrence). Since there was a paucity of documented aerial dogfighting across the southern Russian front, a few fictionalized air-battles were inserted towards the beginning of the book to enhance the narrative structure. Later on in the campaign, a number of those actual strafing and support sorties which helped earn Aten his Distinguished Flying Cross were not included. Additionally, a few of the minor characters are composites that serve to explain the political background to the struggle or to carry the narrative along and Orrmont continually questioned Aten as to what these characters might plausibly have said. Finally, although the female characters are real and the relationships also existed, most of the romantic sentiments expressed are largely fictional. As the unvarnished story of Marion Aten's experiences in Russia is as fascinating as it is unique, it is worthwhile to attempt to separate fact from construction in *LTORB*.

The book was, of course, a commercial project on the part of Julian Messner and it was never the intention of any of the parties that it would be a work of strict historiography. Indeed, it was hoped by all that the story would be made into a Hollywood feature film.

Orrmont produced a 420-page manuscript and this was submitted to Messner in January 1961. A freelance editor hired by the publishing company opined that it was 'sprawling' and asked whether the battle scenes and the material relating to the disagreements between Wrangel and Denikin could perhaps be condensed to one scene each! Thankfully, such radical surgery was not done, but a number of authentic action scenes, to Aten's disappointment, were not included in the final edited version.

It is evident from the taped interviews and correspondence that Aten and Orrmont developed a very close working relationship founded on mutual respect. Aside from a squabble over an initial chapter on the Aten family ranch which Messner's editor had insisted that Orrmont write and which Aten demanded be scrapped, the only other area of serious contention was over the presentation of Aten's relationship with the nurse, Nina Anohina. Although Aten was audibly highly emotional when discussing her on the tapes, he was adamant that their relationship was not one of grand passion, but more of a passing wartime romance. Orrmont wished to, and did, make the relationship between Marion and Nina the backbone of the narrative, whereas Aten, after initially approving the manuscript, later wanted the central female character to be Kitty, the dashing Kuban Cossack sotnia leader. Eventually, a compromise was reached in which Marion's relationship with Nina was toned down somewhat.

One major area of confusion arose through Aten's mis-remembering of his date of arrival in Russia, which he maintained was June 1st 1919. Official RAF records place him on active duty on August 19th, and even allowing for his month-long quarantine in Batum, it is unlikely that he arrived in June. Orrmont then 'stretched' the time-frame for narrative purposes to have Aten arriving in Russia at the end of March 1919. Moreover, Orrmont wrote to Aten: *Because of a paucity of material between July, and the capture of Tsaritsyn and Kotluban, I've had to slow-down the action and have you move up to Kotluban in late July rather than October. In other words, we must get to the retreat more slowly, otherwise we have no book. I hope to hell this doesn't do too much violence to the facts. …don't worry; I have a chronology of battles for 1919 and 1920 and Wrangel's memoirs to set me straight on actual dates and places.*

Throughout the preparation and writing of the book, Orrmont was ever scrupulous in discussing with Aten where events depicted would deviate from strict historical accuracy.

Concerning the aerial victories described in the book, there is no historical evidence that Aten shot down five enemy aircraft. At best he shot down or, more likely, damaged one or possibly two Red Russian planes, as described in the *Liberty* magazines articles. Aten's later synopsis (and presumably, the now-lost manuscript) included dog-fights and victories which were placed there to enhance the excitement value, and thus, the commercial potential of his memoirs.

As described in *Aircraft of the* (Russian) *Civil War*, the aerial forces that the Reds used to engage the White and British airforce units in southern Russia were mostly a mixture of worn and thread-bare French, Russian and German aircraft, relatively few in number. The book notes the aerial victories of Samuel Kinkead, Raymond Collishaw and several other British pilots, and mentions Aten as having no confirmed aerial victories. According to this book, no historical reference has yet been found to a Black Fokker terrorizing the skies. The other Bolshevik Fokker Triplanes described in the text of *LTORB* were also fictional elements added by Aten. No evidence has yet been found that the Bolsheviks possessed any Fokker Triplanes, but they did own one Sopwith Triplane, which was never used in southern Russia. However, Aten did did not lack for bravery in the face of the enemy and he received the DFC for the fighting skills he displayed in Russia. Probably, it was awarded for his missions to attack Red armored trains, gunboats and cavalry – far more dangerous undertakings than might be supposed. The details of these strafing missions are accurately captured in the text of *LTORB* and are mostly consistent with the earlier *Liberty* accounts. These events were so dramatic and perilous that they needed no enhancement.

The Oxford Don and eminent Russian Civil War scholar, David Footman, made the following comments in his 1962 *Slavic Review* piece on the American edition of the book:

> *He [Aten] was not concerned with Russian politics. But in so far as the political, social and military background comes into the book the facts are generally correctly stated.*
>
> *To some readers the earlier pages may bring a twinge of doubt. Of all the London clubs the R.A.C. was and is the least likely to house elderly baronets. There are pages of verbatim dialogue which, after forty years, can hardly be authentic. The language too is not quite the language of the young officers of 1918 (of whom the writer of this review was one). The battles, when we come to them, are rather too tidy, the girls all rather too good looking. The appearances of Nina (who plays the role of heroine) come just as they should in the succeeding acts of a well-constructed drama.*
>
> *And yet, as one reads on, conviction comes. The language may not be quite right, but it is very nearly so. And B Flight is completely authentic. Young pilots were free from the drab exhaustion of trench routine. Their death rate was enormous, but, in their quarters behind the line, the going,*

while it lasted, was very good indeed. Sorties were a sport – highly skilled and highly dangerous – but still a sport; and life was a round of drink, girls, parties, and absorption in the techniques of air combat. …

Convincing too are their relations with the Russians whom they met. White officers, refugees, women, and girls all come to life as these young men would have seen them. We are made to share their moods, the rosy hopes of summer, the doubts, and then the crisis as, almost overnight, B Flight with its panache, its gaiety, and its comradeship was immersed in the confusion and the misery of utter defeat. And finally, on the squalid crowded quays of Novorossiisk, we are made to share the ultimate bitterness – that of leaving behind loyal friends and partners, while the Cheka squads closed in from the frozen hills above the town.

Nowhere else in the literature about the Russian Civil War are we given such an intimate account of events or made to feel that we are there alongside the participants as we find in *Last Train Over Rostov Bridge*.

★

For the preparation of the new edition the main source of information was, of course, Aten himself. As mentioned here in the Introduction to the New Edition, his Russian experiences had been serialized in *Liberty* magazine during 1935. These accounts, published 'as told to H. Bedford-Jones', make far more modest claims with regard to aerial victories than those that appear in *LTORB* and may be regarded as more accurate in this respect.

The recent discovery of the correspondence between Aten and Orrmont has both amplified and clarified a number of events in the book. The manuscript Aten prepared about his adventures in Russia before his collaboration with Orrmont is yet to be found, but just before the present book was readied for press, some twenty-five hours of the taped interviews dating from 1960 were discovered. Once again, Aten's deep – and occasionally booming – voice could be heard as he answered Arthur Orrmont's probing questions.

Original historic documents were consulted as much as possible. Included among these are Aten's RAF service record, his medical card, promotion certificate, 47 Squadron Daily Status record, ships' manifests, patent records, London Gazette announcements, pilot's license and many rare photographic images from the collections of both Aten and George Treloar, some of which are reproduced for the first time in this book.

A variety of standard works on the subject of the Russian Civil War and the memoirs by the salient participants were also consulted. Of particular note is historian Richard Pipes' series of books focused on the period surrounding the Russian Revolution and the resulting civil war: *A Concise*

History of the Russian Revolution, Russia Under The Bolshevik Regime and The Formation of the Soviet Union: Communism and Nationalism, 1917-1923. These works provide a broad scope and framework for understanding the military, political and cultural situation that 47 Squadron faced while in Russia, as well as assessing the impact that foreign intervention had on future international relations with the Soviet Union.

In addition, research done by aviation historian Frank Olynyk and Russian Civil War historian Thomas Hillman have also helped greatly. Olynyk's research of 47 Squadron records, performed as part of his exhaustive project to document aerial victory claims by the 'aces' of the era, indicate where events described in LTORB were not consistent with official records.

Aircraft of the (Russian) Civil War, written in Russian by A. Kondratyev (English translation by Thomas Hillman) is a well-researched and exhaustive overview of the aerial operations conducted by the White Russians and by 47 Squadron. It also provides rare insights into Bolshevik efforts to deploy aircraft against the British and White Russian forces during the Civil War. Footnotes added to Hillman's translation focus on the claims that Aten makes in LTORB and compares them to the research of the Russian authors.

The history of 47 Squadron, *Over the Balkans and South Russia (Being a History of 47 Squadron)* by HA Jones is also an important source of information. This volume covers 47 Squadron's activities in Macedonia during WWI, as well as detailing its early operations during the first months in Russia. However, coverage ends in October, 1919, due to the (*de jure* but not *de facto*) deactivation in that month of 47 Squadron by the British government.

CE Bechhofer's *In Denikin's Russia and the Caucasus,* is an eyewitness account of the collapse of the White forces in the areas of Rostov, Ekaterinodar and Novorossiisk that offers a man-on-the-street view of the panic, the disease and the misery of this pivotal period of time during the civil war.

Letters by Raymond Collishaw, Marion's 47 Squadron commander, written to Marion's sister Imogen Aten soon after Marion's death in 1961, also serve to reveal some of the events of 1919-1920. (These letters are included here in Appendix Two.) Collishaw later wrote an autobiography entitled *Air Command: A Fighter Pilot's Story* that presents a good overview of 47 Squadron's activities in southern Russia, as well as being a gripping account of Collishaw's personal experiences while there. However, as with Aten, there are inconsistencies. For example, Collishaw's letter (first letter in Appendix Two) of September, 1961, provides a detailed account of the gruesome deaths of hundreds of Russian refugees on board his train after it was rammed from behind by a runaway locomotive set loose by the pursuing Bolsheviks. In his autobiography, Collishaw states that: *Fortunately, the damaged wagons held stores and equipment rather than passengers and after making sure that we left nothing serviceable behind for the enemy we were able to proceed.* As ever, a murkiness obscures the sight of events during the Russian Civil War.

Extensive notes on *LTORB* by Colonel George Devine Treloar, an officer attached to the British Mission in the areas around Novorossiisk, Taganrog, Rostov-on-Don and Tsaritsyn during the Russian Civil War, were also very useful. They offer another eyewitness perspective on many of the events described in the book.

Dr Julian Lewis MP, provided material gathered in research for his recent book, *Racing Ace: The Fights and Flights of 'Kink' Kinkead DSO DSC★ DFC★* which helped clarify several matters relating to the members of B Flight.

Several museums were consulted for information relating to the life and the times of Marion Aten. The San Diego Air and Space Museum, the RAF Museum in London (Hendon), England and the Imperial Valley Historical Society Museum in El Centro, California (located on Aten Road!) all proved to be good sources of information.

Appendix Two:

The Collishaw and Kurbas Letters

✳

After Raymond Collishaw learned of Aten's death and read the book, he sent the following three letters with Marion Aten's sister, Imogen, and the texts are included here with the kind permission of Marion's nephew, Gary Boyce Radder. A typed copy of the Kurbas letter is in the possession of Gary Boyce Radder and the text is included here with the kind permission of Arthur Orrmont's widow, Léonie Rosenstiel. The spelling and punctuation in the original documents have been retained.

First Collishaw Letter

September 23, 1961
Dear Miss Aten,

Your letter and book seemed like a message from another world. Your brother promised to keep in touch with me, but all I ever had were several Christmas cards from the 1920s and he did not provide an address. I am very glad that Marion took the trouble to write the book and it is a great pity that I do not know the address of anyone alive from the campaign in Russia, as I should like to send some copies of Marion's book. How unfortunate that Marion should have died before his book was published. Nevertheless, he must have had quite good fun in the writing of the story. I went to see some of Kinkead's family in South Africa in 1941. They had only the vaguest ideas concerning Kinkead's adventures in South Russia. Kinkead served with me in Iraq, after the Russian affair and we quite enjoyed two small wars there.

The story of the retreat of the R.A.F. in South Russia is really in two parts; those who retreated across the Rostov bridge to Ekaterinodar and Novorossiisk and those who arrived too late at Rostov to get across the bridge and thus, had to escape into the Crimea. I was with the latter party. We had an R.A.F. train that had enlarged to 90 vehicles hauled by three locomotives and the voyage to the Crimea took us three weeks. The "White" Army was organized into three Armies, with the Kuban Cossack Army in the East, the Don Cossack Army in the center and the so-called "Volunteer"

Army in the west. The "Volunteer" Army consisted principally of Ex Imperial officers serving as rankers and Russian style, a multitude of wives and children were in attendance as camp followers. A great panic beset the Volunteer Army in the retreat and wives and children were handed over to us in droves, as they believed that safety lay only with the English, who would reach the sea. Finally, we must have had thrust upon us perhaps 2000 people and it was a terrible handicap. As our great train set out for the Crimea, we soon found that our rear had turned "Red" and that we could not officially obtain coal and water for the locomotives, nor food for the mass of people; so we had to obtain supplies by force. To obtain water, we had to use the women to carry snow to the locomotives, using their skirts as conveyors and to capture fuel, we had to take people's furniture by force of arms. While all this was in progress, our train was invaded by typhus and hundreds of people died daily. Our train was passing through a prairie covered by 3 feet of snow and I gave orders that the dead were to be thrown out of the train. All, excepting the R.A.F., were herded in cattle trucks. For obvious sentimental reasons the survivors hoped to get a proper burial later. As we advanced toward the Crimea, local inhabitants became actively hostile and they began to remove the tracks in front of us. Consequently, our only recourse was to pick up the tracks behind us and fasten them down in front of us. We had 100 aircraft machine guns manned by Englishmen on the roofs of the train, in order to keep the hostile natives at bay. And so we went on day and night, "The slow boat to China". All this time we knew that a hostile armored train was close on our rear, but we were comforted by the thought that we were taking up the rails behind us. We struggled for three weeks to get near the Crimea and eventually reached a town which was a railway locomotive repair station. It lay in the hollow of a basin-shaped terrain and while we were replenishing supplies by force of arms, hostile forces managed to send a run-away locomotive down the hillside. It collided with our train with a terrific impact and caused the mass of wooden cattle trucks to collapse and telescope one another. The stoves in those trucks set our train on fire from end to end. The only undamaged part of the train was the steel coaches occupied by the R.A.F. The result of the collision was pitiful for the refugees, hundreds were killed and injured. It was obvious that I had to act at once, otherwise the R.A.F. coaches would burn too. We got some enormous cable chains out of the round houses and tickled by English bayonets, we rounded up the masses of Russian workers. With the chains pulled by the workers, we were able to pull the burning masses of train wreckage off of the tracks and finally managed to attach the R.A.F. steel coaches to the locomotives. While these activities were in progress, hostile forces had managed to get a second locomotive in position ready to reach us with a second attack. With heavy hearts, we had to abandon all the Russian people in our train who had come to us for succor and so we steamed out of that hell hole just in time. Quite soon after this shattering and bitter experience, we were able to reach the safety of the Crimea.

In the Crimea, we went to an aircraft repair Depot and prepared some more aircraft, as we had lost all ours in the ice and snow excepting those that had been flown to Ekateraskaya. In a very short time we had several dozen aircraft and so we continued the war from the Crimea. We helped the white forces in the Crimea to repulse successive Red assaults aimed at gaining access across the narrow peninsula leading in to the Crimea. Finally, it was obvious to the British Government that the game was up in South Russia and so we were recalled.

[A short paragraph with details unrelated to the book, Marion Aten or Russia has been deleted here.]

Reverting to Marion's Book story; what actually happened to bring about the collapse of the "White" Army in South Russia was that all three armies comprising the "White" Army were enjoying immense success everywhere over an extended front 1500 miles wide. As the White Army advanced, the Russian people welcomed the liberators with joy and acclaim. It seemed obvious that the Bolshevik regime would totter and fall. The political banner of the White Army so far depicted only the relatively harmless motto - "Liberation, Liberty and food, clothes and housing for all". When all seemed to be won by the White Army, some of the Ex grand Dukes and Ex rich land owners serving in the Volunteer Army, managed to persuade General Denikin (who was a bad politician) that the time was ripe for a speech revealing the true colours and intentions which would follow as a consequence of the White Army victory. Consequently, Denikin made an extremely stupid speech, in which he depicted a return to the ancien régime and to the restoration of the Russian land to its former rightful owners. One can imagine how such a policy would rest upon millions of people, who by that time had each grabbed a piece of land for himself. He was now called upon to disgorge his spoils and to revert to the serfdom and slavery of his ancestors. Both in Red Russia and in the rear of the White Army, there was a wholesale revolution and in a very few days, a White Army Glorious Advance was turned into a retreat and a collapse. Even the Cossacks in the White Army defected. The Volunteer Army were the principal sufferers in the collapse. Only a week before they had been day dreaming of the recovery of their properties and their riches and now, suddenly, they became the object of destruction from all sides. Civil war between the rich and the poor is far more cruel than international wars. It deliberately embraces the women and children in its destruction. Only a relatively few of the poor Volunteer Army women and children escaped.

As Marion mentioned my typhus in South Russia, I thought you might like the story from my point of view. I went out in an aircraft with an observer to conduct a reconnaissance well over the Bolshevik lines. When well out the aircraft engine failed and we had no choice but to set out to walk and return to our part of the country, a matter of about 50 miles. We took shelter in remote isolated poor shepards' huts. In these huts, the brick stove is the main feature and built in the centre so that each part of the hut has part of the same flat stove. In cold weather the people in each room sit and lie on the stove. Eventually, we reached one of the White Army railways and as there was no alternative we had to get in a cattle truck with a mass of soldiers. We were all huddled together and I must have contracted typhus from the lice with the soldiers. The disease then took hold of me and I was sent by another train down to the base, as Marion explains. I was delirious for weeks and when I regained consciousness, I was in a one room cabin with a woman. She explained that she had discovered me abandoned in a cattle truck and in a bad way so she persuaded the railway employee to help her move me to her cabin. The woman turned out to be a refugee Countess who had trained as a nurse. I could speak very little Russian and she could speak less English. This woman had voluntarily suffered the frightful ordeal of looking after a helpless man for a month. As a trained nurse, she realized that it was wise not to mentally upset me and the result was that every question I asked her she answered in the affirmative. I had no idea where I was or how I got into the cabin and I was still mentally muddled by the reality of the dreams commonplace in delirium. I had dreamed I was in different countries and whenever I asked her if I were in this or that country, she always answered "yes". The result of all this was that I did not know whether it was Xmas or Easter.

Eventually, the R.A.F. got to know where I was and an aircraft appeared and I was taken to the base. Quite soon afterwards the Bolsheviks captured the place I had been with the Countess and the consequence was that I was never able to thank her for all she had done for me. Unfortunately I never saw or heard of her again.

Yours sincerely,
Raymond Collishaw

Second Collishaw Letter

October 15, 1961
Dear Miss Aten,

I just returned from abroad and found your letter awaiting me. I understand that an article appeared in "True" magazine concerned with Marion's book: but I have not seen it.

Yes, I fully agree about the love interest in Marion's book, but Mr. Orrmont doubtless had in mind that movie directors almost invariably introduce spurious female characters into historical sketches, so as to introduce reactions from an interplay of passion, pathos, tragedy and I fancy the popular writers tend to follow similar lines. Manifestly, Orrmont told Marion that it was essential for him to introduce a thread of love interest into the part of the story and so poor Marion weaved a web of fanciful female characters in to the picture.

Yes, I have no objection at all to the idea of Mr. Orrmont having my letter. As you are interested in Russia, perhaps you might like to read "Peter the First" i.e. Peter the Great, recently published in cheap edition. This book gives a picture of life two hundred years ago in Russia and when I read it, it seemed to me that the common people had not changed much by 1919-20. The Cossack tribes had for centuries enjoyed a wider measure of freedom than the other Russian people, but locally the Cossack leader domination was equally barbarous. In return for non-interference with Cossack tribal freedom, the Russian government possessed the power to command the Cossack chiefs to produce Army forces at Call, much as was done in England and elsewhere under the federal system. Thus, the Czarist regime used the Cossacks as a weapon to enforce discipline in recalcitrant elements elsewhere in Russia. This historic Cossack background bore significant consequences after the Russian Revolution; for while there developed wholesale changes in the possession of lands elsewhere, the Cossack organization remained untouched by the revolution and the Cossack tribes (not unlike Scottish clansmen in character) became hostile to the Bolshevik administration. A natural reaction was for escapees from Revolution fever and dangers to migrate in to the Cossack areas and naturally these elements joined forces in active hostility to the central government. Our campaign in South Russia emerged when the Cossacks became united under a combined leadership and the Cossacks were the main military force involved with us. The Ex officers corps and army entered the picture almost exclusively for selfish motives.

The Cossacks contrastingly fought well because they were defending their homeland against invasion by what seemed to them to be a breach of the freedom they had always enjoyed. The collapse of the white army was in no way a Cossack collapse. What happened was that the ex officer Army lay on the left flank and when this Army collapsed, the central government army penetrated deeply behind the Cossack Armies. When the Cossack troops discovered what happened, they abandoned all forward positions in hastily retired with the intention of returning to protect their homes, but they were too late.

The Bolshevik success gave them the opportunity to wipe out the Cossack clannish system and install a socialist organization in its place. The Cossack fighting elements were either destroyed, or forced to flee abroad and many thousands of Cossacks ended their days in foreign lands. The historic Cossack tribal lands extended from Odessa to Georgia and many millions of people were involved in the Consequence.

My wife, Neila, has just returned home after visiting relatives in Toronto and near San Francisco. We are contemplating making a trip by ship around South America, so we cannot say, at this time, when we shall be in California. Curiously enough, I have been in Imperial Valley in recent years and I have been in all the towns there. It is a great pity that I did not know that Marion lived there, as I should have liked so much to see him. My wife passed through Burlingame the other day enroute to San Francisco from visiting her sister, at Saratoga, but, of course, we had not had your letter then.

Marion's book seems to be getting round, because several people have written and telephoned to me about it. Perhaps it was the love interest that did it!

Yours sincerely,
Raymond Collishaw

Third Collishaw Letter

October 24, 1961
Dear Miss Aten,

Thank you for your Oct. 22nd. letter. No, I cannot recall Carl Ashton Dixon, but by his official number, I fancy that he was undergoing flying training early in 1918. It is rather a curious thing that the pioneer airmen were not given official numbers and I never had one.

I thought that you might be interested to hear about the last interesting thing that I can recall about your brother in the Royal Air Force. At that time, we were both out in Baghdad and your brother had a forced landing in the wilderness of the desert, hundreds of miles from Baghdad. It was a case of engine failure and a crash. We searched for the lost aircraft, but did not find it and eventually we had to give up the search. About a fortnight after the disappearance, your brother suddenly reappeared back in civilization. He had constructed a huge raft out of sheep skins bought from desert natives and he had fastened the floatation skins to the wooden members taken out of the aeroplane wings and, on the raft, he had salvaged the aeroplane engines and all the valuable aircraft parts. With this contrivance, the aircraft party had embarked on the raft and floated with the river current at about 25 miles each day until the river eventually brought the raft back to civilization. It was said at the time, that only "Bunny" Aten would have contemplated such an idea!

Whereas, Marion had been flying the small fighters in Russia, he had, in the meanwhile, taken a flying conversion course and in Baghdad he was flying the large troop carriers. It is not without interest that, at the time, 1922–1923, we conducted the earliest successful R.A.F. special effort to clothe, feed and keep equipped an army in the field. A field force of about 6,000 cavalry and all arms was sent into Kurdistan (the country bordering Iraq in the North East) on a primitive expedition, designed to offset damaging raids executed on the Iraquis, by the Kurds. I went with the British Army column, as R.A.F. Liaison officer and your brother's troop carriers were used to drop supplies to the army. It was the earliest attempt to supply a mobile army force from the air and proved a success. The most amusing incident I can recall occurred when when the army demanded 5000 horse shoes and horse shoe nails to match. For reasons not clear to me, your brother's squadron decided that the most convenient way to accommodate and deliver the horse shoes and nails was to pile them in the huge body of the the troop carrier and then to shovel them out over the army camp. Without any warning, suddenly 10 of your brother's troop carrier aircraft appeared over our army camp and proceeded to rain down horse shoes and nails. Happily only 2 soldiers were hurt, but 10 horses and mules were killed. I had quite a time explaining this onslaught to the General in charge of the column, but in any event, the army got its horse shoes!

The General Mudd, mentioned in Marion's book, was in reality acting Brigadier General Maund of the Royal Air Force. Maund did a dastardly thing in stealing Kinkead's locomotive. Maund was the R.A.F. representative with General Holman's mission, whose business was exclusively concerned with the provision and supply of British military equipment being provided to General Denikin's army. When the R.A.F. was formed in April, 1918, the R.A.F. adopted army ranks but the naval officers were unhappy with army ranks and so in 1920, the air ministry introduced the new style R.A.F. ranks. A curious experiment in uniforms occurred at that time. The general officer responsible for equipment in the Air Ministry was friendly with an English leading actress and he took her advice as to how to dress the R.A.F. officers. So we were all dressed in a light blue sky uniform, much adorned in gold lace. At that time, the open pit aeroplanes splashed a good deal of castor oil about and in a very short time, the beautiful uniforms were much marked and damaged. There was such an outcry by the boys in blue, that it was not long before the comic opera uniforms were discarded.

Reverting to Brigadier Maund, he reverted to Major and eventually became an Air Vice Marshall and he was in charge of administration at R.A.F. Headquarters in Cairo in the last war, when he became ill and was flown to England where he died in a R.A.F. hospital. Through one of the rare lapses in service administration, no official action was taken to notify his next of kin, about Maund's death. The result was that Mrs Maund (a Russian) was living in Cairo for some months, in ignorance of her husband's death and it was only when she heard persistent rumors and when she instituted official enquiries, that the facts became known.

Bill Daley, when he left the R.A.F. went to South Africa and when he returned to England he became involved in a frightful divorce scandal, the sordid details of which were publicised in the English Press. It was a bad case of washing one's dirty linen in public. After that I lost sight of his history.

I liked the character study of Clarence Cowderdrill. I remember him as a dim wit with a hanging mouth. It is strange how people with small minds think about big riches.

My Russian diamond story might amuse you. As you know, Russian noblemen escapees had plenty of jewels which they desired to exchange for English pounds and in one of the large South Russian cities appeared a large diamond of about 10 carets for which 1,000,000 roubles was asked. I set out to try to find the money and eventually did so, but before buying the diamond we subjected it to all available tests, such as, burning and acidic reactions. Finally, I bought the diamond and wore it in a belt round my tummy. I had a special railway carriage, formerly the property of a Grand Duke, and in the hectic retreat while our train was halted at a railway station for refuelling, I decided to have a bath so I told my Bolshevic servant to run the bath in the adjoining bath room. While in the bath, massive flames enveloped the car windows and my natural reaction was to immediately get out of the train. I opened the bathroom window and jumped naked through the flames into about 3 feet of snow. When my legs felt the cold snow my wits were restored to me and I began to think what a fool I had been not to grab the diamond on the way out.

It transpired that local hostile people had cut gasoline 4 gallon tins in half and placed half can tins full of gasoline under my coach before setting them on fire. The fire completely burned out the coach and although we eventually carefully examined the ashes for the diamond, it was not found. Some skeptical friends went out of their way to remark pointedly that the so-called diamond had melted in the fire.

Yours sincerely,
Raymond Collishaw

Letter from Vsevolod Kurbas

February 2nd, 1962

"What's that, sir?" the private asked me. I drew a long breath of relief. 'Four-inch guns. An armored train's come up behind us."
"Last Train Over Rostov Bridge", page 313.★

Dear Mr Orrmont,

This is a very interesting book, especially for me, because I happened to be the commander of that particular armored train. To be exact, the commander of our "Ioann Kalita" was a certain Col. Kuntsevich, and I, as a 1st Lieutenant, was the "Second Senior Artillery Officer" and the commander of the fighting unit that about 42 years ago saved Captain Aten and others, if not from death then from captivity and humiliation. Sure, the Greens were not so bloodthristy as the Reds, but they were rough fellows, too.

The other parts of the book are very interesting and all new for me. The purpose of this letter is, first, to thank you for your excellent co-authorship, and second, to ask you whether you could be so kind and able as to provide me with the addresses of other valiant members of the same group and so to help me get in touch with them. I am simultaneously writing to Mr. Reynolds to help me get in touch with them.

Imagine me having been in the US for 12 years and by chance, browsing in the Public Library these days and striking the book, only to learn that Mr. Aten died 9 months ago!

The train incident was written exactly except for the number of assailants. My memory says that there were no more than 100–120 of them. Besides, Makhno had nothing to do with this group. Nestor Makhno, an anarchist leader and former convict (died in Paris in the 1930s of natural causes) was active in the Southern Ukraine, roughly between the Lower Dnieper and the Donitz Mining region. Between us, the Commander in Chief of Green Bands in the Black Sea-Kuban region was a certain Nicholas Voronovich, former Colonel of Czarist Guards (now living at 405 Pennsylvania Ave., Brooklyn 7, N.Y.)

With regards and many best wishes,
Sincerely yours, V. Kurbas

★ This page number refers to the original US edition. See page 281 here.

Appendix Three:

After the Civil War

*

Marion Aten was evacuated from Novorossiisk, along with B, C and Z Flights, on March 24th 1920. Though the option to return to Britain was available to him, Aten made another choice, as he said in an interview during the writing of LTORB:

> *When we* [Eddie Fulford and Marion Aten] *left Novorossiisk, they asked. They said they were going to the Crimea. We had a choice to go to the Crimea or go to Constantinople and home, back home. But Eddie and I volunteered for the Crimea… We were going to help in the offensive, when it started … everybody thought that Wrangel would reorganize the army, and have a jumping-off point to make an invasion that summer, but it never happened. And then, after about a month, we all left! The Bolsheviks captured the Isthmus, and they started coming down the Crimea.*

Ultimately, the remaining elements of 47 Squadron, Aten included, were withdrawn in May. While the months that he spent in Russia were some of the most dangerous and adventuresome of his life, Aten's subsequent duties with the RAF were almost as challenging.

After a brief stay in Constantinople, he was sent to Egypt to fly with 70 Squadron. That July, with the award of the Distinguished Flying Cross (DFC) earned in Russia on his chest, he re-enlisted in the RAF with a commitment for a further seven years.

70 Squadron had been recently activated and it flew the large, twin-engined Vickers Vimy bomber. This was Aten's first encounter with the Vimy and the experience that he gained in learning to fly it would later serve him well when flying a freighter and passenger version of the venerable Vickers bomber called the 'Vernon'.

In November 1920, Marion took an extended leave and returned to visit his family in California. After sailing back to England in February, 1921, he attended an RAF flight instructor's course. Later in the year he was deployed to Iraq along with the rest of 70 Squadron as part of the British force being sent there to put down a growing Arab uprising in the region.

Sam Kinkead, Marion's former Flight leader in Russia, was also sent to Iraq as a Flight leader in 30 Squadron, with Raymond Collishaw assigned as his overall squadron commander. Both 70 and 30 Squadrons were based at Hinaidi Aerodrome, just south of Baghdad.

Once again, Aten was thrust into a chaotic situation in a land that was undergoing violent change. Under the terms of the 1919 Treaty of Versailles, the Arab regions of the old Ottoman Empire were put under control of the victorious British and French. Britain became responsible for Palestine and Mesopotamia (approximately modern-day Iraq), while France had authority over Syria and Lebanon. The emerging Arab nationalist movement rejected this arrangement, compelling the British to maintain a resident garrison of British and Indian troops.

The British also deployed four squadrons of RAF fighter-bombers in the region. Their mission was to patrol the lines of communication between Baghdad and Mosul, and to support the ground forces in internal security operations.

Previously, in mid-1920, growing Arab resentment over British taxation, coupled with a burgeoning nationalist movement, had led to a series of up-risings against the British authorities. Insurgents had laid siege to the towns of Samawa and Rumaitha, cutting off the British garrisoned there. The RAF air-dropped supplies to the defending garrisons and conducted bombing and strafing operations to relieve the defenders. The sieges were soon lifted. Further air and ground operations helped put the rebellion down, at least temporarily. Winston Churchill, then the Minister of War and Air, reported to the British Cabinet that operations had been successful. Both the government and the RAF took note of the effectiveness of this relatively new form of aerial operation. They would soon make use of it again.

Such was the volatile environment that Aten found when he arrived in Baghdad in 1921, soon after the Hashemite ruler Emir Faisal had been installed as the King of Iraq under British supervision and protection. Faisal had been one of the leaders in the Arab rebellion against the Turks during WWI, with British support that was spearheaded by TE Lawrence ('Lawrence of Arabia'). The photograph below shows a pith-helmeted Marion and his fellow RAF officers posing in a group photo with Faisal and the British senior advisor, Sir Percy Cox, who was one of the architects of the political boundaries of the Middle East.

The violence in Mesopotamia did not end with the crowning of King Faisal. In 1922, the Kurds in northern Iraq rose up in rebellion against the British Mandate. Kurdish separatists, led by the popular Sheik Mahmoud Barzanji, had been attempting to establish an independent nation in northern Iraq sporadically since 1919. Raymond Collishaw related an extraordinary incident during the Kurdish uprising when Aten flew a load of horseshoes and nails to a cavalry unit that was marching into Kurdistan:

A field force of about 6,000 cavalry and all arms was sent into Kurdistan ... designed to offset damaging raids executed on the Iraquis by the Kurds. ... It was the earliest attempt to supply a mobile army force from the air and proved a success. ... the army demanded 5000 horse shoes and horse shoe nails to match. ... your brother's squadron decided that the most convenient way to accommodate and deliver the horse shoes and nails was to pile them in the huge body of the the troop carrier and then to shovel them out over the army camp. Without any warning, suddenly 10 ... aircraft appeared over our army camp and proceeded to rain down horse shoes and nails. Happily only 2 soldiers were hurt, but 10 horses and mules were killed. I had quite a time explaining this onslaught to the General in charge of the column... ★

During the revolt of 1922, bombing missions were flown against Kurdish strongholds. Aten's duties with 70 Squadron during this campaign included supply and patrol flights over the remote desert and mountain countryside between Mosel, Kirkuk and Baghdad, as well as supply and mail flights to points as distant as Cairo. He flew mainly DH-9As and Vickers Vernon transport aircraft for 70 Squadron during this period. These were often flown in pairs for safety in case of engine failure.

The flights that Marion piloted on the 900 mile route from Baghdad to Cairo were part of a twice-monthly air mail service being established from Great Britain to India. These flights presented special challenges. Marion faced the formidable task of flying long distances over the sparse, featureless and poorly mapped country of the Middle East. Local weather stations and radio direction navigation did not yet exist. Aircraft engines of the day were not entirely reliable. Navigation was done visually. Communication with aircraft was limited to slow and not wholly reliable two-way Morse-code radio transmissions. In a featureless desert, Aten could often only estimate his likely location by dead reckoning.

Before the route could be established, the RAF had to solve the navigational problem of flying 470 miles of desert between the refueling stations at Ziza, Jordan and Ramadi, Iraq, 80 miles north of Baghdad. With no physical features such as rivers, railroads or paved roads for the pilots to follow, the RAF used tracks scratched into the soil by tractors to mark the route. Flying along this route became known as 'flying the Furrow'.

Emergency landing fields, really just flat or semi-flat strips of earth that had been cleared of rubble and brush, were built about every thirty miles along the route. These fields were not manned. Fuel was made available at two of them in underground storage tanks, protected from theft by a locked metal cover.

★ See the full text in Appendix Two, third Collishaw letter.

From altitude, the 'Furrow' would often be visible only as a thin line drawn on the flat desert. Navigating along this faint feature often strained flight crews, who found it difficult to follow the dim line for hour after hour. Eventually Marion, along with many of the other pilots who flew the Desert Airmail Service, tried to memorize as much of the terrain along the route as they could, so that every small wadi, hill, dune and distant mountain took on major navigational significance. One of Marion's flight maps of this region that has been preserved is annotated with many hand-written notes indicating route details and directions that were gleaned from hard-won experience.

In a letter to Marion's sister, Imogen ,written in 1961, Raymond Collishaw related a remarkable incident that, occurred during a flight in 1923:

> Marion had a forced landing in the wilderness of the desert, hundreds of miles from Baghdad. … About a fortnight after the disappearance, your brother suddenly reappeared in civilization. He had constructed a huge raft out of sheep skins bought from the desert natives and he had fastened the floatation skins to the wooden members taken out of the airplane wings and, on the raft, he had salvaged the aeroplane engines and all valuable aircraft parts. With this contrivance, the aircraft party had embarked on the raft and floated with the (Tigris) river current at about 25 miles each day until the river eventually brought them to civilization. It was said at that time, that only 'Bunny' Aten would have contemplated such an idea!

Aten flew many different types of aircraft during his career with the RAF, including Avro 504Ks, Sopwith Camels, Vickers Vimy bombers, Vickers Vernon transport planes, De Havilland DH-9s and 9As, and Fairey Fawn reconnaissance aircraft. He also flew in some of the world's most spectacular locales, including overflights of the Pyramids of Giza, the Nile River, the Sahara and Mesopotamian deserts, the Russian steppe, and the mountains of Kurdistan. In 1924, before returning to El Centro for a well-earned vacation to visit his parents, he was mentioned in dispatches for his brave service during the Kurdish uprising.

Aten's next posting was a tour of duty in England with No. 12 Bomber Squadron, after which he left active duty with the RAF in 1927 to return to California for good. Marion remarked to Arthur Orrmont during the taped interviews:

> Flying is now going to be more or less conventional … but in those days, it was, every time you took off in a plane, it was an adventure! It was a challenge. You didn't know whether you were going to have a forced landing

---

★★ See the full text in Appendix Two, third Collishaw letter.

or not. Even as late as out in Baghdad in 1924. … It got so dull, the routine flying, the training, that I got tired of it.

At a somewhat loose end for the first time in ten years, Aten used his new found freedom from the military to travel throughout the west and neighboring Mexico. While taking on duties to manage the 8-N Ranch with his father, Marion also took up deep-sea fishing, leading to fishing trips in later years that Marion's nephew, Gary Radder, fondly remembered. Aten's inventive mind applied itself to developing improvements to aircraft similar to those that he had flown for the RAF. In 1929, he was granted a patent for an aircraft braking device and he was granted three more patents in the ensuing years; one in 1934, for a shaving brush, another in 1937, for an innovative car-door locking device to prevent the lock from being forced open and, lastly, a patent filed in England for an automatic flushing mechanism for commodes. Both Marion and his father, Ira Aten, were founding members of the Pioneers Society (later known as the Imperial Valley Historical Society) and the Atens hosted many society events at their ranch house. They were also active in the El Centro American Legion Post, which was named the Boyce Aten Chapter, after Marion's brother who had died in WWI.

During the 1920s, to escape the extreme summer heat of the Imperial Valley, Ira Aten built a residence in the San Francisco suburb of Burlingame. Ira's wife and daughter (both named Imogen) resided there. Daughter Imogen was a career employee at Stanford University and Marion split much of his time between the Burlingame residence and the Aten Ranch in El Centro.

Ira Aten, one of the last of the 19th century Texas Rangers, died on August 5th 1953 at the age of ninety-one and was buried in the family plot at El Centro's Evergreen Cemetery. All of Ira's offspring, as well as Ira's wife and many of his in-laws, would later be buried in the same plot.

The Atens sold off some of their Imperial Valley acreage through the years, but retained land amounting to 320 acres until the 1990s. (This is referred to in surveying jargon as 'a half-section', which is the equivalent of half of a square mile.) The original ranch house, with its surrounding grove of eucalyptus trees, was removed from the 8N Ranch in the 1960s. The road that ran along the north end of the property is named Aten Road, and this formerly rural dirt-road has gone on to become one of the main east-west thoroughfares through El Centro, running from the main gate of El Centro Naval Air Station, in the west, to the grounds of Imperial Valley College, in the east.

Marion suffered from a heart ailment towards the end of his life. A year and a half before his death he began working with Arthur Orrmont on the project which would become Last Train Over Rostov Bridge. Marion was able to see the book in final form but he died on May 10th 1961, before its publication. Marion Aten never married.

Memories of my Uncle, Marion Aten

Stuffy, remember how he used to crow at back door for food? Peacocks and guineas learned that when Stuffy crowed it meant food. They came, ate his food and chased him away. He could see no profit in that and for 3 days he was silent. Thinking. Don't laugh, listen to this: then one day I heard him crowing his heart out at the barnyard gate. Guineas and peacocks gathered around him looking heavenward for manna – that was the way Stuffy figured. He disengaged himself and ran as fast as his little legs could move to the back door [and] squatted silently trying to hide behind his shadow. I gave him a royal feed, well deserved and undisturbed. And he still plays his deceitful decoy game on the slow-witted barnyard fowls. Tell me a rooster can't think, anyway Stuffy can…

Marion Aten writing to Arthur Orrmont

In his later years, Uncle Marion spent most of the time on his 320-acre ranch near El Centro, California, which was situated about 20 miles north of the border with Mexico. My mother, Eloise Aten Radder, was Marion's youngest sister and we lived in Burlingame, approximately 500 miles to the north, near San Francisco. I got to know my uncle well, when as a teenager I spent parts of a number of summer vacations with him on his 8N Bar Ranch. El Centro is in the Imperial Valley and some forty-five peaks are visible in the surrounding mountain ranges. Uncle Marion lived alone in the main house, and his handyman, Pancho, lived with his wife, Lucy, in a little house under a section of the eucalyptus trees on the property. My mother and Marion had decided it would be educational as well as fun for me to visit regularly, and (hopefully) to provide some good company for my uncle. As a city boy, the Imperial Valley seemed to me to be a very rural and different, yet potentially an interesting and exciting place.

The main ranch house was surrounded by dozens of chickens, guinea hens, several peacocks, three horses and various other 'creatures' (a pet desert turtle, for one). My uncle, with his affinity for animals and his tendency for finding humour in little things, named one of his horses, a mare who had been born on the ranch, 'Yard Arm'. He gave her this name because (you guessed it) he once took a tape measure and found that her front leg was 'exactly one yard' (or so he said). He had trained her to 'shake hands' and she would come up to the back door and he would say, 'shake, Yard Arm,' and she would lift up her right front hoof and let him 'shake hands' and then he would give her a carrot from a supply which was kept in a basket just inside the door.

The ranch offered plenty of room to roam and my uncle let me, starting when I was just fourteen, drive his tractor all over it; big stuff for a city kid. I did some work for him too, gathering hay with the tractor at night (it was too hot during the day with temperatures invariably exceeding 100°F), helping Pancho irrigate the crops, and, seemingly forever, feeding the chickens. At this time Uncle Marion was in his early 60s, heavy-set and barrel-chested, about 5'9" tall, with a ruddy complexion. He radiated an air of striking vigour. Out on the ranch, he always wore a pith helmet and usually a short-sleeve type of polo shirt (which after no more than 15 minutes in the sun would be soaked through) as he saw to the never-ending tasks of ranching.

He had steely grey-blue eyes and the habit of looking directly into yours as he spoke, so I was more than a little intimidated by Uncle Marion my first summer there. I believe it was in that first summer that I accidentally drove his car, a new Chrysler Imperial no less, off a dirt ditch bank and got stuck. Try as I might, I couldn't free it. So I had to walk back about a mile to the house and tell him the news. Boy, did he come unglued – calling me a bunch of names and asking how I could be so stupid, etc. Somehow, I mustered the courage to ask him if HE had ever got stuck, and with that he started laughing and said, 'Only about once a month, my friend!' We both ended up laughing and so it often was, my uncle's hair-trigger temper passing almost as fast as it came. After I returned home to Burlingame and told my mother the story, she laughed and said, 'That's Marion, for sure'.

As the years passed we became closer and Uncle Marion's positive and adventurous approach to life became a model for me. Over the half-dozen or so of my visits, we took many trips out into the desert to shoot his .45 pistol at tin cans, and shoot his shotguns at just about everything. He showed me how to get water out of a certain type of cactus, which he believed was important to know in the desert. Several times we went down to Ensenada, Mexico to go deep-sea fishing and many times he and I (occasionally accompanied by his lady-friend, an elegant widow by the name of Julia) visited points of interest in Southern California including the Anza-Borrego desert, the Algodones Sand Dunes, the Salton Sea and, a couple of times, the San Diego Zoo.

Although Uncle Marion had photographs and maps relating to aviation displayed in one room of the ranch house, as well as a propeller from a Sopwith Camel, and an altimeter mounted on his car dashboard, he never spoke much to me of his flying days. This wasn't due to any reluctance on his part (after all, some of his exploits in the RAF had appeared in national magazines), but because I was more interested in driving his tractor, riding his horses and doing what a young teenager was wont to do rather than listen to stories of times long ago. However, I did ask once what he liked most about flying and he replied that he 'liked the feel of the wind in my face'. I took that to mean that when closed cockpits became the norm, the thrill and fun and freedom of flying, for him, were gone.

My uncle had a very strong, low-pitched voice with a deep throated, hearty laugh. For him, it was important that one be of 'good humour' and accentuate the positive while maintaining an even perspective on life. He led by example with flair and flourish and his spirit of gentility easily rubbed off on others. He often encouraged me to believe that many things were possible in life and that I could accomplish them if I would but try. Most of all, I remember how kind he was and how much of his time he gave to me. Perhaps in some subconscious way his influence led me to eventually becoming a helicopter pilot.

In and around the town of El Centro (the ranch was about five miles to the north), my uncle was very well known and was greeted as 'Marion' or, for those who knew of his time in the military, as 'Captain'. He had many friends in the community and at one time was a volunteer deputy sheriff. The 8N Bar Ranch with its huge eucalyptus grove, was a haven for town-folk to have socials, BBQs and picnics. Almost every weekend in the summer there was some sort of community function held there.

Uncle Marion usually spent Christmas with the family in Burlingame. He always had a presence that naturally made him the centre of attention; he would play the piano (by ear) and recite poems from memory (his favourite was Ruyard Kipling's 'If'). His sisters, (my mother and Aunt Imogen) adored him and he was always very loving and respectful towards them. I know that my Uncle Boyce's death (my mother named me after him), in World War I in the battle of Argonne Forest, hit Uncle Marion, and the family, very hard. I think that is one of the reasons he returned to the farm after his flying days ended, as his father (my grandfather), Ira, badly needed his help on the ranch.

For several years before his death, my uncle was being treated for heart problems, but these were not thought to be too serious. We subsequently learned that he had either felt a heart attack coming on, or had actually had one and, although he had the strength to drive himself alone to the hospital in El Centro, he subsequently passed away there several hours later, on May 10th 1961. Of course, we were all shocked and deeply saddened; perhaps since he had never married, this had caused him to make the effort to be much closer to the immediate family. To me as a young man, he was a great inspiration as well as a role model and I still, fifty years on, remember him with the greatest respect and affection, and with deep appreciation for the time he spent with me and for the good times that we shared.

Gary Boyce Radder
June, 2011

Appendix Four:

Short Biographies

＊

RAYMOND COLLISHAW was born on November 22nd 1893 in Nanaimo, British Columbia to Welsh parents who had emigrated to Canada. When war broke out in 1914, Collishaw initially wanted to enlist in the Royal Navy but instead joined the Royal Naval Air Service in 1915 and was transferred to the RNAS 3rd Wing in France in August, 1916. By the end of the war, he was one of the highest scoring allied 'aces' and had received promotion to Lieutenant Colonel. After commanding 47 Squadron in South Russia during the Civil War, Collishaw went on to command Royal Air Force units in Iraq and in Persia (Iran) during the Kurdish revolt against the British Mandate. In the 1930s he was given command of No. 5 Wing. After the outbreak of World War II, Collishaw was promoted to Air Vice-Marshal and was given command of No. 204 Group in North Africa, which faced elements of the formidable German Luftwaffe during the desperate early days of the North African Campaign. Collishaw retired in 1943, but then served as a Civil Defence Regional Air Liaison Officer in Scotland. Following the war, he returned to Canada where he was active as part-owner of a mine near Barkerville, B.C. His long awaited autobiography, *Air Command: A Fighter Pilot's Story*, was published in 1973. Collishaw died in Vancouver on September 28th 1976 at the age of eighty-two.

ROWAN HEYWOOD ('BILL') DALY was born on March 30th 1898 at Leigh-on-Sea, Essex. He served in an airship at Imbros and Mudros in the Aegean, between 1915 and 1916, prior to deployment to the United Kingdom for Home Defence duties. Qualifying as an RNAS pilot in February 1917, he shot down a Gotha bomber 15 miles off Ostend on 7 July, for which he was awarded the DSC. Joining 10 (Naval) Squadron in France, he was wounded during the course of his fifth victory, east of Houthulst Forest, in September 1917. After the war, he volunteered for service in Russia where he earned his DFC during the Civil War. By 1924, he was a bomber pilot in 39 Squadron and while he was practising formation flying on 5 June, over Spittlegate Aerodrome, near Grantham, his undercarriage became fixed in the top plane of another machine which had pulled up beneath him. The press reported that both DH-9As 'commenced to descend locked together. Turning into [a] half-circle, they hit the ground just as Daly, after enormous effort, had pulled his machine out of the top of [Flying Officer] Lucas' plane.' Bill Daly, aged twenty-six, was killed and was buried in Grantham Cemetery. Only in 1925 were parachutes finally issued to RAF pilots.

ANTON IVANOVICH DENIKIN was born on December 16th 1872, in Szpetal Dolny, then a part of the Russian Empire but now located in Poland, to a Russian father and a Polish mother. His father had been a career soldier in the Imperial Russian Army and young Anton enlisted in the army at the age of twenty after attending military college. By 1905, he was serving in the Russo-Japanese War. Having risen steadily through the ranks, he spent WWI as Chief of Staff to the commander of the Kiev Military district. By 1917, he was commander of the Russian VII Corps, fighting in Romania. After the overthrow of Tsar Nicholas II, Denikin supported an attempted coup known as the Kornilov Affair. Its failure led to his imprisonment, and after the October Revolution of 1917, he escaped to southern Russia where he became part of a group of ex-Tsarist officers who formed the anti-Bol-shevik Volunteer Army. After the death of Kornilov in April, 1918, Denikin assumed command of the army. A push towards Moscow in 1919 gave the Volunteer Army some initial victories, but ultimately the Red Army tri-umphed and Denikin resigned his command the day that he arrived in the Crimea, where the remnants of the White Forces had collected. Denikin then briefly lived in several European cities before finally settling in France in 1926. In 1945, Denikin moved to New York City. He died on August 8th 1947, while vacationing in Ann Arbor, Michigan.

EDGAR ('EDDIE') FULFORD was born in 1892, and served in the Canadian Signals Corps before being commissioned into the RFC in 1918. Subse-quently joining 23 Squadron RAF on the Western Front, he was reported missing in late September when his Sopwith Dolphin failed to return. After two months as a prisoner of war, he was repatriated at the end of November. He flew RE8s, in reconnaissance, for 'Z' Flight of the RAF detachment in South Russia, not with 'B' Flight of 47 Squadron, though he certainly was a close friend of Marion Aten. Awarded a Mention in Despatches by Gen-eral Holman at the end of the Allied intervention, Fulford was granted a Short Service Commission on returning to the United Kingdom. He was transferred to the Reserves in 1927, joined the De Havilland School of Fly-ing, moved to British European Airways and took part in expeditions in Africa (with Sir Malcolm Campbell) and the Dutch East Indies. During the Second World War, he was recalled from the Reserves and promoted from Flying Officer to Flight Lieutenant, eventually retiring from the RAF as a Squadron Leader early in 1947.

SAMUEL KINKEAD was born on February 25th 1897 in Johannesburg, South Africa, to an Irish father and a Scottish mother. He joined the Royal Naval Air Service (RNAS) in September, 1915. After training in Eastbourne, he was first attached to 2nd Wing of the RNAS, serving in the Dardanelles and Eastern Mediterranean. An outstanding fighter pilot, by September 1917 he was serving on the Western Front in France, flying Sopwith Tri-planes and, susequently, Sopwith Camels. By the war's end, he had achieved at least thirty-three victories. Kinkead served in command of (RAF) 47 Squadron's B Flight in Russia during the Civil War where he secured three aerial victories (one of which was 'Driven Down') against the Bolsheviks. After Russia, he served with the RAF in Iraq as part of the British Mandate in the early 1920s, and, by 1927, was a member of the British team that competed for the Schneider Trophy, a speed competition for seaplanes. Kinkead was killed in a crash while flying a Supermarine S.5. (a forerunner of the Spitfire) near Calshot, England, on March 12th 1928 while attempting to break the world air-speed record.

NESTOR IVANOVYCH MAKHNO was born October 26th 1888) was a Ukrainian peasant who embraced anarchist and revolutionary politics while still a teenager. The Tsarist regime condemned him to death in 1910, but his sentence was commuted to life in prison with hard labour. He was released in 1917 after the Tsar abdicated and subsequently went on to unite most of the various Ukrainian revolutionary groups under the black banner of his 'Revolutionary Insurrectionary Army of Ukraine'. In an uneasy alliance with the Bolsheviks, Makhno's forces opposed the White Armies during the Russian Civil War, forcing the Whites to divert sorely needed battalions during their drive towards Moscow. In 1920, Makhno's forces helped to defeat the last of Wrangel's White Army in the Crimea. Immediately afterward, the Bolsheviks arrested Makhno's staff and executed them along with many of his followers. In 1921, he went into exile and eventually took refuge in Paris, where he was employed as a carpenter and as a factory worker. There he wrote his memoirs and various anarchist tracts. He died of tuberculosis in Paris in 1934.

WILLIAM ('TOMMY') BURNS THOMSON was born on August 31st 1897, in Scotland, the son of Revd. Edmund Thomson, senior minister of the East United Free Church of Brechin. Keen to enlist in 1914, he had to wait until the following year to join the RFC, where he served as an air mechanic until 1917, when he qualified as a pilot and was commissioned. After brief service in France, he was posted to the United Kingdom until volunteering in 1919 for service in South Russia, from where he returned the following April, having earned a DFC. Subsequently an instructor with 1 Flying

Training School, he returned from leave, soon after the death of his father in March 1922, to take up a post in Egypt at 4 FTS, Middle East, based at Abu Sueir. On November 4th, stunting at low level while off duty, he misjudged a manoeuvre and fatally crashed into a building. Tommy Burns Thomson was twenty-five and was buried in the Ismailia War Memorial Cemetery, Egypt.

GEORGE DEVINE TRELOAR was born on April 23rd 1884 in Ballarat, Victoria, Australia. He had been a touring actor before volunteering in 1915. He was commissioned in the Coldstream Guards and served in France and Belgium, winning the DSO and MC as a captain. In 1919, he was appointed Assistant Military Secretary to the British Mission supporting the White Russian cause on the southern front in the Civil War. When the British Military Mission withdrew in March 1920, Treloar remained and served with General Wrangel's army as a colonel. After the White Army was evacuated from the Crimea, he commanded a camp for Russian refugees near Constantinople, and then left the army in October 1922 to be League of Nations Commissioner for Refugees in Thrace. He returned to Australia in 1927, where he became a noted radio commentator. He was an eyewitness to many of the events described in Last Train Over Rostov Bridge, and made detailed notes on the book. George Treloar died on November 29th 1980.

BARON PYOTR NIKOLAYEVICH WRANGEL, a Russian descended from German nobility, was born on August 15th 1878, in Lithuania. He enlisted in the Life Guards Cavalry of the Imperial Russian Army in 1902 and received military training at the Nikolaev Cavalry Academy, after which he received an officer's commission. He resigned his commission to work for the Governor of Irkutsk, re-enlisting at the start of the Russo-Japanese War in 1904. At the beginning of WWI he was promoted to Captain and led a cavalry unit, eventually rising to the rank of Major General. After Russia withdrew from the war, Wrangel lived in the Crimea, where he was arrested by the Bolsheviks as a potential opponent. After his release, he joined the anti-Bolshevik Volunteer Army led by Anton Denikin and was given command of the 1st Cavalry Division, later known as the Caucasian (Volunteer) Army. Wrangel opposed General Denikin's strategy of immediately marching on Moscow, believing that a link-up with the eastern anti-Bolshevik army of Admiral Kolchak would consolidate their recent advances and allow them to gain strength for a more powerful push on Moscow. Known as an aggressive campaign general and an able administrator and strategist, he is often recognized as perhaps the most effective of Denikin's sub-commanders. Forced to retreat to the Crimea in the face of the superior numbers of the Red Army, Wrangel accepted command of the remaining White forces after Denikin resigned. A series of defeats forced the evacuation of the White forces into exile where he continued as their nominal head, before they were eventually dispersed. Wrangel moved from city to city in Europe until he settled in Brussels in 1927, where he died suddenly – poisoning was suspected – on April 22nd 1928.

Thanks to Frank Dorber for providing information (via Julian Lewis) relating to the members of 47 Squadron.

Index

*

INDEX

INDEX

Published in Great Britain by:

Thin Red Line Books

an imprint of:
Hollydata Publishers Ltd
27 John Street
London WC1N 2BX

First published in Great Britain by:
Cassell & Company Ltd

revised text © the estate of Marion Aten
& Léonie Rosenstiel, 2011

ISBN 978 185398 159 3

Third Edition, 2013
Reprinted 2015

Book design by Brad Thompson
Printed and bound in the UK